East-Central Europe Under the Communists

ALBANIA

EAST-CENTRAL EUROPE UNDER THE COMMUNISTS

ROBERT F. BYRNES, *General Editor*

Albania

Stavro Skendi, Lecturer in Program on East Central Europe, Columbia University, and Research Supervisor, Mid-European Studies Center, editor.

Bulgaria

L. A. D. Dellin, Research Supervisor, Mid-European Studies Center, editor.

Czechoslovakia

Vratislav Busek, Former Professor of Canon Law at Charles University in Prague, and Nicholas Spulber, Associate Professor of Economics, Indiana University, editors.

Hungary

Ernst Helmreich, Professor of History, Bowdoin College, editor.

Poland

Oscar Halecki, Professor of History, Fordham University, editor.

Romania

Stephen Fischer-Galati, Assistant Professor of History, Wayne University, editor.

Yugoslavia

Robert F. Byrnes, Director, Mid-European Studies Center, editor.

ALBANIA

STAVRO SKENDI, *Editor*

with the assistance of

MEHMET BEQIRAJ

GEORGE BOSSY

FRED PISKY

QEMAL VOKOPOLA

Published for the
MID-EUROPEAN STUDIES CENTER of the
FREE EUROPE COMMITTEE, INC., by
FREDERICK A. PRAEGER — New York

Second Printing, June 1958

BOOKS THAT MATTER

First published in the United States of America in 1956 by
FREDERICK A. PRAEGER, INC., *Publishers, 15 West 47th Street*
New York 36, N. Y.

This is VOLUME NUMBER 46
of Praeger Publications in Russian History and World Communism

Library of Congress Catalog Card Number 55-11625
Printed in the United States of America

FOREWORD

The Mid-European Studies Center, a unit of the Free Europe Committee, Inc. (formerly the National Committee for a Free Europe), was founded in the summer of 1950 principally to help maintain the intellectual traditions and cultural heritage of the peoples of Central and Eastern Europe now under Communist control, to assist exiles of scholarly competence to continue their work against Communist tyranny, and to increase the fund of information available on this area, which is a *terra incognita* for even educated Americans. The Center has completed and published a large number of studies, and has probably been the principal research institute in the world concentrating on East-Central Europe.

This volume, *Albania under the Communists,* is one of a series of seven. The series was conceived in the spring of 1954 by Mr. Stetson S. Holmes, then Director of the Mid-European Studies Center, by Mr. Jacob B. Hoptner, then Director of Research of the Mid-European Studies Center, and by Dr. Stephen Fischer-Galati, then a staff member. It was organized as a joint project of refugee scholars and of American specialists, and it was hoped that the volumes would not only increase the fund of information, but would also help define the boundaries of our knowledge and the areas in which research and analysis were most needed. The books are designed to provide thorough, accurate, and well-organized information on Albania, Bulgaria, Czechoslovakia, Hungary, Poland, Romania, and Yugoslavia since they have been under Communist rule. Eastern Germany and the Baltic states, Lithuania, Latvia, and Estonia, all important parts of the Soviet empire in East-Central Europe, were omitted because the Center lacked both the personnel and the materials for volumes on these states.

The series is a massive project, which the Mid-European Studies Center is particularly well qualified to prepare and to publish. As the research division of the Free Europe Committee, it possesses a small but highly qualified staff of experts on this area. Some of these specialists lived for years in East-Central Europe, were educated there, and held important positions in cultural, political, and government life; others have American academic training. In addition, the Center has developed close relations with specialists on this area teaching in American colleges and universities or working in research institutions. Finally, the Free Europe Committee of which the Center is a part, has the largest collection of materials available in the non-Communist world, particularly on developments within the last six years.

However, this material is often fragmentary. Moreover, Communist data must be examined with great care, because all Communist material has a political purpose. In addition, little analysis has been made anywhere in the world of recent developments in East-Central Europe, so that there are few secondary studies available. In a sense, each chapter of each volume—in other words, the 150 chapters in the series—represents pioneer research, with all the faults and weaknesses from which such research suffers. This explains why each volume contains quantities of useful information, but lacks generally the kind of analysis one would find in studies of areas where American research has had a longer and richer tradition.

Dr. Fischer-Galati at the beginning was entrusted with the administration and direction of the series. He prepared the outline for the seven volumes, selected the original contributors, reviewed most of the preliminary drafts, and managed the enterprise generally until he accepted appointment as assistant professor of history at Wayne University in the summer of 1955. At that time, I assumed editorship, with Dr. Alexander Rudzinski and Dr. Bernard Ziffer as close associates, and all the resources of the Center were mobilized to complete the series by the summer of 1956.

When the editorial process was begun by the Center's staff and the editors of the individual volumes, we discovered that some chapters were excellent, but that others failed to meet the standards set for the work as a whole, because of the wide variety of training, experience, and political points of view of the authors. It also became clear that many important and interesting issues and problems had not been included in the general outline prepared in 1954. Consequently, within a limited budget and period of time, some additional chapters were added, and substantial editing, revising, and in some cases complete rewriting of other chapters were undertaken. This task was assumed and completed with skill and diligence by the staff of the Mid-European Studies Center.

The difficulties were all grievously compounded when, as the various volumes were nearing completion, the flow of information from the Soviet Union and from the countries under Communist control suddenly increased sharply. In some cases, the new data constituted the first solid information on important aspects of the economies of these countries; in other cases, the new information supplemented or replaced estimates derived from many scraps of information. All this information had to be carefully analyzed and incorporated. Just as this task was being completed, the Twentieth

Congress of the Soviet Communist Party, and the extraordinary attacks on Stalin and Stalinism which accompanied and followed it, brought considerable revisions to some sections of the books, particularly those dealing with the Communist Party and biographies of Communist leaders.

This volume reflects the state of American scholarship, and of Western scholarship generally, on developments within Communist Albania. Its authors and editors have sought to ensure that it be an accurate and objective description and analysis of what has happened in Albania under Communist rule. The manuscript was delivered to the publisher in January 1956, so that it reflects data available at that time, although minor additions and revisions were made later as new information became available.

The editor of this volume, Dr. Stavro Skendi, is Lecturer in the Program on East-Central Europe at Columbia University and Research Supervisor of the Mid-European Studies Center. He was educated at Robert College, an American institution in Istanbul, from which he obtained a B.S., and he later attended the Geneva School of International Studies. In his native Albania, Dr. Skendi taught in the Commercial Institute of Valona and the Lycée of Korçë, where he was a colleague of Albania's Communist dictator, Enver Hoxha. Because of his patriotism and his democratic beliefs, he was interned for eighteen months on the island of Ventotene, soon after the occupation of Albania by Fascist Italy. Released in 1941, he took an active part in the underground, escaping in 1943 to Istanbul to make known to the West the struggle of the Albanian people against the Axis powers. In 1946, he came to this country, where he received a three-year fellowship for Balkan studies from the American Council of Learned Societies. He obtained a Ph.D. from the Department of Slavic Languages of Columbia University.

Dr. Skendi has been a prolific scholar. In addition to studies in periodicals of prewar Albania and political articles in the press of Istanbul during World War II, he has contributed to several American and Western European learned journals. Dr. Skendi is also the author of a comparative study on Albanian and Yugoslav epics, published by the American Folklore Society in 1954.

Robert F. Byrnes

PREFACE

ALBANIA is not only the smallest of the captive countries, but one of the smaller countries of Europe, both in area and in population. However, she has been a Soviet outpost in the Mediterranean. This volume is the first comprehensive study of Albania under Communist rule ever undertaken.

There have been many obstacles in the preparation of this book. Albania, unfortunately for those seeking information about her, is the least known of the countries within the Soviet orbit. Prewar literature is scarce, and postwar material is far from abundant, particularly with regard to economic developments. There are few scholars in the United States qualified and prepared to write about Albania. As chapters first assigned to individual authors had to be reworked by other researchers, sometimes by a team, questions of unevenness of style and approach were involved.

The general reader does not usually read a volume of this kind from cover to cover, but only the chapters in which he is interested. Consequently, background information has been given at the beginning of each chapter, its length depending upon the need, and allowance has been made for overlapping in some chapters.

An effort has been made to maintain chapters of uniform length, but more space has been devoted to those on agriculture, literature and the arts, and historical background. By the very nature of the country, agriculture and husbandry are the most important fields of Albanian life. The chapter on literature and the arts contains a section on the Albanian language because little is known about this subject, even by the educated public. The lengthy chapter on historical background was imposed by the scant knowledge of Albania's past and the lack of scholarly treatment in English. We have included a review of Albania's international relations, primarily in the postwar period, and we have also sought to provide a historical framework for the reader.

With regard to the number of spellings that exist for toponymies in Albania, we have chosen for consistency's sake the native spelling, which is also used by the Albanian government. The only exceptions are the English spelling of Albania's capital, Tirana, and for uniformity, the Albanian indeterminate form—Shkodër and not Shkodra, Elbasan and not Elbasani—this being the form commonly used in Albanian maps. To help the reader pronounce the names of the Albanian localities correctly, a note has been attached at the beginning of the volume about Albanian pronunciation, including also a list of toponymies, with their corresponding spelling in Western literatures. The note also contains a short table of continental and American units of measure, as well as lists of exchange rates of the Albanian lek at different periods.

It was our intention at the outset to have a separate bibliography for each chapter. However, it was found that, in general, books on Albania dealt with many aspects of her life, rather than specialized topics, and that sources frequently overlapped. The editor therefore decided to prepare a country bibliography comprising, under a more general heading, publications pertinent to separate chapters.

The project of a volume on Albania was initiated by the Mid-European Studies Center as early as 1951 and the draft of a short handbook was prepared. The present study, however, is part of the series which was initiated in the spring of 1954. It was largely prepared by the editor. However, it would not have taken its present form had it not been for the active participation of Dr. Robert F. Byrnes, Director of the Mid-European Studies Center, and for the unselfish work of the members of the Center's staff, particularly Miss Pendleton Garrison and Mr. Neal Buhler of the editorial staff, and had it not been reviewed by competent scholars. To all these collaborators we would like to express our warm thanks.

Stavro Skendi

CONTENTS

Appendix

TRANSLITERATIONS AND EQUIVALENT VALUES

1. In Albanian, the following letters are pronounced differently from their English counterparts:

Letter	*Pronounced as*		*Letter*	*Pronounced as*	
c	ts in	ca*ts*	l	l in	*l*eaf (soft)
ç	ch	*ch*urch	ll	l	*l*ord (hard)
x	ds	go*ds*	j	y	*y*es
xh	j	*j*am	y	German ü (*ü*ber)	
g	g	girl	ë	i	f*i*rst (but less rounded)
th	th	*th*in	gj is a palatalized	g	(*g'*)
dh	th	fa*th*er	q	k	(*k'*)

2. The following important Albanian place names have various Western spellings:

Albanian	*Western*
TOWNS	
Butrint	Butrinto
Durrës	Durazzo
Dibër	Dibra or Debar
Gjirokastër (Gjinokastër in Geg)	Argyrokastro, Argyrocastro, Argirocastro
Këlcyrë	Klissura
Korçë	Korcha, Kortcha, Koritsa, Corizza
Krujë (Krue in Geg)	Croya
Lesh (Lezhë in Geg)	Alessio
Përmet	Premeti
Sarandë	Santi Quaranta
Shëngjin	Shën Gjin, San Giovanni di Medua
Shkodër	Scutari or Skutari
Vlorë (Vlonë in Geg)	Valona
RIVERS, MOUNTAINS, ISLANDS	
Bojanë (Buenë in Geg)	Bojana, Boyana
Shkumbî (Shumbin in Tosk)	Shkumbini
Çermenikë	Chermenika or Tchermenika
Sazan	Saseno or Sasseno

3. The American equivalents of continental measures used in this handbook are as follows:

   1 kilometer (km.) = 0.62 mile
   1 square kilometer (km^2) = 0.386 square mile
   1 hectare (ha.) = 2.47 acres
   1 kilogram (kg.) = 2.20 lbs. avoirdupois
   1 quintal = 220.46 lbs. avoirdupois
   1 hectoliter = 2.84 U.S. bushels

   References to "tons" indicate metric tons (1 metric ton = 1.1023 short tons). As quintal is a measure of weight and bushel of capacity, it is difficult in the measurements of crop yields to convert quintals into bushels, each bushel varying with the crop.

4. The exchange rate was 15 leks to the dollar in 1938, 125 in 1945, 13.85 in 1946 (after the monetary reform), and 50 after 1947.

5. The following symbols have been used in the tables:
   Dots (. . .) indicate that data are not available.
   A dash (–) indicates that the amount is nil or negligible.

Part I – Introduction

1. HISTORICAL BACKGROUND

ALBANIA lies at the northwestern edge of the Balkan Peninsula and is separated from Italy by a channel only forty-seven miles wide. This geographic position has been an important factor in Albanian history, for every strong power which has arisen in the Italian Peninsula has had the tendency to expand into the Balkans by using Albania as a bridgehead. On the other hand, whenever a powerful state has emerged in the Balkan Peninsula, it has tended to reach the Adriatic coast and to use Albania as a springboard for expansion to the West.

ANTIQUITY TO OTTOMAN INVASION (1385)

The Albanians are considered descendants of ancient Illyrian tribes, Indo-European in origin, which may have come to the Balkan Peninsula even before the Greeks. Their neighbors in the West were the Thracians, another ancient Indo-European people of the Balkans, with whom they intermingled and intermarried.

Owing to their contact with the Hellenic world, the Illyrian tribes along the Adriatic reached a high degree of cultural development. There were several Greek colonies on Albanian soil, the most important Epidamnos (Durrës) and Apollonia, between Vlorë and Durrës. Greek civilization did not spread far into the hinterland, and there was no fusion between Greek colonizers and native Illyrians, for the Greek settlers were satisfied with preserving their principal settlements. Their colonies were like scattered islands of Greek culture in the middle of an ethnically Illyrian sea.

The Illyrians of the Adriatic formed a kingdom in the middle of the third century B.C. which comprised Shkodër and parts of the Albanian coast. Their piratic ships endangered Roman trade, and in 167 B.C., Rome conquered their Kingdom of Illyria and became mistress of the Adriatic. Unlike the Greeks, the Romans spread colonies and military stations through Albania. They also created an excellent network of roads, which had as its backbone the Via Egnatia (a continuation of the Appian Way), the great road to the Orient. Via Egnatia crossed Albania along the Shkumbî River, passed through

Macedonia, and reached Salonica, thus connecting Rome with Byzantium.

The roads built by Rome spread her civilization in Albania, but some parts of the country were not reached. The mountains which run roughly parallel to the coast made communication difficult. A conservative spirit developed among the natives of the mountains, and they put up strong resistance against Roman power. The Illyrian tribe which retained the most independence was the Albani or Albanoi, whose city Albanopolis was mentioned for the first time in the second century A.D. by the Alexandrine geographer Ptolemy. This tribe lived in the region of Mat, north of Tirana.

A new influence appeared in A.D. 548-49 when the Slavs crossed the Danube and "spread desolation throughout the whole of Illyricum as far as Epidamnus [Durrës]." During the ninth century, a part of southern Albania was annexed to Bulgaria. Toward the end of the century, the Bulgarians expanded more in the south. In 996, they went as far north as the Drin River, including also the city of Durrës, reconquered by the Byzantines one year before the collapse of the First Bulgarian Empire (1018). Their traces are seen even today, particularly in place names.

The second Slavic pressure was from the north. The most southern South Slavic tribe, the Diocletians (Duklijani), built a state centered in Montenegro which came into conflict with Byzantium. In the eleventh century, Shkodër was already included in their territories, but the Diocletians were not able to hold the lands they seized. Only toward the end of the twelfth century (1190) were the Serbs of the hinterland, in Raška (Rascia), able under Stefan Nemanja to occupy Montenegro and northern Albania.

The expansion of the Serbs during the Middle Ages brought about an interesting symbiosis. Pastoral Albanian and Vlach elements were mixed with Slavic agriculturists. During this period, Albanians reached farther north along the coast than today. While the Serbs lived in settled villages in *župas* (Slavic districts), the Albanians and the Vlachs usually lived in shepherd villages called *katuns*.

Forgotten for many centuries, the Albanians re-emerged on the historical scene in the eleventh century. The half century 1025-1081 in Byzantine history was a period of anarchy. In the frontier provinces, chaos reigned, and various generals tried to bring about the fall of the Empire. The Albanian warlike tribes entered the service of generals of the *thema* (Byzantine province) of Durrës who pretended to the Byzantine throne. When a capable emperor, Alexios I Comnenos, came to power in 1081, the Albanian tribes were quieted, and remained so for a century.

In the eleventh century appeared also the name Arbanon (Albania) and Albanoi or Arbanitai (Albanians), the latter a designation for the successors of the old Illyrians, who had survived in the mountainous regions comprised in the quadrilateral Shkodër-Durrës-Ohër-Prizren. Today the Albanians call themselves Shqyptarë or Shqiptarë (Sons of the Eagle) and their country Shqypní or Shqipëri. Their older names were respectively Arbneshë or Abreshë and Arbní or Arbëri, from which the European forms Albanian and Albania are derived.

While the Balkan States were expanding into Albanian territory, new powers which had arisen across the Adriatic endeavored to occupy the Albanian shore and penetrate into the Balkans. East and West clashed in Albania. This clash was basically political, but it also had a religious aspect.

Christianity was introduced in Albania in the first centuries of its era. When the division of the Roman Empire into East and West occurred (A.D. 395), Albania constituted administratively part of the Eastern Empire but ecclesiastically was dependent on Rome. In 732, however, she was detached from Rome by Leo the Isaurian and subordinated to the Patriarchate of Constantinople. The situation changed in the following centuries, when the two churches were drifting apart, but in general Albania tended to follow Constantinople. When the definite schism took place in 1054, the northern part of the country had come under the jurisdiction of Rome. After the consolidation of their rule in southern Italy, the Normans landed in Albania, taking Durrës in 1082. They extended their conquests in the Balkan Peninsula until they were driven out by the Byzantines in 1107.

By the eleventh century, Venice enjoyed commercial privileges in Albanian towns. After the Fourth Crusade (1204), however, she received nominal control over Albania and Epirus and took possession of Durrës and the surrounding region. The northern part of Albania remained under small semifeudal lords and Serbian princes, Venice's policy being "equilibrium among [ruling] families." Venice did not exercise rule over Epirus because a new state, the Despotat of Epirus, had been formed there under a dynasty of energetic rulers.

What was called Epirus by the ancient writers contained today's southern Albania and part of northern Greece. It was inhabited by the Epirotic tribes, related to the Illyrians and Thracians. When it became the Despotat of Epirus (1204-1358), it was a comparatively large state with Yannina and Arta as centers. In 1259, Michael II, the ruler of the Despotat, who looked for support from the West, married his daughter to King Manfred of the Hohenstaufen, giving him as a dowry the island of Corfu and some towns in Albania, including Durrës. This marriage introduced a new factor into Albania—the kings of Naples.

Although the preliminaries started with the Hohenstaufen, the actual penetration of Italy into the Balkans was conducted by the Neapolitan Angevins. In 1272, the great Angevin army crossed the sea and occupied Durrës. Charles I of Anjou issued a decree for the formation of the "Kingdom of Albania" (Regnum Albaniae) out of his dominions in that country and became its first king. The Albanian nobility submitted to the Captain General, the representative of Charles I of Anjou in Albania. Nevertheless, the mountain Albanians were often at war with the Angevins, and Albanian noblemen were held as hostages by the King.

In 1281, Charles I of Anjou made a campaign against Constantinople. The Angevino-Byzantine wars gave an impetus to the great southern expansion of the Albanians, who reached as far south as Thessaly. The presence of the Angevins in Albania, moreover, curbed the advance of the Serbs to the Adriatic shores and made the Albanians appreciate outside support. The Angevin "Kingdom of Albania" lasted one century; the rule then passed to the Albanian house of the Thopias.

Another Albanian expansion occurred during the reign of Stefan Dušan (1331-55). Owing to the weakening of Byzantium as a result of party struggles, this young Serbian King extended his sway from Shkodër to Berat and Vlorë (1345). In his southward march toward Epirus and Thessaly, as far as the borders of the Duchy of Athens, his troops were composed to a considerable extent of Albanians. The Greek noblemen and *stratiotes* (feudal soldiers) were driven out of their land, and their property passed over to Albanian chieftains and fighters as far as the district of Arta. Epirus became partly Albanian.

After the collapse of Stefan Dušan's empire, Albania fell under the domination of local lords. These were the product of the mountainous interior and of the prevailing feudal systems of the invaders: Serbian in the north, Western in the center and south, and Byzantine in the interior. Some of the important Albanian semi-feudal lords were the Balshas and the Dukagjinis in the north, the Thopias and the Muzakis in the center, the Arianitis and the Shpatas in the south. It was under the Shpatas that the Albanians spread into the mainland of Greece, settling later in the Peloponnesus and some of the Aegean islands.

The various Albanian local lords had known at different times not only the political influence of Eastern and Western powers, but also the influence of their respective religious creeds; Eastern Orthodoxy and Roman Catholicism, between which they wavered according to their momentary interests. On the eve of the Ottoman invasion of Albania, the Catholics were mainly in the north and the Orthodox in the south and center.

Ottoman Domination, 1385-1912

The division of Albania into small territories ruled by independent semifeudal lords facilitated the occupation of the country by the Turks, who first invaded Albania in 1385 upon the invitation of an Albanian lord. It appears that after the Ottoman victory the principal Albanian lords recognized the suzerainty of the Sultan. They were allowed to maintain their positions, on condition that they paid the *harac* (tribute), sent their sons as hostages to the Sultan's court, and furnished auxiliary troops.

The Ottomans made extensive use of the system of *timars* (military fiefs) for the conquest of Albania and followed a conciliatory policy. Nevertheless, revolts did occur. The Albanian lords rose against the Ottoman army, and their victories attracted the attention of the Christian West, particularly when Albanian resistance was led by the national hero, Gjergj Kastrioti Skënderbeg (Scanderbeg).

Gjergj Kastrioti was born in 1405. When he was in his late teens, he was sent as a hostage by his father, an Albanian lord, to Sultan Murad's II palace, where he was trained, converted to Islam, and named Skënderbeg (Commander Alexander). He took part in military expeditions both in Asia Minor and Europe and distinguished himself among the commanders of the Sultan.

In 1443, the Ottomans, at war with the Christians, headed by Hunyadi, King of Hungary, were defeated in a battle near Niš. Skënderbeg left the battlefield, rushed to Albania, seized the fortress of Krujë (Croya), and raised the banner of revolt—the red banner with the double-headed eagle. Popular support enabled him to occupy his father's domains in a few days. He renounced Islam, returned publicly to Christianity, and declared a Holy War against the Turks.

Skënderbeg knew that he could not face the wrath of the Sultan alone, so he attempted to form alliances with the neighboring Albanian lords and the Venetian Republic. A convention of local lords was held in 1444 in Lesh (Alessio), which was under Venetian sovereignty. A league was formed, and Skënderbeg was elected commander in chief of its army. For twenty-four years, Skënderbeg fought the Turkish army, twice led by the Sultans themselves. He was aided by the kings of Naples and the Popes, and Pope Nicholas V called him "Champion of Christendom." The death of Skënderbeg in 1468 did not break Albanian resistance, but gradually the Turks extended their territorial conquests in Albania and regained control. The memory of the national hero and his accomplishments has never died among his countrymen.

The collapse of Albanian resistance resulted in a great exodus to Italy. Albanians had begun emigrating to Italy at the end of the thirteenth century, but the emigrations had been small and sporadic until late in the fifteenth century. The refugees settled in the southern part of Italy, particularly Calabria and Sicily. Almost all belonged to the Greek Orthodox Church. Later, some were converted to Roman Catholicism, while the rest established a Uniate Church, preserving the Orthodox liturgy but recognizing the Pope as supreme spiritual head.

The arrival of Islam with the Turks introduced a third religion in Albania. The conversion of the people to Mohammedanism was a slow and uneven process. At the outset, the Ottomans do not seem to have emphasized conversion, but Skënderbeg's death was followed by a tide of apostasy, for the war between the Albanians and the Turks had been long and bloody and had borne the stamp of Cross against Crescent. The new faith encountered obstacles.

In the north and part of the center, Islam was opposed by Roman Catholicism. There were several forced conversions in the seventeenth century. One took place after 1690, when the Pasha of Pejë (Peć) deported inhabitants of northern Albania into the plain of Serbia and compelled whole villages to change to Islam. It was at this time that the Albanians spread in Kosovo. By the close of the century, the Catholics were outnumbered by the Mohammedans. Political advantages and exemption from taxes contributed heavily to the increase of converts. Although no subsequent period appears to have witnessed such widespread apostasy, occasional accessions to Islam continued until the end of Turkish rule.

Being at the height of their power and not fearing intervention from an Orthodox Christian force, the Turks did not use force in the south. The Orthodox Albanian, who was considered a rayah, embraced Islam for the same motives as the Roman Catholic of the north. Islamic pressure on Albanian Orthodox Christians began with the decline of the Empire and the Russo-Turkish wars of the eighteenth century, when conversions became more numerous.

As the economic-political basis of the Ottoman Empire was not nationality, but religion, the conversion of Albanians to Islam was of great consequence. Moslem Albanians not only ruled Albanian provinces, but also served elsewhere in the Empire. From the beginning of the conquest, they distinguished themselves in the Turkish Army and administration.

The eighteenth century saw the appearance in Albania of feudal latifundists, the landowning beys. The military fiefs of the spahis tended to become more and more hereditary, and the spahis, far from Constantinople in a declining empire, were able to affirm more strongly possession of the lands. Their timars were gradually transformed into *çifliks* (estates), cultivated as a rule by Christians, and the beys in effect became rulers in their own regions. The most powerful among them had at their disposal armed contingents and at times could even oppose the governors of the Sultan. To prevent their union, the Porte played one off against the other.

Toward the end of the eighteenth and the beginning of the nineteenth centuries, the influence of the beys in Albania diminished, for strong rulers emerged in both the north and the south. The Albanian family of the Bushatis had become powerful in northern Albania. Toward the end of the eighteenth century, they brought under their rule almost the whole of northern and central Albania. This situation could not be tolerated by Sultan Mahmud II (1784-1839), who destroyed the power of the Bushatis after the Russo-Turkish War of 1826-29.

It was inevitable that Sultan Mahmud II should come into conflict with the independent ruler of the south, Ali Pasha Tepelena (1790-1822), who by 1812 had extended his authority over all southern Albania, Greece, and southwestern Macedonia. He ruled for thirty-two years as a despot and "possessed more gold and soldiers than the Sultan himself." Owing to the strategic position of the coast and Epirus, which he controlled, the Pasha played an important role in the Napoleonic Wars. Both France and England courted him. In 1820, however, the Sultan ordered a military campaign against Ali Pasha Tepelena, who, after two years of war, surrendered and was decapitated.

The destruction of the Bushatis and Ali Pasha did not bring the war against the Porte to an end. The beys and the agas re-emerged and renewed the conflict as new taxes, officials sent from Constantinople, and compulsory military service infringed upon their privileges. The highlanders of the north (Gegs), among whom there was a tribal organization left intact by the Ottomans, also opposed the *Tanzimat* (reforms). They enjoyed autonomy, paying no taxes and serving as soldiers only in time of war. Among them, particularly in Mirditë and Malësi e Madhe, the customary law of the mountains, the Code of Lekë Dukagjini, was in force.

It was not until the Treaty of San Stefano and the Congress of Berlin in 1878 that the Albanian movement began to take a different course. When Russia defeated the Turks at the end of 1877, she imposed the Treaty of San Stefano, which accorded the Balkan Slavic nations large pieces of Albanian territory. The Great Powers refused to accept the provisions of the treaty, and a meeting of their representatives opened in June 1878 in Berlin to consider its revision. Afraid of decisions detrimental to the integrity of their country, Albanian leaders met at Prizren, a city in Kosovo, and created the Albanian League for the Defense of the Rights of the Albanian Nation, often called the League of Prizren. Few events in the history of modern Albania have been as crucial as the formation of the League.

Although the Congress of Berlin pushed back the San Stefano boundaries, Albania did not escape serious amputation. The first act of the Albanian League was therefore to protest to the Great Powers. The League did not oppose Serbia, which had already occupied the lands accorded her by the Treaty of Berlin. However, when Montenegro's turn came to annex Albanian territory, a clash took place. In the lengthy battle that ensued, Montenegro failed to occupy these regions. England then proposed that the province of Ulćinj (Dulcigno) alone should be ceded to Montenegro. In order to enforce this decision, the Powers resorted to coercive measures, and their combined fleets appeared off Ulćinj in September 1880. A Turkish army was sent to subdue the Albanians and deliver the town to Montenegro.

While the northern branch of the Albanian League was resisting Montenegrin encroachments, the southern branch was occupied with the problem of the Greek frontiers. At the Congress of Berlin, the Greek representatives demanded Thessaly and Epirus. The Great Powers adopted a French proposal that Turkey and Greece should come to a direct agreement on the frontier. The discussions between them failed, and in 1881 the Conference of Ambassadors in Constantinople extended the frontiers of Greece in Thessaly and cut off from Albania the region of Arta.

The Congress of Berlin had made Albanian leaders aware of the shaky structure of the Ottoman Empire, supported by interested powers solely for political motives. They feared that, should the Empire collapse, a disunited Albania would be partitioned. The potentially divisive factors in independent Albania would make the new state easy prey for partition among her neighbors. The population was politically unsophisticated and largely illiterate. The Albanian Catholic minority in the north consisted mainly of warlike mountaineers. The larger Albanian Greek Orthodox minority was settled in the south, adjoining their Greek co-religionists, and were greatly under Greek cultural influence. Finally, the Moslem majority, while concentrated in the center and in the Kosovo region, formed scattered minorities in north and south. The Albanian patriots thought that, under the circumstances, union of the Albanian people could be achieved by remaining for a time within the framework of the Ottoman Empire. They therefore demanded administrative and cultural autonomy for all Albanian lands united into one vilayet.

However, autonomy ran contrary to the centralistic policy of the Porte, and the Albanian claims to autonomy were ignored. The Albanian League therefore decided to resist the Turkish government, denying the authority of its officials and refusing to send recruits. The Turkish government could not permit its rule to be challenged by the League and dispatched an army under Dervish Turgut Pasha. In 1881, the Albanian League was destroyed. Its program, however, continued to influence Albanian political thought and revolutionary activity in the decades to come.

An important role during this period was played by the Italo-Albanians, those Albanians who had settled in Italy and preserved the language, customs, and traditions of their fatherland. With the linguistic congresses of 1895 and 1897, the Italo-Albanians entered the field of collective manifestations. An Albanian National Society was founded, with branches in all the Italo-Albanian colonies. Its organ was *La Nazione Albanese,* in which the best Albanian writers from both sides of the Adriatic collaborated.

The post-League period also witnessed the interest of the Great Powers in Albania. Russia, Austria-Hungary, and Italy interfered directly or indirectly in Albanian affairs. Russia aimed at restricting Austrian influence and at supporting Montenegro, a Slavic country, the aspirations of which were contrary to those of the Dual Monarchy. Austria-Hungary and Italy were concerned about the Adriatic. As neither of them could occupy Albania, they formulated the policy of the *status quo* of the "Ottoman coasts" of the Adriatic, and, if this were impossible, at least to preserve Albanian autonomy. Both Italy and Austria-Hungary, however, diligently attempted to enhance their prestige in the country.

In the beginning of the Young Turks regime, the Albanians, who had greatly contributed to its establishment, were very active. In November 1908, a congress of representatives from all parts of Albania and the Albanian colonies abroad convened at Monastir (Bitolj) to decide upon a common alphabet. The Congress unanimously adopted the Latin alphabet, thus making a great step toward Albanian unification. During the first ten months of Turkish constitutional government, cultural and political clubs were founded in Albania and in other parts of the Empire for the propagation of Albanian culture and the defense of Albanian rights. Schools were opened. For months, the Albanian educational movement was supported by newspapers and periodicals which appeared in all the important towns of the country and in other parts of the Empire. The very names of the publications are symbolic of the nationalistic trend.

However, it soon became apparent that the Young Turk policy was fundamentally opposed to that of the Albanian nationalists. The real aim of the "Committee of Union and Progress" was not the free development of the nationalities, but the "Ottomanization" of all subjects of the Empire and a centralized government. The Albanians sought decentralization. A series of revolts followed, coming to a climax in the summer of 1912.

On August 10, 1912, the Albanian leaders of the north, acting in the name of the four vilayets of Yannina, Monastir, Shkodër, and Kosovo, were strong enough to present substantial demands: a special system of administration and justice according to the requirements of the country; Albanian regional military service; use by government employees of the language and customs of the country; creation of Albanian schools; construction of roads; a general amnesty, and indemnity for damages suffered during the insurrection; restitution of arms. On September 4, 1912, the Constantinople government accepted all demands, except that for regional military service. This amounted to virtual Albanian autonomy, but soon the First Balkan War broke out.

Independence, World War I, Congress of Lushnjë, 1912-1920

For some time the Balkan governments had been preparing for war against Turkey. A Balkan League, composed of Serbia, Bulgaria, and Greece (later joined by Montenegro), was formed at the instigation of Russia, whose purpose was to prevent further Austro-Hungarian expansion in the Balkans, but the Balkan States' real motive was their desire for territorial expansion. The Albanian revolution had proved the weakness of the Ottoman Empire, and the virtual autonomy of Albania disturbed the members of the League, whose expansionist aims could be realized only by preventing the formation of a "Greater Albania." Albanian patriots therefore realized that it was time to abandon the sinking Ottoman ship, to follow a policy of neutrality, to stress the ethnic individuality of their countrymen, and to rely for the preservation of Albanian territorial integrity more upon the jealousy and rivalry of the Great Powers than upon their good will. The leader who played a great role at this critical time was Ismail Qemal Vlora, head of the Liberal Opposition in the first Turkish parliament. While the First Balkan War was being fought, Ismail Qemal left Constantinople for Vlorë, where, on November 28, 1912, before representatives from various parts of the country, he proclaimed Albania's independence and was made head of the Provisional Government.

From the very beginning, the new government faced great difficulties. Parts of Albanian territory were occupied by the belligerent powers, while Esad Pasha Toptani, an Albanian from one of the most influential families of Tirana who had ceded Shkodër to Montenegro and had been allowed to leave that city together with the Turkish Army under his command, was a threat to the newly born Provisional Government.

The Albanian problem raised by the First Balkan War became the concern of the conference of ambassadors, representing the Great Powers, which convened at London late in 1912 to attempt a general settlement. In the discussions at the London Conference, the chief powers supporting Albanian independence were Austria-Hungary and, to a lesser extent, Italy. Both feared the expansion of Serbia. The Dual Monarchy supported the creation of a "Greater Albania," which would include such peripheral regions as the districts of Gjakovë (Djakovica) and Prizren in Kosovo, inhabited mostly by Albanians. However, there was strenuous opposition on the part of Russia. Concessions were finally made on both sides, and on December 16, 1912, the Conference accepted a compromise proposal for an independent Albania whose boundaries were to be determined later.

The question of demarcating the frontiers was a difficult one. Under the provisions of the March 22, 1913 settlement, Shkodër was assigned to Albania, while Kosovo and Metohija were assigned to Serbia. The boundaries of 1913 were very similar to the present frontiers between Albania and Yugoslavia.

In the south, Greece claimed Northern Epirus—the area generally referred to as that part of southern Albania located between the present Greek frontier and a line drawn from a point north of Korçë, near Lake Prespë, to a point south of Vlorë on the Adriatic. This was an area of approximately 2,800 square miles comprising the present prefecture of Gjirokastër and Korçë. Its population included both Moslems and Orthodox Christians. The Conference decided that the boundaries of southern Albania should be delimited upon "ethnographic bases" and empowered a commission to act. On December 17, 1913, the Commission drew up a protocol at Florence. A key document in the Northern Epirus controversy, the protocol assigned the region to Albania. While some 35,000 Greeks were thus incorporated within Albania, an Albanian minority of roughly the same number in Çamëria (Tsamouria) became part of Greece. The Albanian delegation accepted this settlement.

On July 29, 1913, the London Conference decided on the constitution of the new state. Albania was proclaimed "an autonomous principality, sovereign, and hereditary by order of primogeniture, under the guaranty of the six Powers," who were to choose her prince. Control of her civil administration and budget was vested in an International Control Commission composed of an Albanian delegate and delegates of the Six Powers. On March 7, 1914, the new Prince, Wilhelm zu Wied, arrived at Durrës, then the Albanian capital. The Prince was of good will but lacked knowledge of his new country. He also made the mistake of appointing to the key positions—Ministry of the Interior and Ministry of Defense—Esad Toptani, whose ambition was to become King of Albania. Shortly after the Prince's arrival, a rebellion broke out around Durrës, at the instigation of Esad Toptani; a revolt occurred in the south and a provisional and autonomous government of Northern Epirus was established at Gjirokastër with Greek support. On September 3, 1914, on the advice of the representatives of the Great Powers and the International Commission, Prince Wilhelm left Albania, though he did not formally abdicate.

During World War I, Albania was occupied by the armies of several of the belligerent powers. The Serbs, Montenegrins, and Greeks remained for a short time; the Italians, French, and Austro-Hungarians remained for a long period. The Great Powers turned Albania into a battlefield. In order to attract the population of the occupied territories to their side, they conceded a certain measure of home rule, Italy even proclaiming on June 3, 1917, "the unity and independence of all Albania under the aegis and protection of the kingdom of Italy."

At the end of World War I, Albania was occupied by the Allied Powers, with Italy holding the larger part. Italy's policy at the Paris Peace Conference wavered between partition, independence, and complete control of Albania. Yugoslavia demanded Shkodër and Durrës, and Greece again laid claim to Northern Epirus. With respect to the latter question, Italy and Greece concluded the Tittoni-Venizelos Agreement in July 1919, which provided for mutual support in furthering their respective claims. At the Peace Conference, Albania had on her side only the principle of "self-determination" and President Wilson's firm opposition to dismemberment.

Confronted with this situation, Albanian leaders improvised a congress of representatives hastily elected by provincial councils, which met at Lushnjë on January 21, 1920. This body drafted a protest to the Paris Peace Conference against partition, demanding the independence of Albania "within its ethnic and natural frontiers." A government was formed, with Sulejman Delvina as Premier, which started its activities in Tirana in opposition to the government which had been previously formed in Italian-occupied Durrës. A Council of Regency was established, composed of representatives of the four religious denominations prevailing in Albania: a Roman Catholic, a Greek Orthodox, and a representative of each of the two Moslem sects, Sunni and Bektashi. The Congress of Lushnjë is a landmark in Albanian political life, being the manifestation of the nation's will to bar foreign intervention and to defend her territorial rights. In June 1920, an Albanian partisan army expelled the Italians from Vlorë, and the Italian government requested the intervention of the Tirana government to end the war. A treaty was signed in August 1920 by which Italy recognized Albanian independence and the Tirana government, and renounced the occupation and administration of Vlorë, though retaining the island of Sazan (Saseno). Italy's policy was to have on the opposite side of the Adriatic a free and independent, but friendly Albania.

The Reborn State, 1920-1939

The position of the Tirana government was now strengthened. On December 19, 1920, Albania was admitted to the League of Nations as a sovereign and independent state, with international boundaries yet unsettled. The Conference of Ambassadors did not reach a decision in this matter until November 1921, when the 1913 boundaries of Albania were confirmed, with the exception of small changes in the north.

The state was formed, but it had to be governed. Those who came to the top were in general the bureaucratic beys. They were the only Albanians who had any experience in administration, for they had served in the Ottoman Empire. They were supported by the landowning beys, who dominated the Christian and Moslem peasantry in the western and central plains. The beys thought of the state in terms of the interests of their own caste. Their predominance was contested by a rising Orthodox middle class, no longer under Greek cultural influence and some members of which had taken part in nationalist movements or had studied abroad. The Catholics of the north were sensitive about Moslem domination. Led by an influential and patriotic clergy, they formed a compact force and their voice carried weight in public affairs. Like the Orthodox, they had no governmental experience. It was not easy to reconcile the interests of these various groups, but the highlanders of the north, both Christians and Moslems, made matters more difficult for a government in Albania. The highlanders, who had enjoyed autonomy for many centuries, were reluctant to relinquish it.

Since the new government could not respect regional autonomy, Marka Gjoni, chieftain of the Catholic and unruly tribe of Mirditë, instigated a revolt in June 1921 and proclaimed the "Republic of Mirditë" at Prizren under Yugoslav auspices. As the government forces acted to suppress the revolt, Yugoslav troops crossed the Albanian frontier. Britain proposed the following November that the League of Nations take action against the invader, and the Yugoslav forces withdrew. Thereupon the Republic of Mirditë collapsed.

In 1921, a chamber of deputies began to function and Albania's first political parties—the Popular and the Progressive parties—appeared. Their labels were Western, but neither was a political party in the Western sense of the term. Supporters of the Popular

Party, known as the party of reform, were nominally led by the Orthodox Bishop Fan S. Noli, but the actual leader was Eshref Frashëri, a Moslem bey from Korçë. Another leader of this party was Ahmet Zogu, the future King Zog. The Roman Catholics, although inclined to prefer the Popularists, held aloof for the most part, due to the presence of Zog, whose increasing influence they feared. In general, they tended to play a political moderating role. The Progressives, who bitterly opposed agrarian reform, were dominated by Shefqet Vërlaci and other beys advocating feudal tenure.

The parliamentary contest between the two rival combinations brought about the formation of unstable coalition cabinets. Zog emerged as the most capable and energetic politician. However, when he began to exercise power dictatorially, he alienated influential Popularists and drove Bishop Noli and other exponents of Westernization to form a new group, the Opposition Party, which fomented disaffection in the army so that early in June 1924 two columns of troops marched on Tirana. On June 10, Zog fled to Yugoslavia, and a new government was immediately formed under Bishop Noli.

Noli was far too radical to command the support of the coalition that had ousted Zog. He did not seem to realize that there was almost no popular support for radical reforms in Albania. He alienated some of his supporters and alarmed the neighboring states by recognizing the Soviet Union. Finally, his government was paralyzed by a rivalry for office among its members, who split into factions.

Securing Yugoslav support, Zog conquered Albania, re-entering Tirana on December 24, 1924, a date which became known as "Legality Day." Bishop Noli fled to Italy, and the period of parliamentarianism (1921-24), remembered in Albania as one of great freedom, came to an end.

Zog's first act after triumphing over the Noli government was to purge the ranks of the army and gendarmery of those who had participated in the revolution against him in June 1924 and to place his own men in all responsible positions. On January 21, 1925, a constituent assembly, over which Zog's control was virtually complete, proclaimed Albania a republic and named Zog President for a term of seven years. The new constitution, promulgated the following March, vested the President with extensive powers.

Zog's next goal was to obtain the protection of a foreign power. He considered ties with Italy more advantageous than those with Yugoslavia. Moreover, Italy's claims to special interests in Albania had been recognized by the Great Powers in the Protocol of 1921. On May 12, 1925, the Albanian government therefore signed an agreement with Rome dealing with exploitation of natural resources. This, in effect, inaugurated a new stage of Italian penetration in the country.

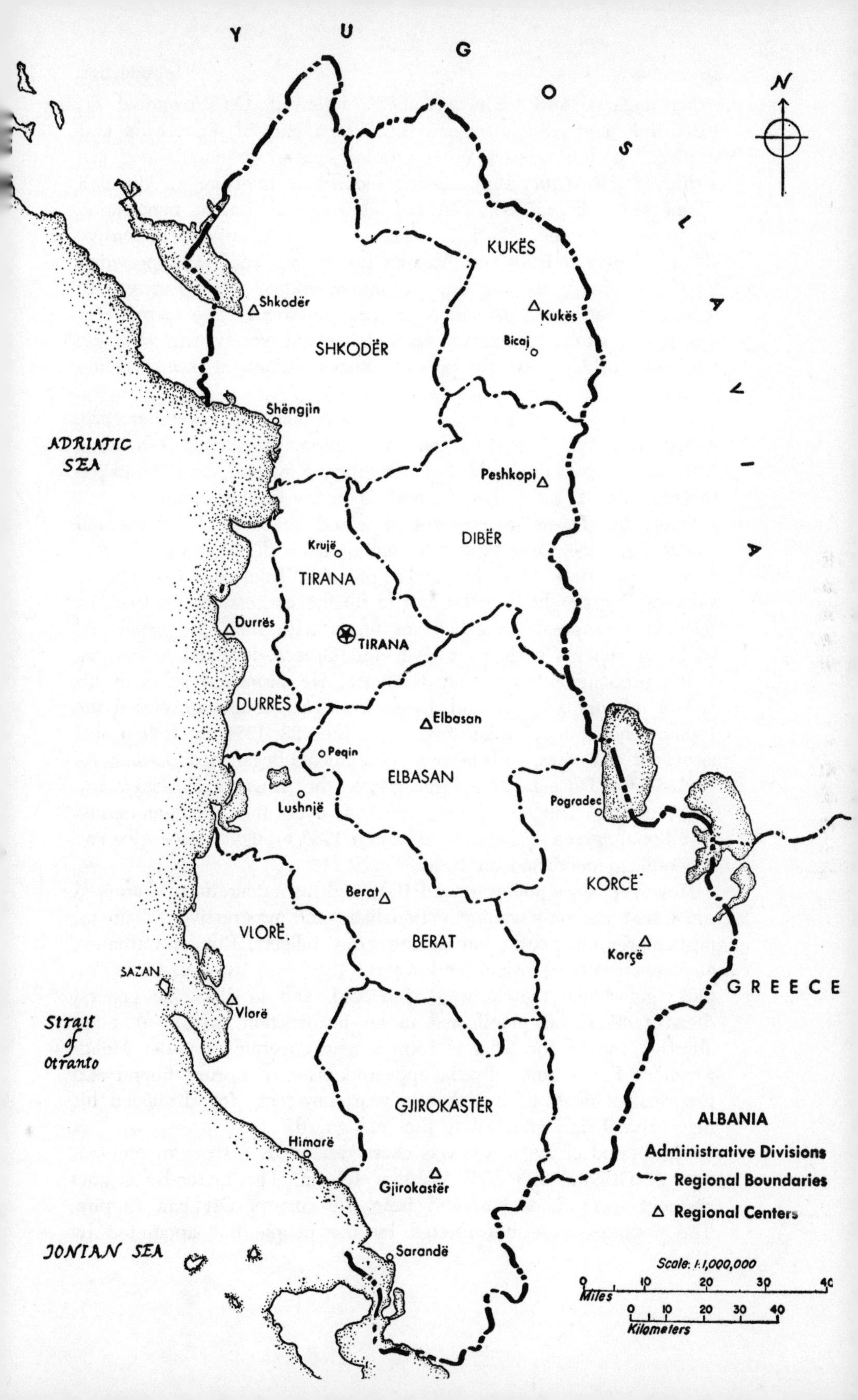

YUGOSLAVIA
ADRIATIC SEA
Strait of Otranto
JONIAN SEA
GREECE
N
SHKODËR
Shkodër
Shëngjin
KUKËS
Kukës
Bicaj
DIBËR
Peshkopi
TIRANA
Krujë
TIRANA
DURRËS
Durrës
ELBASAN
Elbasan
Peqin
Lushnjë
Pogradec
KORCË
Korçë
BERAT
Berat
VLORË
Vlorë
SAZAN
GJIROKASTËR
Gjirokastër
Himarë
Sarandë
ALBANIA
Administrative Divisions
Regional Boundaries
Regional Centers
Scale: 1:1,000,000
0 10 20 30 40
Miles
0 10 20 30 40
Kilometers

Other financial and trade agreements followed. On November 27, 1926, Italy and Albania signed the Tirana pact of "friendship and security," promising each other mutual support in maintaining the territorial *status quo*. Italy also agreed not to interfere in Albanian affairs unless requested. The second stage of Italian penetration began on November 22, 1927, when a treaty established a defensive alliance between Italy and Albania for twenty years and provided for close military cooperation. An Italian military mission arrived to reorganize the army; Italian arms and munitions were introduced. The public works constructed with Italian aid were mostly strategic roads and bridges, and the port of Durrës underwent reconstruction to make it suitable for large-scale landings.

The final step in Zog's rise to power was taken in September 1928. A special assembly revised the constitution, proclaimed Albania a "democratic, parliamentary and hereditary Kingdom," and bestowed the title "Zog I, King of Albanians" upon the former President.

While the Tirana government increased its control over national affairs, Albania's sovereignty was impaired by the King's many concessions to Italy. Finally, under pressure from his nationalistic subjects, Zog sought to call a halt to further concessions. In 1932, he rejected a proposal for a customs union with Italy. He concluded trade agreements with Yugoslavia and Greece designed to weaken Italy's predominant economic influence. He dismissed some of his Italian military advisers and, by nationalizing education, closed the Italian schools in Albanian towns. On June 23, 1934, an Italian fleet appeared at Durrës, and the two governments began new discussions. In 1935 the Duce made a large gift to the Albanian Treasury, and Zog accepted further Italian control over the Albanian army. Additional agreements signed in March 1936 brought closer Albanian economic dependence on Italy.

However, Zog's policy toward Italy and his autocratic rule aroused discontent not only among nationalistic and progressive Albanians, particularly the youth, but among army officers, Roman Catholics, and conservative Moslem landowners (the beys) as well. In 1932 a plot against the regime was uncovered, and in 1935 the general dissatisfaction was manifested in an insurrection, which, although abortive, moved the King to form a new government under Mehdi Frashëri. For a time Albania appeared oriented toward liberal and progressive ideas. In less than a year, however, Zog dismissed his new cabinet and returned to the "old guard."

The period of Zog's rule was characterized by a strange combination of Oriental rule and Western reform. The methods of government were those inherited from the corrupt Ottoman Empire. The deputies were not elected by the people but appointed by the King. On the other hand, substantial improvements were made in various fields as Albania came under greater Western influence. The vendetta and the tradition of carrying arms, prevalent especially in the highlands, were outlawed. Efforts were undertaken to collect taxes and recruit young men for the army, measures hitherto disobeyed by the population. A penal code patterned after that of Italy, a new civil code patterned on Napoleonic law, and a commercial code modeled after the French and Italian examples were introduced. Education was reorganized with the aim of creating a national educational system. There were no universities in Albania, but students went abroad to pursue higher studies. Although the regime later began to fear Western democratic ideas, it could not prevent their propagation and the creation of an intelligentsia. The creation of the Albanian state and the improvement of the means of communication brought the northern and southern Albanians—isolated for centuries mainly due to the topography of Albania—nearer together and created favorable conditions for a more unified country.

Axis Occupation and Resistance, 1939-1944

On April 6, 1939, King Zog left Albania and went into exile. The next day Fascist warships began bombarding the coast and Italian troops made landings at several points, seizing control of the country easily. Count Ciano announced that the invading army had come "to restore order, tranquility, and security to the country."

Italy's invasion of Albania aroused little reaction among other nations. Yugoslavia accepted the occupation as a *fait accompli* and appeared satisfied with the Duce's pledge that Italy was not interested in the Albanians of the province of Kosovo. Greece, not wishing to incur Mussolini's displeasure, made no move. Though the equilibrium among the Mediterranean countries had been upset, Neville Chamberlain made no vigorous protest. Only the United States raised her voice. In a statement on April 8, Secretary Hull denounced the attack as a "forcible and violent invasion" which constituted "unquestionably an additional threat to peace."

Fascist Italy rapidly put into effect its plans for the "new order." While the occupation was still in progress, an administrative committee under Xhafer Ypi, former Prime Minister and Inspector General of King Zog's court, was set up. On April 12, 1939, the Albanian National Assembly directed Shefqet Vërlaci, a long-time opponent of the King, to form a new government. At the same time, the Assembly abolished the constitution of 1928 and offered the crown to the Italian monarch, Victor Emmanuel III. The new King of Albania was represented by a royal lieutenant, or viceroy; this post was held by Jacomoni, who until the invasion had been Italian Minister to Tirana.

The foundations of the "new order" were laid on April 21, 1939, when the Albanian Fascist Party was formed. On June 3, the Albanian army was incorporated into that of Italy. A new constitution was promulgated on the same day, vesting all legislative and executive power in the King, who was assisted by a Fascist Corporative Council. The convening of this body, the appointment of its president, and the consideration of its agenda were reserved to the crown, which thus exercised complete control.

As Italy took over Albania's foreign representation, the Albanian Ministry of Foreign Affairs was abolished. Its liquidation was followed by a guaranty of equality in civil and political rights between Italians and Albanians. Albania's personal union with Italy was hardly distinguishable from outright annexation.

Italy's main object in occupying Albania was to secure control over the Straits of Otranto, the gateway to the Adriatic, and to establish a bridgehead in the Balkans for an attack on Greece. As a pretext for its contemplated invasion, and to enlist the support of Albanian nationalists, the Italian government emerged as the champion of Albanian Irredentism: Çamëria should be liberated. Italy declared war on Greece. On October 28, 1940, her army crossed the border. Albania was automatically at war with Greece.

Although some Albanians fought against the Greeks, many deserted, and others, including officers and enlisted men, joined the Greeks. Considerable Italian forces had to be left behind to safeguard their rear.

Early in December 1940, the Greeks hurled the Italians back into Albania, overrunning approximately one-fourth of the country by March 1941. The Greek forces were welcomed at first despite memories of bitter experiences during previous Greek occupations; but Greek press references to Korçë as the "most Hellenic Koritza" and the subsequent establishment of a Greek administration in the occupied regions caused general disillusionment among the Albanian people.

The German army was forced to come to Mussolini's rescue. In a characteristic blitzkrieg, the Nazis compelled both the Greek and the Yugoslav forces to capitulate in April 1941. Italy was then able to incorporate into Albania the province of Kosovo and other districts of southwestern Yugoslavia, which contained a population variously estimated at from 470,000 to 850,000 persons. Çamëria was also nominally administered from Tirana. German and Italian propaganda heralded the claim that Albania had at last secured her ethnic frontiers.

Albanian public opinion, however, was not won over to the Axis by these territorial aggrandizements. In December 1941, following directives from Rome for the inclusion in the Tirana government of new elements from the intellectual groups and the people rather than the beys, a cabinet was set up under Mustafa Kruja. To this Italy made some concessions toward Albanian autonomy.

Despite the concessions, resistance to the invaders increased in the country. Encouraged by the example of Yugoslavia and Greece, guerrilla bands succeeded in effecting acts of resistance in 1942. The resistance movements soon assumed great proportions under the leadership of the National Liberation Movement and the National Front.

The National Liberation Movement was created by the Albanian Communist Party. Before 1941, there were a few Communist groups in Albania, the most important the group of Korçë. To this group belonged the former Premier, now First Secretary of the Workers' (Communist) Party, Enver Hoxha, while he was still an insignificant teacher at the Lycée of Korçë. All these groups, however, were extremely small, and they frequently worked at cross purposes. Their contacts with Communist elements outside the country were tenuous.

Some months after the attack on the Soviet Union by Nazi Germany, two emissaries of Tito, Miladin Popović and Dušan Mugoša, members of the regional committee of the Yugoslav Communist Party for Kosovo and Metohija, arrived in Tirana, entrusted with the task of forming the Albanian Communist Party. In a brief time, they succeeded in uniting the various groups and in forming the Albanian Communist Party (November 8, 1941). They also chose the members of the central committee, among whom were Enver Hoxha and Koci Xoxe.

It was obvious that the new party was to be dependent on the Yugoslav Communist Party. In point of fact, it was a branch of the older organization. Tito's emissaries stayed in Albania throughout the war, and they were the real leaders of the Albanian Party, Miladin Popović the political organizer, and Dušan Mugoša the military organizer.

The Party took immediate steps to add new forces from the workers and the peasants. Since the peasants constitute the preponderant part of the population, the Communists promised that the land would belong, after liberation, "to those who tilled it." As Albania was a small country, whose lands were coveted by neighbors, they made propaganda for a Balkan federation. At the same time, the Communist Party worked for the ideological and political education of its cadres on the basis of Marxist-Leninist theory. It developed devotion to the Soviet Union and popularized the Soviet role as the vanguard in the fight against fascism. Above all, it strove to prepare the people for armed insurrection.

The Communists were a small, well-disciplined political party, but as the word "Communist" was unpopular and they needed popular support, they resorted to a political stratagem which had proved successful in neighboring countries. On September 16, 1942, they organized a conference at Pezë, to which Communists, non-Communists generally favorably disposed toward them, and some nationalists were invited. They aimed to present the conference as a union of nationalists and Communists and so to gain control of the whole resistance movement.

The Albanian nationalists at the Pezë Conference saw through the Communist stratagem and did not sign the resolution that proclaimed the creation of the National Liberation Movement. Nevertheless, the Communists claimed that the union between them and the nationalists "had been cemented," and that they would fight the invader together. As a tactical maneuver, Enver Hoxha included Abaz Kupi, chieftain of Krujë, a nationalist then not unfavorably disposed toward the Communists, in the National Liberation Council which was to direct the war against the Axis. Behind the façade of the National Liberation Movement, the Communists cynically prepared civil revolution under the guise of national liberation.

It was only after the Pezë Conference that Balli Kombëtar (The National Front) emerged under the leadership of Midhat Frashëri. Frashëri, a veteran democratic patriot and writer, had formed a clandestine resistance movement centered at Tirana during the early days of the Italian occupation. Balli Kombëtar extolled the principles of freedom and social justice within the country, championed the objective of an ethnic Albania, and recruited its following from all except Communists. Balli Kombëtar was essentially republican.

On December 10, 1942, Secretary Hull broke the silence on the part of the Allies. He declared that the United States was not "unmindful of the continued resistance of the Albanian people to the Italian forces of occupation" and looked forward to the day when effective military assistance could be given to the resistants. He stated also that American policy would be based on the Atlantic Charter, which respected the right of people to choose their own government, and wished to see sovereignty and self-government restored to those who had been forcibly deprived of them. This statement was followed by that of Anthony Eden, British Foreign Secretary, which was substantially the same, although it added the reservation that the frontiers of the Albanian state after the war would have to be considered at the peace settlement, if direct agreement between Albania and her neighbors should fail. Molotov's statement, similar to the American, followed suit. The Communists gave to this statement the greatest publicity.

For some time, efforts to secure the collaboration of Balli Kombëtar with the National Liberation Movement failed. However, when the Allies landed in Sicily, public opinion, pressure exerted by the British Military Mission, which had arrived a few months before, and the belief in an Allied landing in Albania led to a new effort toward cooperation of the two groups. On August 2, 1943, representatives of both organizations met at Mukaj, a village near Tirana. After compromises on both sides, the two parties agreed on unity of action and on the formation of a common committee, corresponding to a revolutionary government and called the Committee of National Salvation, which was to direct the war.

The agreement of Mukaj, however, was soon torn up by the Communists. The Yugoslav emissaries wrote on October 13, 1943:

> The [Albanian] comrade delegates have fallen in Mukaj on the positions of the Nationalists and, being full of opportunism, were satisfied with the simple change of a word or a sentence [in the agreement]. At that time, Comrade Tempo [Tempo was the sobriquet for Vukmanović, the principal Yugoslav Communist leader in Macedonia] was there [in Albania]. We discussed and studied together with the Central Committee the whole matter, the situation, etc., and decided to reject the manifesto and to refuse to recognize the manner in which the Committee for the Salvation of Albania was organized and its function as the supreme authority in the struggle for national liberation.

In September 1943, the Albanian Communists accepted the decision of their Yugoslav superiors and agreed to launch a full-scale attack against Balli Kombëtar.

Meanwhile, Albania's internal situation had deteriorated, and Italian intervention began to increase. In January 1943, Kruja, the cabinet head, resigned, and Italy sought the support of the beys by forming a cabinet under Eqrem Libohova, who had been Foreign Minister during King Zog's regime. However, as it became apparent that Italy would fall to the Allied forces, even the "faithful" beys abandoned the Axis cause.

Upon Italy's capitulation to the Allies, the German army took over the occupation of Albania, drove the guerrillas back into the hills, and decided on a policy of political conciliation. Germany paid lip-service to Albanian independence and neutrality, supported an ethnic Albania, and allowed the formation of a parliament and the institution of a regency council, in which Mehdi Frashëri was a prominent member.

In the mountains, however, the Communist guerrillas held sway. They branded the partisans of Balli Kombëtar traitors and fratricides; the latter, unable to combat both the Communists and the Germans largely gave up the struggle against Germany. Armed combat between the rival Albanian groups suited German purposes, for it reduced the pressure on German troops. On the other hand, in order to secure their rear during retreat from Albania, the Germans mounted a strong offensive in the winter of 1943-44 which almost annihilated the Communist forces.

After their recovery, the National Liberation forces met on May 24, 1944 in Përmet, a town in southern Albania, and created the Anti-Fascist National Liberation Committee, with attributes of a provisional government. The Albanian Communist Party still did not dare appear without some camouflage. This duplicity is manifested in the declaration of the Congress of Përmet, which, on the one hand, maintained that no party or group dominated the National Liberation Front (Movement) and, on the other hand, stated that the Communist Party showed to the people the road to liberation and assumed leadership.

In June 1944, Germany sent the 1st Mountain Division, one of her best units, from Greece to Albania. Even this offensive did not destroy the Partisans, whose main field of action was southern Albania. During the last stage of the fighting, the Communists, confident of their ability to seize power, met at Berat and on October 22, 1944, changed the Anti-Fascist National Liberation Committee into the Provisional Democratic Government of Albania. Enver Hoxha, who had assumed the military rank of colonel general and had become the acknowledged Party leader, was named Premier, and other Tosks (southerners) got in general the leading positions in the party and in the government.

Everywhere in Eastern Europe, the national Communist parties in the war and postwar periods sought to remove all obstacles to political power. In Albania the job was relatively easy. Balli Kombëtar, the major opposition, was eliminated by military action, by internal disintegration, and by propaganda favorable to the National Liberation Movement broadcast over the Allied radios. The same fate befell the less important "Legality Movement," which, formed in November 1943 under Abaz Kupi, had proclaimed loyalty to ex-King Zog. Albania had no goverment-in-exile like Greece or Yugoslavia, nor were there any Allied forces in the country. Further, the National Liberation Movement had the support of Tito's forces and of the Communist-controlled Greek EAM. When the German armies withdrew from Albania, the government chosen at Berat installed itself at Tirana on November 28, 1944 as the government of Albania. Enver Hoxha remained Premier.

Albania Under Communism, 1945-1955

Hoxha's Communist government employed every means to consolidate its position. Many of its most bitter opponents, leaders of the

National Front or the Legality Movement, fled to Italy. Others were brought before the People's Court as "war criminals" or "enemies of the people." The object of the trials was not so much to punish collaborators as to eliminate those persons who had influence and might oppose the Communist regime. Of course, the government did not neglect the drive against the remaining anti-Communist guerrillas, who were still resisting in the mountains.

The Tirana government asked for recognition by the West. The United States sent an informal mission to survey conditions and developments in Albania. At the same time, England also sent a formal military mission there. In order to create the impression that it was anxious to collaborate with non-Communist elements of the resistance which were willing to cooperate, the Tirana government changed the name of the National Liberation Front to the Democratic Front, which became the peace-time camouflage of the Communist Party. At the same time, Hoxha's government endeavored to show that it desired relations with the West. Western literature was distributed as freely as that from the East, and American films assembled by OWI were shown for large civilian and army audiences.

On November 10, 1945, the United States government expressed its readiness to enter into diplomatic relations with the existing regime in Albania. In establishing such relations, however, the American government requested assurances, according to the Yalta declaration, that the forthcoming elections for a Constituent Assembly should be held on a genuinely free basis; that all democratic individuals and groups should enjoy freedom of speech and the right to present and support their candidates; and that foreign press correspondents should be permitted to observe and report freely on the elections and the work of the Assembly. The note stated further that the United States desired that the government should confirm that the treaties and agreements which were in force between the United States and Albania on April 7, 1939, remain valid. Free elections were also a condition for recognition on the part of England.

Elections for a Constituent Assembly were held on December 2, 1945. In order to create the impression of a free election, the regime made provision for the casting of ballots for "the opposition." Since no organized opposition appeared because of the prevailing terror, the Democratic Front scored a triumph. According to official returns, 92 per cent of the qualified electors voted, and 93 per cent of these voted for the Democratic Front.

The Constituent Assembly on January 10, 1946 abolished the monarchy, proclaiming Albania a "People's Republic." On March 15, it promulgated the new constitution. The Constituent Assembly became the People's Assembly, or parliament, which chose the members of the Presidium. This followed the Communist pattern in Yugoslavia, which in turn had followed the Soviet pattern.

As the grip of the Communist Party became tighter, and as Yugoslav advisers for the ministries and experts for the army increased in number, dissatisfaction and disillusion among fellow-traveling members of the Democratic Front grew and became more vocal. There was also discontent among the rank and file members of the Communist Party and the army, who resented control by the Yugoslavs. They suffered ruthless persecution at the hands of Koci Xoxe, Minister of the Interior and head of the secret police, who with the backing of the Yugoslavs had become the most powerful man in the Party.

Albania's ties with Yugoslavia were particularly close. When the Germans retreated, the Albanian Communists even sent two Partisan divisions to fight alongside Tito's Partisans in Kosovo and elsewhere in Yugoslavia. In June 1946, Premier Hoxha visited Marshal Tito and concluded a Treaty of Friendship and Mutual Assistance with Yugoslavia. In November 1946, a series of economic agreements were signed between the two governments which provided for the absorption of the Albanian economy into that of Yugoslavia. The currency of the two countries was made interchangeable, and a customs union was put into effect. In all Albanian schools, the study of the Serbo-Croatian language was made obligatory, and many young Albanians were granted fellowships to study in Yugoslav universities. Albania had actually become a Yugoslav satellite and there were plans for Albania's incorporation into Yugoslavia as a federal republic. These plans were discussed by the Eighth Plenum of the Central Committee of the Albanian Communist Party, held in February 1948, but did not materialize because of the Stalin-Tito dispute.

During 1946, relations between Albania and the Western powers rapidly deteriorated, one reason being that the Western governments refused to deliver to Hoxha's regime leading Albanian nationalist politicians, who had fled to Italy or Greece, as "war criminals." Restrictions were imposed upon the American and British missions. Their travel was curtailed and their alien employees were expelled, while diplomatic members assigned to their staffs were kept from entering the country. The facilities of UNRRA were supervised.

For nine months, the Albanian government remained silent on the request of the United States regarding recognition. On August 13, 1946, it finally answered, accepting the multilateral treaties and agreements to which both the United States and Albania were parties, but failing to affirm recognition of the validity of bilateral instruments between the United States and Albania.

When the Peace Treaty was signed in 1947, Italy renounced in favor of Albania all property, "rights, concessions, interests and advantages of all kinds in Albania belonging to the Italian State or Italian parastatal institutions" (Article 29) and recognized "that the island of Saseno (Sazan) is part of the territory of Albania and renounces all claims thereto" (Article 28). The Greek delegation, however, asked for the inclusion of the Northern Epirus question in the agenda of the Paris Peace Conference in 1946. Molotov, whose government had recognized the Albanian regime on November 10, 1945, and Kardelj, Yugoslav Vice Premier, whose government was the first to recognize the Tirana regime, strongly opposed this. It was Secretary Byrnes' influence, however, that was most strongly felt in the withdrawal of the Northern Epirus question from the agenda.

Yet when Premier Hoxha returned from the Paris Peace Conference to Tirana, he accused the United States of being the principal obstacle to Albanian rights. Confronted with the hostility of the Tirana regime and the latter's unsatisfactory answer to her note of recognition, the United States government, on November 5, 1946, delivered to Premier Hoxha a note stating that there was no "further reason for the [American] mission to remain in Albania."

Following the announcement of the withdrawal of the American mission, the Albanian regime instituted trials of Albanian saboteurs, and trumped up charges that H. T. Fultz, an officer of the mission, together with other employes had instigated and subsidized sabotage activities at a drainage project on Lake Maliq, near Korçë. This was a way of simultaneously justifying the failure of the project and striking at opposition elements. The grip of the Communist Party was becoming stronger.

England, which had offered to recognize the Albanian government on November 10, 1945, refused to send her minister-designate to Tirana, when the British military mission there was charged with having organized a plot to overthrow the regime. On October 22, 1946, two British destroyers were blown up by a mine in the Corfu Channel. The United Nations Security Council later decided that the mines had been placed there "with the knowledge of the Albanian government," and Britain was later awarded damages by the Hague Court of Justice.

When the Tito-Cominform break occurred in 1948, the Albanian Communist Party took the side of the Soviet Union. Koci Xoxe, head of the secret police, and some of his henchmen were arrested and condemned on charges of Trotskyite and Titoist activities, and Xoxe was executed. The Albanian government denounced all agreements with Yugoslavia, except the Treaty of Friendship and Mutual Aid, and expelled all Yugoslav experts, advisers, and representatives. The Central Committee of the Albanian Communist Party declared that the Yugoslav leaders "have tried to destroy the independence of our country and our Party."

In the years after the Tito-Cominform rupture, the Tirana regime treated Yugoslavia as an enemy country. As early as September 30, 1948, the Premier of Serbia (a unit within the Yugoslav federative state), P. Stambolić, said in the parliament that Albanian armed bands had crossed the Yugoslav frontier, tempting the Albanian minority (Kosovo and Metohija) with promises of eventual annexation. Later, a Committee of Albanians, composed of members of the Albanian minority in Yugoslavia and some Albanian escapees, was created on Yugoslav soil. The frontier incidents multiplied and Tito's government protested to the Tirana regime, denouncing on November 12, 1949 the Treaty of Friendship and Mutual Aid.

As long as Yugoslavia was within the Russian orbit, Albania was of considerable strategic importance for the Soviet Union as a window on the Mediterranean which controlled the Straits of Otranto. With the expulsion of Yugoslavia from the Cominform, Albania's importance was reduced, although from the Soviet viewpoint she still had importance for Soviet Mediterranean strategy, Soviet prestige, and as a propaganda weapon in the Balkans.

Some months before the Tito-Cominform rift, several Russian advisers had arrived in Albania. After the break, Russians replaced Yugoslav advisers and experts in the ministries, in the army, in schools, and in almost all activities of Albanian life. Mehmet Shehu, a Moscow-trained man, became Minister of the Interior and head of the secret police. The Constitution of 1946 was amended in July 1950 along the lines of that of the Soviet Union. The Albanian Communists (in 1948 the Party changed its name to the Albanian Workers' Party) were less uneasy under Russian control than they had been under Yugoslav control because the Russians had a prestige which the Yugoslavs lacked. With the change, Albania advanced from the status of a subsatellite to that of a satellite.

Communist enslavement in Albania began with the advent to power of Hoxha's regime. By the agrarian laws of 1945-46, the government confiscated the land and redistributed it among the farmers, each family of 5 members being allowed to use 5 hectares (approximately 12.35 acres). Although deeds were issued, the farmer gets only a small fraction of his produce, the rest being procured by the government under the quota system. Collectivization of land started later, although the Albanian terrain is not suitable for it, and little has been done so far.

Hoxha's regime levied taxes on businessmen so high that they were unable to pay them. As a result, their property was confiscated, and the businessmen were sent to prison or labor camps. Factories were confiscated by the state, regimentation into government-controlled groups was the lot of the liberal professions, and the Albanian middle class was destroyed. With the expansion of industry under the present regime, such as the Stalin textile combine or the Çerrik oil refineries, the number of workers has greatly increased. Labor is organized within the narrow framework of trade unions formed and directed by the state.

The Communists began a war on illiteracy in 1946, largely so they could obtain control over the minds of the illiterate majority of the population. They increased the number of schools and courses. The schools, of course, are under Party control. Textbooks conform with the teaching of Stalin and Lenin, and in class the ideological aspects of each lesson are stressed. The student is urged to identify himself with the world Communist movement and to regard the Soviet Union as the realization of the Communist ideal. Everything Russian is extolled, while everything Western is belittled or disparaged.

Owing to the diversity and loose organization of the Albanian religious communities, their enslavement was easier in Albania than in other captive countries. A November 26, 1949 law required the religious communities to develop among their members the feeling of loyalty toward "the people's power" and the People's Republic of Albania. This law also gave the government the right to veto the election of the heads of religious communities. The government has divided the Moslem forces and has accentuated the Sunni-Bektashi opposition by allowing the Bektashis to constitute a community of their own. The ties between the Albanian Orthodox Church and the Russian Patriarchate became closer in the spring of 1951, when a delegation of Soviet religious leaders, headed by Bishop Nikon of Odessa, visited Tirana. On June 26, 1951, a "general assembly" of malleable Catholic clergymen was convened at Shkodër, the center of Albanian Catholicism. In August 1951, the Presidium of the People's Assembly approved the "decisions" of the "general assembly," which turned the Catholic Church in Albania into a national church. All the three major religious heads were used by Moscow in support of the Stockholm peace campaign and other Soviet moves.

The press and all other media of information and propaganda are under complete government control and have been employed to propagate Communist policies and the regime's programs. Several publications are issued by the Albanian-Soviet Friendship Society, Moscow's powerful and all-pervading propaganda agency in Albania.

Forced labor has been used extensively in Albania since the present regime seized control. Some 16,000 persons are said to have perished in Communist camps and prisons in Albania.

The Communists have placed great stress on the industrialization of the country. However, the Soviet Union seems more interested in increasing the production of Albania's farm products and mineral resources (petroleum, copper, chrome ore, and bitumen), the bulk of which are exported to Communist countries with which Albania has trade agreements.

In the Western world, Albania maintains diplomatic relations only with France and Italy. The Soviet Union and the other Communist states have strongly supported Albania's application to the United Nations but the Western Powers, particularly the United States and England, opposed until 1955. The Tirana regime has a record of disturbing peace in the Balkans. As early as November 1946, when Greek rebel bands began their attacks on the legitimate government of Athens, Albania was accused of giving them assistance. When some months later, General Markos took over command of the guerillas, that country became one of their chief bases.

In December 1946, the United Nations Security Council decided to send a Commission of Investigation to the Balkans. During May 1947, the Commission prepared a report which presented detailed evidence of Albanian support for Greek guerrillas. After the Soviet Union vetoed the recommendations of the Commission, the General Assembly of the United Nations established in October 1947 a Special Balkan Committee for the purpose of being "available to assist" Greece and her three northern neighbors in settling their differences and to inform the United Nations about conditions along the northern boundaries of Greece.

The Tirana government refused all facilities and information to that Committee. Even after the Tito-Cominform break, Albania continued to help the Greek rebels. On September 21, 1949, the United Nations Special Committee on the Balkans advised the General Assembly to declare the government of Albania "primarily responsible for the threat to peace in the Balkans" and call on Albania (and Bulgaria) to cease aiding the Greek guerrillas. In later years, whenever the Soviet bloc has proposed Albania's membership to the United Nations, the West has opposed it on the ground that the regime is not peaceful. In November 1954, when Albania's application for membership in UNESCO was considered, the United States representative, Preston Hotchkis, opposed because her regime had proved itself unable or unwilling to fulfill the obligations of the UNESCO constitution. However, on December 15, 1955, when the package proposal for the West- and Soviet-supported states was voted upon, Albania became a member of the United Nations, with the United States government abstaining.

On February 28, 1953, Yugoslavia, Greece, and Turkey signed a treaty of friendship and collaboration. In Athens on July 11, 1953, the foreign ministers of the three countries declared that they agreed "that the independence of Albania would constitute an important element for the peace and stability of the Balkans." This was a statesmanlike step, because the Tirana regime has made use of Greece's claims to southern Albania to strengthen its positions before the people as a government determined to defend the national interest. Since the Athens declaration recognized the independence of Albania, but not her territorial integrity, certain doubts began to arise. The regime, therefore, denounced the Balkan Pact as an instrument of agression and interpreted the Athens declaration as a program for dismembering Albania and subjugating it to the neighboring Balkan States.

In order to convince the Albanians of the friendliness of the United States government, Secretary John F. Dulles made clear its policy toward Albania in a letter addressed to the President of the National Committee for a Free Albania on August 26, 1953. This Committee, formed in Paris in August 1949 under the leadership of the patriot Midhat Frashëri, has enjoyed the support of the Western Powers. In his letter Secretary Dulles stated: "To the United States, which has traditionally supported the right of all oppressed peoples to freedom and liberty, the tragic plight of the Albanian people is a matter of deep concern. . . ." He warmly welcomed "the recent declaration by Albania's neighbors of their peaceful purpose toward Albania and their intent to support the right of the Albanian people to freedom and independence." As far as territorial claims were concerned, Secretary Dulles declared: "The United States recognizes that the problem of future relationship between a free and independent Albania and its neighbors is a matter primarily of bilateral discussion and solution."

Another American expression of friendly feelings toward the Albanian people was manifested on March 4, 1955, when President Eisenhower offered $850,000 worth of food in order to ease the food shortages in Albania. The food was to be distributed by the League of Red Cross Societies. However, the Tirana regime rejected the offer.

Following Stalin's death, some developments took place in the international field. On December 22, 1953, diplomatic relations between Albania and Yugoslavia were resumed. On May 14, 1955, the Eastern Security Treaty, called the Warsaw Treaty, was signed with Albania one of the signatories. The only pact of collaboration and mutual aid Albania had until then was with Bulgaria. With the Warsaw Treaty, not only the other captive countries guaranteed her security but also the Soviet Union, thus strengthening her position in the Balkans. The Bulganin-Khrushchev visit to Yugoslavia which followed made Albania's attitude toward that country friendlier, although with certain reservations, for it was difficult for the Albanian Communist leaders to make such a shift. On July 3, 1955, the Tirana regime, in a message to Greece through the Secretary General of the United Nations, expressed the desire for normal diplomatic and good-neighborly relations. Greece's reply was conditional, and relations were not established. The "Geneva spirit," which originated in the same month, had its effects on Albania, which is always likely to reflect Moscow's shifts in attitudes.

2. THE LAND

Location and Area

If one thinks of the Balkan Peninsula as a large triangle with its base along the southern edge of the Sava and the Danubian lowland, and with its apex at the southernmost tip of the Peloponnesus, then the western side of the triangle rests upon the Adriatic and Ionian shoreline across the sea from the Italian boot. Along that western line of the Balkan Peninsula, washed by the Adriatic and athwart the Dinaric Alps, stretches rugged Albania, smallest of the Balkan States, with a maximum length of about 215 miles northwest to southeast, and with a width ranging from approximately 90 miles between Lake Prespë and the Adriatic to less than 50 miles in the north. With a total area of 10,629 square miles (27,529 square kilometers), (according to the *Encyclopaedia Britannica* staff), it lies between 39°38′ and 42°41′ N. and between 19°16′ and 21°03′ E. Albania borders on Yugoslavia in the north and northeast, and on Greece in the south and southeast.

Albania has a fairly wide coastal belt which provides a gateway to the interior of the Balkans. The ports of Durrës and Vlorë are convenient heads of communication for penetration into the peninsula. Another vital town, Shkodër, near the port of Shëngjin (San Giovanni di Medua), though somewhat less favored, is only half as far from either Salonica or Belgrade, the two principal trade centers of the Balkans, as these two cities are from each other.

Principal Landforms and Their Underlying Rocks

Albania is a predominantly mountainous country, as is illustrated by Table 1, which shows that 70 per cent of the country lies above the 1000-foot contour line. The balance of the area includes the lowland and the low hills of the coastal region, as well as the lower reaches of the valleys which open onto the coastal plain in fiordlike manner.

The mountains rise abruptly from the coastal lowland to elevations above 6,500 feet (see map, page 33). This escarpment stands out most prominently in the following ranges: the Himarë (in the Ionian folded coastal range), the Kurvelesh, Tomorr, Ostravicë, Shpat, the Dajt-Krujë wall, and the western edge of the Mirditë highland. This physical phenomenon has been a leading factor in the economic and cultural separation of the lowland from the upland population of Albania.

The discharge of Albania's rivers is heavy, especially during the winter, even though their lower courses are short. These rivers have created a broad alluvial lowland which is constantly being enlarged in a seaward direction. The Albanian lowland, however, does not form a continuous belt. It is interrupted by several hill ranges. It is of geologically recent origin. Its youth may be judged from the lagoons and marshes that cover certain parts of it year-round, and from the shallow depressions that are flooded during the rainy season and following the snow melt.

Table 1. DISTRIBUTION OF HYPSOMETRIC LAYERS

Elevation above Sea Level	*Area*	*Per Cent of Total Area*
(*in feet*)	(*in acres*)	
0-1000	21,004,670	29.4
1000-2000	13,303,440	18.6
2000-3000	12,791,640	17.9
3000-4000	10,683,910	15.0
4000-5000	7,551,040	10.6
5000-6000	3,904,580	5.4
6000-7000	1,632,550	2.3
7000-8000	487,020	0.7
8000-9000	58,320	0.1
Over 9000	2,000	—

Source: Mario Michelangeli, *Il problema forestale albanese* (Rome: Reale Accademia d'Italia, 1940), p. 6.

In the north, a massive limestone extension of the Dinaric Alps reaches inland some 20 miles in depth and 25 miles in width from adjacent Montenegro. This massif reaches the imposing height of 8,525 feet in the Maj' e Hekurave. Several narrow valleys radiate from this mountain mass; their upper end is at an elevation of 4,900 feet, just below the timber line. Heavy snowfall in this area has prevented tree growth at higher altitudes. Strong erosive forces have been at work here: torrential rains, sudden spring thaws, and warm southerly winds in late spring. These erosive forces have given rise to typically Alpine landforms. Above the timber line, bare rock surfaces are more common than Alpine meadow land. In the deeply incised valleys, the accumulation of till and gravel has left little room for cultivable land or low-altitude pastures. In general, most of the cultivable fields and meadows are found in forest clearings, where Albanian peasants have been able to arrest soil erosion by skillful terracing.

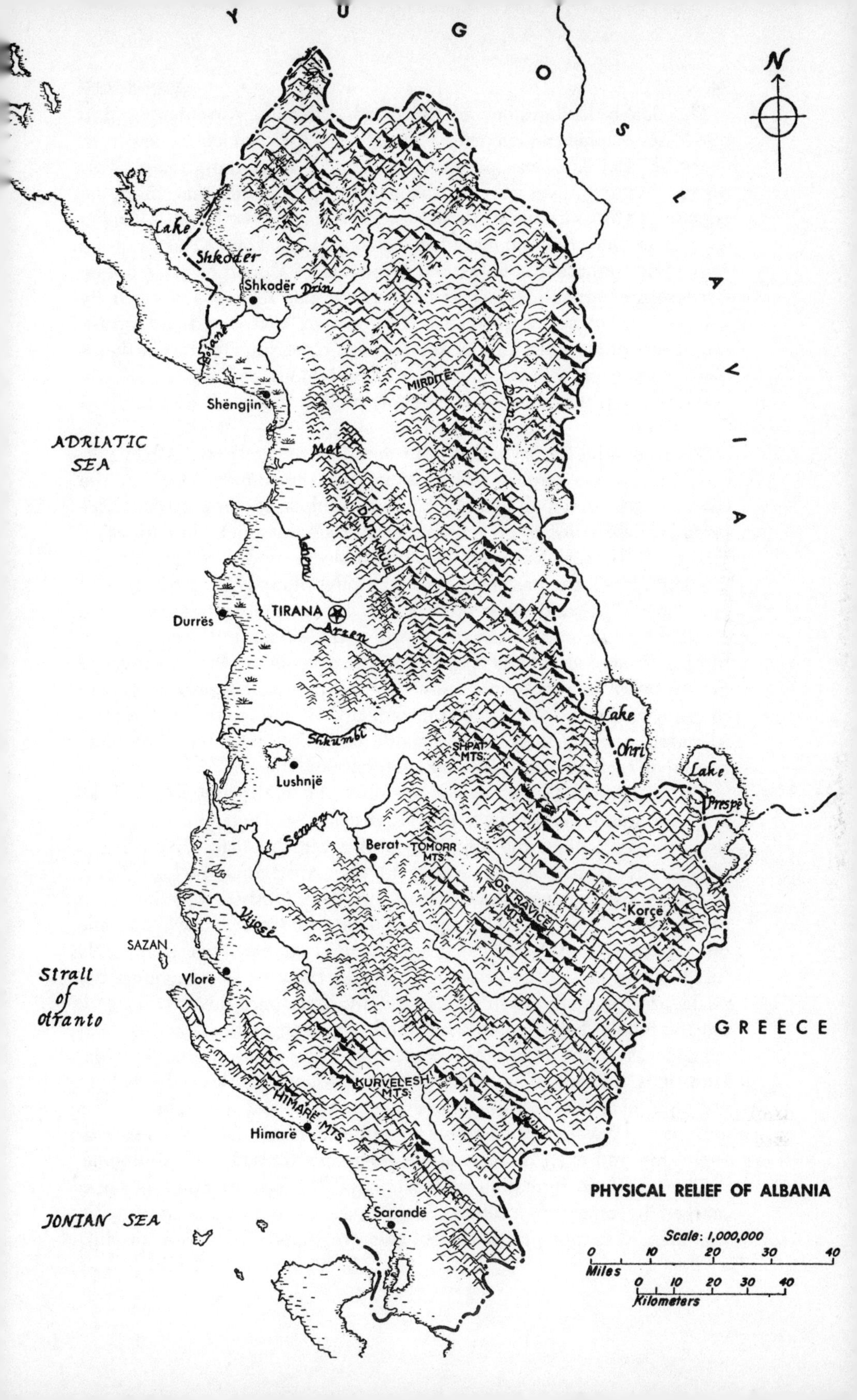

PHYSICAL RELIEF OF ALBANIA

The dolomitic limestone of the North Albanian Alps merges into the lesser Alpine region called Malsi' e Vogël, which is lower in elevation and less precipitous in character than the former. This region, in turn, gives way to the gently rolling hills that form the edge of the Shkodër basin. In an easterly direction the North Albanian Alps pass into the mountainous region of Gjakovë. This massive serpentine formation is imbedded in alluvia of Upper Tertiary origin. Because the serpentine rock is impervious, this region is watered by a dense net of surface streams. The springs that rise here furnish the agricultural water supply for an area extending to the northernmost border of the country. The mountainous region of Gjakovë is bounded on the south by the deeply incised valley of the combined Drin rivers.

South of the Drin valley, the interior of northern Albania is occupied by the largest and most compact mountain block in the country. Its principal heights have a north-south orientation. This central range consists of serpentine overlain by thick formations of limestone. Toward the west, the limestone thins out in the Mirditë highland. Since the basement rock, the physiography, and the vegetal cover in the Mirditë differ only in detail from the central range, the entire mountain mass is usually considered a single unit. This massive block is bounded by the Dajt-Krujë escarpment in the direction of the central Albanian lowland, and by the marginal Korab ranges on the side facing the interior of the Balkans. Where it faces the central Albanian upland, there is a smooth transition into the serpentine basement rock of the Çermenikë Mountains.

The Mirditë highland, which includes the entire district of Pukë and the southernmost part of the district of Dukagjin (over 580 square miles), gives the appearance of a high plateau, even though structurally it is not. According to the Austrian geologist, Ernst Nowack, two general levels may be distinguished on this high plateau—one between 2,600 and 4,000 feet above sea level, and the other between 4,000 and 4,600 feet. Several summits rise from 1,300 to 1,950 feet above the plateau. Wherever the rock is serpentine, the peaks are rounded; wherever topped by limestone, they are jagged. On the whole, however, this hill land has none of the grandeur and ruggedness of the North Albanian Alps. Perched atop a high tableland, it is difficult of access from the lowland. Most of the valleys are high, over 600 feet above sea level, and almost uninhabited. The soil mantle developed from the serpentine parent material is exceedingly thin and even more erodible than soils formed from limestone.

The limestone formation which tops off the central range is pockmarked by numerous dolines. Since there is no surface drainage in this area, watering places for animals are found exclusively in sinkholes where shallow ponds or puddles outlast the summer drought. Between the central range and the mountains bordering this region on the east lies the valley of the Drin i Zi (Black Drin) River, which is really a succession of three basins separated by thresholds of high hills. Each smaller in area and lower in elevation than the preceding one (from south to north), the basins of Dibër, Peshkopi, and Kukës were carved out of Upper Tertiary sandstones partially overlain by younger argillaceous alluvia. Sheep are raised on the gently sloping eastern flanks of these basins. Even here, however, it is not possible to take full advantage of the excellent summer pasture because of the shortage of watering places.

The Mat basin lies between the previously described central mountain range, the Mirditë Mountains, and the western escarpment. It was also carved out of a mixture of Upper Tertiary sandstones and argillaceous alluvia. It owes its origin to the erosive action of mountain torrents. The valley floor is lined with coarser materials than are found in the Drin valley; it is dissected into numerous tributary gorges which reduce the amount of arable land in the basin and impede communication.

From the Çermenikë upland, which forms the northern border of the basin of Elbasan, mountains of serpentine and limestone extend into southern interior reaches of Albania. They flank the middle Shkumbî valley and encircle part of the Shkumbî basin. The sandstone which forms the floor of this basin also extends over the Kamje Mountains to the south and into the substantial high basins of Korçë and Bilisht. The upland of Voskopojë, which bounds the Korçë basin on the west and merges with the Kolonjë basin in the south, consists of superimposed limestone, sandstone, and serpentine layers. The eastern margin of the Kolonjë basin is formed by the towering Gramos range which consists primarily of serpentine. North of the Gramos range, the Moravë ridge forms the divide between the basins of Bilisht and Korçë. The upland of Kolonjë forms the southernmost enclosure of Albania's mountainous interior.

The following important differences distinguish the northern part of the interior from the south: the average elevation of the northern part of the country is just over 6,500 feet, with the intramontane basins ranging from 1,000 to 1,600 feet above sea level; in the southern part of the country the respective figures are 5,000 to 6,500 feet and 2,600 to 3,3000 feet; only the Shkumbî basin (1,600 feet above sea level) falls markedly below this average. This comparison of regional elevations points up the fact that the southern part of interior Albania has more rounded topographic features and a less pronounced local relief than the northern section—its basins are larger and more easily accessible. The tectonic alignment of the principal intramontane depressions, on the other hand, is a feature common to both the northern and southern sections of inner Albania: the most shallow depression is the basin of Kolonjë; directly to the north of it lies the somewhat deeper basin of Korçë. Somewhat farther north another depression, its floor some 1,000 feet below the level of the Korçë basin, holds Lake Ohër (Ohrid). A similar series of steplike depressions occurs in the row of small basins which constitute the valley of the Drin i Zi River.

In the mountains of Kolonjë, the massif of Gur' i Topit, and in the narrow valley system of Rapun-Shkumbî (Librazhd area), the lack of arable land, severely eroded soils, and meager pasturages have all contributed to the very low population density. Only the basin floors and a narrow belt of land along the lower slopes are suitable for settlement, but even so the proportion of lands occupied by humans exceeds the proportion of usable land in the northern districts of the country. This region furnishes excellent examples of how the interior basins are sealed off from the Albanian lowland by such topographic obstacles as sheer mountain barriers and escarpments.

The folded mountains of southern Albania begin south of the basin of Kolonjë and run along a northwest-southeast axis. But for the interruption by a low coastal strip, they constitute a southern extension of the Dinaric Alps. Like the former, they are characterized by strictly parallel crestlines, by deep and rather wide valleys, and by a variety of topographic features typical of massive limestone formations. Along the valley floors a Flysch formation (sandstone) comes to the surface. The southern folded mountains consist of four major parallel ranges: (1) the coastal range; (2) the ranges of Murganë, Mal' i Gjërë, and Kurvelesh; (3) the ranges of Bureto, Lunxhëri, and Shëndëlli; and (4) the ranges of Nëmerckë (or Douskon), Dhëmbel, and Trebeshin. The intramontane valleys in this area suffer from a water shortage.

The hill land: the Flysch formations that run along the whole western border of the Albanian upland gradually disappear at the inner edge of the lowlands. Although it narrows down considerably, this Flysch belt extends as far as the basin of Shkodër and the Cukal Mountains. The soils of the hill country are very shallow, seldom deeper than one foot; over vast stretches bare rock appears at the surface. Only in a few small valleys and depressions do soil accumulations as thick as three feet occur.

The lowland: There is no continuous lowland of any extent in Albania. The low coastline recedes in the shape of deep bays between the forelands built up by the several deltas. The Albanian lowland is best described as a series of disconnected level areas interrupted by the hill country which parallels the coastline. Each of these level areas has its own drainage and water-supply problems. They are often described by the collective term "Myzeqe," a name which more specifically applies to the lowland between the Shkumbî and Seman rivers, the largest of all the low regions.

The soils in these lowland regions are predominantly alluvial. Only the younger, lighter alluvial soils which line the numerous river courses lend themselves to easy cultivation; they are rich in minerals and are periodically renewed by flooding. Although their agricultural yields are potentially very high, these flood plain belts are constantly threatened by inundation.

Climate

Albania has a greater number of climatic regions than one would expect within so small an area (see Table 2).

Table 2. CLIMATIC DATA FOR SELECTED LOCATIONS

		Average Temperature (in F.)			
			Extreme Month		*Average Annual*
Place	*Altitude*	*Winter*	*Summer*	*Annual*	*Precipitation*
	(*in feet*)				
Berat	223	43.0	75.4	58.6	472
Durrës	23	46.9	76.6	61.0	430
Elbasan	361	40.8	78.4	59.2	441
Krujë	1,936	39.2	70.7	54.5	665
Pukë	2,825	33.8	70.3	50.7	717
Shkodër	72	39.9	77.9	58.8	573
Tirana	361	41.5	75.6	57.7	402
Vlorë	36	48.2	77.0	61.9	425

Source: Mario Michelangeli, *Il problema forestale albanese* (Rome: Reale Accademia d'Italia, 1940), p. 13.

The main reason for this climatic variation is the country's topography. The tectonic fault which separates the mountain massifs and folded ranges from the hills and the lowland also forms the dividing line between a typically Mediterranean climate and the continental climate of the Balkan interior. The zone of Mediterranean climate is limited to the coastal lowlands of Albania, where rainy and mild winters are followed by arid, hot, and almost cloudless summers. According to V. Conrad, an authoritative climatologist of the Balkans, a temperature of 86°F. may be reached at Shkodër during the four hottest months; in Vlorë this maximum may occur for as long as six months. Furthermore, on the basis of thirty-year records, Conrad has found that Shkodër is likely to experience sixty days of temperature ranging from 77° to 86°F., and eighteen days with temperatures from 86° to 95°F. In the mountainous interior of Albania, the average August temperatures may be seven degrees lower than in Shkodër (Shkodër 78°F., Pukë 71°F.). In the mountains summer rainfall is much more frequent because the warm air condenses as it rises from the lowland. Although the northern part of interior Albania, and especially the Krujë range, is more receptive to humid, warm sea winds than the mountains of the southern interior, this region is also under the influence of cold Bora winds which sweep in from the northwest. It is thus possible to distinguish three types of summer climates, listed here in order of decreasing rainfall: the northern mountains, the southern mountains, and the coastal lowlands. In the mountains the maximum temperatures are also high, but average temperatures are lower and the cool nights provide ample relief from the heat.

In the winter the number of climatic zones is reduced to two. Strong Balkan winds collide with humid, warm air masses from the Mediterranean directly over Albania so that heavy and frequent thunderstorms blanket the country. However, the cold continental air mass loses much of its force before it reaches the coastal plain. Freezing temperatures are carried only seldom into the lowland, and average temperatures remain rather high throughout the winter—the climate is still Mediterranean. In the mountains, on the other hand, one encounters cold waves of increasing severity as one proceeds eastward. All the upland therefore has a continental climate during the winter.

The climatic impact on human activities is partly shown in Conrad's description of summertime in the coastal plain. Conrad found that: "The high temperatures which frequently prevail during the night and in the morning weaken the body and deprive man of his energy. The monotony of the heat which prevails in the Albanian lowland is something that the Central Europeans find difficult to endure. Average temperatures are high, with little variation and infrequent cooling-off periods." The productivity of the farmer is impaired not only by the high relative humidity and by the coincidence of the hottest season with that of greatest agricultural activity, but also by the primitive tools he is forced to use.

Conditions are hardly more satisfactory in the densely populated intramontane basins. In the summer season, air masses come to a standstill above these basins. The lower layers of air are kept warm, hence the night temperatures are not lowered as they otherwise would be at such altitudes.

The highlands proper, on the other hand, have a very healthful climate. Maximum temperatures are bearable, the air is cool at night, summer rains are frequent, and the relative humidity is low. Unfortunately, however, the highlands cannot support a dense population because the soils have been damaged by erosion, the topography is rugged, and drinking water is lacking.

Native Vegetation

The climatic, topographic, and geological diversity characteristic of Albania is reflected in the variety of natural vegetation types developed. Riverine forests extend along alluvial belts and into the delta regions, as well as into the slight depressions found within the lowland. These forests contain mixed stands of willows, poplars, elms, pines, oaks, and white beeches. Those found in the vicinity of transportation routes have been heavily logged and in some areas have given way to sheep pastures. Because virgin forests help maintain a humic top, the lowland farmer places a high premium on clearing such land for cultivation. Wherever forests do not protect the ground, the soil is either washed away or blown away during the summer drought. Even during humid months, the grass cover is so sparse that it cannot be said to constitute a true meadow. The annual grasses have a growing period of only six to seven months. The perennial varieties require extensive root systems in order to survive the summer droughts. The aridity of the summer and the flooding of low-lying areas during the fall and winter are the principal reasons for the sparse and clumplike growth of Albania's grasses.

Maqui is very widely developed in the drier parts of the lowland and in the hill land. This shrub is a typically Mediterranean plant form. Transpiration from this kind of plant is kept at a minimum by leaves which are small, shiny, hairy, and of waxy or leathery texture. In southern Albania, maqui is found up to an elevation of 1,600 feet; in the north, 1,300 feet above sea level is the limit of growth because the plant is not frost resistant.

Beyond the maqui, one finds sparse deciduous forests which contain several species of oak and hazel shrubs. In the southern part of Albania, especially in the interior of the country, settlement occurs in a concentrated village pattern. In this area the climax forest has been cleared, producing second-growth forests of immature trees whose regeneration is impeded by drought, erosion, indiscriminate felling, and tree-grazing by sheep. This "dry forest," as it has been called by Dr. Friedrich Markgraf, covers the sandstone areas; it is also almost coextensive with the red earth districts of the limestone country.

In the treeless portion of the limestone, low rock plants and karst pasture grasses predominate. These pastures lack the organic matter that develops in forest areas of falling leaves. According to Markgraf, the thousand-meter line (3,300 feet) marks the lower boundary of the cloud forest. This vegetation stratum begins along the lower edge of the more or less permanent cloud cover and is therefore moderately well protected against drought. In limestone areas, the cloud forest consists predominantly of beeches whose leaves provide organic matter to the soil mantle. Black pines make up the cloud forest over serpentine rock formations. In southern Albania, karst heath and meager rock vegetation extend from the timber line to the mountain tops. In northern Albania, there are a few humic meadows above the timber line. Their area is so limited, however, that they are of no more than local economic importance.

Fauna

The mountain areas of Albania are not a favorable wildlife habitat because they are so heavily grazed by livestock during the summer and because they suffer from a shortage of springs during that season. Besides, the naturally scanty fauna has been almost decimated by huntsmen. Wolves, deer, and boars have been pushed back into the remotest forests of the country. Only rarely does one encounter any chamois. Wild fowl, on the other hand, is found in great abundance in the forests of the lowland.

Water Resources and Drainage Basins

The only tributary of the Danubian drainage basin which rises within the boundaries of Albania is a minor mountain stream whose source is on the northern slopes of the Albanian Alps. An even smaller stream empties southward into the Kastoria basin of northern Greece. All the other rivers reach the sea within Albanian territory. Five of the smaller basins discharge their waters into the Ionian Sea, while sixteen of the major watersheds empty into the Adriatic Sea. Table 3 shows Albania's principal drainage basins.

Table 3. Principal Drainage Basins and Rivers

Basin	*Length of River*	*Surface of Basin*
	(in miles)	*(in square miles)*
Erzen	56	301
Bojanë with Lake Shkodër	27	623
Drin	174	2,263
Ishem	43	244
Mat	65	964
Semen	157	2,305
Shkumbî	91	918
Vijosë	147	1,682

Source: Mario Michelangeli, *Il problema forestale albanese* (Rome: Reale Accademia d'Italia, 1940), p. 9.

A distinctive feature of Albania's rivers is the considerable elevation at which they flow prior to reaching the coastal plain. For this reason most of the streams, including the largest rivers, reach the lowland zone as mountain torrents. Within the mountain zone, the rivers have cut deep channels into the soft sandstone formations of the valley floors, forming gorges with almost vertical walls as high as 300 feet above the stream. Because of this, it is difficult to conceive of irrigation works along the upper course of Albania's rivers. Irrigation along their lower course is also fraught with difficulties because the sediment-laden streams build their channels above the level of the flood plain, break out from their natural levels, and shift their channels. Hence, the only segments of the drainage basin where irrigation is feasible are the valley bottoms near the headwaters of the streams and in those parts of the tableland that have perennial drainage. Wherever natural conditions along streams are favorable, the Albanian farmer has built irrigation structures and canals with considerable ingenuity. His skill is so great that he has acquired the reputation of a specialized craftsman, and in former days of unrestricted movement within the Balkan Peninsula his services were in demand far beyond his home district.

Another characteristic of most of Albania's rivers is the attenuated shape of the successive basins they traverse. Geologists have described these basins as former lakes or arms of the sea. Upon leaving their basins, the rivers break through mountain barriers to reach the lowland. These break-throughs have occurred mostly along fault lines. They are clearly discernible along the Drin and Mat rivers, along the upper Shkumbî and Devoll rivers, on the Vijosë near Këlcyrë, and on the Drin shortly before its influx into the Vijosë. As such canyons form the only outlet of many of Albania's mountain-fringed upland basins, it has been easy to defend the isolated settlements located there against invaders. However, the physiography has also been an important contributing factor to the economic and cultural isolation of the population, and to the long-term hostility of tribes inhabiting adjacent basins. In the North Albanian Alps, population clusters within a single basin are sometimes entirely cut off from each other by variations in elevation.

In terms of future economic development, however, these break-through gorges offer favorable sites for major dam structures capable of supplying Albania as well as adjacent countries with cheap hydroelectric power. The advantages of the sites are further enhanced by the hardness and impervious nature of the bedrock and the seasonal abundance of stream flow. The first project of this kind is currently under construction on the Mat River.

The harmful consequences of erosion are visible throughout the mountainous part of Albania. Soil erosion is so active because little of the rainwater percolates into the ground; most of the rain comes in the form of brief but intense downpours and runs off the land with great velocity.

The stream flow of Albania's rivers is highly irregular, with fluctuations which mirror the alternating periods of rain and drought. The Vijosë River, for example, has an average depth of 23 feet during the month of November; during August, this depth is reduced by nine-tenths. Such marked fluctuations are typical of the southern part of the country. The Drin River, on the other hand, is a steadier stream. It maintains an average depth of almost 16½ feet between the months of November and March; the lowest stage, reached during the month of August, is but a third below the highest. The Drin owes this regularity to the summer rainfall characteristic of this part of the country. Also, its drainage basin has not been as ruthlessly deforested as those in the southern part of Albania.

The irregularity of Albania's mountain streams is also felt in the lowlands. Flooding is a chronic occurrence during the rainy winter months, and the lowlands remain inundated for weeks at a time. Life and property are endangered; economic activity and communication come to a near-standstill for several months.

Timberland

With but a few exceptions, southern Albania no longer has any continuous forests. (The exceptions are provided by the small riverine forests of Butrint in the basin of Delvinë, the forest of Karavasta along the Lake Tërbuf lagoon, and the oak forests of the hill country of Belsh—located between Peqin, Berat, Lushnjë, and Elbasan.) The republics of Venice and Ragusa on the Adriatic used Albanian timber to build their sailing ships. E. Vlora, an Albanian scholar, has found the record of a sixteenth-century trading agreement between the Republic of Ragusa and the ruler of Vlorë, whereby the latter contracted to supply the former with 400 boatloads of oak stems. Albanian oakwood was used until recently by builders of fishing boats along the treeless coast of southern Italy. Vlora has also uncovered the eighteenth-century record of a fire set deliberately in the Mal' i Gjerë upland forests near Gjirokastër to rout a group of outlaws from their forest hideout. The Austrian geographer Herbert Louis has stated that, probably as a result of this action, the summer water supply has been seriously impaired in this area.

Furthermore, because there were no laws to protect Albania's forests, charcoal was burned in great quantities in the southern part of the country. Charcoal remains in great demand throughout the

Mediterranean region as the most popular cooking fuel. Several other causes may be listed for the progressive destruction of southern Albania's forests: deliberate burning in order to create additional pastureland; intensification of goat raising (harmful to seedlings), and the concentration of villages on valley slopes.

As one proceeds northward from the deforested zone, the first dense forests occur in central Albania. Here, in the valley of Krujë are the well-known forests of Mamuras. Despite former damage to the stands, a considerable area remains under forest to this day. As long as a hundred years ago, J. G. v. Hahn, an Austrian Consul who made the first serious studies on Albania, reported that trees with a ten-inch diameter were being felled, with eight- to ten-inch diameter trees next in line. Other continuous forests in central Albania cover the upland near Elbasan, the region of Librazhd, and the Kamje Mountains. In all these forests, oak is the principal type at the lower elevations, while black pines or beeches, depending upon type of soil and amount of shade, form the upper tier.

The mightiest mountain forests are found in the north of the country—on both slopes of the central mountain range, in the valleys, and along the higher reaches of the Mirditë Mountains, as well as in the North Albanian Alps. As previously stated, these forests have maintained their virgin appearance because the region is so inaccessible and sparsely populated. Taken together, the forests of Albania occupy about 2,250,000 acres. Of this surface, second-growth forests cover about 1,500,000 acres, half of which are being rapidly destroyed. In 1940, Michelangeli computed that the annual domestic demand for construction lumber amounted to 24,700,000 cubic feet, of which 19,200,000 cubic feet were annually made available in the process of clearing. Another 84,70,000 cubic feet were needed for firewood. Since tree growth is limited by the summer drought to about 70-100 cubic feet per 2.5 acres, Michelangeli assumes that in 1940 Albania needed about 2,470,000 acres of medium-aged forests to check progressive erosion. It can thus be seen that Albania is suffering from a serious shortage of forests and forest products. Although the Communist government claims that 69,200 acres of degraded forest area is to be reforested during the current Five-Year Plan, the increased demand is likely to swallow up this increment.

Wasteland

According to Dalip Zavalani, an Albanian agronomist, 1,379,181 acres, or 19.43 per cent of the country's surface, consists of lakes, marshes, and other wet or useless land. By adding to this figure the pasture and scrublands that are too eroded to be of any value, we find that the category of unused lands is swelled to 1,980,000 acres, or 29 per cent of the total area of Albania. (Mario Michelangeli estimated the unproductive land as a third of the country's area.) Included in the wasteland are the rocky surfaces of the Albanian Alps, the diorite "desert" of Pukë, the sparse summer pastures of the Mirditë highland, parts of the Korab range and of the eastern marginal ranges, the deeply eroded lands of the southern highland, and, specifically, the districts of Kolonjë, Leskovik, Frashër, Skrapar, Përmet, Mallakastrë e sipërme, Tepelenë, and Kurvelesh. About one half of these 1,980,000 unproductive acres, or 14.5 per cent of Albania's area, consist of low-lying lands which could be improved through drainage. Most of the other areas classified as wasteland have soils so heavily eroded that restoration would require great physical effort over a long period of years as well as a very heavy capital investment in a soil conservation program.

Agricultural Regions

Land use data for 1940 in Table 4 are taken from the Italian forest engineer Mario Michelangeli.

Table 4. LAND USE, 1940

Classification	*Area*	*Per Cent of Total Area*
	(*in square miles*)	
Cultivated land	997	9
Forests	3,474	33
Open pastureland	2,703[a]	25
Unproductive land	3,457	33

[a] Of which 772 square miles were protected winter pastures.

According to recent Communist data, area under cultivation had reached 1,397 square miles by 1954 and 1,544 square miles by 1955. This extension has probably taken place at the expense of the winter pastureland acreage.

Lowland agriculture in Albania has always been so organized that each year 75 to 80 per cent of the cultivated area was planted in corn, with the remainder in wheat and oats. There was little room for crop rotation. A less lopsided distribution of corn and cereal acreage could be found in the wider valleys of southern Albania and in northern Albania. Here the winter pastures are far from the villages, the forests take up a larger acreage than the summer pastures, and the severity of the winters has set definite limits to the raising of sheep. The very opposite factors are at play in the southern districts of Gjirokastër and Vlorë. Here, winter pastures are available in quantity and are easy of access, summer grazing grounds at high elevations are plentiful, and the winters are mild. Hence these two districts are the centers of livestock raising in Albania.

Rural Settlements

Most of Albania's villages may be described as tribal or fortified villages. The houses are built next to each other in the south but are more widely separated in the north. The distance between village and fields has hindered the development of the peasant economy. During the day, the farmer has little if any time to spend near his home or in his yard. Only rarely can he help his wife in the more arduous duties required for the maintenance of the farmstead, such as carrying the drinking water from the well or stream, and planting and cultivating the garden. In areas where livestock raising is the dominant agricultural activity, the work load is shared even less efficiently, because the pastures are scattered and at a greater distance from the farmstead than are the cultivated fields. In central and southern Albania, the shortage of surface water is a contributing factor to the spacing of cultivable fields and to their distance from the villages, which were established in the vicinity of springs. In the highlands, the springs usually come to the surface only at the line of contact between the overlying limestone and the impervious layers of serpentine or Flysch. This line of contact occurs at an elevation of approximately 1,300 to 1,600 feet above sea level. Hence, most of Albania's mountain villages are found at this elevation. In the areas of serpentine exposure, on the other hand, small surface springs occur in abundance and settlements are scattered. This, then, is the picture of the typical Albanian mountain settlement: seventy to a hundred farmsteads lost in a rocky wilderness thinly covered by scrub oak trees or maqui with no roads and with almost no water during the summer drought.

At lower elevations, the fields are likely to be laid out around the village, and the patriarchal settlement pattern prevails. Farm homes are more substantial, and the division of labor between the sexes is more equitable and efficient. However, several negative factors come into play. With malaria, flooding, or enemy attacks a constant threat, the Albanian peasant settled in the lowland only if no land could be found elsewhere. Most of those living there were only tenants. Even the tenants, however, prefer to build their homes on hillsides and to walk to their fields in the lowlands.

Urban Centers

With the exception of a small asphalt plant in the vicinity of Vlorë and of several small salt works along the coast, there was no mining or industrial activity until thirty years ago. Gjirokastër and Korçë excepted, the principal cities of Albania are located either along the coast or along the border line between lowland and highland. We have already described how this physiographic boundary has separated the population of the plains from that of the mountain hinterland, both from an economic and cultural standpoint. Because of this separation, Albanian coastal towns have a small hinterland and have not extended their influence and trading activity deep into the interior of the country. Even along the coast, there has been only limited economic development.

In former times, it was less difficult and less hazardous to travel by sea than overland between the ports of Vlorë and Durrës or between Durrës and Shkodër (with its port of Shëngjin). Overland travel in the summertime was endangered by malarial swamps; in the wintertime, ferry-crossings of flooded rivers provided the major hazard. From this, we conclude that the coastal towns had but one *raison d'être*, that of moderately important trading centers. They served as shipping points for exportable agricultural surpluses and for livestock, and as distribution centers for cereals imported in years of short harvests. In the past two decades, the importation of cereals has grown so considerably as to make a sizable dent in the national budget. Rapid population growth is responsible for this trend.

Berat, Elbasan, and Tirana are the traditional gathering and distribution points for agricultural surpluses grown in the central lowlands. The animal products of the southern mountain regions have long been delivered to and processed in the towns of Gjirokastër and Korçë. Tobacco, hides, wool, furs, silk, and wax produced in the interior of Albania are generally shipped to the ports, particularly Durrës.

During the early part of the twentieth century, when the port of Salonica in northern Greece grew in importance, Albania's Adriatic seaports, which were geared to sailboat and small steamship traffic, lost the trade originating in or destined for the Vardar valley. Moreover, the rapid development of the rail nets and river navigation systems of Central Europe brought about an almost complete reorientation of Balkan commerce to the detriment of Albanian ports.

The construction of new administrative buildings, hotels, slaughterhouses, and power plants dates from World War I, when Shkodër was occupied by Austro-Hungarian forces, Korçë by the French, and Durrës, Vlorë, and Gjirokastër by the Italian army. These cities continued to grow during the years of Albanian independence (1920-39). These two decades saw the introduction of motorized transport; the construction of a cement mill, several cigarette factories, and a brewery; the beginning of mining activity; and the erection of fine government buildings and urban residences for civil servants and well-to-do merchants. The attractive small port of Sarandë on the Ionian Sea was built. All of the main towns continued to expand as modern quarters were built to absorb the overflow from the crowded old cities. During the years of Italian occupation and more recently under Communist rule, the growth of Albania's cities has been even more pronounced.

3. THE PEOPLE

ALBANIA has been neglected in the standard textbooks on East European demography, and little statistical material is available on this sparsely populated country. Albania has had little opportunity to develop an adequate system of administration. The first statistical surveys did not appear until 1930; these were based on the 1930 population census. The growing Italian interest in Albania, which culminated in the occupation of the country in 1939, also brought about the publication of some demographic material.

During World War II, Albania was under Axis military occupation and became the site of extensive guerrilla activities. Information gleaned at that time by the Allies for intelligence purposes and released at the end of the war added some valuable facts and observations concerning the general structure of Albanian society and its settlement patterns. However, statistical material concerning wartime population changes, birth rates, etc. was not obtained.

After the war, Albania fell under Communist domination, and little or no information has been made available by the Communist government. The facts and figures published in the *Bolshaia Sovetskaia Entsiklopedia* (*Great Soviet Encyclopedia*), by the Russian and Albanian Communist press, and by Radio Tirana have been carefully selected for the purpose of demonstrating the alleged success of the regime's economic-political course.

The demographic information in the following pages should be examined with this background in mind. Estimates were necessarily based on earlier observations, and the scarcity of accurate records of the past posed considerable difficulty. The estimates and projections of the Statistical Office of the United Nations, the Office of Population Research of Princeton University, and the United States Bureau of the Census have proved to be extremely valuable. The Free Europe Press of the Free Europe Committee has rendered good service by its interpretation of fragmentary news reports emanating from behind the Iron Curtain.

DEMOGRAPHIC FACTORS

Number of Inhabitants

According to the population census of October 2, 1955, the total number of inhabitants was 1, 394, 310. On September 30, 1945, the population census totaled 1, 115, 350. There is no satisfactory method of checking these statistics, according to which the population of the country is considerably greater that estimated by the Statistical Office of the United Nations. Table 1 compares the mid-year estimates of the United Nations to the available official figures which point to a population increase of 278,960 during the 10-year period from 1945 to 1955.

Table 1. POPULATION INCREASE 1945-1955

Year	*Qualification*	*Total Population*	*Increase*	*Per Cent Increase*
1945	Census	1,115,350		
1946	Estimate	1,132,000		
1947	Estimate	1,154,000		
1948	Estimate	1,175,000		
1949	Estimate	1,186,000		
1950	Census	1,208,943	93,593	8.4
1951	Estimate	1,200,000		
1952	Estimate	1,246,000		
1953	Estimate	1,250,000		
1954	Estimate	1,260,000		
1955	Census	1,394,310	185,367	15.3

Sources: Dispatch No. 274 of the American Mission in Tirana to the State Department, Washington (July 16, 1946); *Zëri i Popullit* (The Voice of the People), Tirana (November 13, 1955); United Nations, *Demographic Yearbook,* 1948, p. 82; 1949/1950, p. 79; 1952, p. 97; 1953, p. 77; 1954, p. 105; 1955, p. 109.

The differences between the above-quoted United Nations projections and the official Albanian figures seem to reveal an important fact: the rate of population increase has been considerably higher than expected, particularly since 1950, indicating a rather rapid decline in the formerly high death rate, including infant mortality rate. Meanwhile, the traditionally high birth rates must have remained at the same level.

The population movement of postwar Albania shows a picture quite different from that of prewar years. According to the census of 1930, the population was 1,003,097. If this figure is accurate, the annual population increase was only 5.6 per thousand over the eight-year period from 1930 to 1938, which would make Albania differ greatly from the other Balkan countries, where the rate of increase was almost four times as high. However, due to the difficulties of census-taking in a primitive and largely illiterate country with no previous accurate population statistics, it is more than likely that the actual population was somewhat lower than the 1930 census figure. If the later population figures were more accurate, which seems likely, the actual Albanian population increase was almost certainly much higher in the period than the indicated annual figure of 5.6 per thousand.

The population figures above pertain to Albania's present territory, which—oddly enough—cannot be accurately established. While the *United Nations Demographic Yearbook* for 1953 refers to a territory of 28,748 square kilometers (11,097 square miles), population density is estimated by the *Encyclopaedia Britannica* staff on the basis of an area of 10,629 square miles (27,529 square kilometers). Other sources give varying area estimates, up to 11,300 square miles. In this chapter, the figures established by the United Nations are used in computing population density.

Large Albanian settlements are located in Yugoslavia (approximately 900,000 according to Albanian sources, and 750,500 according to the Yugoslav population census of 1948), in Greece (estimated at 30,000 by the *Great Soviet Encyclopedia* and at 50,000 to 60,000 by the *Notes et Etudes Documentaires*), and in Italy and Sicily (approximately 250,000, according to the *Encyclopaedia Britannica,* and 150,000, according to the *Notes et Etudes Documentaires*). The number of Albanians by birth all over the world is estimated at 3,000,000, including approximately 50,000 living in the United States.

Population Changes and Migration

During the last fifteen years, Albania has undergone many crises, which have affected the population movement. The various inward and outward movements counterbalanced one another to a large extent. During these turbulent years, births, deaths, and migration were inadequately recorded or not recorded at all. Guerrilla warfare made it impossible to determine war casualties. The early postwar estimates concerning the population also included "temporarily displaced persons," who had their legal domicile in Albania but were not in the country at the time.

The first group of population shifts consists of those which resulted from the country's occupation by foreign military forces during World War II. During the years of Italian occupation, a considerable number of Italian skilled workers—Ciano's diary refers to some 25,000—were shipped to Albania. In 1943, the Italian surrender resulted in a partial return of Italians from Albania and a similar return of Albanians to Albania.

During the Greco-Italian war in 1940-41, the Greek armies repelled the Italian attack and succeeded in occupying part of southern

Albania. There must have been both inward and outward migration in this region at that time. In April 1941, when Germany invaded Greece and Yugoslavia, that part of southern Albania occupied by the Greek forces came again under Italian occupation. It is likely that the switch from Greek to Italian occupation was accompanied by some migration of the civil population, although this was perhaps limited. Furthermore, in 1943-44, during the German occupation, there were some deportations.

Another type of population shift is related to temporary Albanian territorial gains in 1941. In August 1941, Italian-occupied and "protected" Albania annexed the so-called Kosovo region (Kosmet), a predominantly Albanian-populated area of Yugoslavia with a total population of approximately 810,000 persons, and some parts of southwestern Yugoslavia. The region was administered by Albania until the end of the war, when the area was returned to Yugoslavia. A number of Kosovars went to Albania. Çamëri (Tsamouria), in northern Greece, was also under nominal Albanian control. Upon the defeat of the Germans, most of the Albanian Çams moved to Albania, where they settled. A minor wave of outward migration from Albania to Yugoslavia apparently occurred as tension grew between Yugoslavia and the Cominform countries.

An increase in the population of Albania took place during Markos' guerrilla war against the legitimate government of Greece (1947-49). Albania was a base of the Communist Greek guerrilla bands, and there was a constant movement across the border. The Greek guerrillas and their captives left Albania after the collapse of the rebellion.

War losses form the third item in Albania's population balance sheet. The number of casualties was estimated at 9,000, which seems low, considering the extent of Albanian guerrilla warfare during the occupation period.

Table 2. POPULATION AND POPULATION DENSITY, SELECTED YEARS 1930-1955
(Area: 11,097 square miles, 28,748 square kilometers)

Year	*Total Population*	*Density per Square Mile*
1930	1,003,000	90.3
1938	1,046,000	94.2
1945	1,115,350	100.5
1950	1,208,943	108.9
1955	1,394,310	125.6

Sources: 1930, *Statistical Yearbook of the League of Nations 1941/42* (Geneva, 1943), p. 16; 1938, *Albania: Basic Handbook* ([London], 1943), Pt. 1, p. 29; 1945, 1950, 1955, listed under Table 1, p. 49.

Density of Population

Albania is the least densely populated of the Eastern European countries. It is approximately the size of Maryland, but its population is only half as large. The average density of population (number of inhabitants per square mile) is reported as 125.6 as of October 1955. Table 2, however, reveals a rapid increase in population density from 1930 to 1955 and offers some idea of probable future trends.

The Albanian population is unevenly distributed, with the bulk of inhabitants concentrated around Durrës, on the Adriatic coast, and in the area of Tirana and Korçë. The rest of the country is sparsely populated, particularly the North Albanian Alps, where some areas fall below six persons per square mile.

Regional Distribution of Population

Until 1949, Albania was divided into ten prefectures, or administrative districts. The number and density of population in these districts for 1930 and 1942 is shown in Table 3.

Table 3. Population and Population Density by Prefecture, 1930 and 1942

Prefecture	*Area*	*1930*		*1942*	
		Number	*Density*	*Number*	*Density*
	(*in sq. km.*)				
Berat	3,666	143,000	36.3	173,000	47.2
Durrës	1,556	78,000	48.8	93,000	59.7
Elbasan [a]	3,548	111,000	37.7	114,000	32.1
Gjirokastër	4,116	144,000	34.7	161,000	39.0
Korçë	3,750	148,000	44.5	172,000	45.8
Kukës [a]	2,038	49,000	23.0	47,000	23.2
Peshkopi [a]	2,140	87,000	36.5	85,000	39.7
Shkodër	5,575	132,000	27.2	164,000	29.5
Tirana [a]	910	58,000	68.0	61,000	66.8
Vlorë	1,449	53,000	39.3	58,000	39.9
Total	28,748	1,003,000	34.8	1,128,000	39.3

[a] Minor administrative reorganizations between 1939 and 1942 help to explain the difference in number and density of population.

Source: "Die Verwaltungseinstellung und die Entwicklung der Bevölkerung in Albanien," *Wissenschaftlicher Dienst Südosteuropa* (Munich: Südost Institut), III, No. 10 (1954), 211-16.

The Communist regime has effected three major administrative divisions since it seized control of the country. In March 1949, the former prefectures were abolished, and *Këshilla Popullore* (Soviets) were created; these included districts (*rethe*), cities (*qytete*), localities (*lokalitete*), and villages (*fshatra*). There were 26 districts with a total of 185 administrative units. The second major change occurred in July 1953 when 10 regions were created corresponding to the previous 10 prefectures, with 53 districts and 47 localities. A further change took place in January 1956, when the country was divided into four regions, 34 districts and 140 localities. The following list refers to the 26 districts created in 1949 and their approximate population:

District	*Population Density per sq. km.*	*District*	*Population Density per sq. km.*
Berat	20-30	Lesh	30-40
Burrel	50-80	Lushnjë	80-90
Çorovodë	20-30	Përmet	20-30
Durrës	89	Peshkopi	40-50
Elbasan	30-40	Pogradec	40-50
Ersekë	20-30	Pukë	17
Fier	50-80	Rshen	20
Gjirokastër	40-50	Sarandë	30-40
Gramsh	20-30	Shkodër	40-50
Kolgecaj	10	Skrapar	50-80
Korçë	50-80	Tepelenë	20-30
Krujë	40-50	Tirana	30-40
Kukës	27	Vlorë	40-50

Source: "Die Verwaltungseinstellung und die Entwicklung der Bevölkerung in Albanien," *Wissenschaftlicher Dienst Südosteuropa* (Munich: Südost Institut), III, No. 10 (1954), 211-16.

Table 4. POPULATION OF LARGEST TOWNS, 1930, 1938-1939 AND 1949-1950

Town	*1930*	*1938-39*	*1949-50* [a]
Tirana	30,806	25,043	80,000
Shkodër	29,909	28,855	34,000
Korçë	22,807	26,139	24,000
Durrës	9,739	8,665	16,000
Elbasan	13,796	13,633	15,000
Vlorë	9,106	9,306	15,000
Berat	10,403	10,152	12,000
Gjirokastër	10,836	12,101	12,000
Kavajë	8,208	7,000	5,000-10,000
Krujë	4,835	4,500	5,000-10,000
Fier	1,800	1,450	5,000-10,000
Lesh	3,000	1,637	under 5,000

[a] The figures for 1949-50 are estimated.

Sources: "Die Verwaltungseinstellung und die Entwicklung der Bevölkerung in Albanien," *Wissenschaftlicher Dienst Südosteuropa* (Munich: Südost Institut), III, No. 10 (1954), 211-16; *Albania: Basic Handbook* ([London], 1943), Pt. 1, pp. 8-10.

Industrialization has affected Albania, although considerably less than it has the other East European countries. The Communist-engineered economic plans have resulted in the gradual increase of city population, particularly in the capital, in mining towns, and in the port cities.

Table 4 reveals that in 1930 approximately 14.5 per cent of Albania's total population lived in towns and communities of more than 5,000 inhabitants. The same category amounted to 20.2 per cent in 1949-50. Since the launching of the Five-Year Plan in 1951, the proportion of urban-industrial population has probably increased, perhaps by 1955 to about 25 per cent of the total population. The rest of the inhabitants live in small but concentrated settlements, rendered almost inaccessible by poor roads and mountainous terrain and nearly self-sufficient from an economic point of view.

Vital Statistics

The most serious obstacle to an adequate demographic study of Albania lies in establishing the so-called vital statistical data, such as crude birth and death rates, net reproduction rate, average age, and life expectancy. The incomplete birth and death registration, the variation of birth rates from one year to another in the available fragmentary reports, etc., leave much room for speculation and interpolation. However, certain basic characteristics and the general trend of population movement can be ascertained.

Sex Distribution. In prewar Eastern Europe, only Albania and Bulgaria had more male than female population. In 1937, there were 540,836 males and 497,020 females, or a total population of 52 per cent male and 48 per cent female. The ratio of males to females was 109:100. In the 1945 "census"—better called an official estimate—which included "temporarily displaced persons," the ratio of males to females was 104:100. It can be assumed that the majority of the "temporarily displaced persons" who have not returned to the country were men. The low number of females seems due to the little care given the infant girl—a girl is not as highly appreciated as a boy—which raises female mortality, and to the hard work of the Albanian woman in comparison to that of the man.

Age Composition. Only a speculative estimate can be made concerning the age composition of the Albanian population (see Table 5). The proportion of the various age groups shows that Albania's population is still the "youngest" of the East European countries. According to the projections, the percentage of the population under 15 years of age will decrease from 29 per cent in 1955 to 25 per cent in 1970. On the other hand, the proportion of the group over 65 years has thus far been declining very slowly. The other East European countries have already reached the stage where the number and proportion of people over 65 years is growing annually. Albania will probably follow the same pattern. According to the projections, her oldest age group will grow to 5 per cent by 1970.

Table 5. DISTRIBUTION OF POPULATION BY AGE GROUP, SELECTED YEARS 1940-1955
(*in per cent of total*)

Age Group	*1940*	*1945*	*1950*	*1955*
Under 15 years	36.4	31.2	29.8	29.0
15-39 years	40.5	44.2	44.1	44.5
40-65 years	18.7	20.4	22.1	22.6
Over 65 years	4.4	4.2	4.0	3.9
Total	100.0	100.0	100.0	100.0

The main bulk of the population is in the so-called working age groups, between 15 and 65 years. The labor force is still expanding and has not yet felt the effects of the very slowly declining fertility. It is expected, however, that the number and proportion of the 15-39 years age group will gradually decline during the 1955-70 period. Parallel with this decrease, a gradual increase will be observable in the number and proportion of the 40-65 years age group.

Birth and Death Rates. Although Albania has the highest birth rate in Europe, with the exception of the Soviet Union, the death rate has also been high, so that from 1920 to 1930 Albania's rate of natural increase was not higher than that of the other Balkan countries. During the early 1930's, there was a comparatively sharp drop in the birth rate, while the death rate was the second highest in Europe. Between 1935 and 1939, however, the birth rate rebounded to such record heights that, despite the continuing high death rate, the average natural increase for the 1930-40 period maintained the trend of the previous decade (see Table 6).

Even these incomplete statistics reveal the dynamic yet primitive character of the Albanian population movement before the end of World War II. Due to the general lack of medical care, infant mortality was extremely high and the average life expectancy very short. At the time, Albania's death rate exceeded 17 per thousand, the same ratio in Bulgaria was 13.4 (1939), 13.0 in Greece (1939), 13.7 in Hungary (1939), and 13.8 in Poland (1938). The highest rates of natural increase in Albania were reported from the districts of Shkodër and Berat (over 20 per thousand) and the lowest from Tirana (under 10). The highest death rates were registered in Vlorë (18 per thousand), Kosovë, Durrës, and Berat (between 16 and 17).

The highest infant mortality rates were that of Vlorë (183 for every 1,000 live births), Peshkopi (180), Durrës (177), and Elbasan (169). The high rates of Vlorë, Durrës, and Elbasan were undoubtedly due to the prevalence of malaria.

Table 6. BIRTHS, DEATHS, AND NATURAL INCREASE PER 1,000 PERSONS, SELECTED YEARS 1931-1942

Year	*Births*	*Deaths*	*Natural Increase*
1931	24.9	16.6	8.3
1932	25.0	17.8	7.2
1935-39	32.4	17.1	15.3
1940	30.9	16.4	14.5
1941	27.8	16.6	11.2
1942	32.8	14.2	18.6

Source: Statistical Office of the United Nations, *United Nations Demographic Yearbook, 1952* (New York, 1952), pp. 228, 268.

After World War II, an increase in the number of births was observed almost everywhere. Meanwhile, the general progress of medical science rapidly decreased the high death rates in every East European country. The expansion of the population—a "vital revolution"—is greatly encouraged by the Communist regimes by means of maternity benefits, special family allowances, etc. The lack of education as well as the general unavailability of contraceptives also contribute to the high rate of natural increase.

Very little information is available as to postwar birth and death rates. The reported crude population increase—2.4 per cent yearly—points to an extraordinarily high natural increase. Radio Tirana reported on September 10, 1955 a birth rate of 40.2 per thousand and a death rate of 12.9 per thousand for 1954. Although it is assumed that this report represents a better than average picture of the Albanian population movement, it appears that Albania is still ahead of other European countries insofar as birth rates are concerned. Death rate averages seem to be slightly higher than those of Romania and Poland.

Life Expectancy at Birth. The term "life expectancy at birth" refers to the future lifelength of all individuals born in a given year. The advance of medical science has, of course, greatly increased average life expectancy. The lifetime of males in general is usually from two to six years shorter than that of females. Albania, in terms of general East European progress, is lagging behind by some thirty years; today, taking into account the rapid development of medical care during the postwar years, life expectancy may be somewhere around 45 to 50 years.

Socio-Economic Factors

The Albanians have the best claim to have "come first" to the Balkans. Of the two ancient peoples of the Balkans, the Illyrians and the Thracians, it is not clearly ascertained which is the ancestral stock of the Albanians, but this historical role is usually attributed to the Illyrians.

The Albanians themselves are divided into two major groups. The Gegs in the north and the Tosks in the south. The natural dividing line between the groups is the Shkumbî River. There is a notable difference in the outlook as well as in the social behavior of the Gegs and Tosks. The Gegs are taller and considered racially less mixed than the Tosks. Among the Gegs in the northern mountains, the traditional family system is still in existence; it resembles the old clan system of the Scottish Highlands. Whereas the Tosks are generally outspoken and imaginative, the Gegs are reserved. The Tosks are more industrious, but the Gegs are held better fighters. Two thirds of the ethnic Albanians are Gegs, including those living in the Kosovo area of Yugoslavia, while the Tosks include the Albanian minority groups in Greece.

These two Albanian ethnic groups form the overwhelming majority of the country's population. Estimates for 1952 set their combined proportion at about 98 per cent of the total population. The most significant minority group in Albania is that of the Greeks, who number around 30,000. There are Vlach settlements in the Pindus Mountains area, as well as in Fier, Vlorë, and Korçë. Some Bulgarians live in the Albano-Macedonian border zone, near Lake Prespë. Serbs are located in and around the city of Shkodër, and gypsies are widely dispersed.

Distribution of Population by Religion

According to the official newspaper *Bashkimi*, in October 1945, the overwhelming majority of the country's population, 70.2 per cent, was Moslem. The Eastern Orthodox Church claimed 19.7 per cent of the population and the remainder were members of the Roman Catholic Church. A few declared themselves atheist under the Communist regime.

Table 7 sheds some light on the geographic distribution of the religious groups in 1941. (As has been mentioned, the present administrative units, *oblasts*, are more or less identical with the prewar prefectures.) This table reveals that the only significant Catholic group is located in the Shkodër district, while large Orthodox groups live in the districts of Gjirokastër, Korçë, Berat, and Vlorë. Moslems are spread all over the country and form groups of considerable strength even in those districts where the other religions are dominant, but they are concentrated most in the center.

Table 7. DISTRIBUTION OF RELIGIONS BY PREFECTURE, 1942

Prefecture	*Total Population*	*Moslem*	*Orthodox*	*Catholic*	*Other*
Berat	173,165	126,857	46,243	58	7
Durrës	92,851	79,397	6,523	6,931	—
Elbasan	113,724	104,770	8,920	29	5
Gjirokastër	161,416	80,105	81,258	13	40
Korçë	171,834	108,091	63,723	20	—
Kukës	47,340	47,136	4	200	—
Peshkopi	85,004	83,563	1,152	289	—
Shkodër	164,287	55,785	1,377	107,116	9
Tirana	60,745	56,385	2,788	1,557	15
Vlorë	57,777	37,328	20,332	46	71
Total	1,128,143	779,417	232,320	116,259	147

Source: Istituto Centrale di Statistica del Regno d'Italia, *Annuario Statistico Italiano 1943 - XXI* (Rome, 1943), p. 203.

Literacy

As shown in Chapter 17, "Education," illiteracy has been very high in Albania. In 1938, approximately 80 per cent of the population was illiterate. In 1945, 679,000 persons, roughly 70 per cent of the population, were illiterate. This figure apparently did not include children under 7 years of age, who numbered about 175,000. Thus the percentage of illiteracy was, in fact, much higher.

One of the main cultural aims of the Communist Five-Year Plan is the rapid reduction of illiteracy. According to Radio Tirana, the number of illiterates decreased to 375,000 in 1950, or 33 per cent of the total population. By 1954, the number of illiterates was reportedly 95,000, or 7.6 per cent of the population. These figures seem exaggerated, although all Communist governments carry on a determined campaign against illiteracy to promote "political education" and to make party literature and directives effective. Another Radio Tirana report, according to which the number of schoolchildren and students was 192,000 by 1954, apparently indicates that the compulsory school program already reaches approximately 70 per cent of the school-age population.

Distribution of Population by Occupation

In 1930, roughly 800,000 of Albania's 1,003,000 inhabitants, or 80 per cent of the population, were dependent on agriculture. Taking into account the numbers of people engaged in the state administration, the armed forces, transportation, and communications, there were obviously few engaged in industry.

According to W. E. Moore's *Economic Demography of Eastern and Southeastern Europe,* at the beginning of the '30's, the ratio of males gainfully occupied in mining and industry to males gainfully occupied in agriculture was 8.33:100. From the same book, it is also clear that the Albanian agrarian "surplus population" ratio (unemployment and/or under-employment) was the highest in Europe.

In 1955, if the various targets of the Five-Year Plan are fulfilled as planned, 70 per cent of the "Albanian working population" will be employed in agriculture. Allowing a modest estimate of 15 per cent for the army, the police, and state services and administration, the remaining 15 per cent of the population would be employed in the country's newly developed industry. Reports on idustrial expansion show a rather slow development. In the light of these reports, it seems plausible that 15 per cent of the population is now engaged in industry.

Part II – The Political System

4. THE CONSTITUTIONAL SYSTEM

ALBANIA had five different constitutions from 1914 through 1939. The first was elaborated by the International Commission of Control after Albania's declaration of independence, but the most important was that of 1928 which replaced the Republic established in 1925 with a monarchy. This change was brought about by President Ahmet Zogu, who in the summer of 1928 instructed the Chamber of Deputies and the Senate to convene as a National Assembly and to consider revision of the Constitution. A Constituent Assembly elected in August 1928 then abolished the Republic and on September 1, 1928 made Albania a monarchy. The Constitution of December 1, 1928 with minor amendments remained in force until the Italian invasion of 1939.

Under this Constitution, power was granted to the King, who exercised it through the government; to the Legistlative Power, exercised collectively by the King and Parliament, composed of one Chamber; and to the Judicial Power, exercised by the Courts of Justice, whose decisions, based on law, were pronounced and executed in the name of the King. Minor changes, such as those authorizing a preventive censorship without constitutional safeguards and the nationalization of schools in 1933, were made by the 1932-36 Parliament.

Under the Constitution, the King was absolute. He represented the state both in the country and abroad, he directed domestic and foreign policy, and he was authorized to conclude pacts of friendship and alliances, and other treaties with foreign states. The Council of Ministers, or Cabinet, was directly dependent upon the King and each Minister was responsible for his own department. In theory, the Cabinet was also responsible to Parliament.

The armed forces of the state were under the direct control of the King. They were composed of the national army (land army, marine, and air force) and the gendarmery. Military service was obligatory for every Albanian citizen. Appointment of officers of the rank of company commander and higher were made by the King, to whom they swore allegiance. The Commander of National Defense and the Chief of Staff were advisers to the King in military matters.

Under the 1928 Constitution, personal liberty was guaranteed, and all citizens were equal before the law. Home and the right to property were inviolable. The liberty of speech and press, the right of association, and "peaceful assembly" were also guaranteed.

The Fascist Constitution of 1939

Immediately upon their occupation of Albania on April 7, 1939, the Italians introduced an Albanian Fascist regime. On April 12, the Italian authorities in Tirana, under the personal guidance of Foreign Minister Ciano, convened a Constituent Assembly, which abrogated the Constitution of 1928 and offered the Albanian crown to the King of Italy, in effect establishing a personal union of the Italian and Albanian kingdoms.

A new constitution, prepared and signed in Rome on June 3, 1939, was given to the Albanian Constituent Assembly, which approved it without question. This constitution provided that: (1) Albania was an autonomous constitutional monarchy, the throne being hereditary in the dynasty of King Victor Emmanuel; (2) the King was represented in Albania by a *Luogotenente* (Viceroy or Governor General); (3) the King, through the *Luogotenente,* ruled through Albanian ministers, but he alone could command the armed forces, declare war, make peace, issue administrative ordinances, and appoint officials; (4) in civil administration, the *Luogotenente* was assisted by a sort of "shadow Prime Minister," an Italian known as the Chief Adviser to the *Luogotenente* and to the Albanian Prime Minister, and the Inspector General of the Albanian Fascist Party; (5) justice was administered in the King's name by judges appointed by him; (6) the legislative power was vested in the Crown, assisted by a Superior Fascist Corporative Council which took the place of Parliament; the Crown retained a right of veto over legislation proposed by this Council; (7) the King could issue decrees having the force of law, which were later presented to the Council for formal conversion into law; and (8) the Council was to consist of members of the Central Council and Directorate of the Albanian Fascist Party and of regular members of the Central Council of Corporative Economy, who were in turn named by the King on the recommendation of the President of the Council of Ministers, in agreement with the Secretary-General of the Albanian Fascist Party.

The Albanian Fascist Party was founded soon after the Italian occupation, but it was not until March 1940 that the Directorate of the Party was organized. The statute of the Party, signed in Rome by Achille Starace, then Secretary-General of the Italian Fascist

Party, was decreed on June 3, 1939, the same day as the Albanian Fascist Constitution.

The Albanian Fascist Constitution remained in force with minor modifications until Italy's capitulation early in September 1943, when Germany became the occupying power.

The Germans recognized Albania as an "independent" state and on September 13 appointed an Albanian National Committee, which in turn created a Provisional Executive Committee, under the Presidency of Ibrahim bey Biçaku, to act as a provisional government and to convene a Constituent Assembly. The Assembly convened on October 16 and passed a number of fundamental decrees, renouncing union with the Italian Crown, revoking all laws passed after April 7, 1939, and declaring Albania neutral. On October 20, the Assembly established a Supreme Regency Council of four members, with Mehdi bey Frashëri, an old Albanian patriot, as Chief Regent. The Regency was vested with the supreme executive power for the duration of the war, and the legislative powers were vested jointly with the Regency and the Assembly, in accordance with the provisions of the Constitution of 1928. For the next twelve months, with Albania in civil war and anarchy, the Regency was unable to control the country, chiefly because of the activities of the Communist-controlled Partisan groups. Finally, on October 25, 1944, the Regency and government resigned as the German forces withdrew. The Communist provisional government, headed by Enver Hoxha, Secretary-General of the Albanian Communist Party, entered the capital city on November 28 (Albania's Independence Day). The following day it proclaimed Albania "liberated."

Communist Constitutions

The Constitution of 1946

General elections for a Constituent Assembly were held, in the usual Communist fashion, on December 2, 1945, under the aegis of the Democratic Front, a façade for the Albanian Communist Party, and on the basis of an electoral law adopted by the Albanian Anti-Fascist National Liberation Council on September 27. The Assembly convened on January 10, 1946. On the following day, it abolished the monarchy and proclaimed the People's Republic of Albania. Ahmet Zogu and his heirs were deprived of all their rights and property and were forbidden "forever" to re-enter Albania. On January 12, the Assembly approved a law establishing a Presidium, headed by Dr. Omer Nishani, who had headed the Presidium of the Albanian Anti-Fascist National Liberation Council since May 1944.

The Constitution of the People's Republic of Albania, which was adopted by the Constituent Assembly on March 14 and promulgated by the Assembly's Presidium on the following day, was not difficult to draft. It was almost a translation of the Yugoslav Constitution, which had been adopted a few months earlier and which was based on the Stalin Constitution of 1936. The only substantial difference was that the federal structure of both models was not adopted.

There is, of course, a great difference between the constitutions of the West and those of the Communist countries. A Western constitution aims at limiting the powers of the state and guaranteeing the rights of the citizens against the state. A Communist constitution, based on the principle of the dictatorship of the proletariat, upholds the authority of the state, which is unrestricted in relation to the citizen. In fact, any rights granted to the citizen may be withdrawn at any time.

Definition and Character of the State. In the first part, or basic principles, Albania is defined as a People's Republic with all powers derived from and belonging to the people, who rule through the People's Councils, which came into existence during the War of National Liberation. All representative organs from the local councils to the People's Assembly are elected by all citizens, by "free elections, and by universal, equal, direct, and secret ballot." The constituents have the right to recall their representatives at any time.

Social and Economic Measures. In the articles dealing with social and economic measures, mines and all other subsurface resources, waterways, natural springs, forests, pasture land, airways, postal service, telegraph and radio stations, banks, etc. are declared national property. The state undertook to direct economic life by a planned economy. The trade unions, peasants' collectives, and other organizations of the laboring masses are put under state control to enable it to carry out its general economic plan. Private property, private initiative, and private inheritance are guaranteed by the state, but no one is allowed to use private property to the detriment of the public. The state is given the right to expropriate private property when the welfare of the community demands it. Certain branches of economy or enterprises might be nationalized. The land belongs to those who till it; large estates are under no circumstances to be owned by private individuals. The state, by means of economic and other measures, encourages the working classes to organize against economic exploitation; the state also protects workers and minors by such measures as limited working hours, social security laws, paid vacations, and similar benefits.

Rights and Duties of Citizens. Some twenty-five articles are devoted to the rights and duties of citizens. Citizens are equal before the law regardless of race, nationality, or color; no privileges on account of family, position in life, wealth, or cultural level are recognized. All citizens, including those serving in the armed forces, who have reached the age of eighteen or over are eligible to vote and to hold office. The equality of women is guaranteed. Freedom of conscience and religion are guaranteed to all, the church is separate from the state, and religious groups are forbidden to use the church and religion for political purposes. Marriage and the family are protected by the state. Freedom of speech, press, organization, assembly, and public demonstration are guaranteed. No person can be held under arrest for more than three days without a court warrant, and no person can be punished without a hearing.

Work is a privilege and a duty, and every citizen has a right to be paid according to his work and to receive from society as much as he gives to it. The state has organized health services and promised all classes of people opportunity to attend schools and other cultural institutions; elementary education is free and obligatory; freedom of scientific and of artistic work is guaranteed. Schools belong to the state. Private schools can be opened only by special permission, and all their activities are supervised by the state.

State Organizations. Part two of the Constitution describes the functions of the People's Assembly (legislature), the state's administrative organs, both national and local, the judiciary, and the armed forces.

1. The People's Assembly. In theory, the People's Assembly is the highest organ of the Republic; it exercises all rights under the Constitution except those assigned to the Assembly's Presidium and government. The Assembly is elected for four years by all citizens and is convened by decree of the Presidium twice annually, on March 15 and October 15. The Assembly appoints various committees for specific purposes, and may investigate matters of general interest through general committees. No bill becomes a law until it is passed by a majority in a session in which the majority of its members take part; laws become effective fifteen days after they are promulgated in the *Official Gazette.* The Assembly alone can change or amend the Constitution, but bills for changes or amendments may be proposed by the Presidium, the government, or by two-fifths of the members of the Assembly. An absolute majority of the Assembly's members (since 1950 a two-thirds majority) is required for adopting such change or amendment.

2. The Assembly's Presidium. The Presidium is elected by the Assembly; it consists of the president, three vice presidents, a secretary, and ten members. The functions of the Presidium include convoking the sessions of the Assembly and calling for its election;

deciding on the constitutionality of laws, interpreting and promulgating laws and issuing decrees; exercising the right of pardon; ratifying international treaties; appointing and recalling diplomatic envoys to and from foreign countries upon the recommendation of the government; accepting credentials and letters of recall from foreign diplomats; proclaiming general mobilization and declaring war in case of armed aggression against the Republic when the Assembly is not in session; appointing and dismissing ministers between two sessions of the Assembly; and creating commisions within the government upon the recommendation of the Prime Minister. The Presidium is responsible to the Assembly, which may revoke it, replace it, or dismiss some members and appoint others. When the Assembly is dissolved, the Presidium remains in power until a new Assembly has elected a new Presidium.

3. State administrative organs. The government is the highest executive and administrative organ of the Republic; it is appointed and removed from office by the Assembly, to which it is responsible and accountable. Between sessions of the Assembly, it is responsible to the Presidium. The government issues decrees and regulations on the basis of, and in execution of, laws that are in effect. Other functions of the government include preparation of state economic plans; submission of annual budgets to the Assembly and direction of the monetary system; taking all necessary measures to uphold the Constitution and the rights of citizens; directing the military forces; maintaining relations with foreign countries and carrying out provisions of treaties and international obligations. The government is composed of the Premier, who presides over its meetings and directs all its activities, the Deputy Premier, the Ministers, the President of the Economic Planning Commission, and the President of the State Control Commission.

Organs of the local governmental units are the People's Councils of districts, villages, cities, and regions. They are elected directly for three years, and manage administrative, economic, and cultural matters, maintain order, see that laws are carried out, and uphold the rights of citizens. The executive organs of the People's Councils, except those of the villages, are the Executive Committees; these Committees are responsible both to the People's Councils, which elect them, and to the executive and administrative organs of the state. The People's Councils may create special bureaus and sections to direct various administrative affairs.

4. Judiciary and Public Prosecutor. The judicial organs of the Republic are the Supreme Court, which is the highest judicial body of the country, the regional People's Courts, and the Military Courts. The courts are independent, in theory, and their decisions cannot be

altered except by higher courts. The Ministry of Justice directs and controls all matters of judicial administration and organization. The Supreme Court is elected by secret ballot by the People's Assembly. Courts on the various regional levels are elected by secret ballot by the respective People's Councils.

The Office of the Public Prosecutor is an organ of the People's Assembly. It supervises the execution of the laws by the ministries, other administrative bodies, and by all public officials and citizens. The Public Prosecutor and his assistants are appointed by the Assembly. District attorneys of the regions are appointed by the Public Prosecutor and are independent of the local governmental units. The district attorneys of the military courts are appointed by the Commander in Chief of the armed forces.

5. Relations between the legislative and administrative organs. The People's Assembly may annul or suspend decrees, instructions, and decisions of the government considered unconstitutional. The Assembly and higher People's Councils may suspend any irregular acts of the lower People's Councils. The Presidium of the Assembly and the higher People's Councils may dissolve lower People's Councils or Executive Committees and authorize new elections.

6. The People's Army. The People's Army is the armed force of the Republic. The Commander in Chief of the armed forces is appointed by the Assembly; he directs all the armed forces of the country.

Seal, Flag, and Capital City. The seal of the Republic depicts a field enclosed with sheaves of wheat tied at the bottom with a ribbon on which is inscribed the date of May 24, 1944 (Congress of Përmet, which founded the Anti-Fascist National Liberation Council). The flag has a red field, in the center of which is a black double-headed eagle topped by a star. Tirana is the capital of the Republic.

The Constitution of 1950

The current Communist Constitution in Albania is referred to as the Constitution of 1950 because, although basically the same as that of 1946, certain changes were made on July 4, 1950 to make it conform more closely to that of the Soviet Union. The most important amendments or additions are:

1. The People's Republic of Albania is a state of workers and toiling peasants.

2. All power of the Republic belongs to the town and rural workers, represented by People's Councils.

3. The state regulates and controls all internal trade in the country (in addition to foreign trade as provided by the Constitution of 1946).

4. The state supports the socialist development of agriculture by organizing state agricultural enterprises and machine-tractor stations, and by aiding farmers' cooperatives and other forms of associations of the toiling peasants created on a "voluntary" basis.

5. Work is the basis of the social order in the Republic, and work is a duty and a matter of honor for every able-bodied citizen according to the principle, "he who does not work, does not eat," and "from each according to his ability, to each according to his work."

6. The following organizations are recognized: the Democratic Front; labor unions; cooperatives; youth, women, sports, defense, cultural, technical, and scientific organizations. The "most active and politically conscious citizens from among the working class and other strata of workers unite in the Albanian Workers' (Communist) Party, which is the organized vanguard of the working masses in their struggle to construct the basis of socialism and is the leading core of all organizations of workers, public as well as state."

7. Every citizen is obligated to defend and strengthen socialist property (state and cooperative) as the "sacred and inviolable basis of people's democracy, the source of strength of the Fatherland and the welfare and cultural life of the working people." He who encroaches on socialist property is an "enemy of the people."

8. Legislative initiative is vested in the Presidium of the People's Assembly, government, and deputies.

9. Justice is dispensed by the Supreme Court, people's courts, and military tribunals, and special courts for special purposes may be created by law.

Since the publication of the amended Constitution in July 1950, a few other amendments have been adopted by the People's Assembly dealing with the number of ministries, the organization of local administration, and the organization of the judiciary, the last being the most important change. The Assembly passed a bill on June 11, 1951 merging the Military Supreme Tribunal with the Supreme Court of the Republic, and the General Military Prosecutor's Office with the General Prosecutor's Office of the Republic under the names, respectively, of the Supreme Court and of the General Prosecutor's Office. The civil head of the Supreme Court, Andrea Nathanaili, was replaced by Shuaip Panariti, a major in the Sigurimi (State Security), and Colonel Siri Çarçani, also a Sigurimi officer, was appointed General Prosecutor.

Analysis of the Constitution

The Albanian Constitution serves only as window dressing for the Communist regime. Neither the promises made in the Statute of Labinot, which were repeated at the Congress of Përmet and of

Berat, nor the provisions of the current Constitution have any relation to the realities of Communist governmental practices, which flagrantly violate the most elementary human rights of the Albanian people. A brief analysis of the basic principles and the provisions dealing with state organizations and the judiciary as described in the Constitution itself and their application by the Communist regime reveals that the Constitution is in part violated by the supreme organs of the state and Party and in part used as a means of legalizing the arbitrary activities of a police state.

The Basic Principles

The allegation made in the first six articles of the Constitution that the Republic is a "state of workers and toiling peasants" and that supreme authority rests with the people is in contradiction to the true state of affairs, for all authority rests in the hands of a small group of men, the Politburo of the Albanian Workers' (Communist) Party. The citizens have no voice in electing their representatives. In all local and national elections, they are simply herded to the polls to approve candidates previously hand-picked by the Party. Anyone who dares to oppose the Party candidates or its policies and directives not only has his right to vote revoked but is in danger of being arrested by the political police as an "enemy of the people." The People's Councils (Soviets), which are described in Article 3 as the basis of political power, are simply tools of the Party. Local Party organs choose, control, supervise, and interfere arbitrarily in all their activities. The Republic is actually a private Party preserve.

The social and economic clauses (Articles 7-13) are nothing but a cover for state capitalism. In all state enterprises, power rests not with the workers but with Party "responsibles"; workers in these enterprises have responsibilities, but no privileges. Workers are requested to work overtime without pay (called "voluntary" work), work under rigid discipline, and are paid starvation wages. The clauses in Article 11 stating that "no one has the right to use private property against the public interest" and "private property can be limited and expropriated if such action is demanded by the public interest" make meaningless the principle stated in the same article that "private property and private enterprise are guaranteed." The so-called new "social order" destroyed the middle classes, the backbone of Albania's social and economic development in the towns and in the countryside, and created an entirely new exploiting class, headed by the Party hierarchs.

The principle enunciated in Article 13 that "he who does not work does not eat" is actually a threat and a means of the cruelest political pressure. Thousands of people have been denied work and ration cards either because of their past social status or for real or suspected opposition to the regime. The statement in Article 14 that "all citizens are equal before the law" is at variance with Article 21, which assigns a special place to the "most active and politically conscious citizens," who are Party members. Such citizens as "kulaks" suffer discrimination; they are subject to higher taxes, they are assigned heavier obligatory delivery quotas of produce to the government, and they pay higher prices for purchases in state stores.

As for the guarantees of freedom of religion, press, and assembly, the right to elect and be elected to office, and so forth, the facts are as follows: (1) All churches in Albania have been brought under the control of the Party and are used to further its program of Sovietizing the country; after its bishops and high clergymen were executed or imprisoned, the Roman Catholic Church in Albania was made into a national church by a decree of the Presidium of the People's Assembly of August 1, 1951. (2) All means of printing, distribution of publications, and radio facilities were nationalized soon after the regime came into power, and no independent or opposition newspaper or other publication has appeared in Albania since November 1944. (3) Article 21 makes the existence of any organizations other than those enumerated an impossibility, and those permitted to exist are under the control of the "organized vanguard of the working class," the Albanian Workers' Party. (4) The statements made in Article 16 that all citizens eighteen years of age or over have the right to vote in elections and to be elected to office, and that "suffrage is universal, equal, and direct, and voting is by secret ballot" have no basis in fact. Only those picked by the Party can be presented as candidates. The Party gave a lesson to those who dared present themselves as candidates outside the Party's electoral list in the first general elections, held on December 2, 1945, when Hasan Reçi, Jani Konomi, and Koço Dilo presented themselves as independent candidates. Reçi, a Party member, went through the usual torture chambers of the political police and was executed, and the other two, both Communist sympathizers but not Party members, were put into jail. (5) The inviolability of person, home, and correspondence, allegedly guaranteed by Articles 22-24, is ignored by the security police, with their forced evacuations and deportations, numerous concentration camps, and rigid mail censorship.

The State Organizations

Articles 41 to 43 of the Constitution provide that the People's Assembly is the "supreme organ of state power" in the Republic.

Actually, the People's Assembly is a rubber stamp created for the purpose of legalizing the measures taken by the Party. The deputies usually meet twice a year for a day or two, unanimously pass laws or decrees that have already been promulgated by the Presidium, and then disband. The parliamentary immunity that the deputies allegedly enjoy does not exist. On several occasions, deputies who have failed to follow the Party line or have fallen into disgrace have had their immunity revoked by the Minister of the Interior and have been arrested and imprisoned. In the spring of 1947, for instance, a large number of deputies were arrested and later tried as "enemies of the people."

The prerogatives assigned to the Assembly's Presidium (Articles 57-60) are on the surface very imposing. However, the Presidium, like the Assembly itself, has no authority of any kind. Ever since the Albanian Anti-Fascist National Liberation Council was founded in 1944, the President of the Presidium, who is nominally the Head of State, has been only a figurehead. An example of the impotence of the Presidium is the decree it issued on February 26, 1951, following the bomb explosion at the Soviet Legation in Tirana six days earlier. Prepared by Mehmet Shehu, then Minister of the Interior, the decree provided for capital punishment of anyone "engaged in terroristic activities" without due recourse to law. This decree was in violation of Article 22 of the Constitution, which provides that "no one may be punished without a hearing or without a defense as guaranteed by law." As Shehu himself admitted in an editorial in the Party's major newspaper *Zëri i Popullit* of March 1, 1951, the decree was "profoundly revolutionary."

The provision in Article 62 that the government is appointed by and is accountable to the People's Assembly is a fiction. The Assembly's role in all governments formed since the advent of communism in Albania is illustrated by the events of July 23, 1953. On July 24, the government issued two communiqués announcing that, in a joint meeting held the previous day, the plenum of the Party's Central Committee, the Council of Ministers, and the Assembly's Presidium took such far-reaching measures as reorganizing and consolidating the national government and the local administration, appointing a new government and accepting the resignation of the Presidium's President, and "recommending" that the Assembly elect Lleshi as the new President of the Presidium. The People's Assembly met on August 1, listened to a long harangue by Hoxha, approved the measures taken on July 23 without a single question, and closed its session, all in the same day. In actual practice the government is an administrative and executive branch of the Party.

The local administrative bodies, or People's Councils, are also merely executive Party organs at a lower level. The members of these Councils must, in the words of *Bashkimi* of August 28, 1952, "love wholeheartedly the Party, the Soviet Union, and Stalin."

The Judiciary

The articles dealing with the courts and the Office of the Public Prosecutor provide that the courts act on the basis of laws and give their sentences in the name of the people (Article 81), that they be independent in the execution of their functions (Article 80), that trials be conducted with the participation of assessors (Article 83), that the trials be public and the defendants have the right of defense (Article 82), and that the courts (except the Supreme Court) be elected by the people and be recalled by them (Article 85).

The above provisions sound truly democratic, but in actual practice they are the antithesis of both justice and democracy. Since June 1951, when a law reorganizing the judiciary was enacted, the task of justice in Albania has been to defend the People's Republic and its "socialist system." The administration of justice has therefore been in the hands of such Sigurimi officers as Panariti and Çarçani who have no legal training and many of whom have no schooling of any kind. It is no exaggeration to say that Albanian "justice" is characterized by terror and a complete disregard for right. Thus, Article 3 of the special decree of February 26, 1951 mentioned above, says a trial may be held without the participation of the accuser and accused; Article 4 states that recourse against a decision rendered by the court and presentation of appeals by the defendants are not allowed; and Article 5 provides that a death sentence be carried out as soon as the court decision has been rendered. The principle of justice is also affected by, if not based on, the "class warfare" and "class enemy" motif, which calls for the liquidation of those citizens whom the organs entrusted with the task of perpetuating the regime consider "bourgeois," "kulaks," or "enemies of the people." As an editorial in *Bashkimi* of July 6, 1951 put it: "We must show no leniency toward the class enemy, because justice is an arm of the People's Democracy."

The Office of the Public Prosecutor, which Article 88 described as an organ of the People's Assembly whose mission was to supervise the "exact execution of laws," is a detachment of the security police. The organic law dealing with the organization and functions of the Albanian Office of the Prosecutor (translated in 1946 almost verbatim from the Soviet law dealing with the same subject) defined the chief tasks of the Public Prosecutor as (1) assuring the legality of the acts of the administration and the activities of political organizations, and (2) strengthening the security of the state. Bedri Spahiu, the first Communist Public Prosecutor in Albania, told his colleagues when he took office: "In our country, the organs of the Office of the Public Prosecutor, by defending and strengthening revolutionary legality which expresses the will of the classes in power, renders invaluable and necessary assistance in fulfilling tasks dealing with the creation of a classless society."

5. POLITICS AND POLITICAL ORGANIZATIONS

POLITICAL TRADITION BEFORE 1944

National Renaissance and Struggle for Existence

The emergence of the national and political consciousness of the Albanians, who had been under the domination of the Ottoman Empire and the Ecumenical Patriarch of Constantinople since the fifteenth century, was inspired by the revolutions and liberation movements of the nineteenth century and by the rapid disintegration of the Ottoman Empire.

The defeat of Turkey by Russia in 1877 and the conclusion of the Treaty of San Stefano (March 1878) produced wide repercussions among Albanian patriots. Imposed on defeated Turkey by Russia, the treaty granted other states large chunks of Albanian territory. Recognizing the dangers posed by the treaty, a group of Albanians convened in Prizren (Kosovo) and on or about June 10, 1878 created the Albanian League for the Defense of the Rights of the Albanian Nation (commonly known as the League of Prizren).

The revisions of the Treaty of San Stefano made at the Congress of Berlin (July 1878) were also detrimental to Albania. This inflamed the nationalist spirit of the Albanians within the Ottoman Empire, as well as those in other countries, especially Italy. As the mouthpiece of these nationalist feelings, the League, by protest and the use of arms, opposed the decisions of the Congress of Berlin to carve up Albanian territory.

In 1881, the Turkish government abolished the League. The Albanian cultural movement, however, which began in Constantinople with the establishment of the Society for the Development of the Albanian Language, survived in foreign lands. Reviews and publications in Albanian as well as the Albanian schools which were opened in the Empire endeavored to affirm Albanian nationality.

Political activity among the Albanians was resumed when the Young Turks came to power (1908). Albanians who had been instrumental in the revolt founded political-cultural clubs in Albania and in other parts of the Empire. A considerable number of newspapers and periodicals were published which aimed at the defense of Albanian rights. The general trend of Albanian political thought was autonomy within the framework of the Ottoman Empire. However, the nationalistic activities of the Albanians disturbed the leaders of the Young Turks, who sought centralization and complete "Ottomanization" of the Empire. A series of revolts took place both in the north and in the south of Albania culminating in the successful insurrection of August 1912.

Political events in Albania after the country was declared independent in 1912 developed in accordance with the interests of the Great Powers and Albania's neighbors and the desires and ambitions of a number of local beys and chieftains, who had been schooled in the corrupt and decadent political life of the Ottoman Empire. The regime of Prince Wilhelm zu Wied in 1914 lasted only six months; the bellicose behavior of such beys as Esad Pasha Toptani, the inexperience of the Albanians in self-government, and the outbreak of World War I rendered impossible the development of distinct political groupings. This state of affairs continued during the war, when the country was occupied by both Austro-Hungarian forces and armies of Italy and France. Toward the end of the war, when the Austro-Hungarian forces began to disintegrate, the large local landowning beys in central Albania and the tribal chiefs in the north assumed control of their local domains, just as they had done during the rule of the Sultans.

Politics, 1920-1944

After the promulgation of the Constitution of Lushnjë in 1920 and the admission of Albania to the League of Nations, political life in Albania began to develop along Western democratic lines. Parliamentary life began in March 1920, when the first National Assembly was elected and convened in Tirana and the first postwar national government was formed, with Sulejman bey Delvina as Prime Minister and Ahmet bey Zogu as Minister of the Interior. A beginning was made at eliminating the semifeudal system and the tribal organization of administration. Political parties began to emerge. The group known as the Liberals included a faction that opposed the granting of posts to former officials of the Ottoman Empire on the grounds that these men were steeped in Oriental conservatism. This group, which dominated the Delvina government was anxious to establish a uniform Western system of state administration, but was generally frustrated by the large landowners, who were known as the Conservatives.

After the elections of 1921, political groupings of a more definite character began to take shape. Thus, the Democratic Party, headed by the American-educated Bishop Fan S. Noli and Luigj Gurakuqi, stood for general social, political, and economic reforms and included young officers and generally democratic elements influenced by

Western ideas. A second group, known as the Popular Party or the "Clique," was nominally led by Sefi Vlamashi, but actually by Eshref Frashëri; this party, too, stood for general social and economic reforms, but it was less radical than the Democrats. In fact, the two groups often collaborated, and were often indiscriminately called the Popularists. A third group was composed of conservatives who called themselves the Progressives. Dominated by Shefqet bey Vërlaci and other beys, the Progressives advocated feudal tenure and bitterly opposed agrarian reforms. A fourth group, led by Iljas Vrioni, was known as the Independents.

Owing chiefly to political wranglings and to the inability of any party to muster sufficient strength in Parliament to form a stable government, coalition governments were generally formed under the leadership of either the Popularists or the Progressives. Because the government changed so frequently, a third general combination, called the Sacred Union, was formed by advocates of the union of all parties. Its most influential members were nationalists, and it attracted a considerable number of deputies from both the Popularists and the Progressives. However, despite efforts at a firm union, the coalition governments seldom lasted for any length of time. The political freedom enjoyed in the country for the first time caused instability, and it was evident by 1923 that Albania was not sufficiently politically mature for representative government. Gradually the Progressives, or beys, consolidated their power and drew toward them young men such as Ahmet Zogu, who had belonged to Bishop Noli's party but who did not share the liberal ideas of the Bishop. The Bishop and a number of his closest collaborators finally left the Popularist coalition and formed what they called the Opposition. In June 1924, the deputies forming the Opposition withdrew from Parliament after the assassination of one of their leaders, Avni Rustemi, and went to Vlorë, where they instigated a revolt. Army officers joined the Opposition, Zogu was driven out of the country, and Bishop Noli became Prime Minister. The revolution of June 1924 put an end to party politics in Albania as they are known in the West, and the country never again enjoyed political freedom.

Noli's government accomplished very little during its short stay in power; it was in fact paralyzed from the outset by a rivalry for office among its members, who split into two factions, the Radical Democrats and the National Democrats. Besides, the Bishop overlooked the fact that popular support for many of his radical reforms was almost completely lacking.

The counterrevolution of December 1924, staged by Ahmet bey Zogu with the assistance of Yugoslavia, resulted in the formation of the Albanian Republic in January 1925 with Zogu as President. Three years later, the Albanian Kingdom was created, with Zogu becoming Zog I, King of the Albanians.

The period from 1925 to April 1939, when Italy expelled Zog, was uneventful, as far as internal politics were concerned. There were no political parties during Zog's regime. Although there were three attempted revolutions (1926, 1935, and 1937), they were minor affairs, except for the one in 1926 which influenced Zog to conclude the "Friendship and Security" pact with Italy. The existence of the regime was never threatened, and it was made doubly secure by the alliance Zog concluded with Italy in 1927. Although Zog held regular elections and Parliament convened and sat as provided by the Constitution, no political issues of importance were decided by the elections or by Parliament. The elections were merely a *pro forma* affair. Zog's cabinets were as a rule composed of conservatives, except in 1935-36, when he appointed a government of younger liberal elements headed by the old liberal patriot Mehdi bey Frashëri. This "government of the young" lasted only a year. It failed to bring about any social and political reforms chiefly because the King never took it seriously. In summary, Zog ruled through a personal dictatorship.

The Italian invasion of Albania in 1939 brought in its wake a Fascist regime and the creation of the Albanian Fascist Party. However, fascism as an ideology had few Albanian adherents. It was imposed by force, identified with the invader, and despised by the people. This was illustrated by the resistance of the Albanian people during World War II and by the general rejoicing when Fascist Italy capitulated in the summer of 1943. The vast majority of the Albanian people also rejected Nazism when German forces replaced those of Italy. Only the threat of communism, which took ominous proportions as the war progressed, prevented the Albanian people from creating a common front against the German occupiers.

Communist Seizure of Power

The Communist Background

The Russian Revolution of 1917 had serious repercussions in Albania, particularly because the Bolsheviks revealed the secret treaty of London (April 1915), which provided for the partititon of Albania. This made a deep impression among Albanian patriots, and a minority group considered Lenin a savior of Albania. When news of his death reached Albania, Avni Rustemi made a short speech in the Albanian Parliament, and a five-minute silence ensued in tribute to the leader of the October Revolution.

Marxism in Albania dates back to the revolutionary government of Bishop Noli (June-December 1924). Although Noli's government was not Communist, the Bishop and a number of his younger associates were influenced by Marxist ideology, or at least were inspired by the October Revolution and subsequent developments in the Soviet Union. One of the first acts of this government was to recognize the Soviet government, an indiscreet political step in those days. This act engendered concern in Belgrade and London and was partially responsible for the overthrow of Noli's regime.

The group of young people who fled Albania with the Bishop dispersed in various European capitals, especially in Vienna, Paris, and Moscow. Among those who went to Moscow were Noli's personal secretary Sejfulla Malëshova, Llazar Fundo, and Tajar Zavalani. Those who remained in Vienna worked with the Confédération Balkanique, a front organization for the Comintern, and founded the Komiteti Nacional Revolucionar (commonly known as KONARE). In the late 1920's and early 1930's, the Bishop and his associates issued a number of appeals calling for Albania's "liberation"; these appeals were printed in the Comintern's official organ.

The Albanian Communists and fellow travelers from abroad who were supported and financed by the Comintern, such as Konstandin Boshnjaku and Ali Kelmendi, made an abortive attempt in 1929 to form a clandestine Communist Party in Albania. In the 1930's, especially after the advent of Hitler in Germany and the consequent Comintern policy to form anti-fascist organizations in Europe, a number of Communist groups sprang up in Albania. One of these, Puna (Work) in Korçë, organized some workers in that city and caused disturbances in the spring of 1936. Zjari (Fire) and Të Rinjtë (The Young Ones) were groups operating in Tirana and Elbasan, and a group composed of poor craftsmen, students, and intellectuals was located in Shkodër. These groups operated independently of each other and were very small, totaling probably no more than a few hundred. Some of their leaders were apprehended and interned. However, these groups were not a serious problem for the Zog regime.

When Italy invaded Albania, some of the leaders of these groups left the country, while the rest held fast and awaited further developments. From the beginning of World War II until the German attack on the Soviet Union, they followed the Comintern policy of approving the Moscow-Berlin *rapprochement*. Once the attack had occurred, the Albanian Communists began to offer resistance to the Italian occupiers. The Albanian Communist Party was founded clandestinely in Tirana on November 8, 1941 by two emissaries of the Yugoslav Communist Party, Dušan Mugoša and Miladin Popović. These two men directed the Albanian Communist Party from its inception until the end of the war. During this period, the Albanian Party was in reality a branch of the Yugoslav Communist Party. Even after the war and until 1948, there was a representative of the Central Committee of the Yugoslav Party in the Central Committee of the Albanian Communist Party, and he wielded commanding power.

Seizure of Power

The Albanian Communist Party could not have seized power in Albania had it not employed the front technique and the big lie. It did not come out in the open during the war and, in fact, remained "illegal" until it held its First Congress in November 1948, when for tactical purposes it changed its name to the Workers' Party.

The Party overcame its lack of popular support by sponsoring the Conference of Pezë (September 16, 1942), in which such nationalist resistance leaders as Abas Kupi participated, and which created the National Liberation Movement (LNÇ), with a Communist-controlled General Council of National Liberation. On the surface, the program of the LNÇ was simple: unification of all nationalist and patriotic forces for the liberation of the country from Fascist Italy. National Liberation Councils were formed in all parts of the country to recruit manpower and to procure supplies for the Partisan forces. In secret circulars to the local Party cells, however, the Party Central Committee ordered that the local Liberation Councils and units of the Partisan formations be led and rigidly controlled by Party men. At its conference of Labinot, held in July 1943, the LNÇ General Council created the General Staff (Shtab) of the Army of National Liberation of Albania (ANLA). On August 15, the ANLA's First Brigade was formed at Vithkuq in the presence of British liaison officers, who had been parachuted into Albania to encourage the creation of guerrilla bands. The Yugoslav Dušan Mugoša was secretly appointed Politruk (Political Commissar) of the First Brigade, and Mehmet Shehu Operational Commander. Shehu had fought in the International Brigade in Spain, and had returned to Albania after the outbreak of the war, along with Dr. Omer Nishani, one of the founders of KONARE in Vienna, Sejfulla Malëshova, and other Communists of the 1924 vintage. Other brigades were created in the following months, and recruitment was based on the idea of joining a struggle for national liberation with that for the creation of a truly democratic state. The First ANLA Division was formed a few days after the Congress of Përmet (May 24, 1944), and several other divisions were formed in subsequent months. In all these Partisan formations, control was vested in the hands of Party chieftains.

From the time the First Brigade was formed until November 1944, the ANLA formations were employed chiefly against the anti-

Communist resistance groups, Balli Kombëtar (BK-National Front), which was officially formed in the fall of 1942 and led by the well-known patriot and writer, Midhat Frashëri, and the Legality Movement, led by Abas Kupi, who bolted the LNC in 1943 after realizing that it was only a façade for the Communist Party. Balli Kombëtar was composed of well-known Albanian nationalists and non-Communists coming from every walk of life. The Legality Movement was formed of former government officials of Zog's regime and mountaineers of Mat and Krujë.

Supervised and directed by Tito's movement in Yugoslavia and materially and morally assisted by the Allied Command in Italy, the ANLA won the civil war, and when the Germans withdrew from Albania at the end of November 1944, it became the undisputed master of the country. On November 28, the "Albanian Democratic Government," headed by the Secretary General of the Albanian Communist Party, Enver Hoxha, entered Tirana.

Various factors accounted for the failure of the two strongest nationalist organizations, the BK and the Legality Movement, to get the upper hand during the fratricidal war in 1943-44, the decisive period for Communist control of Albania. Although the BK was formally organized in October 1942 as a countermeasure to the National Liberation Movement created in the previous month, its existence dates back to the period immediately after the Italian invasion of Albania in April 1939. At that time, Midhat Frashëri and other Albanian patriots decided to oppose Italy's consolidation of power. When the BK came out officially as an organization in October 1942, it published a program of ten points (commonly known as the Decalogue) which defined its political aims. The program was progressive and highly nationalistic in character; it sought the restoration of a free, ethnical, and democratic Albania on a modern social basis, with freedom of speech and thought; it promised to fight for an Albania regulated economically and socially, and for the elimination of "exploiters and exploited"; it required land for landless peasants and a good living for all workers; it promised free education and justice for all, irrespective of age, region, or religion; it called for a fight to the finish against all who collaborated with foreign occupiers and all unpatriotic elements. Despite its liberal and nationalistic program, the BK failed because it lacked a well-knit organization, did not attempt to enlist the active support of the peasant masses, was not sufficiently aggressive against its Communist enemies, and, above all, failed to gain the support of the Western Allies. As the aggressive, ruthless, and well-led LNC increased its pressure on the BK, the latter turned increasingly to the defensive.

In November 1944, most of the leaders of the BK fled to Italy, where they have continued their struggle against the Tirana regime.

The Legality Movement, established by Abas Kupi in November 1943, had a simple political aim: the restoration of the *status quo ante bellum*, including the Zog monarchy. The influence of the organization was confined chiefly to the Mat region; Kupi's organization attracted no substantial support from the people and was unable to offer effective resistance either to the Germans or to the LNC forces. As he failed to obtain material support from the Western Allies, his small forces were dispersed by the LNC formations in the summer of 1944, and he and a few of his closest collaborators fled to Italy in November of the same year.

The ANLA had effectively crushed all anti-Communist opposition by the fall of 1944, and there remained for elimination only a few nationalist groups, such as those led by Jup Kazazi in the Shkodër area and by Mark Gjon Markaj in the Mirditë-Dukagjin areas. Thereafter, the Hoxha regime proceeded to liquidate all "internal enemies" (nationalists) through kangaroo "People's Courts" and to turn Albania into a full-fledged satellite—first of Yugoslavia (1944-48) and after that of Moscow. Consolidation of the Communist regime in Albania amounted to rapid application of the "dictatorship of the proletariat."

The Albanian Workers' Party

Relations with Parent Party

Founded by Tito's emissaries and sanctioned by the Comintern, the Albanian Communist Party was, until June 1948, an appendage of the Yugoslav Communist Party. It was for this reason that Albania was not invited to participate in the meeting in Warsaw when the Cominform was founded in September 1947, Albania supposedly being represented by the Yugoslavs. In fact, the Albanian Communist Party was never admitted to the Cominform. When Tito broke with the Cominform and Albania sided with the latter, direct control of the Albanian Communist Party was vested in the Communist Party of the Soviet Union, which supervises it and issues directives through its own Party representative in the Central Committee of the Albanian Party. Direct relations between the Cominform and the Albanian Party are said to have been practically nonexistent. Although Albanian Communist leaders occasionally contributed articles to the Cominform journal, an Albanian edition of which was issued in Tirana, and the Albanian Communist press dutifully published propaganda material disseminated by the Cominform, there is no indication that directives dealing with policy matters were issued to the Albanian Party by the Cominform; they come directly from the parent Party in Moscow.

Organization

The Statute of the Albanian Workers' Party, adopted at its First Congress in November 1948, defined the organizational structure of the Party as based on the principle of democratic centralization; that is, all decisions have to be made after full and free discussions. Once decisions are made, unanimously or by a majority of votes, all members are to carry them out without question, and the iron discipline of the Party is maintained. The Statute further declared that free and healthy discussion of the problems of Party policy in the various organizations or in the entire Party is an immutable right of each Party member. However, broad discussion of the problems of Party policy, particularly discussion in which the entire Party enters, should be handled in such a way that views of a minority may not be imposed on the will of the overwhelming majority of the Party.

In actual practice, however, Party decisions and policies are made by the seven persons comprising the Party's Politburo and approved by the Party's Central Committee. The rank and file members have no voice in making decisions and formulating policy; their function is to implement these decisions.

According to the Statute, the highest organ of the Albanian Communist Party is the Party Congress, which meets in ordinary session at least once every three years, and which can also be convened for extraordinary sessions. The Congress hears and ratifies reports of the Central Committee and the Auditing Commission; reviews and may change the program and the Statute of the Party; specifies Party tactical lines regarding basic policies; and elects the Party's Central Committee and the Auditing Commission, as well as candidate members for the Central Committee. However, in actual practice, the Party Congress serves no other function than to hear reports presented by the Politburo, approve such reports, and adjourn. Thus, during the First Party Congress in November 1948, the principal reports were delivered by Politburo members Enver Hoxha and Tuk Jakova, both of whom "exposed" the "treacherous" and "Titoist" activities of their former colleagues in the Politburo, Koci Xoxe and Pandi Kristo. Similarly, the Second Party Congress, which opened in Tirana on March 31, 1952, heard Politburo members Hoxha and Mehmet Shehu describe the country's Five-Year Economic Plan, adopted it, and voted the list containing the new members of the Central Committee, which meets at least once every three months, creates a Politburo for the purpose of guiding political and organizational work and forms a Secretariat for the execution of such work. The Central Committee is also authorized to create the following directorates: Propaganda and Agitation; Organization and Inspection;

Cadres; and Agriculture. It is authorized to create sections for propaganda and agitation, for organization and inspection, and for cadres in the city and district committees. It may establish other sections when it deems them necessary. The only mass organization not controlled by the Central Committee is the Albanian-Soviet Friendship Society, which seems to be under the direct supervision of the permanent Tirana representative of the Russian All-Union Society for Cultural Relations with Foreign Countries (VOKS).

The principal functions of the Central Committee are defined as directing all Party activities between sessions of the Congress; representing the Party in its relations with other Parties (presumably Communist Parties abroad) and with mass organizations or institutions; organizing and directing state and Party institutions; appointing the editors of the central organs of the Party and guiding them directly; granting permission for publication of Party organs in the more important Party local organizations; distributing cadres and technical means of the Party; deciding on the payment of Party functionaries and administering the central financial treasury. Other functions of the Central Committee include the calling of a Party Conference at least once a year for discussion and for making decisions upon important questions of Party policy. A conference, of which only two have been convened so far, in 1943 and 1950, can recall and replace members of the Central Committee who do not execute their duties.

The Auditing Commission's tasks are to see that directives of the Party are channeled to its local organs and to the Secretariat of the Central Committee promptly and efficiently, and to audit the Party's fiscal activities.

In cities, regions, and districts, the Party Conferences, which theoretically meet once a year in ordinary session, elect the local Auditing Commissions, hear reports of the local Party Committees, and clarify the Party's directives and policies. City, region, and district Party Committees, which parallel and usually control and supervise the governmental bodies, or Executive Committees, of the People's Councils (Soviets), must meet once a month. They elect bureaus consisting of from seven to eleven members, with two secretaries for each, known as the first and second secretaries; these bureaus must be approved by the Party's Central Committee. The first secretary of the Party is in reality the most powerful person in the city, region, or district; for this reason these posts ar filled by loyal and trusted members of the Party hierarchy. The first secretary of the Tirana region, for instance, is Madame Fiqrete Shehu, wife of the Prime Minister, Mehmet Shehu.

The city, region, and district Party Committees organize and supervise basic Party organizations in factories, transport and construction centers, villages, various institutions, etc.; approve the enrollment of new members in the Party; and administer the Party's local fiscal affairs. These organizations are formed only in those places where there are no less than three Party members. In places where there are less than three Party members, a group of Party candidates is formed under the direction of a Party member designated by city, region, or district Party Committees. All basic Party organizations must be approved by the Party Committee to which they are subordinate.

The principal function of the basic Party organizations, as defined by statute, is to serve as a link between the working masses of cities and villages and the governing organs of the Party. In actual practice, these organizations are instruments employed by the Party to keep close surveillance over every group of persons living or working in communities or work centers. These organizations are, in short, an arm of the police state.

The general duties of the basic organizations are defined in detail by the Statute. These include (1) carrying on agitation and organizational work with the masses and supervising the implementation by the masses of the Party's orders and decisions; (2) mobilizing the masses in work centers, strengthening discipline in work, and stimulating work competition; (3) guarding against chaos and negligence in centers of production; (4) participating actively in the economic, political, and cultural life of the country, and, in particular, attending to the organization and education of the workers and the youths; and (5) accepting new members for the Party, educating them politically, and raising their ideological level. For a basic organization with less than fifteen members, a secretary and a deputy are elected by a general meeting in which the regular members participate; for an organization with more than fifteen members, a bureau is elected in the same manner. All officials of these organizations, although elected by the local members, must be approved by higher Party authorities.

The Statute provides that the work of the basic Party organizations in the army shall be directed by the Party's Central Committee through the Political Directorate, which is on a par with a directorate of the Central Committee; the organization of the Party in the army is based on separate regulations approved by the Party's Central Committee.

The Statute contains an elaborate section dealing with measures for infringement of Party discipline; the most serious infringements are those causing Party disunity, factionalist tendencies, failure to implement decisions of the higher Party and state organs, and deviation from the Party line. Punitive measures for such infringements range from notations in the biographical files of the individual member to expulsion from the Party, the latter requiring approval by the Central Committee.

Party Membership and Composition

Despite the fact that the Albanian Communist Party, through the National Liberation Movement, managed to enlist as volunteers or to recruit large numbers of people by force, Party membership during the war was insignificant. Thus, there were only about 700 members when the First Party Conference was held at Labinot in March 1943 (*Zëri i Popullit,* March 24, 1954). In his report to the Party's First Congress in November 1948, Tuk Jakova placed the Party's membership in November 1944 at 2,800. However, according to Jakova, by November 1948 membership had reached 45,382, of whom 29,137 were regular and 16,245 candidate members; this comprised 3.9 per cent of the country's total population. In his report on March 31, 1952 to the Party's Second Congress, Enver Hoxha said that as of that day the Party had 44,418 regular and candidate members. In an article appearing in the March 24, 1954 issue of *Zëri i Popullit* and dealing with the eleventh anniversary of the First Party Conference, Sadik Bocaj, chief of cadres in the Central Committee, placed the current Party membership at about 43,000.

In his report of November 1948, Jakova gave the following figures on the social composition of Party membership:

Category	*Candidates*	*Regular*
	(in per cent of total)	
	(16,245 total)	(29,137 total)
Workers	15.3	22.6
Poor peasants	51.2	54.3
Medium peasants	13.6	13.0
Kulaks	0.2	0.2
Free professions	0.4	0.1
Civil servants	6.3	2.1
Students	1.3	2.2
Pupils	2.3	2.4
Craftsmen	5.3	0.8
Others	4.1	2.3

In his report on March 31, 1952, Hoxha gave the following breakdown of the Party's social composition as of that day: regular and candidate members of working class origin comprised 8.01 per cent, and 11.5 per cent was composed of elements who were then classified socially as workers. Only 9.73 per cent of the workers then engaged in production were Party members. As of March 1952, said Hoxha,

74.1 per cent of the Party membership came from the poorer classes; 22.2 per cent from the middle classes; and 3.7 per cent from the formerly wealthy classes (*Zëri i Popullit,* April 1, 1952). In other words, the Albanian Communist Party is fundamentally a party of poor peasants.

Party Purges

The Albanian Communist Party has been beset by widespread purges, affecting its members from the Politburo down to the lowest ranks. The first major purge occurred early in 1943, when Anastas Lulo and Sadik Premte, two of the Party's founders, were purged on charges of "Trotskyism"; Lulo was executed and Premte fled abroad. In August 1944, Mustafa Gjinishi, also one of the Party's founders and a Politburo member, was purged on orders from the Yugoslavs because he concluded the agreement of Mukaj with the nationalist organization Balli Kombëtar providing for the creation of the Committee for the Salvation of Albania; he was treacherously assassinated by Liri Gega. From the Congress of Berat (October 1944), when Organizational Secretary and chief of the Communist police, Koci Xoxe, became the most powerful man in the Party (with the backing of the Yugoslavs), until June 1948, many members of the Central Committee were dismissed or purged; these included Sejfula Malëshova, Ymer Dishnica, Mehmet Shehu, Liri Belishova, Liri Gega, and a host of others. Politburo member Nako Spiru was forced to commit suicide (November 1947). When the Albanian Communist Party made its famous "turn" in the summer of 1948 by approving the Cominform resolution against Tito (June 28), heads began to roll again. Koci Xoxe and Pandi Kristo, who had ruled the Party with an iron hand since 1944, as well as a number of other Central Committee members, were purged; in May 1949, Xoxe, Kristo, and other top Party leaders were brought to trial on charges of "Trotskyite" and "Titoite" activities. Xoxe was sentenced to death and executed, and the rest were given long prison terms. Conversely, Shehu, Belishova, and a few others were reinstated in their former positions.

Purges were continued even within the Central Committee appointed after the purges of Xoxe and his associates. It was revealed at the Second Party Congress that of the twenty-one members of the Central Committee chosen by the Party's First Congress, five had been purged, as were four of the ten candidate members elected at the same time. Two others were not re-elected. Tuk Jakova and Bedri Spahiu were other members not re-elected to the Politburo by the Second Congress; Jakova was charged with right-wing deviation; and Spahiu was accused of doing an unsatisfatcory job as the Party's agitaiton and propaganda boss. They were, however, retained as members of the Central Committee. Despite these major purges, Enver Hoxha managed to remain the Patry's Seceretary-General from its establishment in 1941. In July 1955, in accordance with Moscow directives, the position of Secretary General was abolished, and Hoxha became First Secretary of the Central Committee.

In his report before the Party's Second Congress, Hoxha revealed that a complete "verification" of Party documents was initiated on April 1, 1950 and was completed in September 1951. During the "verification" process, 3,776 members were expelled because of "hostile activities," while 2,200 others were expelled "as unworthy of being Party members." From the First Congress to the end of 1951, Hoxha added, 3,909 regular and 7,127 candidate members were accepted by the Party. Actually, on the basis of Hoxha's and Jakova's total Party figure for 1948, 12,000, or more than one fourth of the Party's members, were purged or dropped between November 1948 and the end of 1951. Major purges since then include that of Spahiu and Jakhova from the Central Committee in June 1955.

The rumored rivalry between the top Albanian Communists, Enver Hoxha and Mehmet Shehu, is probably not as important as is generally believed, although some jealousy appears to exist. This is natural, since each needs the other in the power complex in Albania, and Moscow needs both in order to maintain its control over the country. The replacement in July 1954 of Hoxha by Shehu as Premier was due to Moscow's orders to implement the collective leadership principle, rather than to the opposition or rivalry between the two men.

Front Organizations

Article 21 of the 1950 Constitution recognizes, in addition to the "vanguard of the working class" (the Albanian Workers' Party), the following mass organizations: the Democratic Front; labor unions; cooperatives; and cultural, technical, and scientific societies. There are today in Albania a large number of front organizations, all of which are mobilized to implement the policies of the Party and the government. The following are some of the more important.

Democratic Front (DF)

The National Liberation Front (FNÇ), originally known as the National Liberation Movement, was established by the Congress of Berat (October 1944); it was created as a body distinct from the government local National Liberation Councils and the Albanian Anti-Fascist National Liberation Council. A general Council of the

FNÇ with forty-five members was elected with Dr. Omer Nishani as President and Professor Sejfulla Malëshova as Secretary-General. Front Councils were created on village, region, and district levels, as well as in all army units, plants, schools, construction projects, and wherever there was a group of people living or working together. The first FNÇ Congress, held in Tirana early in August 1945, increased the General Council to eighty members, who in turn elected an Executive Committee of twenty and a Secretariat of nine. Hoxha replaced Nishani as President, and the name of the organization was changed to the Democratic Front. Hoxha is still its President.

A camouflaged organization created for the purpose of implementing the program and policies of the Albanian Communist Party, the DF is officially described as the mass organization in which all shades of political opinion should be represented. The Statute of the Party provided that the Albanian Communist Party should lead the DF and should struggle to unite within the DF all the "democratic" and working forces. As *Zëri i Popullit* of March 28, 1954 phrased it editorially, the Democratic Front expresses the "indissoluble unity of the Albanian people." The principal function of the DF at present is to present candidates for local and national elections; no other electoral list is tolerated.

The membership of the DF was officially placed at 645,674 in April 1956. According to Tirana Communist officials, it includes every Albanian eighteen years of age or over, except the "outcast" classes (former bourgeoisie, "kulaks," people considered enemies of the regime, etc.). Next to the Party membership card, the DF membership card is the citizen's most important document; without it, he cannot work, obtain a ration card, shop in state stores, etc.

Union of Working Youth

The Union of Working Youth of Albania, the "fighting reserve" and the "inexhaustible force" of the Albanian Workers' Party, dates back to November 23, 1941, when the Communist Youth of Albania was founded as a junior section of the Albanian Communist Party. From the very beginning, the Party's Central Committee made strenuous efforts to enlist the largest possible number of boys and girls. Through secret circulars, it sent detailed instructions to the local Party Committees to form Anti-Fascist People's Youth Committees in each village and town and in all Partisan formations, and to enlist the most promising recruits in Party cells. By early 1943, many of the Partisan units were composed of young boys and girls who had left school and had been sent to the mountains by the local Anti-Fascist People's Youth leaders. The vast majority of these youngsters had never heard of Marxism; they joined the Partisan forces not because of any Communist leanings but because they associated the term "Partisan" with adventure, active resistance to the Italian forces, and new privileges.

The ranks of the local Anti-Fascist People's Youth Committees must have grown rapidly by May 1943, for on May 9 a national youth meeting in which more then 400 delegates participated was held in Voskopojë (near Korçë). Another large meeting was held August 8-11, 1944 near Panarit, attended by 348 delegates from all parts of the country; it founded the Union of Anti-Fascist Youth of Albania (BRASH). The meeting elected the General Council of BRASH of sixty-one boys and girls. The General Council in turn elected a Secretariat of eleven, with Nako Spiru as President and Liri Gega as Secretary-General, both then militant Communist agitators and leading members of the Communist Youth of Albania. At its third congress in Tirana in 1946, BRASH changed its name to the People's Youth of Albania. On the basis of a Party resolution issued in June 1949 ordering the merger of the People's Youth and the Communist Youth of Albania, a unification congress held in Shkodër on September 15 effected the merger under the name of the Union of Working Youth of Albania. The statute drafted by the congress for the new organization provided that every person between the ages of 15 and 26 who recognized and abided by the program and statute of the organization, worked in one of its branches, obeyed its decisions, and regularly paid his dues was a member of the organization. Each member, added the statute, must work tirelessly for his ideological education, study the principles of Marxism-Leninism, and spread his knowledge throughout the masses of the youth.

The Union of Working Youth is organized along the same lines as the Party. It has parallel basic organizations, city, regional, and district committees, a central Committee, a Political Bureau, a Secretariat (which is headed by Todi Lubonja), and an Auditing Commission. During its second congress, held in Tirana from June 29 to July 2, 1952, it was stated that the Union had 3,220 basic youth organizations and a total membership of 81,700. An additional 25,000 enlisted during 1953.

In addition to the principal task of training future Party members, the Union controls all Pioneer organizations, which include the country's school children from seven to fourteen years of age (current elementary school enrollment is about 140,000); sees that all Party policies and directives are implemented by the country's youth; operates some 2,000 political schools and educational groups; and, above all, mobilizes the country's youth into "voluntary" (forced) labor brigades to work on all kinds of projects. Most undertakings of the present regime—construction of railroads and highways, power stations, agricultural projects of a national character, etc.—have been declared "youth actions."

Union of Albanian Women

Committees of Anti-Fascist Women of Albania were created by the Party parallel with the Anti-Fascist People's Youth Committees for the purpose of collecting clothing and other materials for the Partisan formations, distributing anti-fascist (Communist) tracts, and mobilizing Albanian women behind the National Liberation Movement. These committees recruited some 6,000 girls who fought in the ranks of the Partisans.

A national organization known as the Union of the Anti-Fascist Women of Albania (BGASH), was established on September 23, 1943; a definite form was given at its first congress, held in Berat in November 1944, which chose a Secretariat of nine, with a non-Communist, Olga Plumbi, as President and Communist Liri Gega Secretary General. (They were both purged in 1946.) A second congress, held in Tirana from June 31 to July 6, 1946, was attended by 450 delegates, "elected by 213,000 members of the organization" in 2,021 village councils, 47 district councils, and 10 regional councils. The congress changed the organization's name to the Union of Albanian Women, and named Mrs. Nexhmie Xhunglini Hoxha (Enver Hoxha's wife) President; she held this position until October 1955, when she was replaced by Vito Kapo, wife of Hysni Kapo.

The Union of Albanian Women controls and supervises the political and social activities of the country's women, handles their ideological training, participates in such international Communist organizations as the World Federation of Democratic Women, and mobilizes the country's women for "voluntary" work in state and cooperative farms, industrial projects, etc.

Trade Unions

The first Communist-controlled trade unions were organized on February 11, 1945, when the General Council of Workers' Syndicates of Albania was created in Tirana, with Tuk Jakova as President. A congress held on October 28 of the same year gave the organization a definitive form, adopted a statute, and named it the General Syndical Union. At this congress, it was claimed that the General Syndical Union had a membership of 23,000, or a little more than half the total of about 40,000 prewar wage earners in the country. The second congress of the organization, held in October 1949, made radical changes in the trade union structure to make it conform more closely to that of the Soviet Union, and changed the name to United Trade Unions of Albania. The third congress, in August 1952, placed the membership at 88,105, organized in 1,184 trade union organizations in enterprises, factories, plants, offices, schools, and various other work centers and cultural and social institutions. A network of "activists," mostly Party members, is spread throughout the trade unions for the purpose of controlling and supervising the work of the local organizations, implementing directives issued from above, goading individual workers to fulfill norms and increase output, and furthering political and ideological education. Albanian trade unions are treated at greater length in Chapter 9, "Labor."

Society for Aid to the Army and for Defense

On August 1, 1949, a preparatory committee was organized to create the Society for Aid to the Army and for Defense (SHNUM). On December 12, the first national conference was held in Tirana, with 115 delegates claiming to represent 1,305 local organizations and 41,430 members. The preparatory committee announced that all Albanian citizens who had reached the age of sixteen could join the society, whose aim was to strengthen "traditional patriotic sentiments" and revolutionary hatred and vigilance and to work for the defense of the Motherland and the People's Democracy. At its second national conference, held in May, 1952, Major General Sadik Bekteshi, who delivered the principal report, declared that the duty of the society was to prepare the country's youth by means of special training courses, to train the working masses in self-protection against bombardments and poisonous gases, and to teach them how to organize first-aid centers and to aid the armed forces. Among the courses given by the society are first aid, radio and telephone operations, motor vehicle driving, and marksmanship. The society is actually a paramilitary and civil defense body, and, like the Ready for Work and Defense (GPM) complex in the sports organizations, its purpose is to train people in quasi-military operations. The current head of the society is Major General Spiro Moisiu.

Albanian-Soviet Friendship Society

Founded late in 1945, the Albanian-Soviet Society is a principal agency in Albania for Sovietizing the country. At the end of 1953, it had 3,200 local basic organizations with a total membership of 210,000. The society carries on large scale operations and activities to acquaint the Albanian people with the "achievements" of the Soviet Union; manages the dissemination and application of Soviet methods of work in industry and culture; arranges conferences, lectures, and artistic performances; operates a large number of "popular" courses in the Russian language; distributes Soviet printed matter in the country; and publishes three organs in Albanian, *Friendship, The Soviet Workers,* and *Soviet Kolkhozian.* Its president is Hysni Kapo, who replaced Bedri Spahiu in August 1955.

Other Front Organizations

Among the somewhat less important front organizations are the League of Albanian Jurists; the Albanian Committee for the Defense of Peace; the League of Albanian Writers; the League of Albanian Newspapermen; the League of Albanian Doctors; the Committee for Assistance to Korea; and the Albanian Red Cross Society.

6. THE GOVERNMENT

Pre-Communist Governmental Pattern

Situation under the Ottoman Empire

The Albanians were among the very last European peoples to create a state and, until recently, had no experience in self-government. During the five centuries of Turkish domination, the country was never governed as an entity with definite boundaries, and it never had a centralized authority. The Sublime Porte, finding it difficult to subdue the Albanian people, especially the mountaineers, was forced to recognize the semi-independence of hereditary tribal chiefs who had ruled certain areas in the country since the Middle Ages. In the center and south, it created feudal beys, who were granted large estates in exchange for aid or promises of aid to the Turkish Empire. The Turks then saw to it that the chieftains and the beys were at loggerheads to prevent their uniting against the conqueror. As a result, a certain anarchy on an early medieval pattern prevailed in parts of the country. In addition, many beys were in the service of the Ottoman administration, some of them achieving high positions as ministers and even grand-viziers.

Governmental Life, 1912-1924

On November 28, 1912, Ismail Qemal bey Vlora convened a congress of eighty-three nationalists in Vlorë, declared Albania independent, and formed a provisional government under his presidency, with Dom Nikol Kaçiori as vice president, and seven ministers. A senate of eighteen members was also formed.

The new government met with serious obstacles: most of the beys and chieftains refused to abandon their semiautonomous existence and to give their allegiance to the new national authority, while the rank and file of the people continued to look upon their old protectors as their masters and paid little attention to orders issued by the central government. The situation was complicated by the aspirations of Albania's neighbors, Serbia and Greece, which occupied large sections of Albania. In January 1914, Ismail Qemal bey surrendered the powers of government to the International Control Commission, which drafted an "Organic Constitution," and established Wilhelm zu Wied, the German prince whom the Great Powers chose to be the first Albanian sovereign, as head of the new state. This constitution, which was completed in April 1914, provided for the country's neutrality under the protection of the Great Powers, set up an executive Council of Ministers, and called for a National Assembly. However, the new government did not succeed in uniting the country or in exacting obedience from the local chieftains, the most obdurate of whom was Esad Pasha Toptani, whom Prince Wilhelm had appointed Minister of the Interior and Minister of War. Toptani began arming his followers to revolt against the Prince, and to prepare to ascend the Albanian throne himself. Beset by insubordination and open revolt, Wied fled the country after reigning for only six months, and Albania relapsed into its old condition of semianarchy and rule by local chieftains. Shortly thereafter, the Allied Armies and the Central Powers occupied the southern and northern halves of the country, respectively, in connection with their military operations in World War I.

Some political and social progress was made, however, during this first attempt of the Albanian people to govern themselves. While independence brought neither peace nor stability, it did witness the formation of a central government, the appointment of a single ruler for the whole country, and, for the first time, complete freedom to learn to read and write the Albanian language. It also instilled a certain national consciousness and national pride.

The first serious attempt toward independence after Prince Wilhelm's departure from Albania was made in Durrës soon after the signing of the Armistice on November 11, 1918. On December 25, a group of nationalists convened in that city and created a National Assembly, which in turn formed a Provisional Albanian Government for the purpose of restoring independence. The government was formed under the presidency of Turhan Pasha, and included such patriots as Prenk Bib Doda Pasha, Mehdi bey Frashëri, Midhat bey Frashëri, Luigj Gurakuqi, Lef Nosi, and Dr. Mihal Turtulli. The government then appointed a delegation to present Albania's case before the Peace Conference in Paris. Albania's independence was assured, thanks chiefly to the personal intervention of President Woodrow Wilson, and a national congress convened in Lushnjë on January 21, 1920. From this congress emerged the Lushnjë Constitution and the High Council of State, which was composed of four regents to whom the functions of the monarch were entrusted. The members of the regency represented the principal religious denominations of the country: Sunni and Bektashi Moslems, Catholic, and Orthodox. The Congress also appointed a Cabinet to assist the regency, and elected a Senate with parliamentary powers to serve as a check on the actions of the regency. The first postwar national government, appointed by the Congress of Lushnjë, was installed in Tirana; it was headed by Sulejman bey Delvina, with Ahmet bey Zogu as Minister of the Interior, and five other ministers. The government of Durrës was dissolved.

The foundations of governmental life of the Albanian state were laid by the Congress of Lushnjë. The various Albanian governments formed from 1920 to 1924 undertook the tasks of driving the Italian troops from Vlorë (summer 1920), organizing a national educational system, and establishing a uniform state administration on the Western model. This last task was particularly difficult since the landed aristocracy, which still claimed feudal rights and was steeped in the antiquated Oriental form of government, had always ruled central and southern Albania on behalf of the Sublime Porte, and expected to continue enjoying precedence in governmental positions. Despite the complaints and opposition of the more liberal elements in the country, the landowners managed to fill the most important administrative posts in the new state. However, even with the key positions in the hands of the feudal landowners, the impetus of national feeling following the Congress of Lushnjë made it possible for the state to consolidate Albanian national unity, to prevent the neighbors from destroying the new state, and to make considerable progress in maintaining law and order in the central and southern parts of the country. The northern tribesmen, however, often influenced by foreign gold, proved unwilling to cooperate with the Tirana government, and their chieftains were thus able in many cases to manipulate the local population.

The government's authority was challenged in the spring of 1922, when a group of antigovernment forces marched on Tirana. The situation was saved by Ahmet bey Zogu, Minister of the Interior, who was the only member of the government not to flee Tirana. Zogu defeated the insurgents and prepared his way for higher positions. In December of the same year, he became Prime Minister, which position he held until the spring of 1924, when his prospective father-in-law, Shefqet bey Verlaci, succeeded him for a few months.

The political freedom enjoyed from 1920 to 1924 has never been equaled in Albania; electioneering was wholly free; candidates of the various political parties were generally free from police interference; freedom of press, assembly, and speech were guaranteed in fact as well as in theory. However, in the spring of 1924, the Zogu-Verlaci coalition all but liquidated parliamentary government. The successful uprising staged in June by the Opposition Party brought into power Bishop Noli's left-wing government, which announced far-reaching political, agrarian, and social reforms. However, the Noli project for drastic land reforms and its recognition of the Soviet Union caused alarm in international circles, and the Bishop failed to win economic support from the League of Nations for which he applied soon after he came to power. Moreover, the politicians and army officers who formed the government began to quarrel among themselves over spoils and to form two opposing factions, known as the Radical Democrats and the National Democrats. In the meantime, Zogu, who had spent his exile in Belgrade, acquired foreign aid. On Christmas Eve, 1924, he rode into Tirana, followed by units of Wrangel's (White Russian) armies and Serbian soldiers in mufti, declared the return of "legality" in the country, and set up an authoritarian government.

Albania under Zog, 1925-1939

Zog's regime lasted from December 24, 1924 until Italy invaded Albania on Good Friday, April 7, 1939; from January 21, 1925 to September 1, 1928, he ruled as President Zogu of the Republic, and from September 1, 1928 to April 7, 1939 as King Zog I of the Albanians.

According to the Constitution of 1928, executive power was vested in the King, to be exercised through the government. The Cabinet, consisting of the Prime Minister and the seven other ministers who controlled the departments of government, was directly dependent upon and responsible to the King. When he decided to change his ministers, he simply dismissed the Cabinet and installed another. The legislative power was exercised collectively by the King and the Parliament of one House. However, this branch, composed of fifty-six elected deputies, was also subservient to the King. Since there were no political parties, Parliament was merely an assembly of hand-picked individuals. The deputies were entirely dependent upon the King and always took their cue from him or from his spokesmen. Zog fixed the agenda for Parliament, had the right to veto bills passed by Parliament, commanded the armed forces, and had the authority to declare war.

The independence of the judiciary was often transgressed; the King himself or members of the royal court acting in the King's name constantly interfered with the course of justice. Since his power was personal, license was allowed to any trusted supporter who transgressed the law. Zog played minister against minister, commander against commander, tribe against tribe, interest against interest. He forced everybody to require his protection against a rival. If someone was too strong, the King would either do away with him or, if he was not too dangerous, bribe him.

National elections for Parliament were held in two stages. In the primaries, individual voters assembled at the headquarters of the local commune to appoint electors for the secondary elections. A few weeks later the electors gathered at the district prefecture to choose the deputies for Parliament from a list of official nominees supplied to the prefect by Tirana. Thus, the electoral process merely ratified the King's choice of deputies.

In view of the political immaturity of the country and in view of the traditional autonomy of the northern chieftains and the central and southern feudal beys, Zog's personal and authoritarian government was perhaps well suited for Albania. Probably no other type of regime would have been able to unify the country.

In any case, definite steps toward forming a modern Albanian state were realized during Zog's regime. National education made some progress, illiteracy was reduced, and progress was made in the establishment of law and order. Under Zog, the central government asserted its authority with much effect. The traditional vendetta and brigandage were greatly reduced. Most tribesmen, who before Zog's time went armed as a matter of course, yielded up their rifles. Finally, improvement of communications and the establishment of a disciplined army and gendarmery insured unprecedented peace and order in the country.

The Pro-Fascist Governments

The Fascist regime which was imposed on Albania by force in April 1939 was worked out in detail in Rome prior to the invasion of the country. Nevertheless, Mussolini went through the formal steps of convening an Albanian Constituent Assembly (April 12, 1939), composed chiefly of pro-Italian large landowners, such as Shefqet bey Verlaci, and of former members of Zog's Parliament. The assembly abrogated Zog's constitution, named a government under Verlaci, and offered the Albanian crown to the King of Italy. Verlaci's puppet government and the subsequent government headed by Mustafa Kruja and others until Italy's capitulation in 1943 were Albanian governments only in name; power rested with Italian officials and in the Albanian Fascist Party.

The new constitution of 1939 provided that Albania should be a constitutional monarchy under King Victor Emmanuel; executive power appertained to the King, and was exercised by the King's Viceroy *(Luogotenente)*. A Cabinet of Albanian ministers was provided, but their power was only advisory. Legislative power was vested in the King, and a Superior Fascist Corporative Council, which replaced Parliament, was appointed to assist the Crown. However, in practice the Crown retained all power, and the Council merely discussed bills and rubber-stamped the decree-laws of the

King. Judiciary power was also held by the King, and was administered in his name by judges whom he appointed. The Albanian Fascist Party controlled local government administration for the most part, exercising considerable power over the Albanian population; in fact, this power was actually Italian power, exercised in Italy's interest. The agreement between the kingdoms of Italy and Albania provided that the "conduct of all international relations of Italy and Albania is unified and is centered in the Royal Ministry for Foreign Affairs in Rome" and gave Italians in Albania and Albanians in Italy the same civil and political rights. This made the union with Italy similar to outright annexation.

On September 13, 1943, the last Italian-appointed Cabinet was succeeded by an Albanian National Committee, which in turn, in consultation with and on the approval of Dr. Hermann Neubacher, Hitler's political trouble-shooter in the Balkans, formed the Albanian Provisional Executive Committee under the presidency of Ibrahim bey Biçaku. The Committee acted as a Provisional Government until October 16, 1943 when a National Assembly met to decide on the future form of the Albanian government. The members of this Assembly were generally Albanian patriots who had not collaborated with the Italians, but who were opposed to the Communist-dominated National Liberation Movement and who believed that they could arrange a *modus vivendi* with the German occupation forces. On his part, Dr. Neubacher recognized Albania's independence, arranged for an exchange of diplomatic representatives with the Albanian Provisional Government, and assured that Germany would not interfere with Albania's internal affairs. The Assembly proceeded to nullify all laws passed by the Italian-appointed governments since 1939; created a High Council of Regency, composed of Mehdi bey Frashëri, Chief Regent, and of Pater Andon Arapi, Fuad Dibra, and Lef Nosi; and appointed a government, headed by Rexhep Mitrovica. Mitrovica's government, and those that followed during the next twelve months, did not have much time to govern as the country was in turmoil, and the rising Communist tide consumed their energies.

Communist Penetration and Takeover

The Albanian Communists began preparing to seize control of the country after the Conference of Pezë (September 16, 1942). Using the National Liberation Movement as a cover, and always under the leadership of Tito's emissaries, they calculated every step to lead to the creation of a revolutionary Communist state. The local National Liberation Councils and the ANLA (Army of National Liberation of Albania) formations were made the chief instruments in the Commu nist conspiracy. While in public declarations the National Liberation Councils were represented as expressing the will of the people in liberated areas, and the Partisan units as fighting a patriotic war to rid the country of the foreign invaders, the Communist leaders were issuing secret directives to their local comrades to seize control of both the Councils and ANLA units. This was done through the "Shpati Circulars" in which secret instructions were sent to the local Party leaders. The Shpati Circular of November 3, 1943, for instance, contained the following reference to Party manipulation of the National Councils:

> It must be understood thoroughly that the National Liberation Councils are the backbone of the future democracy of Albania; therefore, the best of our comrades must be placed at the head of these Councils, and the most strenuous activity must be performed in order to give them the necessary status . . . It is through these Councils that the people become conscious of our war and come close to us in our struggle.

The same circular had similar recommendations concerning the Partisan units and the necessity of creating Party cells within the army battalions. However, in the various resolutions and proclamations issued in the name of the LNÇ (National Liberation Councils), it was vociferously denied that the movement was Communist. Enver Hoxha, Political Commissar of the ANLA, reiterated this denial at the Congress of Përmet in May 1944, when he declared: "The traitors are accusing us of making the country Bolshevik and destroying private property, religion, and culture. These lies and calumnies have come out of Goebbels' kitchen."

At the Conference of Labinot in July 1943, the National Liberation Councils were established as the nuclei of Party power, exercising administrative, judicial, and political authority in all parts of the country, ostensibly for the purpose of opposing Italian rule. Although the Statute of Labinot described the Councils as a provisional form of government to function only until such time as the country was liberated from Italian domination, they proved to be the basis of Communist rule in Albania.

Another measure taken at the second conference at Labinot in September 1943 proved decisive in the Communist struggle to seize control. Under pressure from the Yugoslav Communists, they declared open war against the nationalist forces, especially Balli Kombëtar (National Front). The Shpati Circular of September 9, 1943 enjoined the local Party committees to describe Balli Kombëtar as a reactionary organization and tool of the invader to divide the Albanian people. Civil war began on a full scale; the Albanian Communists were determined to crush the nationalist movement so that they alone should fill the vacuum after the defeat of the Germans.

The Congresses of Përmet (May 1944) and of Berat (October 1944) showed the determination of the Communists to have a governmental apparatus ready for any eventuality. The Anti-Fascist National Liberation Council formed at Përmet, together with its executive organ, the Anti-Fascist Committee of National Liberation, prosecuted the civil war with vigor, issued a series of decrees on the Statute on the Councils of National Liberation issued a year earlier at Labinot, and created a Communist judicial system in the liberated areas. The Congress of Berat transformed the Anti-Fascist Committee into the "Provisional Government in Albania," headed by Hoxha and composed chiefly of Communists. The Congress also passed a number of laws dealing with the expanded powers of the National Liberation Councils, which were now confined to governmental functions on the local level. This government under Hoxha acted as the legislative and executive body of the country from the time of its establishment in Tirana on November 28, 1944 until January 11, 1946, when a Constituent Assembly proclaimed Albania a People's Republic and abolished the monarchy. This Assembly also created a Presidium, headed by Dr. Omer Nishani, and drew up a Constitution for the new Republic. The branches of government provided for in this Constitution of 1946 are basically the same as those in the current Communist Constitution, with the exception of a few changes made in 1950 and 1953.

People's Democracy

Official Definition of People's Democracy

The People's Democracy imposed upon the Albanian people by foreign agents, and by a handful of Albanian Communists, was described by Mehmet Shehu in his report before the Party's Second Congress in April 1952 as a "People's Authority" that exercises the functions of the "dictatorship of the proletariat." As such, Shehu explained, the "People's Authority" fulfills three functions: (1) It assures full domination of the country through the "organized and revolutionary violence" of the working masses, with the working class in the vanguard, and the liquidation of resistance by the vanquished "feudal-bourgeoisie"; (2) it guarantees the leadership of the working class over the peasant through alliance with the peasantry; and (3) it assures realization of the economic basis of socialism (*Puna* [Work], April 4, 1952). Manush Myftiu, a member of the Party's Secretariat, declared in a speech in Tirana on January 21, 1954 commemorating the thirtieth anniversary of Lenin's death, that the present regime in

Albania is carrying out the functions of the "dictatorship of the proletariat," and that the People's Democracy was a form of dictatorship.

Nature and Functions of the People's Assembly

The Assembly's rules and regulations were adopted on January 22, 1946 and published in *Gazeta Zyrtare* on February 12, 1946 as Decision No. 196 of the Presidium of the Assembly. The Assembly has permanent and special committees. The Committees on Economic Planning and Finance, Foreign Affairs, Credentials and Immunity, Administration, Petitions and Complaints, and the Judiciary are permanent; special committees are appointed to examine proposed legislation or other questions.

The first general Communist elections in Albania were held on December 2, 1945, when the eighty-two candidates presented in the name of the DF(Democratic Front) won, as no other list of candidates or opposition was allowed. Among those presented by the DF were a number of non-Communists who had been duped into collaboration with the National Liberation Front (FNÇ), either during or immediately after the country's "liberation." During the first few sessions of the Assembly, which convened on January 10, 1946, these non-Communist members naively believed that they could oppose the virtually automatic passage of legislation drafted by a small group of Communist members. As this opposition was strong, the Communist deputies began to intimidate the opposition. In this they were successful, for some members of the opposition group began to vote with the Party program, while others refrained from voting. Subsequently, a number of these recalcitrant deputies were arrested and tried as "enemies of the people." By 1950, when the second general elections were held, about one half of the original eighty-two deputies had been purged; these included both non-Communists and top Party leaders, such as Koci Xoxe and Pandi Kristo.

In the three general elections held so far in Albania, the DF has polled the high percentages usual in all Communist elections. In the first (December 2, 1945), it received 93.16 per cent of the votes cast; in the second (May 28, 1950), 98.18 per cent of the votes cast; and in the third (May 30, 1955), 99.86 per cent of the votes cast.

Presidium of the Assembly

The Albanian Presidium, patterned on the Soviet model, dates back to the Congress of Përmet, when the Anti-Fascist Council of National Liberation created by that Congress chose a Presidium headed by Dr. Omer Nishani. On January 12, 1946, the Constituent Assembly, which later converted itself into the People's Assembly, adopted a law creating the Presidium of the Constituent Assembly, which consisted of virtually the same people who had headed the previous one. This Presidium automatically became the Presidium of the People's Assembly after the Constitution of 1946 was adopted on March 14. Articles 57 to 60 of the Constitution of 1950 deal with the composition and functions of the Presidium. The Presidium, elected by the Assembly, consists of the president, three deputy presidents, a secretary, and ten members. It is responsible to the Assembly. In case of the dissolution of the Assembly, it retains authority until the election of a new Assembly. The current president of the Presidium is Haxhi Lleshi, who succeeded Nishani on August 1, 1953. Its secretary, the most powerful Party figure in the Presidium, is Sami Baholli.

Despite the elaborate tasks and duties assigned by the Constitution to the People's Assembly and to its Presidium, the only functions these two bodies perform are to rubber-stamp legislation introduced by the Party and to give the Communist regime the appearance of legality.

National and Local Government

National Government

The Presidium of the Anti-Fascist Council of National Liberation created by the Congress of Përmet (1944) was authorized to appoint the Anti-Fascist National Liberation Committee, which was described as the "greatest executive committee and operational organ of the People's power," and had the attributes of a "people's provisional government"; it was composed of a president, two vice presidents, and eleven ministers. Enver Hoxha was appointed head of the Committee. Six months later, the Congress of Berat converted this Committee into the "Albanian Provisional Government," with Hoxha as Premier and Minister of National Defense, two vice premiers, and ten ministers. All but two members of this government were Communists. One of the two non-Communist ministers, Professor Gjergj Kokoshi, who resigned a few months later, in 1947 was tried as an 'enemy of the people" and given a long prison term, despite the fact that he had contracted tuberculosis. He died in prison.

Articles 61 to 70 of the Constitution of 1950 set forth the functions and composition of the national government. As reorganized on June 24, 1955, the Albanian government consists of the Premier (President of the Council of Ministers), five vice premiers, twelve ministers, and three commissions (see list of current government and Party leaders at end of chapter).

The government in Communist Albania is in actual practice an executive branch of the Party. While the Party was under Yugoslav control, Yugoslav experts and "advisers" were active in Albanian ministries. Following the Tito-Cominform break, however, they were replaced by Soviet representatives. Most of the actions of the government are carried out not on the basis of laws, but by fiat and administrative measures taken by the Premier and the Minister of the Interior, who are members of the Party's Politburo, and implemented by the Communist security police. The government is composed almost wholly of Tosks (southern Albanians), among whom the Albanian Communist movement had its origins; the Gegs (northern Albanians) have very little voice in the present regime.

The relationship between the Party and government is clearly demonstrated by the fact that every important decree or decision is issued Soviet style, i.e., in the name of the Party and government. Article 21 of the 1950 Constitution expressly recognizes the privileged and "controlling" position of the Party.

Local Government

The National Liberation Councils, which were the nucleus of Party power from the outset, during the war exercised administrative, judicial, and political authority. After the Congress of Berat, however, when the National Liberation Front was made a permanent political organization, the National Liberation Councils were confined to exercising governmental functions in villages, communes, cities, subprefectures, and prefectures. A law was adopted by the Congress of Berat dealing with duties, organizations, and elections of the Councils; and early in 1945 local elections were held for these Councils. In the meantime, the prewar administrative divisions were kept generally intact until November 6, 1947, when Law No. 546 provided for the formation of administrative divisions of the Soviet pattern. On the basis of this law the prefectures and subprefectures were abolished, and 20 city People's Councils, 573 locality People's Councils, and 2,601 village People's Councils were established. The first elections for these new administrative divisions were held in February 1948.

A second administrative division was effected by Law No. 684 of March 11, 1949, which divided the country into 25 districts, one city (Tirana), 185 locality, and 2,597 village People's Councils. On August 1, 1953, the local administration was reorganized once again by Law No. 1,707. This law and Decree No. 1,716 of August 20 (both published in *Gazeta Zyrtare* September 7, 1953) provided People's Councils in 10 regions, 53 districts, 47 localities, and 2,609 villages. Other administrative changes occurred in January 1956 (see page 52).

Articles 71 to 78 of the Constitution, as amended on August 1, 1953, state that the organs of the state power in villages, cities, districts, and regions are the People's Councils, which are elected by the people for a term of three years. These Councils direct the activities of their subordinate administrative organs as well as economic and cultural affairs within the limits of their competence; they maintain public order, supervise the execution of laws, protect the rights of citizens, and draw up local budgets. They also issue decisions and regulations in conformance with the Constitution, laws, and general directives of the higher organs of state power. The executive and managerial organs of the People's Councils are the Executive Committees elected by the People's Councils; the membership of these Executive Committees, as defined by Decree No. 1,210 of January 26, 1951, consists of from five to fifteen members. The activities of the various administrative sections are under the supervision of the Executive Committees and are controlled by the People's Councils, as well as by the corresponding sections of higher People's Councils and corresponding ministries. The Executive Committees are responsible both to the People's Councils which elect them and to the executive and managerial organs of the highest organs of the state. The Executive Committees also have permanent commissions corresponding to the sections.

The local People's Councils, like the national government, have ostensibly been given wide powers both by the Constitution and by specific laws and decrees. However, they are simple administrative bodies through which the Party regulates the life of every citizen. They are a means of placing the stamp of legality and seeming respectability on the authoritarian and unpopular activities of the Party.

The Judiciary

Early Communist "Justice"

The Statute of Labinot provided that the National Liberation Councils in liberated areas create civil courts, that they help the military courts to punish "traitors" and "agents paid by the enemy," and that they confiscate the properties of all "enemies of the people." The section of the Statute dealing with crimes provided capital punishment for political murders, especially if the crimes were committed against Partisans (Communists) and members of the National Liberation Councils. Death was also to be imposed on responsible members of the families of those committing political crimes. If the accused did not surrender and if his family had a hand in the crime, all members of the family were to be punished with death. During the war, the Party, whose principal methods of operation were conspiracy and violence, secretly decreed death sentences for a large number of nationalists and anti-Communist patriots and then assigned teen-age zealots to murder them in the streets in cold blood.

Immediately after its creation, the Presidium of the Anti-Fascist Council of National Liberation promulgated the Law on the Provisional Organization of the People's Courts in the Zones of Free Albania. This law became effective on August 1, 1944. It created People's Courts, District Courts, Courts of Appeal, and Military Courts. The People's Courts and the District Courts were placed in the hands of the village People's Councils and district People's Councils respectively, who appointed their members, usually men with no legal training. The People's Courts could try only petty offenses; the District Courts tried civil cases involving property, divorces, and so on, and some minor penal cases. The Military Courts tried cases involving high treason, offenses aimed at impeding the war of national liberation, and so forth, where the penalty was usually death. These Military Courts, together with the Special People's and Military Tribunals created in December 1944–January 1945 to try "war criminals and enemies of the people," were Albania's revolutionary courts. They sent hundreds of Albanian non-Communists to the gallows during the first two years of the present regime. The "war crimes commissions" prepared the lists of those to be tried by these special tribunals. The most famous of these was the Special People's Court of Tirana, which was headed by Koci Xoxe and which in March/April 1945 tried sixty former ministers, deputies, high government officials, and well-known patriots. Seventeen of the sixty were executed.

The Legal System as Provided by the Constitution

The functions of the judiciary are described in Articles 79 to 90 of the Constitution of 1950, which state that (1) justice is administered by the Supreme Court, People's Courts, and Military Tribunals; (2) courts are independent; (3) higher courts may, within legal limits, control the activities of lower courts; (4) the Minister of Justice directs and supervises the activities of the judicial organs and is responsible for the organization and proper functioning of the courts; (5) courts act on the basis of law, and the accused has the right to defense; (6) the Supreme Court, which is the highest judicial organ of the state, is appointed by the People's Assembly for a term of four years, as are the Military Tribunals, while the lower courts are elected by the people. The Public Prosecutor's Office is an organ of the People's Assembly, which appoints him and his deputies, while local people's prosecutors are appointed by the Public Prosecutor; these people's prosecutors are independent of local state organs.

Reorganizations of the Judiciary

The bomb explosion on February 19, 1951 at the Soviet Legation in Tirana resulted in the issuance of the decree of February 26, which practically abrogated all provisions of the 1950 Constitution dealing with civil rights and with the dispensation of justice. This was followed by the resignation of Manol Konomi, the Communist Minister of Justice, who had held that post since the inception of the Communist government in 1944, and by a widespread purge of the judiciary. In June of the same year, the People's Assembly approved a complete reorganization of the judiciary. The General Military Prosecutor's Office of the People's Army was merged with the General Prosecutor's Office of the Republic, which thereafter bore the latter name and was headed by Siri Çarçani, a former colonel in the Sigurimi (state security police). The military Supreme Court was also merged with the Supreme Court of the Republic (thenceforth known by the latter name), whose presidents, Shuaip Panariti and Aranit Çela, who replaced him in April 1955, were both officers in the Sigurimi. The assistants appointed to Çarçani and Panariti were young Party members who had little, if any, legal training. As the Communist Minister of Justice phrased it, the new magistrates had to dedicate their entire energy to their tasks so as "to become still more resolute defenders of the new society, of our revolutionary legislation, to have at heart the cause of socialism, and to implement the aims of the Party and state."

The New Penal Code

On May 22, 1952, Minister of Justice Bilbil Klosi presented to an extraordinary session of the People's Assembly the draft law for a new penal code for the country based on the class warfare and "revolutionary justice" motif and embodying the basic principles of Soviet justice. The new code was adopted on the following day and became effective on September 1, 1952. In presenting the new code to the Assembly, Klosi implied that the events of February 1951 (the explosion of the bomb at the Soviet Legation) had made imperative a new penal code to guarantee the existence of the "people's authority." He declared that, in view of the increasing attempts to subvert the Albanian regime from abroad, the maximum and minimum penalties provided by Soviet legislation for political and economic crimes be increased in the Albanian code.

Divided into two parts, the code contains general and special provisions. The general provisions state the purpose of the code as that of serving and preserving the "dictatorship of the proletariat" and define the principal element of crime as "endangerment of socialist society." "Social endangerment" is further defined as any activity directed against the economic and political basis of the socialist state, the "people's authority," and socialist property. The lower age limit of general penal responsibility is set at the age of fourteen, but penal responsibility for crimes against the state, damage to state property, and economic sabotage is set at the age of twelve. Individuals who conspire to commit a crime against the state are held penally responsible and may be subject to capital punishment, even if the antistate plan had not been carried out. Equally harsh penalties are provided for persons who give or offer shelter to enemies of the state. In contrast, individuals who commit crimes for the defense of the state and of socialist property are exempted from penal responsibility. The major penalties provided by the code are death, imprisonment, and internment at corrective labor camps. The death penalty is reserved for crimes against the state and for other crimes involving "social endangerment." Life imprisonment is prohibited by the code (*Gazeta Zyrtare*, August 1, 1952; cf. *Zëri i Popullit*, May 23, 1952).

Principal Government Leaders
as of May 1, 1956

People's Assembly

President of the Presidium: Haxhi Lleshi
Vice Presidents: Pilo Peristere
Aleksandër Xhuvani
Myslim Peza
Secretary: Sami Baholli

Council of Ministers

Premier: Mehmet Shehu
First Vice Premiers: Hysni Kapo
Beqir Balluku
Vice Premiers: Manush Myftiu
Spiro Koleka
Koço Theodosi
Secretary General, Office of Premier: Muhamer Spahiu

Ministries

Foreign Affairs

Minister: Behar Shtylla
Assistant Minister: Vasil Nathanaili
Chief of Protocol: Vasil Skorovotic
Chief of First Political Branch: Musin Kroi
Chief of Second Political Branch: Halim Budo

Interior

Minister: Major General Kadri Hasbiu
Assistant Minister: Major General Mihallaq Ziçishti

National Defense
Minister: Lieutenant General Beqir Balluku
Deputy Minister: Major General Panajot Plaku
Chief of Staff: Major General Arif Hasko

Education and Culture
Minister: Ramiz Alija
Assistant Ministers: Kahreman Ylli, Qibrie Ciu
Director of Arts Directorate: Frano Jakova

Industry and Mines
Minister: Adil Çarçani
Assistant Minister: Refat Dedja

Trade (formed July 20, 1954)
Minister: Kiço Ngjela
Assistant Ministers: Zihni Muço, Vasil Kati

Agriculture (formed July 20, 1954)
Minister: Maqo Çomo
Assistant Ministers: Gaqo Tashko, Miti Bozo

Finance
Minister: Abdyl Këllëzi
Assistant Minister: Spiro Bakalli

Construction (formed June 6, 1955)
Minister: Josif Pashko

Communications (formed June 6, 1955)
Minister: Tonin Jakova

Public Health
Minister: Ibrahim Dervishi
Assistant Ministers: Vera Pojani, Eleni Terëzi

Justice
Minister: Bilbil Klosi
Assistant Minister: R. Taushani

Other Agencies and Offices

Prosecutor General: Siri Çarçani

Supreme Court
President: Aranit Çela

Central Council of Trade Unions
President: Pilo Peristere

State Control Commission
President: Shefqet Peci
Vice Presidents: Lefter-Gogo, Ymer Aliko

State Planning Commission
President: Spiro Koleka
Vice President: Ilias Reka

State Procurement Commission
President: Spiro Pano

Top Government and Party Leaders in Order of Importance (as of May 1, 1956)

Enver Hoxha
Mehmet Shehu

Hysni Kapo
Gogo Nushi
Beqir Balluku
Liri Belishova
Spiro Koleka
Rita Marko
Manush Myftiu
Kadri Hasbiu
Pilo Peristere
Shefqet Peçi
Haxhi Lleshi
Nexhmije Hoxha
Fiqrete Shehu

Principal Albanian Workers' Party Leaders
as of May 1, 1956

Politburo

Full Members: Enver Hoxha
Mehmet Shehu
Hysni Kapo
Gogo Nushi
Beqir Balluku
Liri Belishova
Spiro Koleka

Alternates: Manush Myftiu
Rita Marko
Pilo Peristere

Secretariat

First Secretary: Enver Hoxha

Secretaries: Liri Belishova
Gogo Nushi
Rita Marko

Central Party Auditing Commission

President: Koço Tashko

Members: Ismail Caushi, Shefqet Kruja

Union of Working Youth of Albania

First Secretary: Todi Lubonja

Principal Party Committee First Secretaries

Berat: Xhavit Qesja
Dibër (Peshkopi): Jashar Menzelxhia
Durrës: Jordan Pani
Elbasan: Sul Baholli
Gjirokastër: Rrapo Dervishi
Korçë: Haki Toska
Shkodër: Sadik Bocaj
Tirana: Fiqrete Shehu
Vlorë: Gaqo Nesho

7. NATIONAL SECURITY

THE ALBANIAN population has been roughly 70 per cent Moslem for more than a century, a fundamental factor influencing Albanian-Turkish relations and all aspects of Albanian national life. Under the Porte, distinctions were religious rather than national. The Albanians were considered one of the ruling, rather than ruled peoples, which greatly affected their position in the Turkish Army. All subjects of the Porte were legally subject to conscription, but the Balkan Christians were not usually conscripted, as they could pay a tax which exempted them from military duty. Consequently there were proportionately many more Albanians in the Turkish forces than any other European nationality, and many Albanians held high positions under the Turkish Empire, as grand viziers, ministers, and pashas. Although many Albanians desired autonomy, until the beginning of the twentieth century Albania was the only Balkan country under Ottoman control which desired to remain within the Ottoman Empire and in which loyal troops could be raised.

The Young Turk revolution of 1908 greatly altered this situation. Most Albanians, including army officers, supported the new Turkish regime with enthusiasm at the outset, but were first disillusioned and then alienated by its frenzied Turkish nationalism. This led to rebellion by the northern mountaineers, serious revolts in the vilayets of Shkodër and Kosovo, destruction of Turkish arms stores, and defiance of the Turkish authorities by many Albanians, including even officers and men in the Turkish forces.

From the outbreak of the First Balkan War in 1912 and the ensuing Declaration of Albanian Independence in the same year, the military and political situation in Albania remained chaotic until after the end of World War I, during which the country became a battleground for the contending powers. At the Armistice, most of the country was occupied by the Italians, who by various political maneuvers attempted to obtain a Protectorate over Albania. Finally, in 1920, following the battle of Vlorë, the Italian occupation troops withdrew to Italy, and Albania was at last independent.

Under the Ottoman Empire, the internal police system was rudimentary and was effective only in the more important towns and villages. In a country with an extremely poor communications system, where the vast bulk of the population lived in the countryside, and where brigandage was common, outside the towns the only real security a man had for life and property under the Turks was his own rifle. The Turks made only sporadic attempts to increase the size and the efficiency of the police posts and the police force and to eliminate the widespread corruption in the administration of justice.

This traditional lack of law and order affected the pattern of Albanian social and economic life. In the absence of an effective police force, the knowledge that each crime would be avenged by the victim or his kinsmen was a powerful deterrent, and personal vengeance and the blood feud were part of the Albanian code of honor until the most recent times. Economically, the lack of protection in the countryside was a tremendous drawback to the development of both trade and agriculture, and was a factor in the large proportion of tenant farmers: the independent Albanian peasant did not enjoy the protection provided the tenant farmer by the large landowner.

Independent Albania, 1920-1939

Armed Forces

In the first years of independence, governmental stability and national security were threatened by several risings, often encouraged by neighboring powers for political purposes. It was at this time that Ahmet Zogu first distinguished himself. As Minister of the Interior, and later Prime Minister, he showed courage and zeal in maintaining order and governmental authority. A successful rising, in which commanders of the armed forces sided with the revolutionaries, forced him to flee the country in 1924. Upon his return in the same year, an Albanian Republic was proclaimed with Zogu as President. Under its constitution, the President was commander in chief of the armed forces, and one of Zogu's first projects was the creation of a faithful army and gendarmery. When in November 1926 a revolt encouraged, if not engineered, by Italy broke out in the north, the new government was able to dispatch 6,000 troops, and the rising collapsed.

President Zogu became King Zog in 1928, but with the exception of swearing loyalty to the King rather than to the Republic, this change did not greatly affect the army or the gendarmery.

Function. The Albanian Army was fundamentally designed for the defense of the country, but the poverty of the country dictated an army only large enough to hold off an invasion by an enemy until an ally could come to Albania's aid. King Zog attempted to build a small but efficient army large enough to increase national prestige and assure his control.

Organization. The direction of the National Albanian Army was in the hands of the King. Under the King was the Commander of National Defense, with a Chief of Staff, who in turn had a Deputy Chief of Staff. National Defense Headquarters had various sections in charge of planning, training, operations, recruiting, and administration. Although the law provided for the organization of the army by divisions, these were never brought into being, and in practice the basic army formation was the so-called Mixed Group, roughly equivalent to a brigade. Commanded by a colonel or lieutenant colonel, a Mixed Group normally consisted of three infantry battalions, a pack battery of artillery, and an engineer signal section. Not directly connected to any group were additional artillery and engineer units and military training schools. For military purposes the Frontier Guard was considered a group consisting of five battalions. Provision was made for the integration of the gendarmery and the militia into the armed forces in case of war.

Recruitment. Albania, like her neighbors, had compulsory military training by annual classes. After medical examination and selection by a traveling commission (which deferred some of the class for urgent family need or other possible hardship), the conscripts reported to a designated recruiting office, which assigned them to units. Recruits were sent to units stationed in other than their home regions in an attempt to give them a broad national outlook. Of an annual class of roughly ten thousand men, between five and six thousand were generally conscripted for the army. Men were liable for military service and reserve duty from the age of 18 to 50.

Reserves. After army service, trained men went into the reserves. They could be called for further training, and in case of national emergency, mobilized for service in the armed forces. About 3,000 reservists were recalled annually for refresher courses. By the time of the Italian invasion in 1939, there was a reserve of approximately 50,000 trained men.

Strength. Under the monarchy, the usual strength of Albanian armed forces, including the Royal Guard and the Frontier Guard, was approximately 10,000 officers and men (the official figure was 11,450). Of the six Mixed Groups in the Albanian Army, two consisted only of cadre battalions, and the country did not possess sufficient artillery and heavy equipment to bring the six groups to full war strength.

Equipment. Army equipment was virtually all Italian and limited to the needs of an army of infantrymen and mountaineers in rugged country. Mules were used extensively in the army, as they were in regular Albanian life. The basic artillery piece was a pack-mounted 65-mm. gun.

Training. As the bulk of the Royal Albania's Army was drawn from a hardy population thoroughly familiar with outdoor life and accustomed to carrying arms, training was greatly simplified. It was based on Italian methods and supervised at the higher levels by Italian army instructors. In addition to the regular training schools, there was a special school at Tirana for senior officers. By 1939, almost one third of the Albanian career officers had been sent to Italy for training.

Italian Influence. An Italian military mission was established in 1926 shortly after an agreement was signed providing for Italian assistance in the organization of the Albanian Army. This mission remained until 1939, and Italian officers were attached to most important Albanian units in responsible administrative and organizational posts until the Italian invasion. Italian policy dictated maximum control and influence over the Albanian Army, which the Italians insisted be kept large enough to require substantial Italian economic and technical aid, thus to facilitate Italian penetration. In 1928, General Pariani, the Italian Military Attaché, was made head of the Army Department of the Royal Court. By 1930 there was approximately one Italian officer for every six regular Albanian officers, and in that year Italian officers were also assigned to the militia as instructors. Italian influence over the Albanian Army and the number of Italian officers waxed and waned according to economic and political relations with Italy, which deteriorated somewhat after 1933. Although individual Italians connected with the military establishment were generally well liked, Albanian dislike for foreign leadership and the King's covert opposition prevented the Italians from gaining complete control of the army.

The Gendarmery

Not the least of King Zog's accomplishments was the establishment of law and order throughout the country and the elimination of the brigandage and general lawlessness which had been endemic in Albania for centuries. This was largely due to the establishment of an efficient gendarmery, which had been instituted under the Republic in 1925 by a British general and a staff of British Inspectors over the strenuous objections of the Italians, who in the next year demanded the dismissal of the British Inspectors and their replacement by Italians. Italy's obvious attempt to control the gendarmery was forthrightly rejected by the President. Under the monarchy, the gendarmery was expanded and streamlined by Major General Sir Jocelyn Percy and his small staff, who were largely responsible for the excellent reputation and trust the Albanian gendarmery enjoyed among the population. They remained until September 1938, when their contracts expired, despite constant Italian pressure to secure their removal.

Function. The principal function of the gendarmery was the maintenance of internal order and rule of law. As in many respects King Zog was a royal dictator, it also had a political function; it was responsible for watching the King's enemies and preventing revolution.

Organization. According to the Constitution, the King was the supreme commander of the army and the gendarmery, which were nonministerial departments, each headed by a Commandant General, and not part of the political body of the government. The gendarmery was represented in the Cabinet by the Ministries of Justice and of the Interior, for both of which it carried out assigned duties. There was a Gendarmery Command for each of the country's ten prefectures, which carried out the orders of the local Prefect and those of the Gendarmery Command in Tirana. A Gendarmery Commandant was assigned to each subprefecture, and a gendarmery station existed in each commune. Although the gendarmery maintained order in the countryside, there was generally a local armed constable in each village subject to gendarmery authority.

Strength. The Albanian Gendarmery, prior to the Italian invasion, had an authorized strength of 3,130 officers and men. The term of enlistment, which was voluntary, was one year for second-class gendarmes, while first-class gendarmes could re-enlist for five years.

Foreign Influence. There was no foreign influence in the Albanian Gendarmery comparable to the Italian influence in the army. General Percy and the nine British Gendarmery Inspectors were engaged as contract employees of the Albanian state, and their influence was moral and technical rather than political.

Police Departments. The major towns maintained police departments for normal municipal police duties and the enforcement of municipal regulations. The police were independent from the gendarmery but worked in close cooperation. After 1937, the Tirana police constituted an exception, for it was then made the Tirana Police Directory, a special formation under the Gendarmery Command.

Axis Occupation

Armed Forces

When the Italians invaded the country on April 7, 1939, resistance was quickly smothered. The unmobilized Albanian Army was caught completely by surprise. As many units did not even have their full issue of ammunition, the Italians had no difficulty in occupying the entire country in less than a week, in spite of isolated engagements, such as that of Durrës, where the small gendarmery force and Frontier Guard and army personnel gave a good account of themselves.

By a decree-law of March 1940, the armed forces of the new Italian puppet kingdom of Albania were absorbed into those of Italy, Albanian personnel retaining their rank. This measure had little practical advantage to the Italians, who recognized that the few regular Albanian troops incorporated into the Italian Army were unreliable. During much of the Italian occupation, they were issued arms but no ammunition.

When the Italians invaded Greece from Albania in October 1940, some Albanian units in the Italian Army took the opportunity to desert to the mountains to wage guerrilla warfare against the Italians. Anti-Italian and nationalist feeling was so strong that, despite increasing concessions, the Italians were never able to conscript or induce more than a very small proportion of Albania's potential manpower to help their war effort. Anti-Italian guerrilla bands increased steadily throughout the Italian occupation.

Following the surrender and withdrawal of the Italians in 1943, the Germans adopted a new military and political occupation policy. They made little or no attempt to use Albanians in their own forces—except the two battalions they formed of Kosovars— and they made many political concessions to Albanian nationalism. However, by the time of the German retreat in 1944, the Albanian political and military situation was chaotic, with the National Liberation Movement's Partisan formations in the ascendency and the Communists firmly in control of the National Liberation Movement, which they used to impose a Communist government on the entire country. The nationalist Balli Kombëtar and the Legality Movement were labeled Fascist, ruthlessly pursued and exterminated by the LNÇ.

Internal Security

Under the Italian occupation, the Albanian Gendarmery was purged and absorbed into its Italian counterpart, the Carabinieri. Whole units were brought over from Italy, and Italian officers were assigned to all important posts in the new organization. A *Questura* police corps was also created under the Fascist Ministry of the Interior with the same duties as the Italian *Questura,* or local police. There were 15 *questori* in Albania, one for each prefecture, including those in Kuçovë. Total strength was in the neighborhood of 1,500, all Albanians. The Albanian Carabinieri organization was under the jurisdiction of the Supreme Command of the Italian Armed Forces in Albania and was closely connected with the Ministry of the Interior of the collaborationist government. The corps was officially reported to have consisted of 3,088 men in 1940 (roughly the prewar figure), which did not include the very large security forces attached to the Italian Army. The new Carabinieri were a fiasco for the Italians and were held in contempt by most Albanians. Accordingly, in 1942 an attempt was made to reactivate both the disbanded gendarmery and a separate Albanian Army to cooperate closely with the Italian forces. This "Albanization" was not to apply to the unarmed town police, who had remained Albanian and were not held in comparable disrepute. It was admitted in a leading article in *Tomori* (the official Fascist Albanian newspaper) that the suppression of the Albanian gendarmery and its replacement by the Carabinieri had been "a most tragic mistake."

Before the projected measures could be fully implemented, Italy capitulated and the Germans took over Albania. As it was evident that the Axis was collapsing, many Italian as well as Albanian collaborationist units and individuals took advantage of the chaos to desert to the Partisans. When the Germans retreated, the remaining Italians and Albanians in the collaborationist security forces fled with them; many of those unable to escape were summarily executed by the Partisans.

Communist Albania

Under communism, Albania became the Adriatic outpost of international communism, and the Communist Albanian national security organization became the tool and counterpart of the Soviet secret police apparatus. Facts relating to these branches are the most closely guarded state secrets of a regime which considers even nonmilitary economic data secret information, disclosure of which is punishable by severe penalties. Virtually no reliable official information is available.

Armed Forces

Function. Stripped of Communist propaganda declarations, the Albanian "People's Army" has three major functions: in cooperation with the internal security forces, maintaining the regime in power;

implementing governmental directives; and protecting the regime from invasion. Further, like all branches of the other captive governments, it is an instrument of the leadership of world communism, controlled by the rulers of the Soviet Union.

Organization. The armed forces are under the command of the Ministry of National Defense. Until July 23, 1953, the army was under the command of Enver Hoxha, but in an administrative reorganization it was then put under the command of General Beqir Balluku, who was made Minister of National Defense. All that is definitely known about the Albanian Army at the highest organizational level is that Soviet military advisers occupy the most important positions, and that planning is coordinated with over-all Soviet military plans for the captive area. The Albanian Army is thought to be composed of two corps and a number of independent brigades and regiments. There are also auxiliary and technical units, including armored, anti-aircraft, and artillery units, and one "liaison battalion." A Russian colonel or lieutenant colonel is the chief of staff of each Albanian brigade and regiment. There is a parallel political organization, the Army Political Directorate (DPU), whose political commissars are trained in special schools, as in the Soviet Army, and who are administratively responsible to the Party. Although their official function is the "political education" of the army, they are generally members of the secret police, and as such wield more power than regular army officers of the same rank. Major General Ethem Gjinushi has been chief of the DPU since 1954. The army has also published its own newspaper, *Luftëtari* (The Fighter), since 1945.

Recruitment. According to a Russian source, compulsory military service was introduced in Albania in the late 1940's for men from 19 to 35 years of age, who must serve for a period of two years. Albanian regulations actually call for eighteen months' service for trainees. In 1953, this was increased to two years for most units, and to three years for men in aviation, navy, tank, motorized, and frontier units, and for noncomissioned officers in all branches who have taken special training.

Reserves. Men from 35 to 55 are subject to obligatory military service in the reserves. Reserves have been called up at an accelerated tempo in recent years for short training periods, to familiarize them with new equipment and army methods. Reservists who fail to appear when called are subject to heavy jail sentences.

Strength. According to a Russian source, there were 70,000 in the Albanian Army (Partisans) toward the end of World War II. It is probable that the total strength of the Albanian Army in mid-1955 was in the neighborhood of 35,000 officers and men, not counting the

Frontier Guards or the large internal security forces. Of this total, the two effective corps included from 24,000 to 30,000. Since World War II, the Ministry of National Defense has been allotted more money by the budget than any other ministry. It is notable that while the 1955/56 military budgets of Romania, Hungary, Czechoslovakia, and Bulgaria have been cut in "the spirit of Geneva," Albania's military budget for 1955 showed a substantial increase. The government, however, declared that the armed forces were reduced by 9,000 men by December 1955.

Equipment. Until 1948 the equipment for the Albanian Army consisted of World War II German, Italian, and Russian material, as until the Tito-Cominform break Albania was dependent for armaments on Yugoslavia, which then had such material at its disposal. Since that time, there have been increasing reports of the "brotherly help" of the Soviet Union and of the captive countries (particularly Czechoslovakia) in supplying arms and equipment. Although some new Russian army material is evident in propaganda photographs, it is doubtful whether the army has been supplied with the latest Russian material to any large degree. Albania is dependent on Soviet-bloc imports for all military items with the possible exception of small arms and ammunition, the local manufacture of which has been reported. Despite the many purges and the strict discipline, the army is still largely unreliable. Army material is carefully guarded when not used for training or maneuvers.

Training. Army training is now based entirely on Russian methods and is under the control of Soviet instructors. As early as 1945, all officers under the rank of captain commissioned during the war were required to undergo an additional six months of training in a special school. During and after the war, while Albania was a Yugoslav subsatellite, this country provided instructors for training Albanian Partisan forces in the field and in military schools. Tito's political excommunication resulted in the expulsion of all Yugoslav personnel. This vacuum has been filled by an increasing flow of Soviet experts and Russian-trained Albanians. More than 400 Albanian officers have already received training in Soviet military academies. Army training manuals are translated from their Russian prototypes, Soviet army practices are employed, and Albanian officers study Soviet military history and tactics, Communist ideology, and the Russian language under Soviet and Russian-trained Albanian instructors.

Frontier Guard. This body, although armed and organized on military lines, is more closely connected with the Security Police than with the army, and is subject to the Ministry of the Interior rather than the Ministry of Defense. Its duties in time of peace are officially described as "the protection of the borders of the People's Republic, thwarting the activities of diversionists, spies, and criminals at the border." Actually, its principal function is to prevent Albanians from escaping the country. This force is thought to consist of 8 battalions with a maximum individual strength of 350 men, which would give the organization a total strength of 2,800. It is probably less, as many "battalions" appear to consist of smaller formations. Personnel is carefully selected from Communist stalwarts, and a special Frontier Guard school was established in 1953. Major General Teki Kolaneci heads the Border Guard Directorate in the Ministry of the Interior.

Air Force. The small Albanian Air Force consists entirely of Russian aircraft. The obsolete Russian Yaks of which it was first composed have apparently been recently replaced by forty late-model jet aircraft. Pilots are Russians or Albanians trained in the Soviet Union. There are seven known airfields in the country, the most important being those of Tirana, Vlorë, and Berat.

Naval Force. The *Illyria,* a former Italian gunboat, constitutes the nucleus of Albania's naval forces, which reportedly consist of 18 additional craft equipped with machine guns, 23 coast guard boats, and 10 additional small craft.

Auxiliary Organizations. Para-military instruction for boys and girls from 16 to 19 was authorized in 1945 and was made obligatory for both sexes by Law No. 786 of January 21, 1953. Training courses are under regional army command and are given after school or work hours. Trained young people below military age can be organized into auxiliary military units in case of war or emergency.

Major General Spiro Moisiu has been president of the Society to Aid the Armed Forces since 1954. This semiofficial organization was established to arouse public interest and support of the Albanian Army among the civilian population, and to raise morale of enlisted army personnel through celebrations and social activities.

Foreign Influence. Although Italian influence was strong under the monarchy, King Zog was careful to maintain control of the army, and from 1933 until the invasion, Italian influence was on the wane. During World War II, Yugoslav influence was strong in the Albanian Partisan forces, which were subject to operational control by the much stronger Yugoslav Partisans under Tito. An Albanian mission led by Vasil Konomi was accredited to the Yugoslav Army Supreme Command as early as February 1945, and the subsatellite economic and political relationship of Albania to Yugoslavia in other fields applied with equal strength to the Albanian Army in the early postwar years. Soviet control is even closer than was Yugoslav control.

Internal Security

The importance of Albania's Communist internal security forces cannot be overemphasized. Communism was imposed by force on an independent people with a tradition of physical violence and of the most rugged individualism. Forced to adopt an unfamiliar and repugnant economic and political system, the Albanians are kept in check only by the most repressive control and security measures.

Development. The function of the internal security section of a Communist Party not yet in power was fundamentally the enforcement of unquestioning obedience by Party members and close followers and the elimination of "unreliable" elements. Members of this section accused Lazar Fundo of deviationism and beat him to death before the startled eyes of the British Mission in the summer of 1944. Fundo was an Albanian anti-Stalinist, who was political adviser to a non-Communist resistance band. The implementation of such methods helped the few determined Communists among the Albanian Partisans to attain firm control of the National Liberation Movement and the large Partisan forces.

With the LNÇ in control of the country by the beginning of 1945, the so-called People's Defense Division of between five and six thousand men was created from Communists in the Partisan forces to be the nucleus of the Communist secret police apparatus. The head of the DMP was Koci Xoxe, who was not only a Partisan army officer, but also one of the most powerful members of the Party's Politburo and Orgburo. Technically an army division, the DMP was actually the police-terror instrument of the Communist Party, similar to the original Russian Cheka. The so-called People's Police was created in May 1945, but the DMP, later known as the Sigurimi, remained the most feared branch of the Communist police apparatus. All police are now commonly called Sigurimi, but technically that title only applies to the Direction of State Security (Drejtoria e Sigurimit të Shtetit).

Function. The People's Police are charged with maintaining public order in the streets, countryside, and public places, and executing "the laws, decisions, orders, etc., of both the central and local organizations of the People's State concerned with the security of society, . . . the defense of the State property . . . . and the investigation of crimes and their perpetrators." Their political role is clearly spelled out in a decree of July 5, 1954, which stated that "their main duty shall be the defense of the People's Democratic State for workers and working peasants and the enforcement of the socialist juridical order."

There are special branches for different functions. In addition to the so-called General Police, the uniformed People's Police has four subdivisions: Police for Economic Objectives (for guarding state factories, warehouses, construction projects, etc.); Fire Police; Communication Police; and Detention Police. The last is probably the largest uniformed division of the People's Police after the General Police; it includes the forces for the many jails and the forced labor and concentration camps for political prisoners and suspects.

Communist criteria for guilt or innocence is not commission of crime but danger to the regime. Proof is found in the large percentage of Albanian political prisoners sentenced to long terms without having been present at their own trials. Many prisoners have served years in prisons or camps without ever having been "tried" at all. Only in a Communist state such as today's Albania would one of the duties of the police be officially defined as "organizing jails and other places of detention for persons convicted by the courts or arrested as *potentially* dangerous." (Italics added.) (Decree of the Council of Ministers of November 24, 1953.)

The People's Police were officially ordered "to search shops, warehouses, dwellings, etc. in quest of concealed merchandise" on May 23, 1946. They carry out periodic searches for hoarding of a long list of items, possession of which by private individuals is forbidden or restricted. Prison sentences are authorized for the punishment of persons guilty of concealing even grain. Possession of firearms by private citizens is strictly prohibited, and the People's Police is responsible for their control and for the issuance of permits and weapons to approved applicants. It should be borne in mind that the rifle without which every male Albanian mountaineer considers himself undressed is also often his most valuable possession, and that the Communist decree orders weapons turned in without compensation. The fabrication, ownership, and transportation of guns, explosives, and poisons of high potency is forbidden without a license issued by the People's Police, who are also responsible for the enforcement of all regulations concerning printing and the issue of permits to use distinctive seals or marks. These functions are actually euphemisms for the control of sabotage material, underground publications, and propaganda.

Not the least important police function is the control of physical movement of the population. One of the sweeping powers given the Minister of the Interior by a law of August 30, 1946 (not then made public) was the right to regulate the movement of all citizens and foreigners. All residents of Albania had to get identity cards in 1948, and since that time police control of movement has become progressively stricter. After the 1951 bombing of the Soviet Legation, a decree of January 17, 1952 defined the regulations under which every trip or movement, even from one village to another, must be reported. Penalties for noncompliance are imprisonment or forced labor. By a decree of November 24, 1953, the old identity cards were invalidated, and it became compulsory for all citizens between the ages of 16 and 65 to procure cards of a new type. These cards resemble Soviet internal passports, as they are needed for travel (including trips to visit relatives in the nearest village), employment, and benefits, and include all essential information related to the bearer and his family. Acting through the People's Police, the Ministry of the Interior keeps an accurate account of all "passports" and of notations made on them. The Office of Vital Statistics, the Employment Office, the Army, and Frontier Guard (when the notation concerns residence in border areas) are the only other government departments authorized to make notations on the "passports." New ones are issued every five years, except to special population categories, including special workers and government-decorated "heroes," who receive permanent "passports."

The basic function of the Sigurimi police branch is to prevent counter-revolution and to eliminate potential opposition. The most feared and powerful of all government organs, the Sigurimi includes both a uniformed and plainclothes branch, the latter the so-called secret police. Their functions include detection and elimination of members of the anti-Communist underground, as well as elimination of "deviationists," "Titoists," and "Trotskyists" from the Party. The Sigurimi apparently was completely overhauled by Soviet experts after the bombing of the Soviet Legation in 1951. It now reportedly comprises the following six sections, each with a Soviet adviser with more authority than the nominal Albanian section heads: penetration of political opposition; counterespionage; elimination of anti-Communist underground organizations; censorship of press and radio, cultural societies, and schools and teachers; maintenance of political records and supervision of "economic agencies"; political re-education of inmates of labor camps; and a special foreign service section. Members of the last section are believed present in every Albanian legation. For example, the Second Secretary to the Albanian Legation to Italy, who was arrested for espionage in Rome in 1954, was a member of this section.

Organization. The People's Police and the Sigurimi are both adminstratively subject to the Ministry of the Interior. Koci Xoxe was Minister until his purge and execution for "Titoism" in 1949. Xoxe was followed by Mehmet Shehu, who was made Premier in July 1954, and replaced as Minister of the Interior by Major General Kadri Hasbiu.

The Directorate of Police is that department of the Ministry in charge of the People's Police. Indicative of its importance is the fact that the former royal palace is its national headquarters. There is a Police Headquarters in every town, usually headed by a lieutenant colonel or major, who is directly responsible to the Ministry of the Interior. The deputy chief is usually a captain. Regular headquarters personnel generally numbers 140 uniformed men; Police Command stations, 35 men; and police posts, 15 men. The system of police stations and posts corresponds roughly to that of the prewar gendarmery, although the new Communist system is much larger.

Police headquarters have four known sections or branches: Security (Sigurimi) branch staffed by both uniformed and plainclothes men, responsible for keeping the personal dossiers of known or suspected anti-Communist elements; aliens branch, in charge of both aliens and Albanians not born in the district; gendarmery, for standard police duties; and an Office of the Political Commissar.

The Polici e Lokalitetit, or auxiliary local police (see below), are under the command of the People's Police station nearest their community.

Major General Mihallaq Zicishti is the current Albanian head of the Sigurimi, while the People's Police is headed by Major General Delo Balili. Operational and policy control is believed to be exercised by Soviet experts. Like its Soviet counterpart, the MVD, the Sigurimi is believed to be highly compartmentalized for internal security purposes. Government and Party organizations are honeycombed with Sigurimi agents, many of whom hold the highest governmental and Party posts. The Sigurimi also is in charge of the large network of informers. The Sigurimi has its own uniform, which is of a rusty iron color, as opposed to the charcoal uniform of the People's Police.

Recruitment. Physically and mentally fit men and women between the ages of 20 and 35 are eligible for service as commissioned and noncommissioned officers in the People's Police, the minimum term of service being three years. Demobilized army or Ministry of the Interior armed personnel (Frontier Guards) are given preference over civilians. In practice, only the most reliable Communists are enrolled in the police apparatus, which is the key power lever of the Albanian Communist state, and members of the Sigurimi branch are even more carefully screened. As part of the upper government elite, under a law of February 4, 1946, Sigurimi members get pay "double that of other state employees of similar importance." All branches of the People's Police receive free medical aid for members of their families, a privilege not enjoyed by the families of army enlisted men.

Decorations and cash awards are given police members who distinguish themselves in "smashing counter-revolutionary activities."

Training. The first training school was established in Tirana in October 1945. Training was reorganized, and the teaching staff was purged and re-expanded with Soviet MVD personnel after 1948. Since that time, top Albanian instructors and experts have been sent to the Soviet Union for further training. A special Sigurimi school was established in Tirana in 1953 under Colonel Pavlov, a Soviet expert. This school has an enrollment of some 300 students from 18 to 25 years of age. The Albanian teachers are Soviet trained and graduates are sent to Moscow for further training. The Sigurimi appears to be increasingly assuming the character of an Albanian branch of the Soviet MVD. Ideological indoctrination is constant and heavy, due to the sensitivity of the police branch and the consequent emphasis on political reliability. Indoctrination is handled by specially trained political commissars.

Auxiliary Police. An auxiliary local police (Polici e Lokalitetit) was created by a 1948 order of the Ministry of the Interior. Every able-bodied male citizen is obliged to serve for a two-month period in his own locality. The Executive Committees of the local People's Councils prepare lists, revised semi-annually, from which local police are chosen. Their duties include the communication and execution of orders of the local People's Council, the prevention and detection of illegal trade and speculation, assisting tax collectors, and guarding cooperatives. While subject to the orders of the People's Council, the local police are directly under the command and at the disposal of the nearest People's Police Command. The local police are not paid, although they have the same rights and duties as the regular People's Police while on duty. Infractions of rules and regulations are punishable by police regulations, and failure to report for service, or leaving before completion of service, is considered desertion. If they are wounded, fall ill, or die during service, they or their dependents receive regular police benefits. Crimes committed while on duty are punishable by military courts. Local police wear People's Police uniforms on duty, distinguished by a red arm band inscribed PL (Polici e Lokalitetit).

Strength. Any precise estimate of the Communist police apparatus is impossible, as these figures are among the most closely guarded secrets of an almost psychopathically secretive regime. Divulgence of such information is subject to sentence of death, a penalty which has frequently been invoked. It is particularly difficult to make a sound estimate because most of the security forces are not uniformed. Moreover, the government budget is not a reliable index, as the official figures for annual expenditure by the Ministry of the Interior are ridiculously low. When the Communists assumed control of the country, there were between five and six thousand in the DMP alone; this may be regarded as merely the embryo of the Communist security forces. The DMP was augmented by the addition of Pursuit Battalions (Batalionet Ndjekëse) in 1947. Despite the continuous purges and reorganizations of the security forces under the Ministry since that time, the trend has been one of growth and expansion.

A conservative estimate of the number of Communist security forces in 1955 would be 10,000. This figure would include the uniformed strength of the People's Police, an average of 3,000 men serving in the Polici e Lokalitetit, the Frontier Guard, and the uniformed formations of the Sigurimi. It probably does not include the very large plainclothes personnel of the Sigurimi or its network of informers.

8. PROPAGANDA

ORGANIZED propaganda for political purposes appeared clearly for the first time during the rule of King Zog, 1925-39, though the nationalist campaign of the previous half-century had demonstrated some interest and ability in influencing Albanian and foreign opinion, particularly via the press. Albanian periodicals and papers published in southern Italy, Constantinople, Bucharest, Cairo, London, Brussels, and Boston, and a host of publications issued within Albania after the Constitution of 1908, refuted such allegations as "there is no Albanian nationality" and the assertions of Albania's neighbors, especially Greece, that the inhabitants of Albania were not Albanians but "Turks" and "Christians," with the latter automatically Greeks since they attended Greek schools and were members of the Greek Church. These original Albanian publications laid the groundwork for the idea of a general unity among all Albanians, regardless of their religion.

During World War I and for some time thereafter, the press of the Albanian colony in the United States played a significant role in the agitation for Albanian independence and territorial integrity. Enjoying freedom to work and make propaganda for their native land and possessing financial means to support such activity, some fifty thousand Albanian-Americans were able to bring strong pressure on President Wilson to prevent the partition of Albania.

PROPAGANDA DURING ZOG'S REGIME

Zog used propaganda to advance the unification of the Albanian people into a cohesive nation, the development of national consciousness, and the creation of a myth that Zog was a descendant of the Skënderbeg line and tradition, the "Savior of the Nation." This propaganda assumed large proportions just before Zog declared himself King, when he learned or came to believe that other governments, especially the Italian government, would support his assuming the royal power provided he could demonstrate strong popular interest in and support for the monarchy. Zog sought to prove, by means of demonstrations and messages from all over the country, that he was assuming the royal mantle in response to the strongly felt and widespread desire of the people. It was not difficult to produce the required evidence. Demonstrations in the larger cities were arranged during the summer of 1928. Telegrams from all parts of the country were dispatched to Tirana by Zog's supporters, who went to the various localities for this purpose. Tirana publicists, such as the American-educated Konstandin Chekrezi, were temporarily forbidden to publish their newspapers or were locked up for short periods on various pretenses, while pro-Zog newspapers flooded the country. The object of these propaganda maneuvers was not to deceive a strongly republican population, but to keep up appearances before foreign countries.

Once Zog became King, propaganda was confined to having his picture hung in all business establishments, schools, and public institutions, to discussion of his deeds in schoolrooms, and to preventing open criticism of him. In the mid-thirties, a small part of the press, loyal to the King but dissatisfied with his entourage, tried to induce Zog to change the government by propagating the idea that his rule was an "Enlightened Dictatorship." Two semiofficial biographies, by Kristo A. Dako and Gaqo Gogo in the middle 1930's, attempted to enhance his prestige among the people.

Zog's regime was a personal dictatorship, but he did allow a considerable amount of freedom of press, speech, and education. The only subjects prohibited were criticism of the King and of his relations with Italy. From 1925 to 1939, many independent newspapers and periodicals which enjoyed a great degree of freedom often lambasted the government (but not the King) in strong terms. The most notable publications in the 1930's were the two famous democratic and patriotic periodicals, *Hylli i Dritës* (Star of Light) and *Leka,* respectively organs of the Franciscans and Jesuits in Shkodër; *Bota e Re* (The New World) and *Rilindja* (The Rebirth) in Korçë; and *Përpjekja Shqipëtare* (Albanian Effort) in Tirana. Among the more notable independent newspapers were *Demokratia* in Gjirokastër; *Jeta e Re* (New Life) in Vlorë; *Gazeta e Korçës* in Korçë; and *Vatra* (The Hearth) and *Shtypi* (The Press) in Tirana. Although most of these newspapers had financial difficulties and at times accepted subsidies from the Ministry of the Interior, they retained a certain journalistic freedom. They had to abide by provisions of the preventive censorship imposed in 1933. The only paper which could evade such a censorship was the powerful semiofficial *Besa* (The Pledge), which was succeeded in 1936 by *Drita* (The Light).

On the whole, Zog maintained friendly relations with all countries, even with the Soviet Union after diplomatic relations were established in 1935, and there was no antiforeign propaganda to speak of during his regime. However, because of his close financial and military relations with Italy, the semiofficial press expressed sympathy with Italian aims and policies. The Fascist ideology was of course the principal propaganda theme after Italy invaded Albania in 1939, and publications such as *Fashismi* and, later, *Tomori,* were the mouthpieces of the Albanian Fascist Party. Similarly, during German occupation of the country (1943-44), Tirana publications, such as *Albania* and *Bashkimi i Kombit* (Unity of the Nation), represented the Nazi ideology. Most of the other non-Communist publications of this period, such as *Mbrotja Kombëtare* (National Defense) and *Flamuri* (The Flag), both organs of Balli Kombëtar, and *Atdbeu* (The Fatherland), organ of the Legality Movement, were wholly nationalist in spirit and opposed all totalitarian ideologies.

Nature of Communist Propaganda

The Use of Patriotism

From its formation in 1941, the Albanian Communist Party introduced a totally new propaganda approach based chiefly on deceit and misrepresentation and designed to assist in the establishment of a Communist state under the control of the Soviet Union. In view of the strong anti-Slav feelings of the Albanian people, their generally pro-West tendencies, and their deep-rooted love of freedom and independence, the Albanian Communists, actively assisted and directed by Yugoslav agents attached to their headquarters, decided to appeal to the patriotic sentiments of the people and to their desire to rid themselves of the foreign invader. The first clandestine proclamation issued by the Party called on the people to unite for the liberation of the country regardless of their religious beliefs and political tendencies. This tactic was elaborated further after the creation of the National Liberation Movement, which was presented to the people as a purely nationalist movement intended to oust the invader and to establish a truly democratic government. When it became apparent that this movement was Communist-dominated, the Communists engaged in a relentless propaganda campaign to convince the people that the charge was an invention of the foreign enemy and their collaborators at home. Thus, the General Council of National Liberation, which was the executive arm of the National Liberation Movement, or Front, issued at Labinot in July 1943 a declaration denying vehemently that the movement was Communist, inviting the people to "declare war" against all those who called the movement Communist, and declaring that:

> 1. The National Liberation Movement in Albania is an organization comprising all honorable patriots without distinction of religious sect, district, or party. It holds its arms wide open to receive all those who wish to fight against the foreign enemy.
>
> 2. It fights for the liberation of Albania from the yoke of Fascism, and for an independent and democratic Albania.

3. Private property and private initiative in industry and economy remain inviolate.

4. No basic changes will be made in the social life, customs, and traditions, or in the organization of labor.

5. Officers of the old army who enter the Army of National Liberation are guaranteed their rank.

6. After the defeat of the foreign enemy, the people will themselves choose the form of regime they prefer.

These deceiving promises were made just three months after the Party held its first National Conference clandestinely at Labinot (March 1943) and issued secret directives to the local Party bosses and to the commissars in the Partisan formations directing them to assume control of the liberation movement. The resolution adopted by this conference stated that the Party's task was to "popularize the Soviet Union, the Fatherland of the workers and peasants, the leader of the power struggle for the liberation of the peoples enslaved by Fascism."

The deceit and deliberate misrepresentation on the part of the Communists has continued. Hoxha's statement at the Congress of Përmet (May 1944) to the effect that the charges that he and his associates were trying to Bolshevize the country came out of "Dr. Goebbel's kitchen," is well known. Even on the eve of the country's "liberation," Hoxha reiterated at the Congress of Berat (October 1944) that the "democratic authority" which he headed was going to defend all the "democratic rights of the citizens, as well as their beliefs and private property." Concurrently, he issued the secret Shpati (pseudonym for Enver Hoxha) Circulars to the local Party chiefs ordering them to seize and place under Party control the local National Liberation Councils and the Partisan formations.

Propaganda Against Anti-Communists

In addition to deceiving the people by appealing to their patriotic and nationalistic sentiments, the Albanian Communist Party employed every propaganda method to destroy anti-Communists, particularly those truly patriotic elements which had enjoyed widespread and genuine influence in the country. These elements were branded collaborators of the invader. Thus, the Shpati Circular of September 9, 1943 stated that the agreement concluded a month earlier at Mukaj with Balli Kombëtar was to the

> disadvantage of the National Liberation and the Party, and, as such, had been disapproved by the Central Committee . . . Therefore, we must work with the following directives: to discredit Balli before the people by means of a clever exposure and continuous work . . . to introduce Balli to the people as the source of civil war . . . to prepare the people for war against Balli . . .

The Shpati Circular of November 3, 1943 instructed the Party's District Committees that any resistance group outside the National Liberation Movement should be fought without mercy. It ordered that

> the people should be made to believe, that the Reaction [i.e. non-Communist elements] is a tool in the hand of the enemy and that our war against it is not a war of ideologies; that we fight it, first, because it wants to bring back the pre-1939 regime which was against the people . . . that the campaign of the Reaction for unity is all demagoguery; that unity is possible only within the National Liberation Front; that the Reaction is fully responsible for the terror and the civil war; and that the National Liberation Movement has brought order and discipline to the liberated areas, whereas Reaction has always pillaged and plundered.

This type of propaganda was very effective during the war, and it misled large sections of the population within the country as well as high officials of the Allied Military Command in the Mediterranean.

Organization of Communist Propaganda

Organization

The time, energy, and funds allocated by the Communist regime to inculcate the Albanian people with Communist ideology are truly prodigious for a small country.

The propaganda organization of the regime is based on the monolithic system of the Party and government; at the top of the pyramid is the Directorate of Agitation and Propaganda (commonly known as the Agjit-Prop) of the Party's Central Committee, directly supported by the Agitation and Propaganda Sections of the Political Directorate of the People's Army and the Ministry of the Interior. The latter is responsible for propaganda and indoctrination activities in the security, police, and border guard forces. In descending order are the Agjit-Prop sections of the Party Committees in regions, districts, and localities and in industrial plants; the political and Agjit-Prop sections in the central organs of the various mass organizations, especially in the youth and women's organizations, in the Albanian Committee for World Peace, and in the trade unions and their local organizations. Finally, at the base, are the thousands of Party propagandists and instructors, the Party and non-Party "actives," and the political instructors and agitators working through the mass organizations. An illustration of the huge numbers of these agitators may be observed in the trade unions: In 1952, 17,000 young labor union members, or one fifth of the total trade union membership, was engaged in agitation and propaganda work "popularizing" the Soviet Union among the working masses and explaining the Party's and government's policies and program to the laborers.

In addition to the permanent political and Agjit-Prop agencies, "collectives of agitators" are created for special purposes. Thus, during the campaign for national elections (April-May 1954), agitation centers were formed in city wards, districts, and villages; each center had from five to twenty-five militant boy and girl agitators, whose task was to contact every voter and to urge him to "love the Soviet Union." There are, furthermore, "consultative groups" in industrial centers to encourage "socialist competition" and to spread Soviet work methods; there are "collectives of agitators" in the country, composed of "progressive" (i.e. Communist) peasants organized to ensure that the peasants surrender their obligatory agricultural quotas on time, to explain the "peace campaign" to the villagers, and to obtain signatures for various petitions, such as expressions of loyalty to the Soviet Union. These "collectives of agitators" hold frequent conferences, read resolutions and reports, arrange artistic and cultural meetings, explain the country's constitution and laws to the people, etc.; they are armed with immense propaganda material, printed, graphic, and illustrated.

In addition to this organized agitation, every Party member and every member of the Union of Working Youth is expected to engage in daily propaganda; this duty is enforced by the statutes of the two organizations.

Propaganda Channels

Since November 1944, all media of information in Albania have been wholly under Party and government control. No independent or opposition press or other media of information or education are allowed in the country by the present government.

Press and Publications. All newspapers, periodicals, and books are issued either directly by the Party or its mass organizations, such as the Democratic Front, youth and women's organizations, trade unions, and so forth, or by the government, the army, the Albanian Committee for World Peace, or various other Communist institutions. So-called wall newspapers (bulletins) are issued in villages, offices, plants, schools, and wherever there is a group of people living or working together. The two Tirana dailies are the Party's central organ *Zëri i Popullit* (The Voice of the People) and the Democratic Front's central organ *Bashkimi* (Union); both these publications were first issued clandestinely during the war. The Party also publishes a periodical, *Shënime për Agjitatorët* (Notes for Agitators), containing Party matters and distributed chiefly to Party officials, and a monthly theoretical journal called *Rruga e Partisë* (Party Path). At the end of 1953, forty-one newspapers and periodicals were issued with an alleged total monthly circulation (generally through forced subscriptions) of about two million copies; this was in addition to the wall bulletins. By contrast, in 1938 there were twenty-one newspapers and periodicals published in Albania with a total monthly circulation of about 225,000 copies. The current daily circulation of *Zëri i Popullit* and of *Bashkimi* is claimed to be about 45,000 copies each, as compared with *Drita's* 1938 daily circulation of about 5,000.

All printing presses, mimeographing, and other duplicating machines, as well as all printing supplies, are owned and operated by the government; they were seized when the regime came into power, and they were officially nationalized in 1946. In November 1950, all state publishing houses were combined into one, known as Shtëpia Botonjëse Naim Frashëri (Naim Frashëri Publishing House). At the same time, a single distribution center, named Libraria Popullore Qendrore (Central People's Bookstore) was established to handle the distribution of all publications and propaganda material published in the country.

For a small country where nearly 50 per cent of the adult population is illiterate, the number of books and pamphlets published since the end of the war, mostly translations from Russian, is staggering. Radio Tirana on August 1, 1951 claimed that the total number of books circulated from 1934 to 1938 amounted to 840,000 copies, while from 1945 to 1950, 670 different books were published with a circulation of 5,829,000 copies, and during the year 1949/50 alone 260 books were published in 3,500,000 copies. During the period from 1945 to 1950, the broadcast said, 62 works on Marxism-Leninism were published with a distribution of 772,000 copies. Official figures given by the Tirana press at the beginning of 1954 indicated that since 1944 the *Short History of the Communist Party of the Soviet Union* had been printed in four editions totaling some 200,000 copies. From 1944 to 1952, 107 ideological works, mostly Soviet, were published, in a total of 1,231,760 copies. In 1953 alone, 29 Soviet works of a technical and scientific character were translated and published in 182,000 copies, and the Committee for Publishing Stalin's Works, created in 1951 under the chairmanship of Mehmet Shehu, has so far published 12 volumes of Stalin's complete works. In a broadcast on January 4, 1954, Radio Tirana alleged that, during 1953, 150 original works and translations in 1,100,000 copies were published in Albania. It added that this figure did not include 75 school textbooks with a circulation of about a million copies, or literary works for children with a circulation of 100,000 copies.

Another important channel of propaganda is the government-operated Agjensia Telegrafike Shqipëtare (Albanian Telegraphic Agency), the only news agency in the country. This has a monopoly on the collection and distribution of all domestic and foreign news, and it publishes all communiqués issued by the government. Domestic news is gathered by its local correspondents, and nearly all foreign news is obtained from TASS.

Radio. The 50-kilowatt Radio Tirana radio station, built by Soviet experts and opened on the eve of the Second Party Congress (March 30, 1952), and the local stations in Stalin Town (Kuçovë), Korçë, Gjirokastër, Shkodër, and Vlorë are owned and operated by the Committee on Radio Broadcasting, which was created in December 1950 and attached to the Council of Ministers. In 1953, this Committee, as well as the Committee on Publications, was placed in the newly created Ministry of Education and Culture, but in October 1955 it was transferred to the Council of Ministers as the Directorate of Radio Broadcasting. Privately owned radio receiving sets are not common in Albania (17,000 sets in all) and are particularly rare in the rural areas where there is no electric current, so the Tirana regime has installed loudspeakers in the main squares of towns and in work centers, and battery-operated sets in villages to create a radio audience far larger than existed before the war.

Theater and Cinema. The theaters and cinemas are all government controlled and operated. A "People's Theater" was founded in Tirana in the late 1940's under the supervision of a Soviet director. Most of the plays and skits staged by this theater are Soviet propaganda pieces, such as *Voice of America,* a viciously anti-American presentation, or crude domestic comedies and farces dealing with the War of National Liberation and attacking the former upper classes and the "kulaks."

In 1949-50, the foundation of a new film industry, "thanks to the help of the Soviet Union," according to Radio Tirana of January 5, 1951, was laid in Albania. The industry was equipped with projectors, sound equipment, and cameras, and a number of documentaries were begun. In 1948-49, Ilya Kopalin, a well-known Soviet film producer, shot a technicolor propaganda documentary called *New Albania,* which was smuggled into the United States in the spring of 1949 by an Albanian special mission to the United Nations and shown to Albanian-Americans. In early 1952, Kopalin produced another Albanian documentary named *The Glorious Road.* The first film studio, called New Albania, built near Tirana with Soviet technical and material assistance, was opened on July 10, 1952. It was in this studio that a good deal of the work for the technicolor film *Skënderbeg* was done; the film itself was produced by Mosfilm in Moscow.

The importance of films as a means of Communist propaganda was indicated by a general survey of the film industry made by the

Albanian Telegraphic Agency and broadcast by Radio Tirana on January 8, 1954. The survey alleged that during 1953, 123 cinemas, including 20 mobile units, were in operation, or eight times as many as in 1938 and twice as many as in 1950. More than 170 feature films from the Soviet Union and the People's Democracies (no films from the West are exhibited) were shown during that year, and attendance totaled 4,566,000 people (the population of Albania is about 1,394,000). Over 200 documentaries had been shown. The Soviet film *Admiral Ushakov* was seen by 41,000 people, *Arena of the Bold* by 51,000 and *Mysterious Island* by 41,000. The film *Skënderbeg* was seen by more than 82,000 in one month. Mobile cinema units belonging to the New Albania film studio and to local cultural institutions had given more than 2,100 showings during the year in rural areas; these were seen by over 387,000 people.

Albanian-Soviet Friendship Society. Working parallel with the propaganda media of the Party and of the mass organizations is the all-pervading Albanian-Soviet Friendship Society, Moscow's strongest propaganda agency in Albania. At the end of 1953, this organization had 3,200 local branches with a total membership of 210,000. Its political and ideological orientation is handled by an organ known as the Ideopolitical Central Committee, which is reportedly headed by a Russian and is attached to the presidency of the society. Through the central offices in Tirana and the local branches, the society carries out large-scale activities to acquaint the Albanian people with the "successes" the Soviet Union has allegedly attained in the economic, cultural, and social fields. It also manages the dissemination and application of Soviet work methods in industry and agriculture; arranges conferences, lectures, and artistic performances; and operates a large number of "popular" courses in the Russian language for workers. An example of the multilateral and widespread activities of the society is its sponsorship of "Albanian-Soviet Friendship Month" each September. During September, 1953, for instance, the society arranged 44 meetings, addressed by representatives of various Soviet delegations which had come to Albania for the occasion and attended by 156,000 people; 3,500 conferences dealing with life in the Soviet Union, attended by 223,400 people; 314 forums dealing with "dissemination of experience" of the Soviet working people; 721 photo exhibitions; 581 "literary evenings;" and 125 theater and orchestra performances. During the same month, it initiated 34 courses for teaching the Russian language, attended by more than 1,000 workers. During the first twenty days of the same month, 110 Soviet films, mostly documentaries, were shown to more than 250,000 people. In 1952 and during the first six months of 1953, nearly two million persons reportedly attended meetings dealing with political, economic, cultural, and literary topics, and saw film performances shown in rural areas by mobile movie projectors donated to the society by the permanent representative in Tirana of the Russian All-Union Society for Cultural Relations with Foreign Countries (VOKS).

Teaching of the Russian Language. The Russian language is compulsory in all the country's high schools and institutes of higher learning. In September 1953, the Albanian Council of Ministers issued a decree that, effective 1955, the Russian language would be added to the last grade of the seven-year schools and that a two-year language course be organized at the Higher Pedagogical Institute in Tirana to prepare the necessary cadres. The teachers for this course were to be Russian. In addition, a secondary school was opened in Tirana in October 1953 for the purpose of training "hundreds of teachers in the Russian language." A new method by which Albanians could learn Russian was devised by Mina Potapova and published in Moscow early in 1952; 50,000 copies were shipped to Albania.

Basic Propaganda Themes

Domestic Themes

The wartime propaganda line, which stressed liberation from the foreign invaders, the creation of an independent and democratic Albania, and the assurance to all citizens of "bread, peace, and freedom," was replaced by new themes after the Communists assumed control of the country. The new themes, which represented the true character of the Communist movement consisted of the standard Marxist-Leninist lines: class warfare, revolutionary vigilance, people's authority, classless society, dictatorship of the proletariat, economic planning, and so forth.

The class warfare motif was used to consolidate political control; it took the form of ruthless persecution and prosecution of all nationalist and patriotic elements considered real or potential enemies of the regime. It was "revenge with a vengeance," as Koci Xoxe put it in his bloodthirsty speech of February 4, 1945 commemorating the first anniversary of the murder of some eighty-four people in Tirana by the Gestapo authorities. There was to be an end of the "feudal" beys, the bourgeois class, and the former ruling "clique." A new society, based on the alliance of the laboring class and the middle and poor peasantry, and led by the former, was to be formed, with the objective of improving the living standard of the people.

The class warfare motif has been the most persistent propaganda line of the regime and has brought about the incarceration in penal colonies and concentration camps of thousands of innocent Albanian citizens, including children and old people. Vigilance against the "machinations of the class enemy," including Albanian political refugees abroad, is now the daily watchword of all Communist propaganda media in Albania.

In the economic field, the propaganda line has emphasized the promise of a more prosperous life for the "working masses" and the "working peasantry." Alleged achievements in this field are trumpeted constantly and supported by meaningless percentages, combined at times with admissions of dismal failures to fulfill planned goals in industrial and agricultural production. The agrarian reforms effected in 1945-46 are a frequent propaganda theme, despite the fact that those who were supposed to have benefited are generally worse off today than they were before, due to the heavy obligatory quotas and crushing taxes imposed by state procurement agencies. The Party, represented as the "organizer and inspirer of all our victories," calls repeatedly on the people to fulfill "honorably" the Five-Year State Economic Plan.

In the military field, the people are called upon to "love" the People's Army and the police and security forces because they are the "guarantee of the people's victories," purportedly won during the past ten years, and the protectors of the country's independence and territorial integrity, allegedly threatened by its "aggressive" neighbors, especially Greece, supported by "American imperialism." As Minister of People's Defense, Lieutenant General Beqir Balluku said in an order of the day issued on July 10 (Army Day), 1954 that the People's Army, "educated by the Party and government in the spirit of a boundless loyalty to the people's cause, to the Fatherland, and to the Soviet Union," must tirelessly improve its military knowledge and military preparedness, strengthen discipline and vigilance, and increase its spirit of internationalism. On a previous occasion, Balluku had stated that the Albanian armed forces were a part of the Soviet armed forces.

Foreign Themes

During and immediately after the war, the propaganda line of the Albanian Communists was ostensibly friendly toward the West. In the public proclamations issued in the name of the National Liberation Movement, the Albanian people were told that the Anglo-Soviet-American alliance was a guarantee of their country's future freedom and independence. The Congress of Përmet (May 1944) passed a resolution asking that the United States send an official military mission to the Partisan General Staff. In his speech before the Congress of Berat (October 1944) Hoxha stated:

> The great allies, England and the United States of America, which with their hard and continuous bombardments were inflicting on Germany, internally as well as along the whole Western fronts, great damage, opened in France the lightning thrust . . . a thrust which will expedite the liberation of Europe from Nazi Germany . . . The Anglo-American army liberated nearly all France, Belgium, and a part of Holland, and now is at the gates of Germany.

In his long report before the Youth Congress in April 1945, Hoxha declared:

> Think, you comrades of the youth movement, what would have happened if the people of the Great Democracies, of Great Britain, were not strong, those people who placed in the service of the anti-fascist war all their economic and military potential; if it were not for the great English and American Armies which stormed the German fortress from the West; if it were not, in the first place, for Churchill with his rare ability as a leader; if it were not for the great Roosevelt, whose death has grieved our people because we lost one of our great friends, and the progressive world one of the true defenders of democracy and freedom.

This was, until early 1946, the public attitude of the Albanian Communists toward the West. Behind the scenes, however, the picture was different. Thus, Nako Spiru, militant Communist youth leader from 1943 to 1946, repeatedly exhorted his lieutenants to inculcate hatred for the United States into the minds and souls of the country's youth because, as he explained, America was the strongest and richest capitalist country and therefore the most dangerous to the (Communist) "movement." The directives issued by the Party Conference at Labinot in March 1943 instructed local Party hierarchs to do everything possible to popularize the Soviet Union among the Albanian people. The Shpati Circular of September 9, 1943 alleged that it was fear of Hitler that induced England and America to become allies of the Soviet Union. The circular went on to say:

> The English diplomats had refused such an alliance long ago when it was offered by the Soviet Union. They made it when the interests of England were directly threatened by German Imperialism . . . In high circles and in the English government, there are reactionary elements which try to place reactionary forces in power in liberated Europe . . . This must be very clear to the comrades, and they should study it with attention so that their agitation should not be directed against England or America or against the government of England or America with whom we are Allies in this war, but against the reactionary elements in these governments.

The Shpati Circular of November 3, 1943 spoke of the "reaction" that allegedly existed in Anglo-American circles, and declared that "first, we must notice that both Great Britain and America have never tried to crush reaction in Europe, but only to detach it from Hitler."

From 1944 to 1948, while Albania was under Tito's tutelage, the propaganda media of the Tirana regime sought to represent both the Soviet Union and Tito's Yugoslavia as Albania's "liberators." After Tito was excommunicated by the Cominform, the Soviet Union alone received the "boundless love of the Albanian people," while Tito and his Yugoslavia became, in the words of Enver Hoxha, "the greatest mortal enemy of the Albanian people." Since July 1948, the Albanian rulers and the propaganda media they control have expressed the most abject adulation for the Soviet leaders and for the Communist Party of the Soviet Union. "Love" and "gratitude" for the Soviet Union pervades every important speech of the top Communist leaders: it was the Soviet Union which "liberated" Albania from her foreign and domestic "enemies" and brought "freedom" to the people; the Soviet Union protects Albania's "independence" and territorial integrity; the Soviet Union gives Albania "multifarious" assistance for the building of socialism in the country, etc. For these reasons, "eternal friendship" for the Soviet Union and Soviet people has been a fundamental leitmotiv since 1948.

Conversely, the West, especially the United States, has been pictured as mankind's inveterate enemy. American policy toward Albania is presented by the Tirana Communist rulers as aiming at the destruction of Albania's independence and at the eventual partition of the country among her neighbors. A systematic and relentless campaign has been waged to destroy the traditional friendship of the Albanian people for the United States by trying to convince them that the United States government supports Greek territorial claims against Albania.

During and after the Warsaw Conference of May 1955, the propaganda line was to attack the United States for "following the road of creating new military blocs and reviving German militarism." After the Geneva Conference of July 1955, there was a shift. Although Albanian propaganda media protested against discussion of the regimes of Eastern Europe, they upheld "the spirit of Geneva." On August 25, an article in *Zëri i Popullit* commenting on the conference stated: "The conference of the chiefs of the four powers held in Geneva has created a hearty mutual understanding." No praise or approval of the United States replaced the former constant and vitriolic press treatment of this country; with the exception of current political developments reported from the Communist viewpoint, United States news was held to a minimum until early 1956, when the Tirana press began to revert to the standard vitriolic attacks against the "American imperialists."

Part III – The Economic System

9. LABOR

Labor Movements and Organizations

Labor Situation Prior to 1944

A country of peasants and farmers with no industrial establishments of any import, Albania had no labor problem prior to the advent of communism in that country late in 1944. During the interwar period, small cotton, wool, tobacco, and silk plants, flour mills, electric power stations, olive oil presses, and minor manufacturing and processing establishments were set up in the country's major cities; a cement factory was founded in Shkodër; and breweries and alcoholic distilleries were established in Korçë, Elbasan, and Vlorë. In addition, Italian concessions for petroleum, bitumen, coal, copper, chrome mines, and timber employed about 10,000 people. Industrial workers were paid very low wages; a ten- to twelve-hour day was standard, even for children in their early teens, and there was no social or economic protection of any importance.

During the regime of King Zog, labor organizations were not encouraged. However, various professional and manual workers formed local craft organizations similar to medieval guilds, such as the tailors', typographers', and teachers' societies in Tirana; the Puna (Work) organization in Korçë (some of whose chief leaders, like Koci Xoxe, had Communist inclinations), which included shoemakers, tailors, and various other craftsmen; and Shoqënia Puna of Kuçovë (now Stalin Town), embracing the oil field workers—about 2,000 in all. Puna of Korçë was suppressed by the police in February 1936 while it was organizing a "bread" demonstration, and Shoqënia Puna of Kuçovë was disbanded in the same year when it staged a strike.

After Italy occupied the country in April 1939, the manual and professional groups were converted into Dopolavoro (After Work) organizations controlled by the Albanian Fascist Party, but these seem to have attracted very few Albanian workers. Certain Communist-dominated labor groups, especially those of Shkodër, Tirana, and Korçë, which infiltrated the Dopolavoro, formed the nucleus of some of the wartime underground sabotage organizations. In many instances these groups, usually under the leaders of pro-Communist or Communist Party elements, recruited workers and sent them to the mountains to join the Partisan formations.

Communist Labor Movement

Immediately after the Communists assumed control of the country, young prewar labor leaders, such as Koci Xoxe and Tuk Jakova, began campaigning for a single national organization of all manual and professional workers. On January 31, 1945, a preliminary meeting of labor was held in Tirana, and a United Committee, headed by Tuk Jakova was elected to call a conference of representatives of all labor groups to establish a centralized and unified national labor syndicate. The conference was held in Tirana on February 11, 1945 and formed the Provisional General Council of Workers' Syndicates of Albania with twenty-five members, headed by Jakova. It was the standard Communist monolithic organization with regional unions all centralized in the capital.

The organization was given a definitive form by the First National Congress of Workers' and Civil Servants' Syndicates, which was convened on October 28, 1945 by the General Council of Workers' Syndicates. The congress adopted a statute, the first article of which stated that the organization, henceforth to be known as Bashkimi i Përgjithëshëm Sindikal (BPS-General Syndical Union), was to include all workers' and civil servants' societies in Albania. Within the BPS, six syndicates were formed: (1) mine workers; (2) industrial workers; (3) building and other construction workers; (4) civil servants; (5) transportation workers; and (6) distribution and supply workers. At this congress, the BPS claimed a membership of 23,000, or a little more than half of the total of about 40,000 prewar wage earners in the country. By the end of 1947, its membership had reached 46,387, of whom 4,496 were women. At that time, the Union declared that it had 526 branches, 54 local syndicates, and 26 district syndicate councils.

Professor Malëshova, the key speaker at the first labor conference in February 1945, discussed the aims and potentialities of the "proletariat" in Albania and outlined the goals of the syndicates as (1) guaranteeing the future of the "popular democratic authority"; (2) reconstructing the country; (3) improving the economic, political, social, and cultural conditions of the working classes; and (4) helping to develop an independent national economy. At the congress of October 1945, these principles were reiterated and extended to include cooperation with the "democratic workers of the world."

The Second Congress of BPS, which met in October 1949, made radical changes in the statute of 1945 to make it conform to the organizational structure of the trade unions in the Soviet Union and changed the name to Bashkimet Profesionale të Shqipërisë (BPSh-United Trade Unions of Albania). Additional changes were made by the Third Plenum of the Central Committee of the BPSh, which convened in December 1950. In his report before the Third Congress of BPSh in August 1952, Pilo Peristere, its president, described the BPSh as composed of the following seven unions: mine workers; industrial workers; transport workers; construction workers; agricultural and forestry workers; administration, trade, and health workers; and educational and cultural workers.

In addition to the seven unions, the BPSh had at that time 18 District Councils and 43 Locality Committees, all formed on the basis of the reorganization plan of December 1950. The functions of the District Councils and of their auditing commissions were defined as to assist, control, and coordinate the work of the trade union basic organizations. The Councils performed their functions under the direct control of the Central Committee of the BPSh and were financed by it.

The last structural changes were effected by the fourth plenary session of the BPSh's Central Committee, which met in Tirana on November 22 and 23, 1953. Peristere said in his report to this session that organizational changes were necessary for the trade unions to carry out their new duties, to deal with the state economic and administrative organizational apparatus, and to fight bureaucracy and formalism. The seven unions were accordingly amalgamated into three: (1) the trade unions of workers in industry, mines, construction, and transportation formed the Trade Union of Workers of Industry and Construction; (2) the trade unions of workers in the state administration, trade, health, education, and culture formed the Trade Union of Workers of Education and Trade; and (3) the trade unions of workers of agriculture, forestry, and procurements formed the Trade Union of Workers of Agriculture and Procurements. The plenary session also decided to merge the District Councils and and the Locality Committees and to create in their stead regional trade unions in the ten new Communist administrative regions of the country.

The BPSh membership, as revealed by the Third Congress, was 88,105, and at that time there were about 20,000 manual and white collar workers in the country not members of any union. As of January 1953, the membership had not changed materially. There were, as of August 1952, 1,184 trade union basic organizations in enterprises, factories, plants, offices, schools, and various other work centers. A network of 17,049 "activists," Communist propagandists and agitators, mostly young Communist Party members, was spread throughout the trade union basic organizations. Their functions were to control and supervise the work of the local organizations, to implement directives issued from above, to goad individual workers to fulfill norms and increase output, and to further the political and ideological education of all workers.

Table 1 shows the growth of the trade union membership from 1945 to the end of 1952, including government employees and workers on the state farms.

Table 1. TRADE UNION MEMBERSHIP, 1945-1949, 1951, AND 1952

Year	*BPSh Members*	*Total Labor Force*	*Per Cent of Total*
1945	25,000	40,000	62.5
1946	33,000	....	....
1947	46,700	....	....
1948	64,000	72,727	88.0
1949	64,812	80,412	80.6
1951	74,479	....	....
1952	88,105	108,104	81.5

The postwar Albanian labor movement has been under the complete control of the Communist Party and has been used as a mass organization to further the Party's political, ideological, economic, and cultural aims. From 1945 to 1948, the organization was controlled by a small group of Communist Politburo members who had organized craft unions before the war: Koci Xoxe, a former tinsmith and one of the organizers of Puna in Korçë in 1933; Pandi Kristo, a former shoemaker's apprentice and one of the organizers of the Society of Shoemakers and Cobblers in Korçë in the early 1930's; Tuk Jakova, a carpenter from Shkodër; and Kristo Themelko, a tailor's apprentice in Tirana. With the exception of Jakova, these men were eliminated from the Party hierarchy after the Cominform broke with Tito in 1948. At that time, control over the organization passed to Enver Hoxha and his followers. Pilo Peristere, a prewar iron worker active in Puna, was named head of BPSh in the fall of 1950 and re-elected in 1952.

BASIC POLICIES AND LABOR LEGISLATION

Legal Responsibilities

Strict controls over all workers in Albania are vested in the Directorate of Labor and in the BPSh through government legislation and the BPSh rules and regulations. Compulsory labor was legalized in Albania soon after the Communist regime assumed control of the country in November 1944. Thus, on December 15, 1944 all specialists (that is, all professional and skilled workers) were mobilized by the state, and a law passed in April 1945 provided that all persons appointed to public office or to state service, whether temporarily or permanently, were in a state of mobilization. Since then, many additional labor control decrees have provided for freezing workers at their jobs and placing heavy penalties on absentees.

The Law for the Protection of Workers and Regulations of Work (adopted July 9, 1945, and amended on April 20 and August 31, 1946) granted the trade unions sweeping powers to regulate hours, wages, working conditions, and the hiring and dismissal of manual and professional workers. Moreover, both the statute of BPSh and its Ordinance for the Regulation of Work in Enterprises provide for strict discipline of all workers and outline in detail their duties and obligations.

A characteristic government decision taken on July 30, 1947 provided that throughout the government administration, in plants, and in all other work centers, "work which can be done by women must not be done by men, and men must do the work that cannot be done by women." Direct government control of workers in Albania is complete. The Directorate of Labor, which was created in May 1947, was authorized to mobilize all workers through employment offices. The primary function of these offices was defined in the *Gazeta Zyrtare* (Official Gazette) of January 16, 1948 as the distribution of labor in enterprises, economic institutions, etc., both state and private, on the basis of the state economic plans. Under this law, economic enterprises can hire workers only through the employment offices.

Forced Labor

On August 13, 1947, Radio Tirana announced that the government has decided to "introduce forced labor," adding that "all persons who served the former antipeople's regimes and who at present are jobless will be mobilized and employed in construction work." This concept became part of the Labor Code, promulgated on August 25, 1947. Article 7 of Chapter III of the Code provides that: "In exceptional cases (such as disasters or shortage of labor for carrying out works of considerable importance to the state), all citizens shall be liable to be called up for labor service by a decision of the government" (Labor Code published in *Gazeta Zyrtare,* September 16, 1947). On February 8, 1948, Radio Tirana said that the government had recently issued an order providing for the employment of all able-bodied citizens between sixteen and fifty years old who "avoid work." Law No. 726 of August 1949 widened the labor conscription powers of the government, which was empowered to order various categories of skilled and professional workers, including teachers, other specialists, and all other skilled workers to work in construction centers or in the "service of the state." Among the decrees dealing with compulsory transfer or freezing of workers in their jobs, one issued by the Council of Ministers on June 30, 1951 provided that all laborers and specialists must remain at the various state industrial enterprises, regardless of their contracts, until those projects were finished, and that all civil servants and other workers between the ages of sixteen and fifty-five in certain cities must work a minimum of ten days each month on various specified state industrial projects.

The government has made its penal system part of its method of organizing labor to serve the "building of socialist society." The new Albanian Penal Code, which became effective September 1, 1952, is based—according to Minister of Justice Bilbil Klosi—on the principles of "class warfare and revolutionary justice," and it embodies "the basic principles of Soviet justice."

Among the "crimes" punishable by forced or corrective labor terms of from six months to four years are: producing industrial goods of bad quality, insufficient quantity, or in violation of designated standards (Article 90); departure without permission of a worker or civil servant from a state or social enterprise or institution (Article 202); disobeying orders to work permanently or temporarily for the realization of the state's production and construction plans (Article 204).

Legal Rights

Albanian Communist propaganda emphasizes the privileges that labor has won under the Communist regime and the "high" standard of living attained, but there is little evidence to support these claims. The Labor Code guarantees certain rights and privileges for the Albanian workers. It provides, *inter alia,* an eight-hour work day, prohibits children under fourteen years of age from working, classifies workers according to skills, etc. However, these are all only paper guarantees. Most of the state projects, including the railroad lines and state highways built after the war, have been constructed by penal and forced labor and "voluntary" youth labor brigades, the last composed of boys and girls between the ages of ten and twenty-five. Further, the eight-hour work day is only a fiction, for it has been openly admitted at various trade union congresses that norms are set by most industrial enterprises in such a way that the majority of industrial workers must work ten to twelve hours a day. In addition, in order to increase output, most workers are required to work "voluntarily" after regular hours and on Sundays and holidays.

The Communists also proclaim that the collective bargaining agreements assure the worker a proper wage, protect him from accidents, and afford him the power to bargain with his employer. In reality, these agreements, which are contracted between the government-controlled labor unions and government enterprises, contain obligations to increase production in order to fulfill the government's economic plan. Of all the labor legislation enacted by the Albanian Communist regime, only the Law on Social Insurance (adopted August 26, 1947) seems to provide some benefits for the workers. Administered by the BPSh, the law contains provisions for free medical treatment, compensation for certain accidents, and old age pensions.

Labor Supply and Methods of Increasing Output

Chronic Shortage of Labor. There is a chronic labor shortage in Albania. Because of the traditional belief that the woman's place is at home and that the man's "manly" profession is the peasant's plow, the shepherd's crook, or the soldier's rifle, the government's efforts to draw laborers from the countryside have so far met with little success. The economic failures of the regime are principally due to the stubborn resistance of the Albanian mountaineers and peasantry to the pressure to abandon land and to accept work at state industrial and construction projects. For this reason, the government has resorted to the "voluntary" labor system, through which it has regimented the country's youth for heavy work. Nearly everything built in Albania since 1944 has been declared a "youth action" project.

The basic drawback of the Albanian labor force is its inefficiency. There were practically no skilled workers in Albania at the end of the war because the few key industries in operation before and during the war were in the hands of the Italians, who supplied their own technical and skilled workers. Although Albanian labor leaders claim that over 11,000 youth workers have attended various vocational courses since the end of the war and have become "qualified" workers, and that over 5,000 of them had become skilled workers by 1952, they admit the serious lack of skilled workers and technicians to operate the complicated machinery of the new industries. Preparing the necessary industrial cadres, therefore, is the urgent task of the Albanian labor movement. As Enver Hoxha put it at the BPSh's Third Congress, there is a wide gap between the low professional qualifications of the industrial cadres and the knowledge required by the new industries being created in the country. The goal set in the Five-Year Economic Plan (1951-55) was for training 8,500 "medium" technicians and 54,000 "qualified (semiskilled) workers. Some 500 technicians in Albania from the Soviet Union and the captive nations tried to accomplish this program, chiefly through the Labor Reserve Schools which are in operation at various industrial establishments. The Five-Year Plan also envisaged the increase of the total labor force, manual and professional, to about 150,000 by the end of 1955. This is planned through drawing agricultural workers, poor peasants, and kulaks into industrial projects. The goal was not achieved, the present labor force totaling 115,000.

Methods of Increasing Worker Output. Socialist emulation and the Stakhanovite and shock-worker movements in Albania have been used to obtain maximum output from workers. Thus, while some 20,000 workers participated in socialist competition in about 100 collective groups in various enterprises in 1949, by April 1952 the number had risen to 53,910 workers in 269 enterprises. In 1949, there were only 2,304 shock-workers in the country; by August 1952, there were 23,465. While the Stakhanovite movement was nonexistent in 1949, there were 2,027 Stakhanovites in August 1952. The number of Stakhanovites as of June 30, 1954 reached 6,760, of whom 1,082 were women, while the number of shock-workers reached 24,720, of whom 3,482 were women (Radio Tirana, June 30, 1954).

In addition, a new method of driving the workers to higher production was introduced in 1952 through the Brigada të Kulturës së Lartë (Brigades for High Production), which were formed in oil fields and important mining establishments. Composed of shock-workers and Stakhanovites, these brigades are under military discipline. They are separate from the rest of the workers and are subordinate only to the oil field and mining directors. They exercise pressure on the other workers by establishing higher work norms, which are in turn established for all workers.

According to speeches delivered before the BPSh's Third Congress by Enver Hoxha and Pilo Peristere, serious deficiencies still exist in socialist emulation, with the result that enterprises are not able to fulfill their plans. According to Peristere, these deficiencies exist because Soviet techniques (some 46 of which had been introduced in the past few years) and the Stakhanovite movement are being adopted slowly, are receiving little attention from the enterprises and from trade union leaders, and are being opposed by the "class enemy" in some enterprises.

Wage System. In 1949, the Communist government instituted an elaborate system regulating wages and salaries for all types of workers, technicians, civil servants, and professional people. This system is embodied in a 300-page document entitled *The Classification of Workers,* approved by the Council of Ministers Decision No. 661 of December 17, 1949. With minor changes, this classification is still in force.

Classification of Technical Personnel (Workers). All workers are divided into twelve categories, according to the importance of the production sector or services rendered. The successive categories include workers in: (1) chrome, coal, copper, and bitumen mines, and the refining processes for these minerals; (2) petroleum industry; (3) machine shops and electric power stations; (4) sawmills and woodwork and cement factories and plants; (5) agricultural and dairying enterprises, and machine and tractor stations; (6) leather, shoe, tile, and textile factories, as well as handicraft trades; (7) the food industry; (8) land and water transport, including loading and unloading of goods; (9) communal economy, such as roads, vegetable gardens, irrigation projects, postal-telegraph-telephone service, bakers' and photographers' cooperatives, and other services; (10) hotels and restaurants (excluding the managerial staff); (11) construction, installation of machinery, etc.; (12) studies, projects, and geological research of any kind.

Each category is divided into seven classes, with each worker placed in a class according to his degree of skill. Thus the first class includes unskilled workers who have no experience of any kind, while workers with some experience and who have been at work for a short period are placed in the second and third classes. The most skillful workers are included in the last, or seventh, class. Wages are arranged on a progressive scale on the basis of category and class. The base wage of the first class (the most unskilled type of worker) is not identical for all categories; that is, workers in mines, the petroleum industry, and construction are paid higher wages than workers in other economic sectors. This reflects the importance the regime places on priority industries.

Of some 80 leks per day, which the average unskilled laborer receives in Albania (and the great majority of workers are unskilled), a number of reductions and compulsory contributions sharply reduce take-home pay. These include income tax and social security payments; rent and board for those away from home; forced subscriptions to Communist publications; dues for membership in the Communist Party, trade unions, or other mass organizations; and contributions for special causes (such as assistance for the "capitalist victims" of Indochina). Similar reductions and contributions are in force for the technicians and employees of the state and local administration of the state economic enterprises; the average monthly salary for these groups is about 4,500 leks a month.

Table 2 gives the prices of basic commodities on the official as well as free market during 1952 and 1953, when the official Albanian rate of the dollar was 50 leks.

Table 2. COMMODITY PRICES, 1952 AND 1953

Commodity	*Unit*	*Rationed Goods Price*	*Free Market Price*
		(in leks)	
Bread	Kilo	6	100-120
Olive oil	Liter	50	280
Sugar	Kilo	40	250-300
Eggs	Each	5	10-15
Macaroni	Kilo	22	100
Beans	Kilo	14	80
Cheese	Kilo	28-40	180-400
Lamb	Kilo	45	110
Beef (2nd grade)	Kilo	48	120
Butter	Kilo	....	600-800
Salt	Kilo	10	....
Flour	Kilo	....	150
Coffee	Kilo	....	1,500
Onions	Kilo	....	20-30
Cabbage	Kilo	....	7-10
Carrots	Kilo	....	12
Spinach	Kilo	....	30-50

Source: "Food, Fodder and Farmers," *News from Behind the Iron Curtain,* II, No. 10 (October 1953), 23.

It is clear that the average daily wage of an Albanian worker buys on the free market only one kilo of bread, or one kilo of second-grade beef, or one-third kilo sugar, or ten eggs. It is obvious that the lot of Albanian labor in terms of living standards is far inferior to that of Western workers and is even considerably below Soviet and other Eastern European standards.

10. AGRICULTURE

Before the Communists

Agrarian Structure

The primitive farming and livestock raising of Albania had been virtually unchanged for centuries when Albania achieved independence, and Albania in effect emerged from the Middle Ages into the twentieth century. Even the metal plow was almost unknown until after World War I. Albania was and remains the poorest and least developed country in Europe. In 1939, more than 80 per cent of the population—the highest proportion in Europe—was dependent upon the land, and even in 1955, that percentage probably approximates 75. When independence was achieved, the agricultural population consisted of a small landowning class of beys with estates worked by tenants, a larger group of small farmers and hillmen, and a large number of independent mountaineers.

Until the Turkish conquest in the fifteenth century, the coastal lowlands and valleys of Albania were farmed by serfs of local lords, while the sparsely settled highlands were occupied by peasants and shepherds. Under the Turks, the land became the Sultan's personal property, and the system of timars (military fiefs) was introduced. The timarholders did not own the lands, they merely held them for services rendered to the Ottoman state. In the eighteenth century, however, the class of landowning beys emerged, as the Albanian timarholders turned their timars into *çifliks* (estates), owned by them. Gradually the status of the lowland peasant was raised from serf to tenant sharecropper. The free mountain peasants continued to work their small lots. From the beginning of Turkish rule until World War II the tenant farmers of the lowland and the free farmers and shepherds of the mountains tended to stabilize into these two main and distinct strata which comprised the country's basic agrarian structure.

The Lowland Tenant Farmer

All large estates, whether owned by the state, by religious organizations, or by individuals, were partitioned into small tenant farms, usually ten acres or less of cultivable land plus from two and a half to five acres of enclosed pasture and about ten acres of natural pasture land of very low value. The pastures, fields, and villages were surrounded by high blackberry hedges designed to hide the low, elongated sod huts from marauders. Tenant families tended to cultivate the same land for generations, and to form strong and lasting attachments to "their" land and homes. As a rule, tenant villages consisted of only a few dozen small farms.

The crop was divided into ten equal parts; usually one part for the state tithe, three parts for the landlords, and the remaining six parts for the farmer. In some cases the landlord provided the draft teams and seed and received half the crop. The landlords' share not only represented a rent for the tilled land, but also for about 15 acres of pasture which the tenant farmer exploited for his exclusive profit. Landlords with estates larger than 50 acres of plowed land generally lived in houses in the towns. They usually possessed olive groves and invested their capital in town enterprises. The tenant farmers contributed the firewood and transportation for their landlord's town household, as well as such annual presents as a lamb, a turkey, chickens, and eggs.

Until World War I, property enjoyed no protection, and the landlords maintained paid armed guards for their country holdings. Security was an advantage enjoyed by the tenant over the small independent farmer, and a major service and expense assumed by the landlord.

The tenant-landlord relationship was often disturbed by entrepreneurs who leased many large estates—often sharp and adventurous characters who abused their privileges. The tenant farmer was also handicapped by the absence of a credit system. He could usually obtain a loan without interest of corn for bread and seed from the landlord, but he was at the mercy of the usurer.

In the interwar period, the entire rural population learned to desire the goods of the "Franks" (i.e., Westerners). Cash was required for these goods, and the landlords became impoverished even faster than the farmers, and they incurred debts to pay for new "luxury" goods. The Albanian gentry was but a generation removed from the military class and petty bureaucracy of Turkey and demonstrated no interest in improving their estates. It did not possess any "old money," as was the case in the eastern parts of the former Turkish Empire (i.e., in the Arab countries), where the landholding class had developed from the old and rich urban merchant class.

It is impossible to present accurate data on the number of estates and categories of their different sizes up to World War II. Communist figures refer to the expropriation of 7 large estates comprising 35,955 acres; 4,713 small estates with a total of 225,192 acres; estates owned by religious institutions with about 8,400 acres. They also indicate that the state owned about 125,000 acres in 1944. No breakdown of this land (tilled, pastures, or vineyard) is given. The only trustworthy Communist figure in this sphere is that for the number of sharecroppers, 21,544 families. Since Albanian tenant families were unable to work more than 10 acres for spring and fall cultivation, and since the proportion of tilled to untilled land on tenant farms was generally 1 to 3, it may be estimated that in 1939 these 21,544 families worked about 200,000 acres and that roughly 600,000 acres of winter pastures belonged to estate owners of all categories.

The Mountain Peasants

A system of large landholdings and tenant farming did not develop in the uplands, and the extensive forests were never systematically exploited. The exploitation of the land in the uplands was extraordinarily inefficient. The almost hermetic isolation of the upland and the small size of the holdings impeded the development of agricultural exchange markets and the evolution of nonagrarian professions in the mountain areas. The system of cultivation was particularly hard on the mountain woman, who had to execute outdoor labor near the farmstead, while the man went to the hill or valley with the sheep and goats.

The largest economic unit worked in the uplands by one peasant family was 10 acres of tilled land, 50 sheep or goats, and one or two cows (kept for plowing rather than for milk or meat production). The average was nearer the minimal units, which included less than 5 acres of tilled land, less than 10 sheep or goats, and as a rule, no cow, and there were even smaller units.

Annual milk production of a typical mountain farm for a family of five was 1,000 liters from about 15 sheep or goats and one cow. Of about eleven growing lambs, five were sold, three were slaughtered, and three were kept to replace the annual loss of three grown sheep (of which one was usually slaughtered and two were sold). Five acres yielded about 95 bushels of corn, wheat, rye, barley, or oats, of which the farmer had to give 10 per cent for the state tithe. Cereal production of many farms was insufficient even for the family bread supply and the major part of their milk production was used for purchase of bread cereals.

The cold winter and long summer drought of the highlands help to explain the exceptionally small number of livestock, while the structure of the settlements and the generally rugged surface with its far-advanced erosion are responsible for the little tilled land.

Family Communities. Economic cooperation based on blood relationship was a characteristic of Albanian agriculture, especially in the northern highlands. One form was that in which the married brothers of a single family would form a lifetime cooperative under the leadership of the father or the eldest or most able brother. Another was the economic union of several related single families, each of which had too little land and livestock. The division of labor in such communities placed each male member in charge of one branch of agricultural activity and resulted in a degree of specialization and greater efficiency. This union of blood-related families was not uncommon among tenant farmers of the lowlands, who accumulated five or six spans of draft oxen, several hundred sheep, and dozens of cows and mares.

More than half of the Albanian small landholdings were family communities, which had evolved from the successful ownership of migratory herds. Herd owners, too, joined in family communities. Through specialization and mutual aid, they were often able to increase the number of sheep and livestock until the herd became so numerous that neither local summer nor winter pasture sufficed. They then had to organize a regular migratory herd, for which they leased pasture in the lowlands for the winter, while mountain community grazing grounds were available during the summer for little or nothing. Such large herds were passed on in the family from generation to generation. Cultivation of the few tilled acres was never abandoned, as plowing was considered proof that a family was really domiciled. Livestock was sometimes sold to buy land, but land was never exchanged for herds.

There was no evolution from moderate-sized medium holdings to large landed estates. Discounting some usurpation by the beys, the elementary latifundium system could only develop from service under the Turks, from wealth acquired during residence in foreign countries, or accumulated through large-scale trading.

The family community, while important to the Albanian social structure, had served its purpose by 1920, for it had been developed for mutual protection against lawlessness and violence and against extreme economic distress. Many family communities dissolved themselves during the peaceful years of Albanian self rule, especially in the more advanced south, but they retained their importance in the mountains.

Farming Methods

Until the 1920's, the wooden plow was the major piece of farm equipment. More than 30,000 iron plows—one for every second draft team— were imported between 1920 and 1939. As Albania's main crop is corn and as the country lacked the necessary equipment for deep-plowing, fields had to be hoed repeatedly, a waste of time and manpower. The ancient method of threshing has been largely replaced in the lowlands by machines, but mechanized work remained much too expensive for the average farmer. The old method did not require outside help, as harvesting was a community job done by several families together.

Land Utilization

The Albanian land registry showed boundaries between properties only by natural landmarks such as rivers, watersheds, rocks, roads, trees, and creeks. As late as 1939, estimates of land use were collected in the villages by employees of the district chambers of agriculture, who simply registered draft teams and the days they were used in first plowing to determine the sown area. From annual estimates, officials in the central agricultural offices had to estimate total land use. The large variations in such estimates by different writers, based on different sources, is readily understandable. For general land use the best figures are those given by Mario Michelangeli for 1938: 9 per cent of the total surface of the country tilled; 24 per cent forests, tillable and valuable pastures; 67 per cent worthless scrub woodland, eroded mountain slopes, and unproductive areas of little or no value for farming or livestock operations.

Corn was grown on 60 per cent of the cultivated area, not only because of the relatively high yields (average yield per acre in the south around 450 kilograms; in the Korçë basin, about 640 kilograms; in the northern provinces about 720 kilograms), but because the moisture retention character of the soil did not permit a more well-balanced cultivation.

Wheat production was concentrated in the Korçë basin. Wheat was generally grown at medium elevations; it could not be grown at low elevations because of the excessive moisture of the soil in the winter, or at high elevations because of the generally stony structure of the land. Rye was grown in the less fertile mountain regions.

Of all so-called industrial plants, only tobacco (the small-leaved, highly aromatic Turkish-Macedonian varieties) was commonly grown. Cotton, rice, and sugar beets were grown on an experimental basis. In 1938, Albania had 1.6 million olive trees, with an average production of only 16 kilograms per tree, mainly due to lack of proper care. From 1938 to 1942, approximately 210,000 young olive trees were planted. Tables 1 and 2 give the pattern of land use and the area and production of major crops in the interwar period.

Table 1. Pattern of Land Use, 1938

Prefecture	Area	Tilled Land: Sown	Tilled Land: Orchards and Vineyards	Tilled Land: Total	Tilled Land: Per Cent of Total Surface	Productive Untilled Land: Tillable Enclosed Pastures	Productive Untilled Land: Open Pastures	Productive Untilled Land: Forests and Alpine Pastures	Productive Untilled Land: Total	Productive Untilled Land: Per Cent of Total Surface	Unproductive Area: Wasteland and Water Surface	Unproductive Area: Per Cent of Total Area
	(in square kilometers)					(in square kilometers)					(in sq. km.)	
Berat	3,992	423	103	526	13	197	765	535	1,497	38	1,911	49
Durrës	1,596	146	16	162	10	115	62	218	395	25	1,038	65
Elbasan	2,955	833	116	949	32	198	268	356	822	28	1,183	40
Gjirokastër	4,142	144	33	177	4	160	534	179	873	21	2,992	75
Korçë	3,312	264	89	353	11	47	137	176	360	11	2,599	78
Kosovë	2,135	30	3	33	1	19	10	90	119	6	1,984	93
Peshkopi	2,386	82	12	94	4	29	88	1,707	1,824	77	568	19
Shkodër	4,870	87	11	98	2	70	105	167	342	7	4,430	91
Tirana	850	52	3	55	6	18	13	30	61	7	734	87
Vlorë	1,360	113	22	135	10	58	155	27	240	18	984	72
Total, Albania	27,598	2,174	408	2,582	9	911	2,137	3,485	6,533	24	18,423	67

Source: Mario Michelangeli, *Il problema forestale albanese* (Rome: Reale Accademia d'Italia, 1940), p. 16.

Table 2. Specific Land Utilization and Crop Production, 1938

Crop	Area Sown	Production
Grains	*(in hectares)*	*(in metric tons)*
Barley	7,810	5,000
Corn	91,976	144,000
Oats	11,617	9,600
Rice	427	1,000
Rye	3,585	3,000
Spelt	1,861	3,000
Wheat	40,084	39,000
Total	157,360	
Fodder Crops		
Alfalfa	727	......
Hay-producing areas	52,853	67,211[a]
Vetch	1,795	1,400[a]
Total	55,375	
Industrial Crops		
Cotton	208	155[a]
Tobacco	2,063	2,700[a]
Total	2,271	
Truck Produce		
Beans	955	......
Cucurbit	1,104	......
Onions and tomatoes	1,231	2,815[a]
Potatoes	506	2,000
Total	3,796	
Orchards and Vineyards		
Orchards	36,845	28,900[a]
Vineyards	3,955	8,800[a]
Total	40,800	
Total, agricultural area	259,602	

[a] 1939 figure.

Sources: Map No. 8 of *Albania in 10 cartine dimostrative,* compiled by Francesco Pollastri, Chief of the Geographical Office of the Istituto Centrale di Statistica del regno d'Italia (Rome: Tip. Failli, 1939); Dalip Zavalani, *Die Landwirtschaftlichen Verhältnisse Albaniens* (Berlin: P. Parey, 1938); Mario Michelangeli, *Il problema forestale albanese* (Rome: Reale Accademia d'Italia, 1940). Production figures for 1938 are those of Pollastri, augmented by 1939 figures from Allied studies made during the war and since released.

Livestock

Sheep. Sheep are the most important animals raised in Albania, but the average weighs alive only about 0-25 kilograms. There were about 1,600,000 in 1938. As a result of poor shelter and lack of concentrated fodder, the percentage of lambings was low, and little over 60 per cent reached maturity.

There are three main strains: the milk sheep in south and southeast Albania, the Ruda lamb for meat and wool in the Black Drin basin, and the meat sheep of the north. With the exception of the Ruda lamb—an ancient Merino cross—Albanian sheep have the common characteristics of the Dinaric mountain sheep, a small, light, weather-resistant, and extremely agile mountain animal.

Goats. Goats predominate in areas with poor summer and winter pastures. Albanian goats weigh from 5-10 kilograms more than the average Albanian sheep and produce about 400 grams of low butter content milk during their lactation period. There were roughly 900,000 goats in 1938. Their milk, meat and wool products were consumed almost exclusively at home.

Cattle. Albanian cattle do not get sufficient nourishment to develop normally; the average weight is about 180 kilograms, and yearly milk production is approximately 300 kilograms per animal. In 1938, the total of 391,175 cattle comprised 168,180 oxen and steers, 113,245 cows, and 109,750 young animals.

Horses. There were roughly 55,000 horses in 1938, of the Illyric breed, used as riding and working animals. Due to lack of proper nourishment they are small animals, about 1.35 meters high.

Mules. The country's 10,000 mules were used on the larger holdings in isolated and particularly rugged mountain provinces. They can easily carry burdens up to 100 kilograms for 10 hours at a time.

Donkeys. Although the statistics for 1938 indicate only 44,500 donkeys, it is possible that there were more donkeys than horses and mules together.

Pigs. Moslem prohibition limited swine to Christian communities, where they were raised on a very limited scale.

Poultry. There were probably 1.5 million laying hens in 1938. A hen laid only about 80 eggs a year. Turkeys were often raised on small holdings in the lowlands.

The distribution and number of livestock in 1938 is found in Table 3.

Agricultural Taxes and Credit

One tenth of all agricultural products had to be delivered at harvest time to the Ministry of Finance, which sold the right to collect the tithe to the highest bidder, a continuation of the tax-collecting system

Table 3. Livestock Population, 1938

Prefecture	*Horses*	*Mules*	*Donkeys*	*Cattle*	*Buffaloes*	*Sheep*	*Goats*	*Hogs*
Berat	9,500	900	9,000	76,000	12,700	259,000	114,000	372
Durrës	4,300	–	4,900	34,000	3,300	91,000	27,000	1,108
Elbasan	4,400	500	5,500	43,000	2,200	204,000	126,000	–
Gjirokastër	9,900	3,800	7,600	47,000	29	371,000	242,000	715
Korçë	9,800	2,000	6,400	49,000	2,204	146,000	95,000	199
Kosovë	4,200	200	1,100	32,000	13	64,000	42,000	211
Peshkopi	3,200	500	2,600	34,000	–	90,000	60,000	160
Shkodër	4,300	900	3,300	50,000	164	158,000	105,000	4,642
Tirana	2,000	200	1,800	12,000	71	51,000	33,000	13
Vlorë	3,600	900	2,300	14,000	682	137,000	88,000	69
Total, Albania	55,200	9,900	44,500	391,000	21,363	1,571,000	932,000	7,489

Source: Ferdinando Milone, *L'Albania economica* (Padua: CEDAM, 1941), pp. 129, 142, 147.

established by the Turks. This system made the smallholder pay most of the taxes and was inefficient, but it was the easiest method of agricultural taxation.

Under the monarchy there was a yearly head tax of 1 franc for cattle and horses and ½ franc per goat or sheep, a sales tax of 2 per cent of the value of all agricultural products and livestock, and a tax of 2 per cent of the value of all houses and farm buildings. Annual state income from agriculture under the monarchy was about 2.3 million francs from livestock taxation, and about 3.8 million francs from other direct agricultural taxes.

During the economic distress of the mid-1930's, usury became such a plague that several laws were passed establishing debt moratoria. While these measures protected the farmers, they also stopped legal agricultural credit completely. The establishment of an agrarian bank became increasingly urgent, but there was no capital for investment in an agrarian bank, which could only pay low dividends.

When agrarian reform was decreed in 1930, parliament had issued several drastic laws providing specific taxes to raise the initial capital of 5 million francs for a State Agricultural Bank, which finally began operations in 1937 and which did not fulfill its promise. The bank was not primarily designed to fill the credit needs of the small land-owner, but to aid sharecroppers to acquire land. No branch offices were opened, and the bank concentrated on safe loans. In 1939, its capital was transferred to the Bank of Naples, which under the Italian occupation greatly expanded short-term agrarian credit and opened several branches in Albania to increase the local agricultural output.

Agrarian "Reform"

The first agrarian reform law was passed by the Albanian Parliament on March 13, 1930. Under its provisions, the estate owner was permitted to keep 40 hectares (roughly 100 acres) of land for himself, and five hectares of cultivated land and ten hectares of pasture for his wife and each child. One third of the remainder was to be sold to the tenants, who had to pay 20 francs per hectare (about 2.5 acres) to the agrarian bank in 10 annual installments. The estate-owner could keep the other two-thirds for fifteen years if it was "modernized"; otherwise it, too, was subject to sale to the tenant under the same conditions. The landowners were paid in shares of the State Agricultural Bank. For a variety of reasons, very few estates were affected by this law during the following eight years. In practice, it remained more a warning to the traditionally "restless" beys and a sop to the liberal intellectuals than a land reform measure. It further discouraged maximum effort by the tenants on land which did not belong to them, and the landowners were reluctant to make further investments or generally modernize properties of which they might be deprived.

Communist Albania

Period of Transition, 1944-1946

When the Communists seized the government in 1944, the harvest was already in and the sharecroppers had paid their rent. In the following spring, the government declared that sharecroppers were to keep 60 per cent of the produce and deliver the remaining 40 per cent to the landlord, but that henceforth the landowners were to furnish both teams and seed. Communist officials in the rural districts let it be known that the state would not defend the rights of the landowners when they attempted to collect past debts and agricultural rents, and the remaining landowners did not seriously attempt to collect rent from their tenants, and few sharecroppers met their modified obligations.

The first Communist agrarian legislation was approved on August 30, 1945, and put into execution on September 6, when it was announced that forests and pasture land belonged to the state. The main features of this program were:

1. Land belonging to persons who had other sources of income was expropriated without compensation.
2. Landowners having no other sources of income, and working their land with modern agricultural equipment, were allowed to retain 40 hectares of land, of which 10 had to be maintained as pasture land.
3. Landowners having no other source of income, as well as religious institutions working land by manual labor, were allowed to retain 20 hectares of land, five of which had to be maintained as pasture land.
4. Landowners whose lands were worked by tenant farmers were allowed to retain seven hectares of land (of which two had to be pasture land) provided they agreed to work the land themselves.
5. Those to whom land was to be distributed were granted five hectares of land per family unit, plus an additional ½ hectare for each family member in excess of six, unless there was a married son, in which case the additional land was three hectares for each married son.
6. The new landowners were required to compensate the old landowners [if compensation were allowable, see 1 above] by giving them 10 quintals of wheat per expropriated hectare within a period of 10 years.

This program was characterized by its comparative moderation, dictated by the tactical needs of the Party. The large landowners had fled, been executed, or were in jail. Government control had not yet been consolidated, and the measure was designed to rally the landless and dwarf peasants, without threatening the small independent farmers. The food situation was critical, and a premature revelation of things to come might have resulted in the slaughter of livestock. Thus, in March 1945, a Communist spokesman had declared that farmers would "retain their properties and receive government aid," and in April, Hoxha declared "We will give land to farmers, which henceforward will be their own property." Throughout the summer, the peasants and small holders had been exhorted to produce more, assured that small independent farmers would be encouraged and aided. In the mountain regions, People's Committees had been drawing up an inventory of tillable land, while the Committee of Landless Farmers had drawn up lists of undersized holdings. In the lowlands, technical surveys of the most fertile areas had been completed.

Another consideration doubtless influencing the Communists was fear of jeopardizing the flow of UNRRA supplies, which were contributed by non-Communist countries, overwhelmingly by the United States. The importance of UNRRA aid to Albania agriculture at this time (6.3 million dollars worth of food alone) may be gauged by the fact that for much of 1945 UNRRA grain fed more than a third of the population and that in the same year UNRRA delivered wheat seed enough to sow 30 percent of Albania's prewar wheat area.

According to an article appearing in *Bashkimi,* November 10, 1948, after the completed land "reform" of 1945, there were 139,994 individual holdings consisting of a total of 369,000 hectares, while before the "reform" there had been 128,691 families with their own holdings of 237,668 hectares. A total of 21,544 sharecroppers were settled on 14,551 hectares owned by "7 large landowners," 91,134 hectares owned by 4,731 "well-to-do landlords," 50,000 hectares owned by the state, and 3,163 hectares owned by religious institutions. Subsequent Communist legislation reduced the size of individual holdings, made the state the greatest landlord, and gave the state complete control over the previously independent farmers.

"Hard" Agricultural Policy, 1946-1951

After 1945, the initial moderate or "soft" line became harder as Communist control was consolidated. On February 2, 1946, a decree was issued that cattle could be slaughtered only with government permission; in April 1946, military tribunals were authorized to punish anyone concealing grain by prison sentences. All farm tools and draft animals were made state property. The law of June 1, 1946 expropriated orchards, vineyards, olive trees, and fruit trees without compensation and limited the land of religious institutions to ten hectares. On June 8, before the harvest was in, farmers were ordered to deliver wheat, maize, barley, rye, and oats to state centers at listed prices. The delivery quotas were comparatively high and the official prices were low.

In September 1946, the farmers were assailed for lagging on quotas, veiled threats were made against such People's enemies, and the tone of the government toward the farmers began to take on an ominous note. In November, the government abrogated all sales of municipally owned land to individuals, requiring the purchasers to return the land to city authorities (People's Councils) without compensation.

The beneficiaries of the Communist reform were not allowed to rent or sell any part of their new allotments, despite previous promises of full ownership. They now had to lease pastures from the state, and a farmer who wished to use land for pasture or turn it into a meadow still had to meet his assigned delivery quota in grain. During the summer of 1946, grain producers were allowed to retain up to 250 kilograms per person, but after the poor harvest was in and there were no prospects for further UNRRA aid, this amount was cut to 15 kilograms per person. In December, farmers were strongly denounced for their failure to fulfill their delivery obligations, and on the nineteenth of that month an ordinance was passed requiring the registration of all livestock with the Ministry of Agriculture. Well-publicized death, prison, or forced labor sentences were given those who "sabotaged the Agrarian Reform," failed to meet their quotas, or expressed antiregime sentiments. On May 17, 1947, the government was authorized to expropriate all possessions of all individuals at its discretion. On May 30, the warning was issued that persons delivering grain containing more than 14 per cent moisture would be considered People's enemies and saboteurs.

It was in this period that the government began to step up the collectivization drive. Various inducements, notably lower taxes for collective members, were offered, and "forced" collectivization was instituted. Nevertheless, collectivization lagged badly despite the effort made: only 2,428 families joined by 1948 (see below). With the sudden confiscation of all herds of over 50 sheep or goats in May 1948, and the creation of the so-called dairy brigades, a further attempt to control agriculture by putting it under increased state control was made. The recalcitrant peasants would not join the collectives voluntarily, and forced collectivization proved a costly failure, as in neighboring Yugoslavia. After the Tito-Cominform break of June, this policy was dropped in Yugoslavia, but the Albanian leaders in an attempt to convince the Soviet leadership of their loyalty struggled on. Although it had to be admitted in November of 1948 that the collectivization campaign had failed, this was blamed on "Yugoslav sabotage," and many officials of the Albanian agricultural sector were purged. Failures and purges and force continued to be the pattern in Albanian agriculture until 1951.

"Soft" Communist Policy, 1951-1955

The first definite indication of a softening in the agricultural line was a 25 per cent reduction in grain delivery obligations in March 1951. On March 10, a new law permitted private farmers to divide their holdings among members of their families, subject to approval. On May 14, after Hoxha's return from Moscow, the government admitted that the previous decision to speed collectivization was a mistake, and revealed that no new collectives would be created until the existing collective farms had "achieved better organization." This new approach has had some effect on production, even though the planned goals have not been met in most fields, and livestock raising, the backbone of Albanian agriculture, remains a dismal failure.

Despite minor variations in tempo, Communist collectivization policy since 1951 has been one of "make haste slowly." Compulsory delivery quotas and taxes have shown a trend to grow and then to be cut back. Thus, in June 1953, outstanding quotas for all agricultural products for the 1949-52 period were canceled. In July 1954, a substantial reduction of "levies on agricultural economy" was announced, and in April 1955 a 5 to 20 per cent reduction in general taxation of collectives was announced.

Albanian Agriculture Today

The Socialist Sector

State Farm. Article 32 of the Agrarian Reform of 1945 provided for the formation of state farms modeled after the Soviet sovkhozes, and creation of the first state farm followed on December 7. The nucleus of the state farms was the Italian model farms set up before and during the war, and taken over by the Communist Ministry of Agriculture. These were the best and most modern farms in the country, the Italians having made considerable investments in them in drainage work, agricultural machinery, and breeding stock. Later, many of the best olive groves were assigned to state farms.

Workers on state farms are salaried government employees. They do not contribute land nor equipment, nor do they share in the profits, although they may receive bonuses for outstanding production achievements. State farm laborers generally consist of the least ambitious peasants. Albanian state farm managers and administrative personnel have been periodically denounced in the Communist press for "general incompetence, dishonesty, and speculation." Table 4 shows the development of the state farms, 21 of which had cultivated 16,443 hectares of land and at least 230,000 olive trees by 1954.

Table 4. STATE FARMS, SELECTED YEARS 1945-1954

Year	*Number of State Farms*	*Total Surface (in hectares)*	*Olive Trees*
1945	1	8,379	.....
1947	......	13,491	230,000
1948	......	16,390	230,000
1953	21	16,443	......
1954	21	16,443	.....

Sources: Bashkimi, November 10, November 11, 1948; Radio Tirana, May 19, September 15, 1954.

Collective Farms. The collectives are the heart of the government program for agriculture. Located generally in the flat coastal plains, comprising some of the country's richest farmland, and given every advantage, they should be much more productive than official complaints indicate they are. In spite of the advantages and inducements in the form of state credits, a 50 per cent reduction in direct taxes, lower compulsory production quotas, and lower charges for work done by the state machine-tractor stations (MTS), farmers continue to resist joining them. In 1952, their membership comprised only slightly more than 5 per cent of the total farmers and only about 30 per cent of the former sharecroppers, of whom, according to all Communist authorities, collectives are almost exclusively composed. From a comparison of the average number of horses and draft animals brought into the collectives (less than one horse for every 14 families and only one ox team per 9.6 hectares of plowland, according to a March 1949 statement of the Ministry of Agriculture), it is evident that only the poorest of the former sharecroppers have joined the collectives, for the average sharecropper had owned 4.7 working animals and cattle.

An examination of the statutes of the Albanian collective farms as published in a May 1954 series of articles appearing in *Zëri i Popullit* indicates some of the reasons for the stubborn reluctance of all but the poorest farmers to join the socialist sector. Up to 1949, a collective member's share of the net income was based on both the amount of land he brought into the collective and the number of work days. Early in that year, this procedure was denounced as based on "Yugoslav influence." Henceforth, the member's net share was based only on working days. A member family had had the right to one-half hectare as a private plot, and there was no limit to the number of animals they could raise. Henceforth, a member family's private plot was to be one third of a hectare, and the number of animals was limited. The property of a family joining a collective becomes collective property; should they leave the collective, only the tools brought in may be taken out.

Although pregnant women may take six weeks at half-pay before and after the birth of children, members who fall ill receive no sick-leave pay, but may apply to the special collective "invalid fund" for aid.

At the end of the crop year, the collective's quota is delivered first to the state, the MTS is paid in crops, and the balance of the crop is sold to the state at "free market prices." The money thus earned is used first for buying seeds and fodder. From the remaining funds, 15 per cent is deposited for the "war invalid fund," the farm "invalid fund," taxes, social security, salaries, other expenses of the directorate, and various welfare organs of the farm. The remaining 85 per cent is divided among the members according to their "working days," which are not actual days worked, but complicated agricultural work norms, i.e., "A swineherd having charge of six female pigs is deemed to have completed three working days for each piglet born."

The "Executive" of the collective consists of the director, the secretary, and the bookkeeper, "freely elected" as a group by a plenary meeting of the collective members. The executives almost invariably are Party members, chosen by the local Party organ for political reliability and zeal rather than agricultural ability. In practice, the collective members have no voice in choosing the executive group, which has the exclusive right to expel members or admit new ones. It examines and confirms the accomplishments of the working year, controls collective assets and liabilities in cash and produce, establishes labor standards and wages, negotiates annual contracts with the MTS, and plans the work of the collective and its members.

The emphasis in the collectives on cereal and industrial crop cultivation aggravates the inefficient Albanian agricultural employment cycle: underemployment most of the year, and peak demand during the sowing and harvesting seasons.

A new type of collective for the cooperative exploitation of all or part of private holdings was first described in *Bashkimi* of April 21, 1951. These are officially referred to as Class II cooperatives, in which the members retain ownership of the land, as distinguished from true collectives, in which the land and equipment of members become collective property. The few semicollectives created between 1951 and the end of 1954 were seasonal, but in December 1954, statutes for two simpler forms of semipermanent associations were published and several were established in 1955. In July 1955, the Tirana press said that the area of cultivated land in the kolkhoz type of collectives (see Table 5) comprised 10 per cent of the country's total tillable land, while the simpler forms (Class I and II) comprised only 1.2 per cent of all cultivated land. The Party's decision of December 1955 to accelerate agricultural collectivization resulted in the creation of 308 new collectives in the first three months of 1956, or nearly as many as were established between 1946 and 1955. By May 1, 1956, the number of collectives had reached 677, in addition to some 110 associations of the simpler types.

Table 5. DEVELOPMENT OF COLLECTIVES OF KOLKHOZ TYPE, 1946-1955

Year	*Number of Collectives*	*Number of Families*	*Number of Workers*	*Total Surface* (*in hectares*)	*Number of Working Animals*
1946	7	217	570	943	260
1947	21	1,825	1,988	3,672	1,137
1948	56	2,428	6,481	10,870	2,882
1949	58	2,881	......	11,359	......
1950	90	4,500	......	......	......
1951	94	5,561	......	......	......
1952	113	6,291	15,855	......	......
1953	115	......	17,122	27,460	......
1954	128	......	......	......	......
1955	189	10,226	......	41,164	......

Sources: 1946-48, *Bashkimi,* November 10, 1948; 1949, 1953, Radio Tirana, April 20, 1953; 1950-52, Radio Tirana, May 4, 1954; 1954, 1955, *Rruga e Partise* (The Road of the Party) (January 1956).

Machine-Tractor Stations. Patterned after the Soviet MTS, these are an increasingly important part of the Albanian socialist agricultural sector. All tractors, threshing machines, and major agricultural machinery belong to the Albanian MTS organization. The nucleus of the MTS equipment was a total of roughly 100 tractors and threshing machines in the country in 1944 and the 150 new tractors Albania received as part of UNRRA aid after the war. It would appear that Albania did not receive any tractors from the Soviet Union until at least 1952, as an article in *Bashkimi* for April 3, 1952 put the Albanian tractor total at 200. Substantial imports from the Soviet bloc must have been received between that date and a Radio Tirana broadcast of November 28, 1954, which declared that there were then 668 tractors in the country. The August 1955 issue of *Statistische Praxis,* published by Communist Eastern Germany's Central Statistical Institute gave a figure of 16 MTS and 747 tractors in Albania for 1954.

Several articles in the official press have assailed the work of the MTS and accused them of being the weakest link in Albania's agriculture. Mechanical plowing, harvesting, and threshing have been limited to the favored socialist sector, but assignments appear to have been fulfilled late and badly, resulting in crop losses.

It was declared in 1953 that 50 per cent of the MTS working power was to be supplied to the socialist sector, with the other 50 per cent to individual small holdings previously unable to take advantage of these services. Considering the small size of privately owned fields and the high MTS fees, it appears extremely unlikely that individual holdings could afford MTS contracts.

Dairy Collectives. These state-owned organizations, each consisting of 3,000 to 4,000 head of sheep or goats rather than cows, were created immediately after the government confiscated all herds of more than 50 sheep or goats in May 1948, without compensation. This measure had been prepared in the strictest secrecy to prevent the livestock owners from distributing their herds among their relatives, friends, or trustees. The confiscated herds and supplies allowed the state to form the dairy collectives without expense.

Soil Improvement

An ambitious soil improvement project was initiated before World War II, but only 37,000 acres had been affected by 1943. For the Communist government, drainage of the most fertile areas has been a step toward strengthening the favored socialized sector. From 1944 to 1954, over one billion leks were allocated to such land improvement projects, and thousands of political prisoners and "volunteers" were employed as forced laborers.

According to a May 1954 speech by Hoxha, 102,368 acres of arable land had been improved, and 15,085 acres of new land had been gained. Irrigated areas have reportedly been increased from 136,000 acres in 1953 to 178,000 acres in 1954, and were projected to increase to 264,000 acres by the end of 1955. About 250,000 acres along the main rivers and around their deltas are uncultivable because of floods.

Industrial Crops

Agrarian industries based on domestic raw materials have been a major Communist development. The principle industrial crops of the socialized sector are sugar beets (Korçë basin), sunflowers, and cotton (in the lowlands and along the coast). The great increase in these crops, confined almost exclusively to the socialist sector, is cited as proof of the advantages socialized economy has over independent farming. Even for the socialized sector, industrial crop production has not been an unqualified success.

The cotton acreage increased from 520 acres in 1938 to 39,040 acres in 1950, but yields per acre fell to 0.8 quintal per acre in 1950. Sugar beet production rose from trial plantings in 1938 to 3,450 acres in 1950, when the yield was only 18.4 quintals per acre.

Tobacco plantings have increased in area, but the yields per acre have also decreased considerably. The cultivation of sunflowers was completely unknown before 1944. In 1950, however, it covered 16,300 acres. Lin and kerp are the other two major industrial plants introduced under communism. Table 6 shows the area devoted to the production of industrial plants in 1936 and the 1946-50 period.

Table 6. INDUSTRIAL PLANT AREA, 1938 AND 1946-1950
(in hectares)

Year	*Tobacco*	*Cotton*	*Sugar Beets*	*Sunflowers*	*Lin*	*Kerp*	*Total*
1938	2,063	208	—	—	—	—	2,271
1946	3,400	500	—	—	50	50	4,000
1947	5,000	3,200	—	4,000	600	600	13,400
1948	3,700	10,700	1,300	6,400	1,300	1,600	25,000
1949	3,000	10,000	1,100	4,400	800	1,700	21,000
1950	4,600	15,800	1,400	6,600	1,000	1,600	31,000

Sources: 1938, *Albania in 10 cartine dimostrative,* compiled by Francesco Pollastri, Chief of the Geographical Office of the Istituto Centrale di Statistica del Regno d'Italia (Rome: Tip. Failli, 1939); 1946-50, *Bashkimi,* April 3, 1952.

Cereals

Cereal acreage has also been increased (see Table 7).

Table 7. LAND UTILIZATION, SELECTED YEARS 1938-1955
(in hectares)

Year	*Grains*	*Industrial Plants*	*Vegetables*	*Fodder*	*Total*
1938	211,800	2,900	3,800	2,500	221,000
1944	238,885	4,300	3,700	3,700	247,645
1945	211,850	3,120	5,040	3,100	223,110
1946	250,000	4,100	5,930	3,300	263,630
1947	275,000	13,565	8,003	8,247	305,000
1948	269,200	25,120	11,350	11,350	317,000
1949	278,000	21,000	9,000	11,000	319,000
1950	269,000	31,000	12,000	18,000	330,000
1952	......	......	......	......	320,000
1953	......	......	......	......	362,340
1954	......	......	......	......	364,699
1955 (Plan)	274,000	46,000	15,000	38,500	385,000

Sources: 1938, 1944-48, *Bashkimi,* February 5, 1948; 1949-50, *Bashkimi,* April 2, 1952, Radio Roma; 1953, "9.8 per cent more sowed area than 1950," according to Radio Tirana, November 28, 1953; 1954, "65 per cent greater sowed area than 1938," according to Radio Tirana, September 15, 1954; 1955, sowing plan for 1955, *Bashkimi,* April 3, 1952.

There has been an admittedly large decrease in yields per acre under communism: from 5.76 to 3.88 quintals for corn, and from 4.25 to 3.56 quintals for wheat. The proportion of wheat to corn production has risen from a pre-Communist figure of about 1:3 to a current 3:3. Since very high rents are charged by the state for winter pastures, the importance of wheat straw for fodder has risen. In addition, the drainage program and the introduction of early maturing wheat varieties have reduced former damage caused by rust. According to a Hoxha speech of May 1954, approximately 159,000 tons of corn and 122,000 tons of wheat were harvested in 1953, and there had also been an increase in related crops (see Table 8).

Table 8. PRODUCTION OF GRAINS AND RELATED CROPS, SELECTED YEARS 1938-1953
(in thousand metric tons)

Year	*Corn*	*Wheat*	*Rye*	*Rice*
1938	144	39	3	1
1946	136	7	5	2
1948	160	70	8	3
1950	109	85	8	3
1953	159	122	13	7

Source: 1938, 1946, 1948, 1950, *Bashkimi,* April 3, 1952; 1953, Speech of Premier Hoxha, May 1954.

The reported total of 281,000 tons of corn and wheat is close to the planned 284,000 tons of grains for 1954 (*Bashkimi,* April 3, 1952), and this cereal production should supply the country's needs for bread. However, the cut in the bread ration from 16 to 9 kilograms per unit of rural population and the annual import of from 50 to 60 thousand tons of bread cereals from Soviet bloc countries is a good indication that official Communist statistics on grain production are not reliable. Spoilage of grains in the primitive collection centers and warehouses is extremely high, according to escapee reports.

It is difficult to accept claims of efficient new agricultural extension services and technological training in the face of the sharp decrease of crop yields. Even the yields forseen for the end of the Five-Year Plan (1955) for corn, barley, and oats are lower than actual yields per acre for 1938. Factors contributing to the admitted yield decrease under communism may include farmers' declaration of lower yields than they achieve and the migration of the ablest workers to the cities because of the advantages given workers. The greatly enlarged army also removes a substantial number of rural men during a period of their maximum physical strength. The "modern agricultural techniques" which have been introduced consist almost in their entirety of Soviet methods and articles simply translated from Russian. As they are not based on experiments in the Albanian alpine basins, lowlands, and coastal plains, but are imitations of methods employed in Russia, where conditions are entirely different, it is hardly surprising that they have not increased Albanian unit output or efficiency.

Rice, Vegetables, and Fodder

Rice production increased in the 1938-50 period from 1,000 to 3,000 tons, and reportedly jumped to 15,400 tons in 1954.

The cultivation of fodder and vegetables appears to have increased considerably among independent farmers. According to a new law, vegetable production on soil of very low fertility is not taxed, and the required grain quotas for poor regions are lower than in the fertile coastal regions. Table 7 gives the area devoted to fodder production; for rice production see Table 8.

Forestry and Horticulture

Reforestation of 69,000 acres of arid mountain land was planned for the period from 1951 to 1955. Hoxha indicated in his speech to the Second Party Congress in the spring of 1951 that the mountain people would have to "volunteer" for this work: "The mobilization of sufficient people to plant the trees will represent no problem for the Party."

According to the so-called Fifteen-Year Plan (1950-65) for olive production, the number of olive trees is to be increased by 5.9 million, of which 3.6 million are to be planted by state farms and the remainder by private farmers and collective farmers. Apparently, the planting of these trees has not started, as, according to Radio Tirana, there were only 14 per cent more olive trees in 1954 than in 1938, and this increase took place in the first few years after the war. It is probable that nurseries are now being established. It was reported that the number of fruit trees in 1954 was double that of 1938, and that in 1950 this figure exceeded 6 million. The current number of citrus trees is supposed to be three times larger than in 1938. For a description of Albanian trees and their distribution see Chapter 2, "The Land."

Livestock

The major problem of Albanian agriculture since 1912 has been the fodder shortage for livestock. With the increase in acreage for grain production and industrial crops, the natural pastures have diminished proportionately and the fodder shortage has become alarming, in spite of the increase from 6,150 acres in 1938 to 44,500 acres in 1950 in the area devoted to fodder cultivation and the 95,100 acres planned for 1955. Only part of the new meadow land can be irrigated, and grassland farming is unknown to the Albanian farmer. The result will be many years of low average fodder production.

The fodder shortage is revealed by the fact that in 1950 there were 19,000 fewer draft oxen than in 1938. In the mountains, where tractors cannot be used, half of the holdings still do not have their own draft teams due to lack of fodder. The increased acreage of sown land in the lowlands is too large to be worked by the newly established tractor stations alone, and draft animals remain a necessity.

The total number of dairy cows in the country has remained the same since the Communists seized power, but new methods of feeding have apparently increased milk production. According to the Five-Year Plan, average milk production should increase by 1955 from 400 to 800 liters per cow. At the Shkodër experimental station it was reported that in 1952, two cows each gave between 4,400 and 4,900 liters, during a lactation period of 300 to 355 days when fed ad libitum with corn, pollard, and sunflower seeds as concentrated food, and with sugar beets, sunflower leaves, and cereal straw as silage.

From 1938 to 1953, the stock of sheep and goats hardly changed. As the stock belonging to the dairy brigades has severely decreased, the stock of free and collective farmers must have increased accordingly. The wider distribution of the Ruda lamb, for whose wool the new textile industry now pays 40 per cent more, is a further development.

The pig stock has tripled, the continuation of an old trend, accelerated by concentrated feed production, which has also been largely responsible for a 50 per cent increase in chicken raising. Table 9 gives the Albanian prewar and Communist livestock population.

Table 9. LIVESTOCK POPULATION, SELECTED YEARS 1938-1955
(in thousand head)

Animal	*1938*	*1946*	*1948*	*1949*	*1950*	*1955 (Plan)*
Sheep	1,574	1,835	1,730	1,639	1,709	1,844
Goats	932	1,065	847	800	830	847
Oxen	168	142	156	148	149	162
Cattle[a]	134	140	143	134	129	139
Pigs	15	27	22	30	47	127
Mules and donkeys	55	67	68	65	67	124 (mules, donkeys and horses combined)
Horses	54	55	53	60	51	

[a] Includes buffaloes.

Source: "Economic Report, Albania," *News from Behind the Iron Curtain,* III, No. 5 (May 1954), 17, from *Bashkimi,* January 29, April 3, 1953.

Government Marketing

Albania's geographical structure does not permit a highly centralized system of agricultural marketing. State sales and purchases of agricultural produce are operated very inefficiently: transportation costs are extremely high and transport equipment very limited. The state is so fully engaged with the collection, transportation, and sale of the principal cereal and industrial crops that it neglects the purchase of the perishable goods, particularly of dairy products, of which the small mountain holdings have a modest surplus. The Communist press often complains that state purchasing collectives accept only products that can be easily stored. The government's trade monopoly and the lack of rapid turnover at even a small profit is a major fault impeding increased agricultural production.

The Independent Farmer and Agriculture

Independent farmers and their families still comprise the bulk of the labor force and close to 70 per cent of the Albanian population. According to Mehmet Shehu's May 1952 report to the Party Congress, as late as 1950 independent farmers produced 94 per cent of the total agricultural production. Under Communist planning, however, agriculture is treated as an economic stepchild. According to *Bashkimi* for April 3, 1952, agriculture had received only 14.1 per cent of total investments from 1946 to 1950, and was slated to receive only 13.5 per cent of the total planned investments for the 1951-55 period.

As a matter of policy independent farmers are penalized in comparison with the socialized agricultural sector. They were denied any share in the new state lands by a decree of April 24, 1948, which declared state lands were to be divided among collectives and landless farmers, even though by that date the latter category supposedly had ceased to exist. Ironically, the most able independent farmers are made to suffer the greatest hardships. Labeled "kulaks," they are the regime's new whipping boys. On June 12, 1951, all People's Councils were instructed to list all kulaks and to impose special taxes on them based on the agricultural tools in their possession. The term kulak is elastic enough to include even the poorest farmers suspected of hostility to the regime.

Agricultural income is low and the tax burden weighs most heavily on the independent farmer. From the Communist seizure of power until the beginning of 1949, the peasantry had to deliver all agricultural and dairy products to government collecting stations at very low, fixed prices. The government cooperatives established in the villages for the purchase of agricultural produce and the sale of consumers' goods gradually turned into collecting stations for delivery quotas. The urban population received less food, and the farmers became even further removed from urban life. Progressive taxation on gross production and delivery quotas based on a complicated land classification according to soil fertility were established at the beginning of 1949. The high delivery quotas apply to all arable land, cultivated or fallow, and in years when the crops are bad, fulfillment is virtually impossible. Here too the independent farmers suffer discrimination, as the quotas for collective farmers are lower. The classification by soil fertility of the total arable land in Albania gave rise to further difficulties and inequalities, admitted by Mehmet Shehu in a 1952 speech: "The many mistakes made in soil classification and land surveying have proven to be a serious handicap to all farmers."

High rents to the state for winter pasture and the new water tax for irrigation are a form of direct taxation, but the exceedingly high prices for consumers' goods, the production and sale of which is virtually monopolized by the state, and the very low prices paid for agricultural produce are a new and very oppressive Communist form of indirect taxation.

According to *Bashkimi* for November 10, 1948, after the Communist agrarian "reform" of 1946, the average independent farmer had less than 6.5 acres under cultivation. Furthermore, the extensive winter pastures that were formerly village property and on which every village household had the right to keep a certain number of animals free of charge have become state property. Thus in addition to all the other new burdens, income of small holdings from herds has been reduced by about 40 per cent, the equivalent of the rent of the winter pasture.

It must also be remembered that most of the individual small holders are in the hill and mountain regions, and they are being kept from participation in the more fertile lowland areas by the development of the socialized sector. With about half of the tillable land per ox team of the average collective farmer, the independent farmer has reached the subsistence minimum of land. He also has a lower priority than the collective farmer in receiving credits, aid, technical advice, and pasture allotments.

However, the individual Albanian farmer retains many advantages. Individual judgment and initiative enable him to adjust his work much better to unforseen conditions than can the collectivized farmer, who must follow the plans and orders of master planners in Tirana, following Communist agricultural ideology and "the glowing example of Soviet agriculture," both of which are unsuited to Albanian conditions. On the working level, the collective farmer is further handicapped by incompetent collective management.

Finally, the independent farmer is a descendant of a small proud people who for centuries have defended their rights and honor with their blood. The socialized agricultural sector in Albania is the smallest of any of Russia's captive states. Independent farming may be doomed if the country remains Communist, but lacking the weapons the regime has taken from him, the independent farmer will use every possible means his ingenuity and courage can devise to cling to his small holding.

11. MINING AND QUARRYING

Historical Background

Albania is relatively rich in both metallic and nonmetallic minerals, and her mineral resources were known and exploited in ancient Greece and the Roman Empire. Such ancient historians and philosophers as Strabo, Aristotle, Plutarch, Pliny, Livy, and Vitruvius mentioned the bitumen mines of Selenicë in their writings. In the early days of Albanian mining, only the Selenicë mines were exploited with any degree of intensity or continuity. They were also the first yielded to a foreign mining concern as a concession. This concession was granted on July 26, 1875 to an Englishman, who in turn leased the mines to an Italian company financed by the Banco di Santo Spirito of the Vatican. On June 13, 1891, the concession was transferred to the Société Anonyme des Mines Selenitza of Paris. In 1918, the rights to exploit these mines were sold for 1,700,000 lire to the Società Italiana delle Miniere di Selenizza–Albania (SIMSA), with headquarters in Rome.

During World War I, when Albania was occupied by the armies of both the Allied and Central Powers, a number of well-organized exploratory drillings and prospecting activities for minerals were made. Special emphasis was given to geological explorations for petroleum, the presence of which was strongly indicated in the zones of southwestern Albania occupied by the Italian forces. Even before the war, in 1913, the Italians had sent a technical group to carry out geological surveys in the region extending from Tepelenë to the Mat River, south of Shkodër. The attention of the Italians was focused on the vicinity of Kuçovë, where a small oil pool and asphalt deposits were detected. This discovery was announced in 1915.

The first successful commercial oil well was drilled in 1918 near Drashovicë by the Italians, who at that time occupied the area. The Italian occupation forces also developed a coal mine at Memaliaj, near Tepelenë, utilizing the coal for lime kilns and as fuel for their warships. In the northern occupation zone, the Austro-Hungarian army began prospecting for copper in Pukë and for coal in the Krabë mines. The French armed forces exploited the coal mines at Mborje-Drenovë and prospected for gold and silver at Rehovë and Vithkuq. This period first saw the publication of a number of original studies on Albanian minerals by Ernst Nowack, an Austrian geologist, the French geologist Jacques Bourcart, and several other scientists.

The Struggle for Concessions

The competition for Albanian mining concessions began in 1921, when representatives of the Anglo-Persian Oil Company in Tirana obtained a concession which, if ratified, would have given the company a virtual monopoly over Albanian petroleum resources. In December 1922, representatives of seven large oil companies were actively bidding for Albanian oil concessions. Finally, on January 27, 1924, the Albanian Parliament declared the country "open territory" to all bidders for oil concessions. Shortly thereafter, numerous concessions for oil prospecting, covering nearly 12,350,00 acres of land, were obtained by British, American, Italian, and French oil concerns. The most promising area, comprising some 125,000 acres in the vicinity of Kuçovë and Patos, was leased to the Anglo-Persian Oil Company.

During the period from January 1924 through December 31, 1926, concessions were granted to two Italian companies for exploiting the bitumen deposits at Selenicë, coal at Memaliaj, and the copper deposits of Pukë. Additional concessions for the exploitation of the Pukë copper deposits were granted to British and Yugoslav companies. Two private Albanian entrepreneurs held the mining concessions for the exploitation of Mborje-Drenovë coals. By 1926, the Italian State Railroads, which later formed the Azienda Italiana Petroli Albania (AIPA), had increased its holdings from 75,000 to 290,000 acres of prospective oil-bearing land. In 1927, the Standard Oil Company, realizing that prospects for the discovery of new oil were poor, abandoned its concession. The Anglo-Persian Oil Company, which had developed the first well on October 17, 1925, at Ardenicë near Fier and which began the construction of an oil refinery at Vlorë, decided in 1930 to discontinue its unprofitable exploitation drillings at Patos. Two years later, the Anglo-Persian concessions were sold to AIPA, which thus finally obtained a monopoly for exploitation of oil fields. The Italian concern SIMSA, which exploited the bitumen mines of Selenicë, managed gradually to obtain control over the copper mines of Pukë and Rrubig (Rubik), and in 1938 the Italian Azienda Minerali Metallici Italiani (AMMI) obtained a concession for the chromium mines of Pogradec, Kukës, and Klos. Thus, by 1938, all concessions for the exploitation of Albania's important mineral resources were held by Italian concerns. During the Italian occupation of Albania (1939-43), mining activities and mineral output were considerably intensified and increased.

Communist Mining Policies

Confiscation of Italian and German Enterprises

The Communist seizure of power on November 29, 1944 was followed by a series of measures aimed at ensuring Communist control. These measures were legalized as formal decrees or laws issued by the Presidium of the Anti-Fascist National Liberation Council. Thus, on December 15, 1944 the Presidium passed a law (Law No. 19, published in *Gazeta Zyrtare,* December 23, 1944), which stated that "all Albanian industries and enterprises are placed under state control." This was followed by the law of January 13, 1945 (Law No. 36, published in *Gazeta Zyrtare,* January 23, 1945), which confiscated "all wealth owned by the states of Italy and Germany, or controlled by those states indirectly by means of corporate or intermediary enterprises," and placed under state control "all wealth owned by Italian and German nationals and by Italian-German, Albanian-Italian, and Albanian-German corporations, companies, enterprises, firms, and proprietorships which contracted business in Albania." The first confiscated enterprise was AGIP (Azienda Generale Italiana Petroli), which held a monopoly over the distribution of Albanian petroleum. The decision was promulgated in a special law (Law No. 49, published in *Gazeta Zyrtare,* March 29, 1945), under which the Ministry of Finance was ordered to seize the headquarters of AGIP. Similar laws confiscating the other Italian enterprises in Albania were issued in rapid succession.

Nationalization of Mineral Resources

The nationalization of all mineral resources was effected on December 22, 1945, when the Presidium of the Albanian Anti-Fascist National Liberation Council passed a law (Law No. 183, published in *Gazeta Zyrtare,* January 5, 1946) which revoked and rescinded all mineral concessions granted on the basis of the mining law of January 27, 1923. After a preliminary statement to the effect that the mineral concessionaires had exploited the mines to the detriment of the state, the law provided that: (1) all mineral concessions granted on the basis of the old mining law were revoked, without compensation; (2) the state was to take control of the mines on the day the law became effective; (3) all activities prior to the date of nationalization were the responsibility of the former concessionaires; (4) all properties belonging to the mines or to the mineral-processing plants became the property of the state.

Finally, Article 5 of the Constitution of the People's Republic of Albania, passed by the Constituent Assembly on March 14, 1946, stated that "the means of production form that wealth of the people which is owned by the state" and that "the wealth of the people includes mines and all other earth resources."

Albanian-Yugoslav Joint Companies

The Albanian government operated all the mines from the time of their seizure from the Italians until the early part of 1947, when Albanian-Yugoslav joint companies were created in Tirana. Among these were the Albanian-Yugoslav Company for the Prospecting and Exploitation of Petroleum, created by an economic treaty signed in Belgrade on November 28, 1946, and the Albanian-Yugoslav Company for the Prospecting and Exploration of Mineral Ores. Albanian-Yugoslav companies exploited Albania's mineral deposits and mines until July 1, 1948, when Albania rescinded and voided all economic treaties and agreements with Yugoslavia. It is notable that these companies had failed to reconstruct and restore the mines to their previous output level. The expulsion of the Italian technicians and administrative employees who had operated the mines until the end of 1944 resulted in prolonged periods of idleness and the reduction of their production to primitive levels. The Albanian-Yugoslav joint companies suffered from lack of trained personnel, technological know-how, and funds for the replacement of machinery worn out or damaged during the war.

Soviet Control

Following the break with Tito on July 1, 1948 and the appeal of the Albanian Communists to Moscow for assistance, the Soviet Union sent a number of experts, including engineers for the oil fields at Patos and Kuçovë, the bitumen mines at Selenicë, the copper mines at Rrubik, and the chromium mines at Bulqizë.

No Soviet-Albanian enterprises were created to replace the Albanian-Yugoslav joint companies, and the mines remained under the nominal control of the Albanian Ministry of Mines. However, Soviet experts have assumed operative control of the principal Albanian mineral resources. The products of petroleum, chromium, copper, and bitumen deposits are exported almost in entirety to other Communist countries. The Soviet Union has reportedly sent a considerable amount of machinery and equipment to the Kuçovë and Patos oil fields and has mechanized some of the operations at the chromium, copper, and bitumen mines. A number of mining engineers from Czechoslovakia and other European satellites assist the Soviet engineers.

Soviet geological surveyors and prospectors have undertaken several surveying expeditions in Albania, but results of these expeditions have not been published. In two articles published in *Bashkimi* of October 13 and 14, 1950, Reshat Zajimi, an Albanian mining engineer, stated that the country's resources are being explored systematically by Albanian and Soviet geologists. According to several recent reports, Soviet technicians are actively prospecting for, and may be exploiting, silver and gold deposits in the Vithkuq and Lubonjë areas, especially at Rehovë. It was reported in 1951 that Soviet mining engineers discovered uranium deposits in the Fratar area.

Investments and Planning

The Communist emphasis on the development of mining is indicated by the annual investments allocated to that sector of Albania's economy. Table 1 gives the announced actual and planned investments in Albanian mining, industry, and agriculture and shows that the funds allocated to mining exceeded those allocated to industry during the period of 1946-47 and in 1949 and those allocated to agriculture in 1949 and 1950.

Table 1. ACTUAL AND PLANNED INVESTMENTS IN INDUSTRY, MINING, AND AGRICULTURE, 1945-1950
(in million leks)

Year	*Industry*	*Mining*	*Agriculture*
1945[a]	......	23.0	......
1946[a]	20.6	63.0	121.5
1947[a]	65.5	136.3	188.6
1948[a]	309.9	195.9	288.0
1949[b]	383.6	456.0	271.9
1950[b]	720.3	380.0	296.3

[a] Actual investments.
[b] Planned investments.

According to *Bashkimi,* June 4, 1949, total investments in the Two-Year Economic Plan (1949-50) allocated to mining amounted to 836 million leks (or 20.17 per cent of the country's total investments during the two-year period), of which 456 million leks were to be invested in 1949, and 380 million leks in 1950 (officially 50 leks to one dollar). The Five-Year Economic Plan (1951-55) provided for the investment in industry and mining of 8,943 million leks, a considerable part of which was allocated to mining. In 1954, the investment in mining amounted to 720 million leks. The Plan stipulated that the value of industrial and mining output was to reach 11.1 billion leks (in 1950 prices) by the end of 1955, more than three times the value of industrial and mining output in 1950 (3.2 billion leks). The Plan called for a mining and mineral-processing output with a value of 1,382 million leks (in 1950 prices), compared to the value of 452 million leks produced in 1950.

In its issue of November 20, 1949, *Bashkimi* stated that investments in the mining industry during the period of the Two-Year Economic Plan would be provided mainly by the Soviet Union and that they were concentrated in the petroleum industry for opening new wells and intensifying the search for new reserves. This indicates the considerable importance placed by Moscow on the development of Albania's petroleum resources, which constitute a valuable asset. The role of Albania as a mineral supplier to the Soviet bloc was pointed out in the January-February 1950 issue of the Romanian economic periodical *Probleme Economice,* which stated that the bulk of Albanian mine output (crude oil, bitumen, chromium, copper) was slated for export. The increasing demand for Albanian minerals was reflected in the Five-Year Economic Plan, which called for intensified exploration of the country's iron, nickel, manganese, copper, bauxite, argil (clay), and sulphur deposits.

Mineral Fuels and Bitumens

Petroleum

Albania's oil-bearing region is located in the southwest, within a triangle formed by Vlorë, Berat, and Durrës. The probable total petroleum reserves of Albania are estimated at 12 to 15 million metric tons.

Crude oils from the Kuçovë and Patos fields have an asphaltic base and are generally unsuited for good lubricants. Their great density places them among the world's heaviest oils. The calculated average weight of typical Albanian crudes is 7.87 pounds per gallon. Their approximate yields, which were compiled from several prewar Albanian sources, were as follows: gasoline, 13 per cent; kerosene, 8 per cent; gas oil, 18 per cent; asphalt, 40 per cent; sulphur, 3 per cent; and residuals, 18 per cent.

While cracking of Albanian crudes results in an average gasoline yield of 40 per cent, distillation decreases the proportion of gasoline to 18 per cent. A relatively high share of aviation gasoline (roughly 80 per cent) may be obtained through the use of hydrogen in catalytic cracking (hydrogenation process). As most Albanian crudes are unsuitable for distillation or noncatalytic cracking, it is necessary to resort to the costly hydrogenation process for an acceptable yield of oil products. The production of crude oil is likewise extremely expensive, the average cost per barrel amounting to roughly $2.50, more than double the cost in the United States.

The exploitation of Albanian petroleum deposits began in 1918 when Italian military prospectors struck oil at depths ranging from 230 to 410 feet in the Shushicë-Drashovicë area. The first Albanian oil wells yielded about 875 gallons daily, which were chiefly consumed by the Italian occupation forces. The evacuation of Italian troops in 1920 caused an interruption of exploitation and even exploratory drilling activities. In 1923, the Italians obtained a concession for the exploitation of 400,000 acres of oil-bearing land in the Vlorë-Berat-Durrës triangle. Two years later, the Italian Ministry of Communications organized the Azienda Italiana Petroli Albania (AIPA) to survey the oil-bearing regions of Albania. Preliminary drillings on the coast near Vlorë and in the Vijosë valley area were generally unsuccessful. However, drillings along the Devoll River near Kuçovë proved to be more promising, and some ten exploratory oil wells with a combined depth of 20,500 feet were developed there in 1927. As the oil pool in the Devoll area was deposited in dense asphaltic sands, its exploitation required costly machinery which in turn required substantial financial investments. A subsidy of 200 million lire granted to AIPA by the Italian government in 1933 marked the beginning of intensive commercial exploitation of Albanian petroleum. By the mid-1930's, there were 62 exploratory and exploitation wells. The country's petroleum output, which increased from 11,000 barrels in 1933 to 237,000 in 1936, rose steadily up to the beginning of World War II. Albanian petroleum production for the 1933-54 period was as follows (in barrels of 42 U.S. gallons):

Year	*Barrels*	*Year*	*Barrels*
1933	11,000	1944	334,000
1934	10,000	1945	267,000
1935	41,000	1946	1,000,000
1936	237,000	1947	2,000,000
1937	619,000	1948	1,500,000
1938	752,000	1949	2,188,000
1939	934,000	1950	2,335,000
1940	1,497,000	1951	1,200,000
1941	1,334,000	1952	1,100,000
1942	1,601,000	1953	962,000
1943	1,100,000	1954	1,130,000

Sources: American Petroleum Institute, *Petroleum Facts and Figures*, 9th ed. (New York, 1950), p. 446; *ibid.*, 10th ed. (1952), p. 237; *ibid.*, 11th ed. (1953), p. 292; Radio Tirana, May 18, 1954, February 5, 1955.

In the late 1930's, prospecting for oil was carried on in the Patos area, where four exploratory wells originally drilled by the Anglo-Persian Company in the 1920's were successfully reactivated and exploited. The Patos oil field, which covered an area of roughly 1,125 acres, soon developed into one of Albania's leading producers of dense asphalt-base petroleum.

The Italo-Ethiopian War and Italy's preparations for World War II created a heavy demand for Albanian petroleum and resulted in intensified prospecting activities by AIPA. New exploratory drillings were made in the Krujë region, where a large pool was found at a depth of 65 feet. This new oil basin covered an area roughly 7,500 acres and was allegedly five times as large as that of Devoll. Its exploitation was prevented by the outbreak of the war, and the Italians concentrated their efforts on the Devoll and Patos basins. By 1943, the total number of productive oil wells rose to 974, of which 954 were in the Kuçovë area and 20 in Patos. All wells were in workable condition at the time of their seizure by the Communists at the end of November 1944.

The Communist regime began the exploitation of the Kuçovë (later renamed Stalin Town) wells as early as December 1944. By March 1945, the country had nearly 100 productive oil wells which yielded approximately 12 metric tons of gasoline, 12 metric tons of naphtha, and 6 metric tons of kerosene daily. During the late 1940's, the country's crude and petroleum products output was substantially increased. The present annual yield of the Albanian productive oil fields of Kuçovë and Patos exceeds one million barrels, and the number of workers in these two fields amounts to roughly 3,000.

The bulk of Albanian petroleum is shipped to Poland. Roughly 30,000 metric tons per annum are processed at three small refineries at Kuçovë and Patos presumably for local consumption. The oil is transferred through two pipelines constructed by the Italians in the 1930's. The first and major pipeline, with a 20-inch diameter, extends from Kuçovë to Uj'i Ftohtë (Krionero) on the bay of Vlorë, where there is a storage capacity in underground tanks exceeding 700,000 cubic feet. From there, it is usually transported through an underwater pipeline to an anchorage point for tankers. The second pipeline originates at Patos and joins the major one at Fier. The pipelines and pumping stations were thoroughly reconstructed by the Communists in 1947-48. A new pipeline leading from Kuçovë to Çerrik is under construction to connect the country's principal oil wells with the Çerrik refinery, whose 1955 completion was not fulfilled. The refinery, which is located near the town of Elbasan, is expected to process 150,000 metric tons of crude annually. The construction of a thermoelectric power plant with a capacity of 7,500 kilowatts, which will be connected with the refinery, was provided by the Five-Year Economic Plan (1951-55).

This Plan called for a 1955 crude oil output of 263,000 metric tons (roughly 1,750,000 barrels). During the period of the Plan, the exploratory drilling footage was to amount to 137,750 feet, and the exploitation drilling footage was to reach a high of 595,000 feet. No provisions were made in the Plan for the development of the Krujë oil deposits. Crude oil output by the end of 1955 was only about 220,000 metric tons, falling short of the goal set for that year.

Natural Gas

The presence of natural gas in the Kuçovë and Patos oil fields was noted by several Italian experts in the 1930's. According to prewar Italian estimates, Albania's natural gas reserves amount to several million cubic feet. Their exploitation began in the late 1930's on a minor scale, and undisclosed quantities were reportedly used for the production of natural gasoline and as a fuel source for the thermoelectric power plant of Kuçovë. The country's natural gas output reached its peak in 1942 and has presumably declined considerably since.

Coal

Albania's coal deposits consist almost exclusively of relatively high-quality lignites, and the presence of higher coal ranks in the country has not been established. Albanian lignites range from the common varieties with a markedly woody texture to coals with physical properties resembling asphaltic pyrobitumens or even asphaltites. The country's most important lignite basins are found in the following four areas: (1) a triangular plateau with apexes at Tirana, Elbasan, and Lushnjë in the Krrabë Mountains; (2) the Vijosë River valley, mainly at Memaliaj near Tepelenë; (3) the Pogradec-Korçë area, mainly at Mborje, Drenovë, and Alarup; (4) Priskë near Tirana.

The proved lignite reserves of the Krrabë basin are estimated at 7 million metric tons, and those of the Vijosë basin at 5 million metric tons. The Krrabë basin covers an area of roughly 1,360 acres. Its lignite seams, which average 24 inches in thickness, are intercalated with layers of clay 3 to 7 feet thick and sand of Upper Miocene and Lower Pliocene origin. Their quality is reportedly very high. The Memaliaj lignites of the Vijose basin are likewise of excellent quality, and the calorific value of certain varieties exceeds 10,800 B.t.u. A typical dry sample of these lignites contains 46.35 per cent of fixed carbon, 44.42 per cent of volatile matter, and 9.23 per cent of ash. The proximate analysis of Memaliaj lignite is as follows: moisture, 9.50 per cent; ash, 8.35 per cent; volatile matter, 40.20 per cent; and fixed carbon, 41.95 per cent.

The sulphur content of Memaliaj lignites exceeds 6 per cent, and 1 kilogram yields 555 grams of coke. The average calorific value of Priskë lignites exceeded 10,000 B.t.u. and their average volatile matter content amounted to 42 per cent. Most Albanian lignites, which were often classified by the Italians as "brown coals," may probably be designated in the subbituminous class.

The country's first lignite mine was established at Memaliaj in 1918. Albania's annual coal output during the interwar period averaged 4,000 metric tons, and a high of 8,686 metric tons was reportedly reached in 1936. Minor quantities of coal for local consumption were extracted at the Krrabë and Mborje-Drenovë mines owned by private Albanian mining concerns. A considerable increase in production in the early 1940's was due to the development of new mines. During the Italian occupation (1939-43), the Italian mining concern Azienda Carboni Italiani (ACI) developed the mine of Priskë, which yielded roughly 100 metric tons of coal daily, used for household purposes in Tirana, for Italian ships at the port of Durrës and for Yugoslav railroads running through Italian-controlled territories. The Italians claim that Albanian coal output during World War II amounted to 132,000 metric tons, of which 108,000 tons were classified as "brown coals."

During the postwar period, coal output has continued to rise steadily, as can be seen from the following figures for selected years 1938-54:

Year	*Metric Tons*	*Year*	*Metric Tons*
1938	4,100	1950	42,000
1939	7,000	1953	81,546
1948	12,100	1954	115,960

Sources: Bashkimi, June 4, 1949, April 3, 1952; Radio Tirana, November 28, 1954, February 5, 1955.

The Communist regime has concentrated its efforts on exploiting the Memaliaj basin, where new equipment and an aerial ropeway were installed in the 1950's. In addition to Memaliaj coals, which are suitable for steam production without cleaning or sizing, the country's present coal output comes from the mines of Krrabë, Mborje-Drenovë, and Priskë. The Five-Year Economic Plan called for a 1955 coal output of 168,000 metric tons and provided for mechanization of the four active mines, and construction of a coal-cleaning plant with an annual processing capacity of 40,000 metric tons. Extensive prospecting activities aimed at the discovery of new coal deposits were also to be carried out. Coal output fell short of the planned production goal set for the end of 1955 by about 40,000 metric tons.

Asphalt and Bitumen

Albanian bitumen and asphalt deposits are found in a triangular area between Kudhësi Mountain at the village of Selenicë and the

Vijosë River between the villages of Karbunarë, Treblovë, and Armen. The area covers approximately 700 acres of limestone formations and sands of Miocene and Pliocene origin. Asphalt occurs mostly in a semiliquid state in the limestones. Its specific gravity averages 1.1, and the fusion point is as high as 118° F.

The native bitumen deposits formed at Selenicë are of very high quality. Their average hydrocarbon content amounts to 33 per cent. The Selenicë deposits have been worked continuously for many centuries. Their exploitation during the interwar period was controlled by the Società Italiana delle Miniere di Selenizza Albania (SIMSA), which administered the Selenicë mines from 1918 to 1944. During the 1920's, the company extracted an average of 3,500 metric tons of bitumen and crude asphalt annually. This was doubled during the 1928-35 period, tripled in the late 1930's, and stabilized at about 20,000 metric tons annually in the early 1940's. The country's bitumen and asphalt output in selected years 1938-53 was as follows:

Year	*Metric Tons*	*Year*	*Metric Tons*
1938	10,500	1946	10,800
1940	20,000	1948	11,800
1942	18,000	1950	26,300
1945	6,300	1953	28,350

Sources: Albania: Basic Handbook ([London], 1943), Pt. 2, p. 69; *Bashkimi,* September 12, 1945, April 14, 1946, June 4, 1949, April 3, 1952; Radio Tirana, September 19, 1954.

Albanian bitumen and asphalt output has risen considerably during the postwar period. The bulk of Albanian production is used for paving and waterproofing and for the manufacture of insulators and roofing shingles. A number of by-products, such as asphalt-base petroleum and coke, are produced by the bitumen-processing plant of Vlorë, which was built by the Italians in 1941-42. The Vlorë plant is connected with the Selenicë mines by a decauville rail line. Recent reports indicate that the mines are well mechanized and equipped with new steam boilers. They are now administered by the Ndërmarja Minerale e Shtetit Selenicë (State Mineral Enterprise Selenicë), which employs around 800 workers. The Five-Year Economic Plan called for the production of 10,000 metric tons of crude, and 80,000 tons of purified bitumen in 1955. It also provided for extensive prospecting and research activities and for the construction of a new bitumen plant with an annual processing capacity of 80,000 metric tons. The planned output was not reached and the processing plant was not built.

Principal Metallic Minerals

Chromium

Chromium ores of excellent quality are found in many parts of Albania. Prewar Italian estimates placed the country's reserves at 500,000 metric tons, but according to Professor I. Ndoja, who published an article on Albanian chromium mines in *Bashkimi* of February 11, 1949, the chromium ore reserves of Albania "considerably exceed" this figure. Ndoja stated that chromium ores constitute the country's most valuable mineral deposits. They are located in the following four principal areas: the vicinity of Pogradec near Korçë; the Klos area near Mat; the Letaj zone near Elbasan; and near the town of Kukës in northern Albania. The occurrence and tenor of these deposits is outlined in Table 2. Albanian chromium ore output for selected years 1938-54 was as follows:

Year	*Metric Tons*	*Year*	*Metric Tons*
1938	6,240	1948	16,500
1939	22,654	1950	52,000
1940	20,000	1953	54,500
1942	35,910	1954	115,500

Sources: *Bashimi*, April 3, 1952; United States Department of the Interior, *Minerals Yearbook 1949* (Washington, D.C., 1951), p. 1611; Radio Tirana, March 24, 1954, November 28, 1954, February 5, 1955.

The Pogradec and Kukës deposits, which are the most valuable, consist of many irregular lenticles found at depths usually not exceeding 10 feet (maximum 30 feet). Schlieren appear only in the Kukës area. The average Cr_2O_3 content of the deposits is 42 per cent, and the FeO content averages 12-13 per cent.

During the interwar period, the concession for the exploitation of Albanian chromium was held by the Azienda Minerali Metallici Italiani (AMMI) for shipment to Italy. The company's output during the first year of intensified mining amounted to 6,240 metric tons.

Output rose to 22,654 metric tons in 1939, and 18,000 tons of ore were shipped to Italy in 1940. In 1942, which was the peak production year prior to the Communist takeover, the country's chromium ore output totaled 35,910 metric tons, of which 14,353 tons were mined in the Letaj area, 10,385 in Kukës, 8,010 in Pogradec, and 3,162 tons in the Klos area. From September 1943 to July 1944, a few mines were intensively exploited by the Germans.

The first chromium mines worked by the Communist regime were those of Memelisht and Katiel in the Pogradec area. In 1948, the mines in the Kukës and Klos areas were reactivated; only the latter has been in operation since 1950; because of transportation difficulties, the exploitation of the Pogradec mines was discontinued and that of the Kukës mines was not undertaken at all. The Klos area is administered by the Ndërmarja Minerale e Shtetit "Fitorja" (State Mineral Enterprise "Victory"). The Klos mines are connected by highway with the port of Durrës, the country's chromium-exporting center.

Table 2.
OCCURRENCE AND TENOR OF PRINCIPAL CHROMIUM DEPOSITS, BY AREA

Area	*Name of Deposit (as of 1938)*	*Occurrence*	*Tenor*
Pogradec	Memelisht	Undisseminated	High
	Gjerduk	Disseminated	Medium
	Katiel	Undisseminated, isolated	......
	Pishkash	Pisolitic, undisseminated, isolated	......
	Skroskë	Pisolitic, undisseminated, isolated	......
Klos (Bulqizë)	Fortuna	Disseminated (brittle)	......
	Italia	Undisseminated knots	......
	Littorio	Undisseminated	......
	San Luigi	Knots, partly disseminated	......
Letaj	Letaj	Undisseminated, pisolitic, and occasionally isolated	High
	Perollaj	Nodular	High
	Zogaj	Undisseminated	......
	Lejthizë	Undisseminated	......
	Kepenek	Undisseminated, occasional knots	High
	Helshan	Undisseminated	......
	Kam	Undisseminated	High
	Lenic	Undisseminated	Low
	Bityq	Undisseminated, occasionally nodular	High
Kukës	Kalimash	Undisseminated, pisolitic, schlieren	......
	Dukagjin	Mainly knots	......
	Surroj	Mainly knots	......
	Qaf'e Kumbullës	......	Low

The Five-Year Economic Plan called for a 1955 chromium output of 120,000 metric tons, which was not fulfilled, for the mechanization of the Klos mines, and for exploratory surveys of other areas with the help of trained Soviet personnel.

Copper

Substantial copper deposits are found in northern Albania near Derven, Bulshizë, Erzen, Velë, Narel, Kabash, Klos, Dedaj, Firzë, Iballë, Orosh, and Qerat in the Pukë-Mirditë zone, and in the Kukës and Shkodër areas. Minor deposits occur near Kamenicë and Rehovë near Korçë. The copper reserves of northern Albania were estimated by the Italians at 5 million metric tons. The copper sulphide ore reserves of the entire country were estimated by Professor D. C. Lunder at 50 million metric tons. The tenor of Albanian copper ores is generally very low. The average copper content of chalcopyrite is 10 per cent, and that of cupropyrite 3 per cent. The less valuable malachite and azurite are common.

The first Albanian copper mine was developed by SIMSA near Pukë in 1929. Output, which amounted to roughly 50,000 metric tons during the following eight-year period, was considerably increased after the development of new mines at Rrubik near Lesh. The Rrubik mines, which employed over 600 workers, became the site of a large smelter built in the late 1930's. The plant had a processing capacity of 16 tons per hour, and the Italians, who anticipated an output of 6,000 tons in 1940, claimed an average monthly production of 150 tons of blister copper.

The extraction of copper ore and the production of blister copper was resumed by the Communists in 1946. In 1948, production of 195 metric tons of blister copper, and in 1950 roughly 900 tons, was announced, as was a copper ore production of 14,200 tons for the latter year. Output figures for subsequent years have not been reported, but Radio Tirana stated that copper production in 1952 exceeded that of 1951 by 59 per cent, and that the 1954 output exceeded that of 1953 by 14.9 per cent. The considerable output fluctuations were most probably due to technical deficiencies and transportation difficulties. The Tirana press claimed that the Rrubik mines had been thoroughly reconstructed and equipped with new excavating machines, pneumatic drills, and compressors. A new copper-processing plant with an annual capacity of 90,000 metric tons, scheduled to be completed by the end of 1955, was not even begun. Both the mines and the smelter, which employ roughly 1,000 workers, are administered by Ndërmarja Minerale e Shtetit "Një Maj" (State Mineral Enterprise "May First").

The Five-Year Economic Plan called for 1955 copper ore output of 145,000 metric tons, and for blister copper production of 2,500 metric tons. It also provided for the construction of a new copper-processing plant and for an increase of the capacity of the power plant which services the country's copper works. Prospecting in the Rrubik and

Derven areas was to be intensified. There is no indication that these planned goals were achieved.

Iron Ore

Albanian iron ore reserves were estimated by the Italians at 20 million metric tons. Their metal content averages 25 per cent. The principal deposits are located in the Pogradec-Librazhd area, in the Krumë-Kukës area, along the valleys of Fan i Vogël and Fan i Math rivers southeast of Shkodër, and near Peshkopi. Smaller deposits are found in the vicinity of Himarë, Tepelenë, Gjirokastër, and Delvinë. The Pogradec-Librazhd area is noted for its high quality hematite with an Fe content exceeding 60 per cent. Magnetite ores are found in northern Albania, but their exploitation is impeded by the lack of transportation facilities.

Iron ore mining in Albania was carried on only in the early 1940's. The Italian concern Ferralba (Ferro Albania) constructed a few small mines and an aerial ropeway in the Pogradec-Librazhd area and attempted to build a railroad from Durrës to the Labinot mine. The output of these mines was not disclosed, but the production goal for 1941 was set at 1,500,000 metric tons. As all Albanian iron ore was to be shipped to Italy, lack of shipping caused the abandonment of the mines in 1943.

The Communists have made no attempts to resume ore extraction. The ore could not be utilized locally because of the lack of processing plants, and excessive transportation costs prevent export to other Communist countries. The provisions of the Five-Year Economic Plan were limited to survey activities, which may have resulted in in the discovery of new deposits.

Other Metallic Minerals

Gold and Silver

Minor deposits of gold and silver with a tenor suitable for industrial use are found in the Lubonjë-Vithkuq area. Prospecting for gold and silver in the vicinity of Rehovë and Vithkuq was carried on by the French during World War I. It is reported that surveying of the Rehovë area was resumed by Soviet geologists dispatched to Albania.

Bauxite

Residually concentrated bauxite deposits occur in the Llesh area, in the Kakarriq Mountains, and also near Renë, Vlorë, and Krujë. Their exploitation has not been reported.

Nickel

Traces of nickel appear in the Lubonjë-Vithkuq area, and also in the sulphur deposits of Kamenicë and the iron deposits of Pogradec. As the reserves are very small, the metal is not mined.

Miscellaneous

Insignificant quantities of antimony, lead, zinc, mercury, and platinum are reportedly associated with some of the other metal deposits of the country. It was reported in 1951 that uranium was discovered in the vicinity of Kafaranj in the Fratar area.

Miscellaneous Nonmetallic Minerals

Magnesite

Magnesite is found in the Shkodër area in the north, and in the Gramsh and Voskopojë districts in central and southern Albania. Italian sources claim that during World War II production of magnesite reached 2,400 metric tons per annum. Substantial deposits highly suitable for refracting were discovered in 1949 in the Gramsh district by members of a geological team on a field trip organized by the Albanian Museum of Natural Sciences. A 1950 press report from Tirana urged the utilization of these deposits as refractory materials and called for the construction of an Albanian refractory furnace. The report stated that experiments were made with magnesium oxide in an effort to replace zinc oxide in rubber processing. Sufficient quantities of magnesium oxide were obtained from the Bulcar (Gramsh district) magnesite deposits, where mining operations were initiated for this purpose by the Ministry of Industry. The quality of the several hundred quintals of magnesite extracted at Bulcar was very high, and further surveying and exploitation activities were anticipated.

Clay and Kaolin

Albanian potteries, which have existed for centuries, are based on the abundant clay deposits found throughout the country. White and colored kaolins are likewise common. They are used for the manufacture of whiteware and of all kinds of porcelains. Extensive deposits of clay were discovered in the Shkodër district in 1950.

Arsenic

Arsenic is found mainly along the left bank of the Drin River near Mgullë in the north, and was mined for the domestic market during the Turkish occupation. During the interwar period, arsenic was extracted at Komarë, Pukë, and Shijak by an Italian mining enterprise.

Salt

Abundant salt deposits are found in the vicinity of Kavajë and Vlorë. They are exploited by two mines with a combined annual production of roughly 10,000 metric tons.

Sulphur

Minor sulphur deposits of undisclosed origin appear in the vicinity of Kamenicë. The Five-Year Economic Plan calls for their exploration and exploitation.

Limestone

Limestone is found and quarried throughout Albania. It is one of the principal raw materials for the country's building industry.

Significant Factors

Albania should be noted as Eastern Europe's major producer of chromium ore. During the postwar decade, over 50 per cent of the chromium produced in the eight Communist countries of Europe came from Albania. Albanian production, which was higher than that of the United States, constituted about 7 per cent of the Soviet output and over 2 per cent of the world total. Her crude oil output for the 1945-54 period was below 3 per cent of the total for Eastern Europe, but the ratio of 1955 reserves to 1954 output was higher than in the other seven countries.

Albania is also prominent in Eastern Europe as a country whose mining sector generates the highest share of the gross industrial product and employs the highest share of industrial labor force. In 1950, the mining industries of Albania contributed 45 million leks to the gross value of her industrial output of 3.27 billion leks. Although the share of mining declined from 13.7 per cent in 1950 to 7.5 in 1955 (0.77 billion out of 10.21), the sector continues to play a leading role in the country's economy.

12. INDUSTRY

UNTIL 1925, industry was practically nonexistent in Albania, and many factors combined to render the country's industrialization a slow and laborious task. Four and a half centuries of Turkish domination had created none of the necessary bases for economic development. During this period, contact with Western Europe was slight, no development of manufacturing took place, the communications system was neglected, and none of the conditions favoring capital formation existed. When Albania regained her independence, there was an acute shortage of capital, trained personnel, and entrepreneurial skill. Moreover, the domestic market was extremely small because of the poverty of the country.

From 1925 onward, industry slowly started to grow, prodded by the government. To the existing handicraft industry which produced all required cotton, woolen, and silk textiles, as well as other consumers' goods, a nucleus of modern industry was added. After occupying Albania in 1939, the Italians made a strenuous effort to develop industry, but the war shortly put a stop to those plans not directly connected with their war effort. By 1940, Albania possessed several sawmills, two modern olive oil extracting plants (which had an exportable surplus), several power mills, two large and four small cigarette manufacturing plants, one large brewery, one modern cement factory, and several plants manufacturing soap, furniture, cardboard, handmade tools, and carts. There were also thirteen electric generating stations.

COMMUNIST POLICY

Communist industrial policy in Albania can be divided into two periods: that for reconstruction and nationalization, from 1944 through 1947, and that for reorganization along Soviet lines, since 1947.

First Period, 1944-1947

State ownership was extended over industry gradually by a series of laws nationalizing certain categories of properties. Thus, Law No. 41 of January 1945 confiscated all enterprises belonging to any individual arbitrarily labeled an "enemy of the people." Law No. 37 of January 13, 1945 imposed a supertax on war profits, payable in an unusually short period of time. Nonpayment let to government confiscation of inventories of stock on hand, which virtually paralyzed industrial and commercial activities in the important commercial centers of the country. In 1945, all Italian and German properties were confiscated, and all concessions granted to foreigners were revoked.

While private ownership was still permitted under the 1946 Constitution, no private industrial enterprises have been permitted since 1947. The Constitutions of 1946 and 1950 distinguished between state ownership and property of "people's cooperative organizations." The tempo of nationalization of industry is demonstrated by the following figures: in 1944, only 3 per cent of Albania's industrial enterprises were nationalized; in 1945, 7 per cent; in 1946, 79 per cent, and by 1947, 100 per cent. In 1947, there were 45 state enterprises, and 13 enterprises were owned or controlled by organs of local government.

Second Period, since 1948

Coordinated Communist economic planning began with the 1948 One-Year Plan, which was followed by the Two-Year Plan for 1949-50, and the Five-Year Plan for 1951-55.

The One-Year Plan for 1948 was designed to link Albania closely to Yugoslavia. Albania was at that time virtually under Yugoslav control and appeared slated to become an integral part of the Yugoslav economic sphere. The Plan was originally directed and financed in part by Yugoslavia, but with the expulsion of Yugoslavia from the Cominform in 1948, the situation changed drastically. All economic relations with Yugoslavia were severed, and Plan execution went through great difficulties. Total industrial production for that year reached only 84.4 per cent of the planned target. The admitted failure of the One-Year Plan was attributed to "Yugoslav sabotage."

The Two-Year Plan for 1949-50 took into account the change in orientation and was called realistic. Nevertheless, it was only 91.4 per cent fulfilled, the failures being mainly in refined oil, leather, soap, shoes, and wood products. The Five-Year Plan continued the same pattern as the Two-Year Plan, but with somewhat greater emphasis on industry and more emphasis than in other captive countries on agricultural and mineral raw materials. Table 1 shows planned and actual industrial investments, 1946-55, according to Communist sources. It is interesting to note that industry and mining received 31.3 per cent of the total investment during the period 1946-50 and rose in the Five-Year Plan period to 42.7 per cent of the total investment.

Table 1. Planned and Actual Industrial Investments, 1946-1955
(in million leks)

Year	Planned Investments Total	Planned Investments Industry and Mining	Actual Investments Total	Actual Investments Industry and Mining
1946	......	......		83.6
1947	......	......	3,970	201.8
1948	......	......		505.8
1949	......	839.6	......	......
1950	......	1,100.3	......	......
1946-50	......	......	6,824	2,136.0
1951-55	20,943	8,943.0	......	......

Source: "Economic Report, Albania," *News from Behind the Iron Curtain*, III, No. 5 (May 1954), 12-15.

Table 2. Value of Industrial Production, 1938 and 1945-1954
(in million leks)

Year	Total [a]	Consumers' Goods	Capital Goods
1938	826	640	186
1945	200	......	......
1946	801	584	217
1947	1,317	913	404
1948	2,101	1,575	526
1949	2,527	1,930	579
1950	3,266	2,505	761
1951	4,800	......	......
1952	5,760	......	......
1953	7,030	......	......
1954	7,780	......	......

[a] The share of industrial production in the Albanian gross national product amounted to: 20.0 per cent in 1938; 25.0 per cent in 1948; 33.0 in 1949; 40.6 in 1950; and 51.6 in 1953.

Sources: Bashkimi, April 1, 1952, April 3, 1952; *Zëri i Popullit,* January 5, 1955; *Radio Tirana,* June 4, November 28, 1952; November 28, 1953; March 22, March 28, April 13, April 15, April 25, May 18, August 1, August 7, October 19, 1954; February 5, 1955.

Industrial production has increased sharply since 1938. However, one should remember that the amounts shown in Table 2 do not represent a production index, but the value in leks. Due to the inflationary pressures during this period, the figures inevitably show a strong upward and misleading tendency. Consequently, it is impossible to state whether industrial production of 1947 was actually higher than that of 1938. Another point should be made: no figures are given for industrial production during the war years, although it is probable that 1942 production was substantially higher than that of 1938. Roughly speaking, less than one third of the total industrial production consists of capital goods. In the other captive countries, where much more stress is put on heavy industry, capital goods represent a much higher percentage of production.

In the first years of the Five-Year Plan, the original goals for industrial production were revised upward. In 1954, however, the planned goals were revised downward, but production still fell below the targets to 90.2 per cent of the original and 97.5 per cent of the revised plans. The goals for 1955 were also lowered. Some of the spectacular projects of the Five-Year Plan, such as the hydroelectric station on the Mat River, and the oil refinery of Çerrik, were slowed down and their dates of completion set for 1956 and 1957.

Handicrafts are an essential element of the Albanian economy, accounting for an important portion of the total manufactured articles and for most consumers' goods. To control this important sector, the Communist government forced the artisans to enter cooperatives, headed by the Union of Handicraft Cooperatives. There were 46 of these handicraft cooperatives in 1947; 65 in 1948; and 101 in 1954. By 1949, the whole handicraft sector of the economy had been included in cooperatives.

These handicraft cooperatives produce a variety of articles, such as cotton, wool, and silk fabrics, houseware, mats, furniture, agricultural implements, timber, bricks, tiles, electrical equipment, and foodstuffs. Table 3 gives the production of handicraft cooperatives for 1939, 1946-50, and planned production for 1955.

Table 3. Production of Handicraft Cooperatives, 1938, 1946-1950, and 1955

Year	*Production*	*Per Cent of Total Industrial Production*
	(in million leks)	
1938	386	46.7
1946	309	38.6
1947	380	28.9
1948	470	22.4
1949	453	17.9
1950	519[a]	15.9[a]
1955 (Plan)	1,511	13.6

[a] Another source lists this figure as 353 million leks, or 10.8 per cent of the total industrial production.

Sources: *Bashkimi,* April 3, 1952; November 13, February 4, 1953; April 13, 1954; February 5, 1955. "Economic Report: Albania," *News from Behind the Iron Curtain,* III, No. 5 (May 1954).

Until 1950, production of the handicraft cooperatives was consistently below target. With the launching of the Five-Year Plan, more emphasis was placed upon this sector. Investments increased, and the craftsmen received inducements to increase production in the form of raw materials and tax reductions.

Electric Power

Albania possesses a considerable hydroelectric potential, conservatively evaluated at 2.5 million kilowatts, of which only a minute fraction has been developed. The country's hydroelectric potential by power source (river, waterfall, possible dam site) has been estimated as follows:

Power Source	*Kilowatts*
Drin	1,000,000
Devoll	300,000
Shkumbî	70,000
Vijosë	250,000
Kir (Shkodër)	20,000
Pogradec (Lake)	1,000,000
Selitë (Tirana)	21,000
Mat	20,000
Total	2,681,000

Source: "La République Populaire d'Albanie," Pt. III: "Evolution Economique et Sociale," *La Documentation Française: Notes et Etudes Documentaires,* No. 1845 (March 6, 1954), 11.

Early in 1942, the "Ente Generale Italo-Albanese" was founded for the purpose of building reservoirs and power stations. This company began construction of a hydroelectric power station at Selitë, which, due to the war, was not completed. During the Italian occupation, the capacity of existing stations was increased by installing additional generators, so that by 1941 capacity reached 10,000 kilowatts, as compared to 5,000 in 1938.

In 1946, with UNRRA help, electric capacity was increased to 15,000 kilowatts. The Two-Year plan called for the construction of a a new hydroelectric power station of 20,000 kilowatts on the Mat River. This project was carried over to the Five-Year Plan. Although by 1953, construction was well advanced, work has slowed down considerably, and its completion is now set for 1957.

The Selitë hydroelectric station, which was begun by the Italians, was finally completed in 1952. Its capacity is 5,000 kilowatts, and it supplies Tirana, Durrës, and Elbasan with electric power. Table 4 shows the capacity of Albania's hydroelectric plants and their production for selected years, 1930-55.

Table 4. ELECTRIC POWER PLANT CAPACITY AND PRODUCTION, SELECTED YEARS 1930-1955

Year	*Capacity*	*Production*
	(in kw.)	*(in million K.W.H.)*
1930	2,970	......
1938	5,000	......
1941	10,000	......
1946	15,000	......
1947	15,000	......
1948	15,000	10
1949	15,000	......
1950 (Plan)	......	30
1951	......	20
1952	......	30
1953	......	40
1955 (Plan)		120

Source: UNRRA, European Regional Office, London, Division of Operational Analysis, No. 46, "Economic Rehabilitation in Albania"; *Bashkimi,* January 9, May 28, 1952.

In 1950, 56 million leks were invested in this field; 323 million leks were to be invested for 1955, or, 1.7 and 2.9 per cent respectively, of total industrial investment for those years.

Building Materials

The first cement factory in Albania was built in 1928 at Shkodër with an annual capacity of 22,000 metric tons. In addition, two small cement plants were built in the interwar period, one in Vlorë and one in Tirana, with a combined capacity of about 5,000 tons.

Under the Five-Year Plan, a new cement factory, the "Fabrika e Çementos Lenin," erected in Vlorë, began production in 1954 with an annual production capacity of 40,000 tons. Cement production for selected years, 1938-55, was as follows:

Year	*Metric Tons*
1938	12,000
1946	6,667[a]
1948	25,000
1950	15,000
1951	40,000
1955 (Plan)	58,000

[a] Calculated from indices.

Sources: Bruno Kiesewetter, *Statistiken zur Wirtschaft Ost- und Südost-Europas* (Berlin: Duncker and Humblot, 1955), Pt. 1, p. 41; *Bashkimi,* April 3, 1952; *Radio Tirana,* September 6, October 12, 1954.

As clay is found in large quantities in many different locations, bricks and tiles were manufactured all over the country in primitive furnaces. This continued after Communist incorporation of this activity under the Handicraft Cooperatives. There were also four industrial tile and brick producing enterprises at Shkodër, Tirana, Durrës, and Korçë. Brick production, which was 9 million pieces in 1948, was to reach 23 million in 1950 and 35 million in 1955. No information is available as to whether or not these goals were achieved.

There were several sawmills in prewar Albania. Production was 4,000 cubic meters in 1938. The production figures of timber for 1948 and the following years differ considerably, according to different sources. The Five-Year Plan, however, sets a target of only 35,000 cubic meters for 1955. Table 5 gives the value of building materials production. During the Five-Year Plan the "Nako Spiru" Wood Combine in Elbasan, with an annual capacity of 40,000 cubic meters of processed wood, was completed.

Table 5. VALUE OF BUILDING MATERIALS PRODUCTION, SELECTED YEARS 1938-1955

Year	*Value of Production*	*Per Cent of Total Value of Industrial Production*
	(in million leks)	
1938	21	2.5
1945	28[a]	14.0
1946	26	3.2
1947	65	4.9
1948	96	4.6
1949	140	5.5
1950	179	5.5
1955 (Original Plan)	682	6.1

[a] Calculated from indices.

Sources: Bashkimi, November 18, 1949, April 3, 1952. Radio Tirana, October 5, October 19, 1954; November 28, 1954; February 5, 1955.

According to a Radio Tirana broadcast of September 28, 1954, Albanian "house construction" amounted to 105,000 square meters for the 1944-51 period and 60,000 square meters for 1953. The Plan calls for 119,000 square meters in 1955.

Machinery and Metal Products

Vehicles. Truck bodies were built in Albania before the Communist regime, in Durrës, Tirana, and Shkodër, but only in limited quantities. This industry does not appear to have expanded. Horse-drawn carts, now built mainly by the Handicraft Cooperatives, remain an important transportation medium.

Agricultural Implements. In the past, agricultural implements were made by village blacksmiths and local workshops, which have been forced to join the Handicraft Cooperatives, now accounting for almost all the output. In 1954, it was announced that 10,164 plows and 2,064 cultivators were produced and that production of 12,400 plows and 2,000 cultivators was planned for 1955.

Machine Repair Shops. Repair work on agricultural machinery and on vehicles is carried out by the "Enver Hoxha" mechanical establishment in Tirana, constructed under the Five-Year Plan and which also manufactures considerable amounts of spare parts for industrial, agricultural, and transportation machinery, and in the Durrës mechanical workshop, a prewar plant recently enlarged. Railroad rolling stock is repaired at Durrës, in a plant constructed in 1953, the current expansion of which is to be completed in 1955. There is also a small machine shop in Elbasan.

Shipyards. There is one small shipyard in Durrës, which was constructed by IPIS, an Italian fishing company. The Five-Year Plan calls for the enlargement of the yard and the construction of twelve 200-ton motor-sailing vessels, or a total of 2,400 tons.

Miscellaneous. A factory with a capacity of 300,000 metal oil barrels per year is to be completed in 1955 at Çerrik.

Petroleum Products

Before the war, the Italian company, Azienda Italiana Petroli Albanesi (AIPA), a subsidiary of the Italian State Railroads, shipped Albanian crude oil to Italy for refining. A pipeline was constructed from the oil fields of Kuçovë to the port of Vlorë. During the war, the Germans erected three movable refineries at Kuçovë, but damaged them when they retreated.

The damaged machinery of the refineries was repaired with UNRRA help. The combined capacity of these refineries is about 30,000 metric tons per year. Under the Five-Year Plan, the construction of a new refinery was started at Çerrik, about forty miles southwest of Tirana; this refinery, which will be inaugurated in the summer of 1956, has a planned annual capacity of 150,000 tons, which would enable it to refine nearly half the Albanian output of crude petroleum.

Consumers' Goods Industry

Consumers' goods comprise by far the largest part of Albania's industrial production. The value of consumers' goods in 1950 was 2,505 million leks, and it was planned to reach 8,131 million leks in 1955, or respectively 76.7 and 73.1 per cent of total Albanian industrial production. The relative importance of consumers' goods is tending to decrease, but very slowly.

A major role in the production of consumers' goods is played by handicrafts, and, since the Communist regime, by the Handicraft Cooperatives. In 1950, these accounted for 54.7 per cent of the value of the total consumers' goods production. In the 1955 plan target, they account for 34.3 per cent.

Foodstuff Products

In an overwhelmingly agricultural country such as Albania, it is hardly surprising that food processing should represent a large proportion of all industrial activity. The value of the production of this industry in pre-Communist Albania and for the first five years after the Communist takeover is given in Table 6.

Table 6. PRODUCTION OF PROCESSED FOODS, 1938 AND 1946-1950

Year	*Production*	*Per Cent of Total Value of Industrial Production*
	(in million leks)	
1938	194	23.5
1946	211	26.3
1947	338	25.7
1948	478	22.8
1949	311	12.3
1950	339	10.4

Source: Bashkimi, April 3, 1952.

Flour Milling and Processing. There was a sufficient capacity to cover all domestic requirements before the Communist takeover. Modern mills, operated by steam or electricity, existed in Tirana, Durrës, Shkodër, Korçë, Elbasan, and Vlorë, while water mills were found in small communities. No important changes have occurred in this sector under the Communist regime.

A type of macaroni had long been produced in households and in small shops in Albania, and later, macaroni factories were established in Durrës and Shkodër. Under the Communists, macaroni has become a food staple. Under the Two-Year Plan, macaroni factories were built in Tirana and Durrës as a part of the existing mechanical flour mills. In 1938, only about 700 metric tons of macaroni were produced in the country, but 2,440 tons were produced in 1948 and 4,700 tons in 1950. The revised Five-Year Plan calls for a production of 13,060 metric tons in 1955.

Fish Preserving. Fish resources are abundant in Albanian lakes and rivers, and especially on the Adriatic coast, but were consumed only in the larger cities and in the coastal areas. The surplus, which averaged 250 metric tons annually between 1936 and 1938, was exported in fresh, salted, or dried form. In 1930 the government granted a fishing monopoly in the Adriatic waters to two Italian-Albanian companies, IPIS and Pescalba. They built warehouses and refrigerating facilities at Vlorë, and IPIS also began a fish cannery in the same port.

Under the Five-Year Plan, the Vlorë fish cannery was put into operation, with a capacity of 2,000 metric tons per year, and the ice plant built by the Italians was reopened. The only statistical information available indicates that 1948 fish production was 566 metric tons.

Canning. Except for the fish cannery in Vlorë, there was no canning industry in Albania at the end of World War II. The machinery for the Berat canning factory and for the fruit-preserving factory in Elbasan was supplied by UNRRA in 1946-47. With the later completion of additional enterprises, Albania's canning industry now comprises the following establishments: jam and preserve factories at Korçë and Ersekë; a fruit-preserving and canning establishment at Berat; and a fruit and vegetable conserve plant with a yearly capacity of 3,000 metric tons at Elbasan.

Processing of Dairy Products. Dairy production in prewar Albania was mainly in the hands of households. While the cheese factories of Korçë, Gjirokastër, Tirana, Vlorë, and Shkodër had modern equipment, the rest of Albanian dairy production came from households or very small enterprises.

Prewar milk production averaged 14,000 metric tons per year; the 1948 Plan called for a production of 12,270 metric tons. In 1938, butter production was 1,200 metric tons, covering all the domestic requirements; 3,000 metric tons of cheeses, of which 1,000 tons were exported; and 14,000 metric tons of eggs. No statistical data are available for the postwar period, although there is an admitted failure to fulfill planned goals. To induce greater milk output, the government has increased the purchasing price, extended credits, and supplied the peasants with dairy utensils.

Sugar Refining. Prewar sugar consumption was covered by imports, which averaged 4,000 metric tons per year. Annual per capita sugar consumption was in the neighborhood of only 4 kilograms. During the Italian occupation, the Italian company Sacarifera Italiana constructed two small refineries, one in Tirana and the other in Korçë, but their output amounted to only a few tons.

The Communist regime enlarged the Korçë refinery to a capacity of 2,000 metric tons and reopened it in 1951. In 1952, the Kombinati i Sheqerit Tetë Nëntor (Sugar Combine November 8) sugar refinery was completed at Maliq. This has an annual capacity of 10,000 metric tons and with the other refineries is able to fill domestic requirements. Domestic sugar production has risen from roughly 700 metric tons a year in 1949 to a planned figure of 12,000 tons in 1955.

Olive Oil Processing. This industry could be important to the Albanian economy, as the country is particularly well suited for olive growing, especially along the coast and in its central section. Little advantage was taken of this asset in prewar Albania, and olive oil was an important article only in the diet of the population of the producing areas. Prewar national per capita consumption was but 3 kilograms. Some olive oil was refined at Elbasan and Vlorë, while other oil production was obtained through households. In 1939, there were twenty mechanized olive oil presses, and 1,304 hand-operated olive presses.

Under the Italian occupation, one modern olive press with a capacity of eight metric tons a day was built at Berat, and another in a village near Tirana. The residue was sent to Italy for further extraction. Later on, an extraction plant was erected, but the olive oil processing industry was negligible.

Olive oil production greatly diminished in the early years of Communist rule, probably because the olive oil processors were forced into government-controlled cooperatives. The Five-Year Plan called for an increase in olive production which is expected to reach 5,150 tons in 1955.

Distilling and Brewing. Brandies were distilled by many farmers all over Albania, in addition to the industrial distilleries of Tirana, Durrës, Korçë, Pogradec, and Shkodër, which had a combined annual capacity of 2,000 metric tons. The main production was *raki* (from grapes), the national beverage, of which that of Leskovik and Përmet, and *raki manash* (mulberry brandy) were the best known. The present production is not known, but in 1952 Albania exported 900 tons of *raki* to the Soviet Union.

Beer was produced in Albania before the Italian occupation. The Birra Korça Company, half Albanian and half Italian, supplied the bulk of the Albanian market. The company's modern brewery at Korçë, with an annual capacity of 20,000 hectoliters, produced beer of excellent quality. With the Italian occupation, ownership of this company passed completely into Italian hands. Under the Communist regime, production has been kept at a high level, reaching 21,000 hectoliters in 1950. The Five-Year Plan calls for increased output to 30,000 hectoliters in 1955.

Wine is produced only in small quantities, as most Albanians are Moslems.

Textiles

Before the war, cotton, silk, and most wool fabrics produced in Albania were processed by handicraft spinning and weaving and dyed by peasant methods. There was one modern knitting mill in Korçë. During the Italian occupation, the textile industry in general suffered heavily from Italian competition, although the cotton industry expanded its facilities.

The Communist regime attempted to merge the small textile enterprises into larger ones and to force artisans into Handicraft Cooperatives. This led to some disorganization, and production fell during the first years of Communist rule. Measures to increase production were taken under the Two-Year and Five-Year Plans, and new plants were constructed.

Cotton. Contrary to the trend in other textile sectors, the cotton industry expanded during the Italian occupation. Three small modern spinning plants were erected at Shkodër, Korçë, and Sarandë, equipped with Italian machinery.

The Communists also expanded production capacity, adding the following enterprises: Kombinati Tekstil Stalin (Stalin Textile Combine) at Yzberish, equipped with 21,000 spindles and having a production capacity of 20 million meters of cotton cloth, which is due to be in full production by 1955; two cotton gins, one opened in 1951 in Fier, the other in 1952 in Rrogozhinë, with a production capacity of 10,500 metric tons each; and two cotton spinning factories, one completed in 1951 in Shkodër equipped with 5,000 spindles, the other to be completed in 1955 at Yzberish, as part of the Stalin plant, with a capacity of 600 metric tons. In addition, a new textile mill is in operation at Korçë, a small textile plant in Shkodër, and a hosiery factory in Rrogozhinë. Cotton textile production for 1938 and 1950-55 was as follows:

Year	*Million Meters*
1938	0.34
1950	1.10
1951	5.08
1952	5.50
1953	13.80 [a]
1954	20.00
1955 (Plan)	17.91 [b]

[a] Other official sources give the figure as 13.0 and 13.5.

[b] Revised goals. The original goal was 21.5. Other official sources give the revised figure as 16.47.

Source: Bashkimi, April 3, 1952; Radio Tirana, May 13, June 7, June 11, July 5, September 30, November 28, 1954.

Cotton cultivation has been increased, and, if the Five-Year Plan goals for 1955 are met (which appears highly improbable), Albania would not only cover all her raw cotton needs, but even have a small exportable surplus.

Wool. The woolen textile industry, which was concentrated mainly in handicrafts, suffered much during the occupation from Italian competition and the fact that the Italians seized most of the available wool stocks. The shortage of raw materials became more acute during the war. Production of raw wool slackened still further with the Communist collectivization of industry, and failed to reach the annual Five-Year Plan goals. The goal for 1955 is approximately 12,000 metric tons, or about 20 per cent above the 1938-39 average, but it appears doubtful that it will be fulfilled.

Wool material production was 552,000 meters in 1950, and the plan calls for 852,000 meters in 1955. The quality is poor and there are only a few limited varieties of material.

Leather and Footwear

Small tanneries existed in all principal towns in the prewar period. The industry grew steadily, especially during the Italian occupation, when larger factories were erected. The largest factory in use now is the Fabrika e Lëkurëve Gjirokastër (Gjirokastër Leather Factory), the former Habibi and Papavangjeli Company, which has been expanded, equipped with Czechoslovak machinery, and now employs 120 workers. Other tanneries are located in Korçë, Vlorë, and Durrës.

In pre-Communist Albania, all footwear was produced by local shoemakers and cobblers. A small amount of cheap manufactured footwear was imported from Czechoslovakia.

Under the Communist regime, the artisans have been forced into small factories directed by the Central Union of Handicraft Cooperatives. These factories are poorly equipped, as delivery of capital goods from the rest of the Soviet bloc is taking place slowly.

The quality of footwear is inferior to that produced by the prewar shoemakers. The Five-Year Plan stresses that relatively expensive leather should (wherever possible) be replaced in footwear production by such cheaper materials as rubber, cloth, and wood. According to official sources, the original plan for 1955 called for production of 730,700 pairs of shoes of all kinds. The revised plan calls for only 598,000 pairs, including 187,000 pairs of children's shoes.

Miscellaneous Consumers' Goods Industries

Tobacco. After the early 1930's, the privately owned and well-equipped factories in Durrës, Shkodër, Elbasan, and Korçë operated under the Tobacco State Monopoly law. Under the Italian occupation, the tobacco factories worked to full capacity, supplying the Italian market. Their combined yearly output was about 40 million packs of cigarettes, in addition to other types of manufactured tobacco.

The industry continued its development under the Communist regime, and a tobacco-curing factory was erected in Shkodër in 1952 with a capacity of 1,500 tons per year. Another factory, with a capacity of one million packs per year, was completed in Tirana. Cigarette production amounted to 700 tons in 1950, and was planned to reach 850 tons in 1955.

Soap Industry. Prewar Albania possessed four small soap factories, in Vlorë, Tirana, Shkodër, and Durrës, the combined output of which amounted to only 120 tons per year. This did not include a large handicraft production.

There has been some centralization and reorganization of the industry under the Communist regime. Apart from handicraft production, there are now only three industrial plants, in Shkodër, Elbasan, and Sarandë. According to official sources, soap production amounted to 950 tons in 1950, and the revised plan for 1955 calls for a production of 2,760 tons, a figure which was greatly reduced from the original 1955 target of 3,700 tons.

Rubber. There is only one rubber and rubber goods factory in Albania, the relatively modern Durrës plant. In the prewar period, this was located in Korçë, but the machinery was transferred by the Communists to its new location. The factory's production consists of rubber gloves, rubber soles, and rubber shoes. It is also equipped to galvanize automobile tires. Except for its contribution to the shoe industry, this factory is of little importance.

Paper. A paper mill was reported under construction in 1950, but no further details are available. The 1955 Plan calls for paper production of 5,000 tons.

Glass. In 1954, a glass factory with an annual capacity of 20,000 square meters of window glass was completed in Tirana. The 1955 Plan calls for the production of 200,000 square meters of window glass and total glass production of 2,000 tons.

Recent General Statistics

Some new figures relative to 1955 have been disclosed lately. Overall production has increased by 13 per cent over 1954, or to 8,790 leks, thus falling short of the revised plan by 17 per cent (and 21 per cent below the original plan). The plan for 1956 seems to have been more realistically set, demanding an increase of 10 per cent over 1955. 1955 industrial production grew only slowly, by 3 per cent in light industry and 4 per cent in the machine construction industry; only in the building materials industry has there been a large increase, of 54 per cent. The emphasis placed on handicraft production has continued, and 1954 production was exceeded in 1955 by 21 per cent. However, it is impossible to ascertain the share of handicrafts in the total value of industrial production at the end of the first Five-Year Plan. It seems likely that the increases in industrial production which will be set under the second Five-Year Plan will still rely heavily on the contribution of handicrafts.

13. DOMESTIC TRADE AND FINANCE

Domestic Trade Before the Communists

There was practically no industry in Albania before World War II, and primitive cottage industries such as weaving, spinning, and handicrafts fulfilled most needs. Aside from a few state monopolies (i.e., matches, playing cards, and cigarette paper), both wholesale and retail trade in Albania were free up to World War II. A number of business establishments in the larger cities handled all imports. The craftsmen, who represented the largest single middle-class group in the country, generally sold their wares direct to the consumers. They supplied the population with shoes and sandals, household utensils and furniture, homespun cloth, and some foodstuffs.

As far as agricultural products were concerned, the peasant sold his produce in the town markets, usually on market days. However, since Albania had to supplement its grain production with imports, the government and some wholesalers participated in the grain trade; the import of grain totaled 25,300 metric tons in 1936, some 40,000 metric tons in 1937, and 34,600 metric tons in 1938.

After the occupation of the country by Italy, a limited goods rationing system was introduced. Inflation set in, and prices of all goods rose by leaps and bounds, as illustrated by Table 1, which gives the indices of wholesale prices during selected years of the 1939-43 period.

Table 1. Wholesale Price Indices, Selected Years 1939-1943
(January 1939=100)

Month and Year	*General Trade*	*Foodstuffs*	*Other Products*
January 1939	100.0	100.0	100.0
December 1939	147.4	143.8	152.5
December 1940	272.5	278.5	263.7
December 1941	559.3	591.3	510.0
December 1943	1,096.9	1,288.8	789.5

Table 2 gives retail prices of some basic foodstuffs for March 1939, a month before the occupation, and for November 1943.

Table 2. Selected Retail Food Prices, March 1939 and November 1943
(in Albanian francs)

Commodity	*Unit*	*March 1939*	*November 1943*
Wheat bread	Kilo	1.0	16.0
Corn bread	Kilo	0.5	12.0
Macaroni	Kilo	2.5	70.0
Butter	Kilo	13.0	202.0
Cheese	Kilo	5.0	117.0
Beef	Kilo	4.0	60.0
Beans, dry	Kilo	2.0	20.0
Milk	Liter	1.0	18.0
Olive oil	Liter	5.0	158.0

Communist Domestic Trade Policy

Immediately upon assumption of power in November 1944, the Albanian Communist regime issued a series of decrees providing for strict control of all domestic trade. On December 15, 1944, Law No. 19 provided for state control of all industrial and business enterprises. Law No. 24, promulgated on the same day, requisitioned food supplies, medical products, building and construction materials, and means of transport. The latter law also provided for registration of all consumers' goods by the local authorities and the prohibition of purchasing or selling blocked supplies without specific government permission. Law No. 25 of the same date on the confiscation of movable and immovable property of political fugitives, Law No. 37 of January 13, 1945 on the war profits tax, and Law No. 40 of January 14, 1945 on the general disposition of confiscated private property served to place the major wholesale and retail establishments in the country in the hands of the Communist authorities. Thus, by the summer of 1945, the Communist regime had eliminated all private enterprises dealing with wholesale trade and had taken over most of the larger retail concerns.

Law No. 92 of July 17, 1945, creating the state enterprise for the purchase and sale of wheat, corn, barley, rye, and oats, inaugurated the creation in the following years of hundreds of state enterprises dealing with all kinds of activities in wholesale and retail trade. Decree-Law No. 418 of March 22, 1947 (*Bashkimi,* March 26, 1947), which contained sixty-nine articles on the creation of state enterprises in all economic fields, gave a definitive form to state control and operation of nearly all wholesale and retail outlets in the country.

The Three Principal Sectors

The first Albanian Communist Constitution (March 1946) recognized three general sectors in the economy of the country: the state sector, the cooperative sector, and the private sector. According to Article 5 of that constitution, the first two sectors are encouraged and favored by the state, while the third sector is generally restricted and closely controlled.

The State Sector. The state trade sector had its origins in 1945 when the state Autonomous Agency for Grains was created and given a virtual monopoly for collecting and selling grains (Law No. 92 of July 17, 1945). Early in 1946 state stores were established throughout the country to sell all kinds of goods, chiefly to those who held ration cards. As *Bashkimi* put it editorially on February 14, 1946, the "state stores are . . . the foundation for bigger and more developed economic enterprises in favor of the poor classes of the people. Through these stores, the state assists the wide masses of the people in order to guard them against speculation, the black market, and contraband. . . ." In June 1946, a Procurement Branch was created at the Trade Directorate of the Ministry of Economy (Law No. 255 of June 6, 1946) and granted the exclusive right to purchase, stockpile, and sell agricultural, dairy, and industrial products.

The network of state stores was expanded late in 1950 when a series of decisions issued by the Council of Ministers established the People's Stores (generally known as MA-PO–Magizinat Popullore) to sell all kinds of industrial articles, foodstuffs, and dairy and agricultural products. At this time, "special trade enterprises" were created in the country's major cities to sell industrial articles and foodstuffs for "gold and platinum, and articles made of platinum, gold, and silver, as well as precious stones and foreign currencies which are freely exchangeable" (*Gazeta Zyrtare*, November 6, 1950). The purpose of these "special trade enterprises" was to collect hoarded gold and hard foreign currency; they are now commonly known as "dollar stores."

The Cooperative Sector. The creation of cooperatives, which were nonexistent in Albania before the advent of the Communist regime, was authorized by Decree-Law No. 236 of April 20, 1946, which authorized the establishment of village and city cooperatives and the naming of a Cooperative Commission by the Council of Ministers to establish principles for cooperatives and to give general directions on the method of forming different types of cooperatives. Many ordinances and laws have been passed defining the duties and functions of consumers' and selling-purchasing cooperatives, both of which now play an important role in the country's internal trade. In 1947, the Tirana press reported that there were 25 consumers' (chiefly foodstuff) cooperatives with 46,467 members, and 304 selling-purchasing cooperatives with 63,384 members. By October 1952, it was claimed that these cooperatives had over 192,580 members representing 926,225 people. On June 9, 1954, Radio Tirana said that at the end of 1953 there were 1,219 consumers' cooperative shops in Albania, as against 961 in 1948. Goods turnover in these shops during 1953, added the broadcast, was estimated at 4,380 million leks, or 272 per cent more than in 1948.

During the Second Congress of the Consumers' Cooperatives, held in Tirana in May 1953, the basic functions of the cooperatives were defined as carrying on continuous war with private "speculative" trade, exchanging goods between town and village, strengthening the alliance between laborers and working peasants, and, above all, collecting the obligatory quotas of certain goods and collecting and stockpiling all surplus agricultural and dairy products from both the agricultural collectives and individual peasants.

At this congress, the Politburo accused the cooperatives of right-wing deviation as, "in their greed for profits," the cooperatives had all but abandoned barter and the conclusion of contracts for agricultural and dairy products with fixed prices. Instead, they had devoted all their energies to free trade in which there is little price control. Other deficiences of the cooperatives included: (1) inability to supply the villagers with simple agricultural implements; (2) flouting the major provisions of the cooperative statutes; (3) failure to make the cooperatives truly mass organizations; (4) failure to create strong bonds with the agricultural collectives; (5) supplying the countryside with low quality goods; and (6) inability to carry on business steadily and thus to compete effectively with private trade (*Bashkimi,* May 17, 19 and 20, 1953).

The Private Sector. While this sector handled nearly 100 per cent of the retail and wholesale trade until November 1944, it now does no wholesale business and handles less than one fifth of the retail trade. Beginning early in 1945, the Communist regime applied the squeeze to this sector. Law No. 422 of July 2, 1947 gave the government full power over Albanian finance and the economy. On the basis of this law, the government nationalized the collection and sale of grain and corn and of most meat products. Through such laws and orders, private trade by the end of 1947 had been confined to a few small shops located in isolated places where it was unprofitable for the state or cooperatives to operate stores.

Some impetus was given private trade on August 1, 1953, when Enver Hoxha announced Albania's "new course." Hoxha stated at that time that the government would take stricter measures to organize the trade network in town and countryside, to consolidate organization of consumers' cooperatives, and to encourage private trade under the strict control of the state. In subsequent months, the government took a number of measures aimed at encouraging the development of private trade by making more supplies available to existing private shops, by extending credits, and by granting tax reductions to those who opened new shops. As a consequence, a large number of people applied for, and some obtained, permission to open new retail stores, chiefly to sell foodstuffs.

Comparative Status of the Three Sectors

Table 3 gives the percentage breakdown of trade (both wholesale and retail) by sector for selected years 1948-53, compiled from sporadic official statements and data issued by the regime.

Table 3. PORTION OF TRADE BY SECTOR, SELECTED YEARS 1948-1953 *(in per cent)*

Year	*State*	*Cooperative*	*Private*
1948	28.0	29.0	43.0
1950	32.0	45.0	23.0
1951	33.0	45.0	22.0
1953	38.3	45.8	15.9

The regime has also given some figures on the volume of trade since the end of World War II. Thus, in a speech in Tirana on April 18, 1953, Shehu declared that in 1947 goods turnover (probably retail trade) amounted to 2,295 million leks; in 1950, 5,600 million leks, and in 1953, 9,238 million leks. He also stated that the trade turnover figure per capita, as compared with 1947,was 228,2 per cent in 1950 and 351.7 per cent in 1953. On November 28, 1954, Hoxha declared that the over-all trade turnover (presumably wholesale and retail trade) increased from 4.5 billion leks in 1945 to 7.3 billion leks in 1950, and to 12.5 billion leks in 1954 (probably at current rather than stable prices). During the same speech, Hoxha claimed that, compared with 1950, the supply per capita in 1954 had increased as follows, in per cent: sugar, 56.3; fats, 92.3; macaroni, 37.1; meat and fish, 9.5; woolen fabrics, 72.7; cheese, 110.0; shoes, 111.0; sandals, 200.0; laundry soap, 77.8; cotton goods, 81.8.

The Three Principal Markets

There were in Albania in 1955 three principal markets in retail trade: guaranteed (rationed), free, and barter. The guaranteed market handles rationed supplies, which included until January 3,

1956 basic foodstuffs, clothing, fuels, and shoes; these are sold chiefly by state stores to workers and civil servants who hold ration cards. Clothing and footwear were derationed in January 1956.

The free, or commercial, market handles all kinds of goods, including as a rule those rationed, but at from five to ten times the prices in the guaranteed market. These supplies are purchased both by those who have been denied ration cards and by those who possess these cards.

The barter market dealt with the exchange of industrial goods for agricultural products; that is, the farmer was given a certain amount of such necessities as kerosene, salt, sugar, soap, cloth, and so forth in exchange for specified amounts of agricultural and dairy products. This market was abolished early in January 1956.

A fourth market, usually known as *dyqanet speciale* (dollar stores), sells only for precious metals and foreign hard currency, generally American dollars. Those who possess such currency can purchase practically everything they need at these stores, at prices lower than those on the free market, but much higher than those on the guaranteed market. However, since gold and dollars are now very scarce in Albania, this market represents only an insignificant share in the total trade.

Both the free and guaranteed markets are under constant criticism by the Communist press because of their failure to supply the people with foodstuffs. The state stores and the cooperatives are especially accused of making little effort to accumulate and distribute food products. According to newspaper articles, supplies are inadequate and of low quality. Vegetables and fruits rot in state depots and are thrown away. Irregularities in fixing prices in the free market, desire for big profits on the part of the cooperatives, and speculation are other factors held responsible for contributing to the low efficiency of the trade sector.

Finance Before the Communists

The Monetary System

In 1925, Albania adopted the gold standard, with a gold franc of 0.2903229 grams of fine gold as the monetary unit. Prior to this time, Albania had neither metallic nor paper currency of its own; gold pieces and silver coins of adjacent nations, in particular pre-World War I Austrian crowns and silver coins of Bulgaria, Greece, and Serbia, as well as paper French francs and Italian lire, had all been used to supply the currency needs of the primitive domestic economy. For purposes of business accounting, the value of these foreign coins was established in relation to the French napoleon (pre-1914 20-franc gold piece). Foreign coins continued to circulate for some time after 1925 because the government did not issue a sufficient amount of national currency and because of the intrinsic value of the foreign coins.

According to the law of 1925, the National Bank of Albania was granted the exclusive privilege of minting and issuing gold and other coins and of issuing bank notes. The gold franc as the monetary unit was divided into leks (5 leks = 1 franc) and centimes or qintars (100 qintars = 1 franc). Prior to the Italian occupation, 100-, 2-, 5-, and 1-franc bank notes were made convertible into gold coins, foreign bank notes of gold standard countries, and checks or telegraphic transfers drawn on funds available on current account in banks in foreign countries having a sufficiently stable currency in general demand.

During the Italian occupation (1939-43), several changes were introduced in the Albanian currency system. The Italo-Albanian Economic, Customs, and Currency Convention, concluded soon after the occupation began, provided that the provisions of the 1925 law which established the Albanian monetary system were to be considered repealed or modified insofar as they were in conflict with terms of the Convention. The National Bank of Albania was obligated to use the facilities of the Royal Italian Mint for the minting of Albanian coins and to adopt the metals and alloys used in the minting of Italian coins. Several denominations of coins were withdrawn from circulation and replaced by issues stamped with a likeness of King Victor Emmanuel of Italy and the Fascist insignia.

The Banking Convention concluded on March 15, 1925 created the National Bank of Albania and required that the Bank maintain a metallic reserve (gold and silver coin and bullion) of one third the note issue, and that the Bank's statutes prescribe definite rules for the remaining reserves. However, the Organic Law of the National Bank, approved in July 1925, ignored the directive to provide for full coverage and even extended the definition of "metallic reserve" to include "stable and secure foreign exchange up to two-thirds of the required metallic reserve." If the reserves fell below one third of the note issue, the Bank was to increase its discount rate accordingly. Since the National Bank of Albania was for all practical purposes an Italian institution, its gold reserve was kept in Rome. At the time of the Italian occupation, the gold stock of the National Bank of Albania, amounting to 7.6 million francs, was confiscated by the Italians, although the Bank continued to carry this gold on its books as an asset.

After the Italian occupation, the metallic reserve requirement was suspended, and the provision was made that future reserve for bank notes would consist of Italian lira notes or other credits on the Bank of Italy. Bank notes were made exchangeable at the National Bank upon demand for "check payment orders to the equivalent amount of Italian lira to be utilized in Italy," and into other currencies consistent with the National Bank's provisions concerning dealings in foreign exchange and currency. The Albanian franc was pegged to the Italian lira at a rate of 1 franc to 6.25 lire.

Currency Circulation

Prior to April 1939, the National Bank of Albania kept an adequate metallic reserve to cover note circulation. In addition, the Bank's reserve position was strengthened by its foreign securities, consisting mostly of Italian treasury bonds, and foreign exchange, predominantly Italian lira (see Table 4).

Table 4. MONEY CIRCULATION AND RESERVES OF THE NATIONAL BANK OF ALBANIA, 1935, 1937, AND 1938
(in thousand Albanian francs)

End of Year	*Bank Notes in Circulation*	*Total Deposits*	*Gold Reserve*	*Foreign Securities and Exchange*
1935	12,243	9,274	7,556	11,515
1937	11,131	14,280	7,583	14,988
1938	10,529	11,618	7,574	11,320

In March 1939, a few weeks before the Italian invasion, the bank note circulation totaled 11.9 million francs. By December 1939, the total had reached 26.3 million francs; by October 1940, it had reached 70 million francs; and by August 1943, just prior to Italy's capitulation, 240.6 million francs. This is more than a twentyfold increase in less than two and a half years. This increase in bank note circulation was obviously related to the presence of a large Italian army in Albania, the major cause of inflation.

Banking

Credit instruments and even the ordinary facilities of a banking system were never widely used in Albania because of the low level of commerce and industry and the low money income of the population. Banks in Albania, after it became independent and until the Communist takeover, were predominantly Italian owned or controlled.

The most important bank in the country was the National Bank of Albania, which was established by the Banking Convention. This was drafted by the League of Nations and signed on March 15, 1925 by representatives of the Albanian government and of an international financial group headed by the Italian government-controlled Credito Italiano. The nominal capital of 12.5 million gold francs was divided into 495,000 ordinary shares valued at 25 gold francs each, and 100,000 founders' shares valued at 1.25 gold francs each.

Credito Italiano, which represented Italian participation, was to have the 100,000 founders' shares and 125,000 ordinary shares, Yugoslav banking interests were to have 50,00 ordinary shares, and other foreign banking institutions 75,00 shares. Albanian participation was put at 245,000 ordinary shares, but Albanian interests failed to participate to any extent and these subscription rights were taken up by Italians. At the end of 1938, however, less than 4 million of the 12.5 million authorized capital had been paid up.

The Banking Convention of 1925 defined the "rights and powers" of the Albanian National Bank as (1) transacting banking and financial business; (2) issuing all legal tender notes, and minting and issuing all metallic currency in Albania; (3) receiving state funds on deposit and serving as the agent of the Albanian Treasury; and (4) negotiating government and municipal loans.

The first 10 per cent of the Bank's net profits was allotted to the Albanian government. In partial compensation for this payment, the Bank was exempted from the assessment of "any law or impost other than the license duty to the extent provided for by the law at present in force." Up to 1933, the Bank paid its stockholders an annual 5 per cent dividend; from 1933 to 1939, it declared dividends at the rate of 4 per cent annually.

Prior to the Italian occupation, there were three other banking institutions in Albania: (1) a branch of the Yugoslav Export Bank, established in 1934; (2) the State Agricultural Bank, organized in 1937; and (3) a branch of Banco di Napoli-Albania, opened in 1937. In addition to these institutions, a branch of the Greek Bank of Athens operated in Albania for some time during the late 1920's. After the Italian occupation of 1939, the State Agricultural Bank was taken over by the Albanian branch of the Banco di Napoli, and a branch of the Banca Nazionale del Lavoro was opened in Tirana, while the Yugoslav Bank was liquidated.

Prewar Budgets

The prewar Albanian government did not publish accounts of public revenue and expenditures after 1931. The principal domestic sources of revenue were state properties and direct and indirect taxes (notably custom duties and excise taxes on articles under government monopolies), and taxes on agricultural crops. Table 5 shows the total revenue and expenditures during the 1935/36-1938/39 period, and the respective expected deficits.

Table 5. BUDGET ESTIMATES, 1935/36-1938/39
(in gold francs)

Budget Year	*Revenue*	*Expenditures*	*Deficit*
1935/36	17,237,191	18,035,563	798,372
1936/37	22,033,896	22,299,281	295,385
1937/38	26,224,787	26,224,787	—
1938/39	28,235,400	28,565,400	330,000

The revenue figures probably included the secret, but very substantial, annual grant-in-aid from Italy for national defense, inaugurated in the latter half of the 1920's. Even with Italian aid, however, it was impossible to balance the budget in prewar years.

COMMUNIST FINANCE

Monetary and Financial Organization

The Communist regime acted with dispatch in assuming complete financial control of the country. It immediately seized the assets of the National Bank of Albania, as well as those of the Italian Banco di Napoli-Albania and Banca Nazionale del Lavoro, and nationalized all banking and credit institutions in the country. Law No. 37 of January 13, 1945 on "war profits tax" drew to the State Treasury all gold and currency reserves. Subsequent laws dealing with monetary changes, especially those promulgated on July 11, 1946 and July 9, 1947, relating to gold confiscations, state loans, and savings accounts, were intended to divest the individual citizen of all surplus cash and to prevent inflation, which would have otherwise resulted.

The Monetary System

The Organic Law of the Bank of the Albanian State provided for the creation of a bank of issue with a capital of 10 million Albanian francs, endowed with the exclusive privilege of issuing bank notes and minting coins. One of the first Communist regime measures was the prohibition of the import or export of bank notes and the export of foreign exchange and currency. Council of Ministers Order No. 7 of June 2, 1945 provided that the sale and purchase of foreign exchange and currency was to be effected only by the State Bank. Order No. 9 of June 28, 1945 called for the stamping (surcharging) of all Albanian bank notes of 20- and 100-franc denominations issued by the old National Bank of Albania and money orders of all values. All unstamped bank notes and checks were considered valueless.

The first currency issued by the regime was authorized by Law No. 45 of March 17, 1945, which authorized the State Bank to put into circulation "check-currency" totaling 8.5 million Albanian francs by surcharging checks of the former National Bank of Albania. The first major postwar currency reorganization was effected by Law No. 265 of July 11, 1946, according to which all bank notes were withdrawn from circulation. Only bank notes and metal coins of 5, 2, 1, 0.40, 0.20, and 0.10 francs were temporarily left in circulation, with the value reduced.

The State Bank was authorized to issue new 5-, 20-, 100-, and 500-franc bank notes for the withdrawn bank notes and currency. The exchange of old for new francs was set at five to one. On the day that the exchange was effected, all financial transactions were automatically reduced at the ratio of five to one; this included prices of goods of all kinds, public and private services, rents, wages, debits and credits, financial incomes, expenditures, taxes, and all other transactions.

The most devastating provision of this law ordered that the exchange of the old for new currency was to be effected at once when the sum involved did not exceed 5,000 francs (or 1,000 new francs) per family. For any person presenting more than 5,000 francs for exchange, the amount above 5,000 francs was placed on deposit in the Bank and utilized for reconstruction. The deposits were to be paid "later" on order of the Ministry of Finance. State agencies and enterprises, cooperatives, labor unions, and "political organizations" (i.e. the Communist Party) were exempted from this confiscatory clause.

A second basic currency charge was effected on July 8, 1947 when the lek (one fifth of a franc) replaced the franc. Later, a new issue was placed in circulation on the basis of nine leks to one franc (instead of five leks to one franc as formerly). The conversion made the Albanian lek equal to the Yugoslav dinar. Exchange of old currency was effected freely and without any confiscatory features.

A new monetary change was effected on September 28, 1949 (Law No. 737), removing from circulation bank notes of 10-, 50-, 500-, and 1,000-lek denomination of the 1947 issue and replacing them with a new issue of equal denomination on a one-for-one basis. The change was necessitated by the fact that the Albanian-Yugoslav economic treaty of 1946 had been abrogated by Albania on July 1, 1948.

Money Supply

The present Albanian government has never revealed the amount of leks or any other currency in circulation in Albania. When Italy capitulated in September 1943, there were 30 million Albanian paper francs in the Albanian National Bank in Tirana, an additional 120 million paper francs in the Rome branch of the Bank, and more than 400,000 gold napoleons on deposit in Rome. The Germans seized these and shipped them to Berlin. On October 30, 1944, the Germans closed the Bank in Tirana, taking 10 million Albanian paper francs and leaving an equal amount. Thus, when the Communist regime seized the Bank in November 1944, they found a total of 10 million francs, 11,000 of which were in gold napoleons and the rest in paper currency. At the end of December 1944, 240 million Albanian paper francs were in circulation, as well as an unknown but probably substantial amount of gold pieces. Through the war-profits tax, outright confiscations, and other means, the government gradually obtained most, if not all, of this gold.

Unlike the other captive states, Albania has not suffered general runaway inflation. Anti-inflationary factors in Albania have been (1) the very low wages paid the workers; (2) the very low prices paid the peasants for their agricultural products through the obligatory collective system; (3) the confiscatory measure taken in July 1946, when the old francs were changed for new francs and the people were forced to deposit all cash over 5,000 francs in the State Bank for the "country's reconstruction"; and (4) various state loans (actually forced), which have siphoned the people's savings to the State Treasury. Aside from some 160 million leks which are deposited in the government's savings deposits accounts (see below), the Albanian people now have practically no cash reserves.

Price Control and Wages

The State Control Commission, created in 1945, controlled the price structure in Communist Albania until September 15, 1948, when the Council of Ministers created the Directorate of Prices, which lasted until February 2, 1949. On April 25, 1949, another order provided that prices of all goods be set by the Council of Ministers on the basis of proposals of the Ministries of Finance and of Trade and of the local organs of these two ministries. All prices are thus set by government order, although in the free market the state and cooperative stores are granted a wide margin of profits in order to increase or decrease prices according to supply and demand, the season, and other factors. The local governmental organs, or People's Councils, have also been given some authority to set prices on certain locally produced goods, including perishables. By and large, however, the government sets the prices.

No publicity is given to price increases, but much propaganda is made by all the Communist information media when price reductions are made. Since the end of the war, three general price reductions have been announced, the last on September 30, 1954. A joint Party and government decision was published on that day providing for reduction of prices of mass consumers' goods in the private, state, cooperative, and barter markets. This reduction averaged 24 per cent in foodstuffs in the private, state, and cooperative markets; in footwear and garments, nearly 17 per cent; in construction materials, 22 per cent; and in stationery, sports, and luxury goods, nearly 30 per cent. In the barter market, the average price reduction for the industrial articles was a little above 13 per cent, the price reductions thus greatly favoring the urban population. Provision was also made for an average 10 per cent reduction in state restaurants, candy shops, and mess halls, and for a reduction in the prices of some groups of pharmaceuticals by an average of 14 to 24 per cent. The decision also provided for standardizing the prices of salt, kerosene, marmalade, knitted goods, cement bricks, and tiles, which had differed from one part of the country to another. The lists did not include such staple foodstuffs as meat, dairy products, and vegetables; provision was made for price reductions of flour but not of corn and wheat, both of which are more frequently used in rural areas than flour. Some price adjustments were effected on January 3, 1956 for clothing and footwear when these items were derationed.

Several other factors enter the Albanian real wage picture. The peasants sell a portion of their products at prices fixed in advance by the government authorities, but they also sell a part of their products at prices formed in the "free" market, which are considerably higher than the fixed prices. While peasants in general do not obtain supplies at rationed prices, agricultural workers on state farms do. Finally, while the portion of an urban worker's purchases made in the rationed as opposed to other markets cannot be accurately determined, perhaps 75 per cent of all purchases of an urban worker's family are made in the market for rationed goods.

Table 6 shows the prices in leks in the four principal markets as of July 1954, as obtained from escapees.

The Banking System

On January 13, 1945 the Anti-Fascist Council of National Liberation issued Law No. 38, which annulled the charter and shares of the National Bank of Albania, and promulgated the Organic Law of the Bank of the Albanian State (see page 214). This law provided for the creation of a bank of issue in Albania called the Bank of the Albanian State, with a capital of 10 million Albanian francs put up by the state. The assets of the National Bank of Albania were trans-

Table 6. SELECTED CONSUMERS' GOODS PRICES, JULY 6, 1954[a]
(in leks)

Products	*Rationed Price*	*Free Market*	*Barter*	*Special (Dollar Stores)*
Foodstuffs (in kilos)				
Corn bread	5	50	–	16
Wheat bread	6	70	–	11
Corn	3	60	–	–
Wheat	6	60	–	–
Rice	24	250	–	35
Beans	22	250	–	35
Sugar	40	250	90	40
Olive oil	50	280	120	65
Vegetable oil	42	280	120	–
Meat	50	150	100	140
Soap	47	280	100	–
Butter	150	550	–	300
Eggs (one)	5	12	–	8
Cheese	80	350	–	240
Macaroni	24	250	–	–
Salt	5	–	23	–
Flour	–	150	–	–
Potatoes	–	–	–	30
Olives	25	–	–	–
Coffee	–	1,200	500	500
Onions	–	25	–	–
Carrots	–	12	–	–
Cabbage	–	7-10	–	–
Apples	–	60	–	–
Lemons	–	40-50	–	–
Pears	–	80-90	–	–
Oranges	–	40-50	–	–
Grapes	–	25-80	–	–
Spinach	–	30-50	–	–
Figs (dried)	–	40-80	–	–
Shoes and Clothing				
Socks (cotton)	50	300	80	–
Rubber shoes (pair)	500	1,000	–	880
Leather shoes (pair)	–	1,200	–	–
Sandals (pair)	300	1,000	–	450
Shirt (cotton)	250	–	530	760
Woolen cloth (meter)	500	–	–	–
Cotton cloth (meter)	130	–	220	380
Overcoat	1,800	–	–	–
Ready-made suit (poor quality)	6,500	12,000	–	–
Fuels and Power				
Kerosene (liter)	25	75	–	–
Electricity (kw.)	–	9	–	–

[a] These data do not reflect the price reductions effected September 30, 1954.

ferred to the new bank, which also assumed its liabilities. The new bank was to exercise exclusive privilege of issuing bank notes and minting coins; to carry out banking activities; to accept savings deposits; to exercise the functions of fiscal agent of the government; to make advances to the government for the normal needs of the State Treasury up to 30 million Albanian francs; and to finance industrial, agricultural, mining, and other activities.

The Organic Law provided further that the bank notes are legal tender for all payments in Albania; bank notes are convertible into gold and silver coins; the Bank must maintain a reserve equal to at least one third of the bank notes issued, the coverage consisting of gold and silver or money on deposit inside or outside the state, and foreign exchange. The Albanian state was to pass to the Bank all quantities of gold, silver, and other valuable items under its jurisdiction. The convertibility of bank notes into metal coins was suspended, however, until economic and financial circumstances should permit its resumption.

The Organic Law also provided that the Bank be governed by an Administrative Council composed of nine members appointed by the Council of Ministers upon the recommendation of the Ministry of Finance. Profits go into a reserve fund of the Bank, after the deduction of 5 per cent for personnel expenses; in case of loss, the balance is covered by the Ministry of Finance. The Albanian state guarantees all obligations of the Bank assumed on the basis of the provisions of the Organic Law.

The Bank's Organic Law was amended by Law No. 184 of December 22, 1945, raising the sum that could be advanced to the state from 30 million to 100 million francs and making certain administrative changes. On August 2, 1946 (Law No. 268), the Bank was authorized to perform all activities relating to state revenues, that is, handling all receipts and making payments for the state. The Bank's Organic Law was revised on August 8, 1947 (Law No. 522) to correspond with the monetary reform effected on July 8, 1947. An important amendment to Law No. 522 was adopted on November 26, 1949 (Law No. 745), authorizing the Bank to advance credits to private farmers. Previously, this privilege was confined to state and collective farms.

Early in 1948, a savings section was created at the State Bank, and on August 10, 1949 the Directorate of Savings was created to float state loans. The Directorate of Savings was authorized to open agencies in all parts of the country. Every citizen is allowed to deposit as much as he wishes in savings accounts, except in those whose interest is based on lotteries, which are limited to 50,000 leks. All deposits are guaranteed by the state. Although nominally the deposits in these accounts are voluntary, nearly all workers are forced to deposit about 10 per cent of their earnings through payroll deduction plans. Radio Tirana on May 4, 1954 gave the following figures for savings deposited by the people in the State Bank since 1946:

Year	*Leks*
1946	2,580,000
1950	38,788,000
1952	107,600,000
1953	138,541,000
1954 (May)	159,000,000

State loans, however, were a much heavier burden on the savings of individuals (see below page 222).

Government Finance and Fiscal Policy

Budgetory Institutions and Regulations

The Ministry of Finance has the over-all responsibility for preparing national and local budget estimates, collecting state revenues, and executing other fiscal duties. On August 3, 1946, Law No. 271 described procedures for state financial control. Article 1 of this law provided that national budget estimates be prepared by the Budget Directorate at the Ministry of Finance. Law No. 582 of February 2, 1948 provided that each ministry, state institution, and local People's Councils prepare its own budget estimates and submit them for inspection to the Ministry of Finance. The latter then formulates a national budget and sends it to the Council of Ministers, which submits it to the People's Assembly for final approval.

The annual budgets issued since 1945 have described sources of the general state revenues. Thus, the 1945/46 budget (April 1, 1945 –March 31, 1946) provided for revenue of 1,016,220,000 francs for the national budget and 12,000,000 francs for local budgets. The sources of state revenue for that year were as follows:

Source of Revenue	*Francs*
State properties	45,200,000
Direct taxes	71,500,000
Indirect taxes	23,600,000
State monopolies	235,200,000
Stamp taxes	7,000,000
Licenses	2,800,000
Postal-telegraph	5,000,000
Unspecified	11,200,000
Special war profits tax	600,000,000
From state enterprises	14,720,000
Total	1,016,220,000

The budget for 1946/47 was prepared after the monetary reform of July 11, 1946, when five old francs were exchanged for one new franc. The sources of state revenue for the 1946/47 budget were as follows:

Source of Revenue	*Leks*
Revenue from state domains and state enterprises	102,237,400
Duties and taxes	48,850,000
Revenue from the State Treasury	20,000
Revenue from sundry sources	380,900
Special revenue (probably credits)	24,000,000
Total	175,488,300

The state revenue for the 1948 budget (prepared after the lek replaced the franc as the national currency) was shown as 6,231,932,000 leks, some three billion of which represented a paper credit from Yugoslavia. Turnover tax, revenue from state enterprises, income taxes, and agricultural taxes represented the main sources of revenue.

Since 1949 the Albanian budget has contained no details on sources of income; it has confined itself to giving the total revenues and expenditures (see below page 223). During discussions in the People's Assembly, it has been revealed that in 1949 some 38 per cent of the budget revenue was represented by credits and grants-in-aid from Soviet orbit countries; in 1951, 18.4 per cent of the revenue represented credits and grants from these countries; at present, some 20 per cent of the budget revenue comes from these sources. Most revenue since 1950 has derived from the turnover tax (nearly 40 per cent of the total), state enterprises, the income tax, and the tax on agriculture. In addition, the state periodically extracts large loans from the public.

Expenditures

The budgets of 1945/46, 1946/47, and 1948 contained details on the allocation of state expenditures, but since 1949 only general percentages have been given. The expenditures of the local governments in 1946/47 were placed at 41,216,900 francs. A breakdown of state expenditures as given in the 1946/47 budget is provided in Table 7.

Percentages as given since 1949 have indicated that the armed forces (exclusive of the police and security forces) have been allotted from 14 per cent in 1949 to 11 per cent in 1954 of the total expenditures, with the rest going to the national economy and construction (usually about 40 per cent), agriculture, social and cultural activities, public health, and state administration.

Table 7. State Expenditures, by Governmental Branch, 1946/47 Budget
(in francs)

Governmental Branch	*Expenditure*
Supreme Institution	
People's Assembly	507,800
Attorney General	736,000
Planning Commission	896,000
Prime Ministry	5,379,040
Control Commission	315,200
Ministry	
Finance	23,413,540
Justice	2,217,000
Interior	12,913,000
Foreign Affairs	2,858,000
Public Works	30,509,480
Agriculture	7,390,800
Health	10,264,000
Economy	15,828,200
Education	6,785,400
National Defense	107,200,000
Total	227,213,460

In the 1954 budget, financing of the "people's" economy represents 39 per cent of the total expenditures; defense expenditures represent 11 per cent; culture, education, health, and social assistance represent about 20 per cent; and the rest represents investments in agriculture and land improvement, expenditures for the state administration, and miscellaneous expenses.

Summary of Budgets, 1945-1954

Table 8 lists the revenues and expenditures as given in the Communist budgets, 1945/46-54. With few exceptions, the regime has so padded the budgets that they are either balanced or show a paper surplus.

Since no data are available on the sources of state revenue or on state expenditures, no further analysis of the budget figures given in Table 8 is possible.

State Loans

A part of government revenue in recent years has derived from government loans. In the four government loans launched since 1949, the following amounts have been realized: first loan (July 1949),

305,240,000 leks; second loan (February 1952), 405,135,800 leks; third loan (March 1953), 501,453,950 leks; fourth loan (March 1954), 458,000,000 leks. Needless to say, these were forced loans which confiscated the bulk of the people's savings.

Table 8. REVENUES AND EXPENDITURES, 1945/46-1954 BUDGETS

Year	*Budget*	*Revenue*	*Expenditures*
		(in francs)	
1945/46	National	1,016,220,000	1,016,220,000
	Local	12,000,000	137,495,000
1946/47	National	175,488,300	227,213,460
	Local	41,216,900	41,216,900
		(in leks)	
1948	National and local	6,846,837,000	6,846,837,000
1949	National and local	6,550,000,000	6,550,000,000
1950	National and local	7,800,000,000	7,700,000,000
1951	National and local	9,500,000,000	9,100,000,000
1952	National and local	10,300,000,000	10,200,000,000
1953	National and local	11,350,000,000	11,250,000,000
1954	National and local	10,200,000,000	9,900,000,000

14. FOREIGN TRADE

ALBANIA'S foreign trade has been conditioned by her political relations with other countries. Before World War II, Italy received the greatest amount of Albania's exports and was the primary source of her imports. In the early postwar period Yugoslavia took Italy's place, followed by the Soviet Union after the Tito-Cominform break. Albania's foreign trade has essentially been a colonial exchange of goods with these countries.

BEFORE THE COMMUNISTS

Constant Trade Imbalance and Italian Loans

Before World War II, Albania had a large import surplus, the value of imports being almost triple that of exports. Both Albanian exports and imports expanded in value from the end of World War I until 1929; thereafter, they fell to a depression low in 1934 (see Table 1). After the depression low of 1934, foreign trade began to rise, and in 1939, the first year of Italian occupation, imports were almost twice as large as those of the preceding year. This growth was accounted for mainly by the accelerated program of public works and industrialization initiated by the Italians and the consequent large imports of heavy machinery.

From 1925 to April 1939, Albania was on the gold standard, and its currency was considered one of the most stable in Europe, although it was of small international significance. The National Bank of Albania placed no restrictions on foreign exchange operations in the Albanian gold franc, and continued to supply foreign exchange for the needs of the Albanian economy even after Great Britain and the United States abandoned the gold standard. After 1933, the exchange rate between the dollar and the Albanian franc was one to 3.3.

Eighty per cent of all exports consisted of agricultural products, while machinery and manufactured articles constituted the bulk of the imports. Until the early 1930's, the unfavorable balance of trade was offset largely by emigrants' remittances, especially from the United States, and by tourist trade. However, these two sources of foreign exchange declined materially after 1930, and Albania's large import surplus was maintained by Italian loans and subsidies.

Italian capital was supplied chiefly in the form of long-term loans to the Albanian government by the Italian Società per lo Sviluppo

Economico dell'Albania (SVEA) (Company for the Economic Development of Albania), which was set up in 1925 to grant Albania a loan of 50 million gold francs for large-scale public works and for agricultural and industrial development. According to official Italian accounts, the Italian government by December 31, 1945 had expended more than 62 million francs on this loan, in principal and in service costs.

Table 1. FOREIGN TRADE, 1927-1939
(in thousand Albanian gold francs)

Year	*Imports*	*Exports*	*Excess of Imports*	*Value of Exports in Per Cent of Imports*
1927	24,682	11,107	13,575	45.0
1928	32,312	14,694	17,618	45.5
1929	38,644	14,683	23,961	38.0
1930	33,289	12,352	20,937	37.1
1931	29,513	7,509	22,004	25.4
1932	22,814	4,500	18,314	19.7
1933	15,938	5,746	10,192	36.1
1934	12,332	4,284	8,048	34.7
1935	13,730	6,037	7,693	44.0
1936	16,778	7,435	9,343	44.3
1937	20,316	10,175	10,141	50.1
1938	22,668	9,129	13,539	40.3
1939	40,601	9,467	31,134	23.3
Average	24,894	9,009	15,885	36.2

In addition to the SVEA funds, the Italian government in 1931 loaned 100 million gold francs to Albania for public works, economic development, and balancing the budget. On the basis of a later agreement, the Italian government in 1936 advanced Albania 9 million gold francs, of which 2.8 million were assigned to establish the Albanian State Agricultural Bank. Under this agreement, the Italian government also advanced Albania an agricultural loan of 10 million gold francs for livestock raising and agriculture. The total payment made by Italy on this 10 million franc loan amounted to 31,496,000 lire (the official exchange rate in 1939 was 6.25 lire to one gold franc), or slightly more than 5 million francs. By the same agreement, a loan was advanced to Albania to complete the construction work on the port of Durrës. On paper, this loan was made by Banco di Napoli, but in reality it was made by the Italian Treasury. The total payments, according to official Italian claims, made by Italy on the Durrës loan amounted to 7,663,053 lire.

Albania's Foreign Trade by Country

As shown in Table 2, Italy far outranked every other country in Albania's trade, but occupied a much more prominent position as a market for Albanian exports than as a source of its imports. Throughout the 1930-36 period, Italy, Greece, and the United States together

Table 2. DISTRIBUTION OF FOREIGN TRADE, BY COUNTRY, 1937 AND 1938

Country of Origin or Destination	*Value in Thousand Albanian Gold Francs*		*Per Cent of Total*	
	1937	*1938*	*1937*	*1938*
	Imports			
Italy	4,881	8,327	24.0	36.7
Yugoslavia	2,272	2,520	11.2	11.1
Romania	2,173	2,285	10.7	10.1
United States	933	1,355	4.6	6.0
Germany	957	1,255	4.7	5.6
Japan	1,488	799	7.3	3.5
England	1,000	786	4.9	3.5
Greece	639	735	3.1	3.3
Other countries	5,973	4,578	29.5	20.2
Total	20,316	22,668	100.0	100.0
	Exports			
Italy	7,998	6,133	78.6	67.2
Greece	928	1,424	9.1	15.6
United States	861	435	8.5	4.8
England	69	169	0.7	1.9
Yugoslavia	72	66	0.7	0.7
Other countries	247	902	2.4	9.8
Total	10,175	9,129	100.0	100.0

accounted for more than 96 per cent of Albania's export trade, with Italy absorbing over 65 per cent, and Greece and the United States each about 15 per cent. In the same period, the average distribution of Albania's import trade by origin was as follows, in percentages: Italy, 37.9; England, 8.1; Yugoslavia, 7.2; United States, 6.8; Germany, 5.7; Japan, 5.7 and Greece, 4.1. Japan rose from a negligible position to second place during the years 1934-36. As the political ties between Italy and Albania suffered in the early thirties, Albania's imports from Italy declined until 1936. In 1938, however, Italy supplied about 37 per cent of Albania's imports and Yugoslavia 11 per cent of the total.

Principal Imports and Exports

As indicated on Table 3, in 1939 Albania's leading imports were petroleum products; sugar and condiments; cotton and cotton goods; iron and steel; wood and wooden products; wool and woolen goods; cereals and other agricultural products; dyestuffs and chemicals; automobiles, trucks, and other means of transport; agricultural implements; and paper and paper articles.

Table 3. IMPORTS OF PRINCIPAL COMMODITIES, 1938 AND 1939

Commodity	*Value in Thousand Albanian Gold Francs*		*Per Cent of Total Imports*	
	1938	*1939*	*1938*	*1939*
Petroleum products	2,302	4,320	10.2	10.6
Sugar and condiments	1,107	3,000	4.9	7.4
Cotton and cotton goods	4,832	2,100	21.3	5.2
Iron and steel	1,255	1,800	5.5	4.4
Wood and wooden objects	831	1,500	3.7	3.7
Dyestuffs and chemicals	871	1,470	3.8	3.6
Cereals and other agricultural products	3,351	1,360	14.8	3.3
Wool and woolen goods	1,232	1,200	5.4	3.0
Automobiles and other means of transport	838	1,200	3.7	3.0
Paper and paper goods	712	1,200	3.1	3.0
Machines, motors, and parts	738	785	3.3	1.9
Leather goods	636	630	2.8	1.6
Other commodities	3,963	20,036	17.5	49.3
Total	22,668	40,601	100.0	100.0

Table 4. EXPORTS OF PRINCIPAL COMMODITIES, 1938 AND 1939

Commodity	*Value in Thousand Albanian Gold Francs*		*Per Cent of Total Exports*	
	1938	*1939*	*1938*	*1939*
Raw hides and pelts	1,456	2,395	15.9	25.3
Wool and woolen goods	322	1,396	3.5	14.7
Dairy products and fish	1,748	1,366	19.2	14.4
Livestock	804	169	8.8	1.8
Wood and charcoal	695	88	7.6	0.9
Cereals, farm produce, and fruit	1,393	66	15.3	0.7
Combustibles	204	46	2.2	0.5
Tobacco	216	6	2.4	0.1
Dyestuffs and chemicals	534	......	5.8	......
Other commodities	1,757	3,935	19.3	41.6
Total	9,129	9,467	100.0	100.0

Albania's leading exports in order of value, as shown in Table 4, were raw hides and pelts, wool and woolen goods, dairy products and fish, livestock, wood and charcoal, cereals, farm produce and fruit, combustibles, tobacco, and dyestuffs and chemicals.

Wartime Developments

From April 1939 to September 1943, when for all practical purposes Albania was a part of Italy, Albanian foreign trade expanded greatly because of Italian civilian and military operations in Albania. On the basis of an agreement between Italy and the National Bank of Albania, concluded in April 1939 after the union of Albania with Italy, Albania abandoned the gold standard, and the rate of exchange between the new Albanian franc and the Italian lira was fixed at 6.25 lire to the franc. Italy placed no special limitations on Albania's economic relations with foreign countries. After the occupation, Italy sent to Albania supplies of all kinds, including large quantities of foodstuffs and consumers' goods.

According to Italian official figures, after 1939 Albania imported from Italy much more than it exported, the balance for the 1939-43 period being 600 to 650 million Albanian francs, or some four billion lire. Albania derived a twofold advantage from this trade imbalance: she received goods that were not obtainable on any other market at lower prices than on the world market, and she paid for them in her national currency. In point of fact, Albania experienced great prosperity in the 1939-43 period, and many of the country's merchants became rich, by Albanian standards, by exporting supplies imported from Italy to Greece and Yugoslavia.

Foreign Trade, 1944-1948

In August 1944, an agreement was signed in Bari, Italy, between the Albanian National Liberation Army and the Allied Command in Italy for supplying the Albanian Partisan forces with war material. In April 1945, an agreement was concluded between the Allied Military Liaison in Italy and Hoxha's government for sending relief supplies, chiefly food, to Albania. In August 1945, an agreement was concluded between the Hoxha government and UNRRA for delivering relief supplies to Albania. In the course of its operations in Albania between August 1945 and early 1947, UNRRA delivered to that country 130,048 gross long tons of various supplies to the value of $26,251,000. UNRRA supplies gave a tremendous lift to the Albanian economy at a time when no other foreign source of vital supplies was available. With the exception of some imports from Yugoslavia, practically all Albanian imports during that time came from UNRRA. A trade agreement envisaging a two-way exchange of goods to the value of $2,560,000 was signed between Italy and Albania in December 1954, but did not become effective until October 1955. In 1955, Albania also concluded commercial agreements with private firms in West Germany and Switzerland.

State Monopoly

Under the Communist regime, foreign trade has become a state monopoly. On December 15, 1944, just two weeks after the Communists seized control of the country, the Presidium of the Anti-Fascist Council of National Liberation promulgated Law No. 20, Article 2 of which stated that the "export and import of all commodities, whether agricultural products or manufactured articles, are prohibited, except by special permit of the Ministry of Economy" (*Gazeta Zyrtare*, December 23, 1944). Article 5 of the Albanian Constitution of March 1946 provided that "foreign trade is under the control of the state." On June 2, 1945, Minister of Finance Ramadan Çitaku issued Order No. 7 introducing strict exchange controls and providing that the selling and purchasing of foreign currency and foreign exchange be effected only by the State Bank (*Gazeta Zyrtare*, June 9, 1945).

From 1946 to 1948, all Albanian imports and exports were handled by the Albanian-Yugoslav Company for Imports and Exports, a joint state agency of the Albanian and Yugoslav governments. After 1948, they were controlled by the Albanian Ministry of Trade. The principal agency of the Ministry of Trade is Ndërmarja Shtetërore Import-Eksport (NSHIE—State Enterprise Import-Export), which was created by Council of Ministers' Order No. 17 of May 16, 1949. Article 1 of this Order says that NSHIE operates on the basis of *hazreshiote* (Russian abbreviation *khozraschët*, literally "economic accounting"), under the direction of the foreign trade sector in the Ministry of Trade (*Gazeta Zyrtare*, May 25, 1949). An organization known as Ndërmarja Shtetërore Shpërndarjes Mallrave Importit (NSHSHMI—State Enterprise for Distribution of Imported Goods), with headquarters in Durrës, handles the distribution of all imported commodities.

Merging of Albanian and Yugoslav Economies

At its very inception, the Tirana regime became a full-fledged satellite of Communist Yugoslavia, with which it had the closest political and economic ties. As early as March 1945, a commercial treaty was signed between Albania and Yugoslavia. Petroleum, wool, hides, consumers' goods from the then well-stocked Albanian warehouses, and dairy products were sent to Yugoslavia in exchange for corn and army equipment. In May of the same year, the Albanian Minister of Finance and representatives of the Albanian State Bank arranged for closer economic collaboration and for printing the new Albanian francs, a shipment of which was delivered in Tirana from Belgrade in June 1945, but not put into circulation until July 1946.

During 1946, the Tirana government concluded a series of trade and commercial agreements with the Yugoslav government. The most important was the economic treaty of July 1946, which provided for the establishment of an agency to coordinate the economic plants of the two countries; to equate the Albanian currency unit, the lek, with the Yugoslav dinar; to direct the flow of Yugoslav economic aid to Albania; to introduce into Albania the Yugoslav price system; to abolish the customs frontier and to create a customs union between the two countries; and to create a joint Albanian-Yugoslav Customs Commission, seated in Albania, to supervise the single customs area.

The economic treaty of July 1946 was followed by the agreement on economic cooperation of November 28, 1946 which provided for the following: (1) organization for a period of thirty years of joint Albanian-Yugoslav companies for railroads, petroleum, mines and metals, electrification, shipping, import-export, and Albanian-Yugoslav banks; (2) training of Albanian specialists in Yugoslavia, and Yugoslav provision of technical aid and experts for Albanian agriculture and industry; (3) a Yugoslav credit to Albania for the purchase of machines and tools; and (4) formation of the above-mentioned joint companies on a parity basis, with an Albanian option to purchase the Yugoslav shares at the end of thirty years. Thus, for all practical purposes, the Albanian economy became part and parcel of the Yugoslav economy. This lasted until July 1, 1948, when the Albanian government, following the expulsion of Yugoslavia from the Cominform, abrogated all its agreements with Yugoslavia.

In their White Paper on Yugoslav-Albanian relations from 1939 to 1948, which was published in 1949, the Yugoslavs declared that from the summer of 1945 to June 1948 they contributed 704,991,000 dinars (roughly $14,099,820 at the official rate of exchange of 50 dinars to one dollar) for material for the Albanian armed forces. In 1946, they gave Albania 20,000 metric tons of wheat and corn. On the occasion of the widespread floods in Albania in the fall of 1946, the Yugoslav government collected 52 million dinars for "aid" for the Albanian people, although the Albanian government later stated that the Yugoslavs considered this a loan, not a grant. On June 12, 1947, an agreement was signed between the two countries for a Yugoslav credit to Albania of 2 billion dinars. In a speech before the Albanian People's Assembly on July 17, 1947, Deputy Minister of Finance Abdyl Kellëzi said that the 2 billion lek (or dinar) Yugoslav credit represented 57.73 per cent of the Albanian state income for 1947. In their White Paper, the Yugoslavs maintained that by June 1948 over 1.6 billion of the 2 billion dinar credit had been used by Albania.

The Yugoslav leaders now claim that they complained to Stalin in 1947 that Albania constituted too heavy a drain on the Yugoslav economy and asked him for assistance. Stalin's answer was allegedly: "Swallow Albania."

Albanian-Yugoslav trade relations were reinstated in May 1955, when a trade agreement involving exchange of goods to the amount of $1,5000,000 for both countries was concluded. A similar agreement for 1956 was signed in Belgrade on December 30.

Foreign Trade since 1948

Economic Assistance from the Soviet Orbit

Immediately after the break with Yugoslavia on July 1, 1948, the Albanian rulers requested economic aid from the Soviet Union and its captive states. The Soviet orbit countries have been subsidizing Albania's economy ever since that time. In January 1950, the Tirana press admitted that nearly 37 per cent of Albania's national budget of 6.5 billion leks for 1949 had been provided by the Soviet Union and the People's Democracies. The 1950 national budget of 7.8 billion leks was balanced, according to the Albanian Minister of Finance, by "substantial aid supplied primarily by the USSR and the People's Democracies." In the 1951 budget of 9.5 billion leks, 18.4 per cent of total revenue was obtained from the Soviet bloc countries; in the 1952 budget of 10.3 billion, 15 per cent of the total was in the form of subsidies. In the 1953 budget of 11.3 billion leks and in the 1954 budget of 10.2 billion leks, no subsidy figures were revealed, but statements were made to the effect that a considerable part consisted of grants from the Soviet countries. However, in the 1955 budget, 2.4 billion leks out of a total income of 12.3 billion leks were derived from "imports" (credits and grants) from the Soviet bloc countries.

Albania was admitted to the Soviet-sponsored Council of Economic Mutual Assistance in February 1949, and has signed a number of trade and credit agreements with the Soviet Union and the People's Democracies. The texts of these agreements have never been published; usually they have been announced by short communiqués giving the date the agreement was signed and a few details of its provisions. Although most aid to Albania has apparently been given in the form of grants to keep the country's sagging economy viable, some of it is based on exchange of goods and on long-term loans.

The total amount of aid given to Albania has never been published, although the Tirana press frequently describes the types of goods sent to Albania. An Albanian Telegraphic Agency communiqué of April 1, 1949 said that the trade agreements for 1949 between Albania and Poland, Czechoslovakia, Hungary, and Romania provided for a total of $12,080,000 in goods and loans (*Bashkimi,* April 2, 1949). On November 30, 1949, Tuk Jakova revealed that during Premier Hoxha's state visit to Moscow in March-April 1949, he had obtained from the Kremlin a credit for 1949-52, and that in the fall of the same year Poland, Czechoslovakia, Hungary, and Romania had agreed to grant Albania credits for the period 1950-52 (*Bashkimi,* December 1, 1949). In 1952-53, these countries gave Albania additional credits for the years 1953-55. During a state visit to Sofia, Premier Shehu signed on October 28, 1954 a trade agreement with the Bulgarian government providing for a long-term Bulgarian credit to Albania; this was the first Bulgarian grant, so far as is known.

That most of the "credits" granted to Albania by the Soviet Union and its captive states are subsidies is confirmed by Albanian officials, who have repeatedly admitted that Albania is unable to meet its export commitments, consisting chiefly of oil, chrome ore, bitumen, copper, raw hides, wood products, and some foodstuffs. This subsidy in reality represents Albania's current deficit in the balance of payments. It probably amounts to approximately 20 million dollars annually.

Trade and Credit Agreements

During the early stages of the establishment of economic relations between Albania and the Soviet Union, Bulgaria, Czechoslovakia, Eastern Germany, Hungary, Poland and Romania, some details were given concerning the amount and volume of trade involved. Since 1950, however, the information provided has been in general terms and has dealt only with the commodities supplied by the respective countries.

Soviet Union. On July 14, 1947 an Albanian state delegation headed by Premier Hoxha visited Moscow. On July 27, a Soviet-Albanian communiqué stated that "in view of the destruction suffered by Albania during the war and in answer to a request of the Albanian government, the Soviet Union will furnish Albania equipment for light industry and agricultural machinery, on which matter an appropriate agreement has been concluded." A few weeks after Albania broke with Tito (July 1, 1948), Albania dispatched to Moscow a trade delegation headed by the Minister of Industry, Tuk Jakova.

On his return to Albania, Jakova revealed that the Soviet Union undertook to supply Albania large quantities of grain, textiles, trucks, and machinery, and that Albania would receive a sugar refinery with an annual capacity of 10,000 metric tons, a textile mill with a yearly capacity of 20 million meters of cloth, and a large and modern hides and leather tannery. These factories were subsequently built in Albania. By the end of 1948, the Soviet Union had delivered to Albania the following supplies: about 520 metric tons of steel of the 888 tons provided by the treaty; 2,600,000 meters of various textiles, the full amount promised in the treaty; 110 trucks out of 221; and 16,568 metric tons of wheat of the promised 30,000 metric tons.

During a visit to the Soviet Union by Premier Enver Hoxha in March-April 1949, an agreement was signed for the delivery to Albania of equipment and material on credit, and a protocol was concluded on mutual trade deliveries for 1949 (*Zëri i Popullit,* April 13, 1949). On his return from Moscow, Hoxha declared that the Soviet government had again granted his country a "most precious loan" for a large hydroelectric power station, a textile mill, other factories, oil field and mining equipment, and railroad materials. The Soviet government also undertook to supply Albania a quantity of consumers' goods under "very favorable conditions," said Hoxha. Since 1949, a number of other credit and trade agreements have been concluded between Albania and the Soviet Union, but no details have been published.

Bulgaria. The first postwar trade agreement between Albania and Bulgaria was signed at Tirana on August 3, 1948. This was to be valid until the end of 1949. Under it, Albania undertook to supply Bulgaria with mineral products, especially crude oil, asphalt, coal, and chrome ore, as well as olives and cotton, while Bulgaria promised to send Albania seeds, textiles, chemicals, construction materials, and foodstuffs. Trade and payment agreements have been concluded annually between the two countries since 1949, and, as indicated above, an agreement provided for Bulgarian credits to Albania was signed in Sofia on October 28, 1954.

Czechoslovakia. Albania and Czechoslovakia concluded their first postwar trade agreement on March 12, 1949. This agreement, which involved a total of $3,350,000, provided for Czechoslovak exports to Albania during 1949 in the value of 180 million crowns (approximately $3,600,000 at the official rate of exchange of 50 crowns to one dollar), of which 135 million represented a credit to Albania (with interest at 2 per cent per annum) to be repaid during the 1951-55 period by deliveries of copper, chrome ore, crude oil, walnut timber, and other industrial timber. During 1949, Czechoslovakia agreed to deliver to Albania consumers' goods, such as textiles, school and office supplies, glass products and jewelry, porcelain, umbrellas, trucks, electrical and telecommunication supplies, and varying amounts of machinery. The contemplated shipments from Albania to Czechoslovakia for 1949 were valued at 45 million crowns. By October 1949, however, Czech exports to Albania and Albanian exports to Czechoslovakia were revised to 150 million crowns and 30 million crowns respectively. Since then, annual agreements have been signed between the two countries.

Eastern Germany. Eastern Germany and Albania signed their first postwar trade agreement on March 27, 1951; this provided for a 50 million ruble (4 rubles to one dollar at the official rate of exchange) credit to Albania and was to be valid until the end of 1955. Annual agreements and protocols have been signed since then, providing for implementation of the 1951 credit agreement. In 1951, some 10 million rubles' worth of goods were shipped to Albania. The protocol signed between the two countries on February 26, 1952 provided that nearly 18 million rubles' worth of Eastern German goods be shipped to Albania that year. Two other trade agreements were signed in Berlin on February 2, 1953, the first covering 1953 and the second relating to trade exchanges in 1954 and 1955.

On August 4, 1951, Radio Tirana announced that the first goods from Eastern Germany had arrived in Albania, including trucks and agricultural machines. Under the agreement of February 26, 1952, Eastern Germany undertook to supply Albania with industrial equipment, machines, electrotechnical articles, precision instruments, chemical products, and fertilizers, while Albania promised to deliver to Eastern Germany ores, timber, tobacco, and agricultural products. The 1953 agreement, according to a Radio Tirana broadcast of February 2, 1953, provided for delivery by Albania to Eastern Germany of nonferrous metals, chrome ore, industrial and medicinal crops, tobacco, and other products, and for shipment by Eastern Germany to Albania of industrial goods, electrical and food-processing machinery, laboratory and veterinary equipment, medicines, and other items.

Hungary. The first postwar trade agreement between Hungary and Albania, signed in Budapest on March 14, 1949, provided for an exchange of goods and credit in the amount of $1,730,000 in 1949. Hungary undertook to send Albania machinery, spare parts, and consumers' goods. The trade agreements signed annually since 1949 have not revealed the amounts involved.

Poland. The first postwar trade agreement between Albania and Poland was signed in Warsaw on January 22, 1949. Poland undertook to export to Albania rolling stock, textiles, machinery, tools, and electrical equipment. In return, Albania was to export to Poland copper, pyrites, cotton, crude oil, tobacco, and other commodities. Total trade for 1949 was to exceed $4,000,000. Koço Tashko, Albanian Deputy Minister of Foreign Affairs who headed the trade delegation to Warsaw, declared on his return to Tirana that Albania had obtained "large amounts of credits" from Poland for the purchase of two diesel-powered ships of 650 metric tons each, railroad passenger and freight cars, and equipment for a factory to produce barrels. The trade agreement for 1950 signed between the two countries on November 22, 1949 provided for Polish exports to Albania of "considerable" quantities of iron goods, sugar, textiles, chemicals, and other articles, and for Albanian exports to Poland of crude oil, ore, cotton, and other goods. The annual trade agreements concluded since 1950 between the two countries have provided for the export and import of similar products, but have not revealed the amounts involved.

Romania. The first postwar trade agreement between Albania and Romania was signed in Bucharest on April 12, 1949. This provided for the exchange of 3 million dollars' worth of goods and for an unspecified Romanian credit to Albania. Romania agreed to supply Albania with gasoline, grain, timber, cement, chemical products, paper, ink, etc., and Albania was to export to Romania chrome ore, cotton, raw hides, and processed food products (*Bashkimi,* April 2, 1949). According to *Bashkimi* of January 24, 1950, in November 1949 an additional pact for the exchange of goods for the year 1950 totaling 15 million rubles (about $3,700,000) was concluded. On the basis of this pact, Romania was to export to Albania petroleum products, paper, cereals, foodstuffs, and construction materials; Albania in return undertook to supply Romania with copper, chrome ore, raw cotton, hides, and citrus fruit.

Foreign Trade Volume and Consumption

The October 1952 issue of the Soviet journal, *Vneshniaia Torgovlia* (Foreign Trade), stated that 100 per cent of Albania's foreign trade was with the Soviet bloc countries from 1949 through 1951, even though in 1948 only 38 per cent of Albanian foreign trade had been with these countries and in 1937 only 5 per cent.

Radio Moscow on August 18, 1953 broadcast a TASS dispatch, datelined Tirana, which said that Albania imported from the Soviet Union mainly equipment for complete industrial plants, which in 1951 accounted for 42 per cent of its imports from the Soviet Union. In the first half of 1953, the Soviet Union accounted for 39.6 per cent of Albania's foreign trade. Next followed Czechoslovakia, Poland, Hungary, Eastern Germany, Bulgaria, and Romania, in that order.

Sotir Toka, who was section chief in the Albanian Ministry of Foreign Trade until he fled to the West in August 1952, reported that Albania's Five-Year Economic Plan (1951-55) was financed by revenue from taxation and other sources and by assistance given Albania by the Soviet bloc countries in the form of imports on long-term credits. Toka, who in June 1952 had audited the 1952-55 import estimates for Albania, gave the value of imports for the fiscal years 1952/53-1954/55 incorporated in Table 5.

Table 5. VALUE OF IMPORTS, BY COUNTRY, 1952/53-1954/55
(in million rubles)

Country	*1952/53*	*1953/54*	*1954/55*	*Total*
Soviet Union	22.2	26.7	28.6	77.5
Czechoslovakia	14.2	14.2	9.9	38.3
Romania	11.2	7.0	8.0	26.2
Poland	8.1	8.6	8.1	24.8
Eastern Germany	7.4	5.4	5.9	18.7
Bulgaria	5.4	7.3	3.3	16.0
Hungary	4.2	4.3	4.8	13.3
Total	72.7	73.5	68.6	214.8

Some of the imports from the 1952-53 estimates included:

Commodity	*Amount*	*Commodity*	Amount
Wheat	30,000 tons	Cable	170 kilometers
Corn	20,000 tons	Window glass	60,000 sq. meters
Cement	18,000 tons	Trucks	104 units
Dynamite	200 tons	Percussion caps	150,000 units
Paper	13,000 tons	Blankets	18,000 units

According to Toka, Albanian exports to the Soviet bloc countries consist chiefly of agricultural, dairy, forestry, mineral, and petroleum products. Toka supplied from memory the following list of exports for the 1951/52 fiscal year: sunflower seed (5,000 to 7,000 metric tons); cotton seed; raw cotton; olives (1,000 metric tons); olive oil; flax and linseed; tobacco; oranges and lemons (340 metric tons); other fruits and nuts; resin; liquor (100 metric tons); cheese (150 metric tons); butter; wool; goat skins (50,000 pieces); hare skins (100,000 pieces); fox skins; ferret skins; ox and sheep sausage casings; timber; acorns; herbs; crude oil (87,000 metric tons); copper; chrome ore; oil tar; bitumen; soap; and salt.

Trade with Non-Communist Countries

Albanian postwar trade with non-Communist countries has been negligible. This trade has been carried on through the Free Port of

Trieste and has included small amounts of such imports as foodstuffs, chiefly sugar, fishing equipment, precision instruments and telecommunication supplies, medical supplies, leather, industrial fats for soap, and textiles. Albania has exported through the same ports insignificant amounts of herbs, citrus fruit, cotton, timber, raw hides, and chrome ore. According to a U.S. Department of Commerce report for August 1955, Albania imported $232,000 worth of commodities from non-Communist countries in 1954 and exported $122,000 worth (see Table 6).

Table 6. ALBANIAN FOREIGN TRADE WITH NON-COMMUNIST COUNTRIES, 1954

(in U.S. dollars)

Country of Origin or Destination	*Albanian Imports*	*Albanian Exports*
Austria	4,000	5,000
Belgium-Luxembourg	5,000	20,000
Canada	5,000	—
Denmark	5,000	—
Italy	147,000	32,000
Mexico	—	5,000
Netherlands	5,000	—
Norway	—	5,000
Switzerland	1,000	—
Turkey	—	5,000
United Kingdom	10,000	—
United States	—	8,000
Union of South Africa	—	13,000
Uruguay	46,000	11,000
West Germany	4,000	18,000
Total	232,000	122,000

International Finance and Exchange Rate

The Communist government has not published any information dealing with the methods of payments to foreign countries and the gold and foreign exchange holdings of the Albanian State Bank or of other government agencies. In July 1947, the Albanian government issued a decree replacing the Albanian franc, which had been the country's currency since 1925, with the Albanian lek. In this connection, a new set of exchange rates was published which fixed the value of various gold coins and foreign currencies as follows:

Foreign Exchange Rates, July 1947	*Albanian Leks*
Hard Currency	
1 Napoleon (20 gold francs)	326.00
10 U.S. gold dollars	546.00
1 Sovereign	410.00
1 Turkish gold pound	371.00
20 Gold reichmarks	402.25
1 Austrian gold shilling	296.00
10 Gold imperial rubles (1886 issue)	673.00
10 Dutch gold florins	339.00
Paper Currency	
100 Yugoslav dinars	100.00
100 Czech crowns	100.00
1 U.S. dollar	50.00
100 Swiss francs	1,163.79
1 English pound	201.50
1 Canadian dollar	50.00
100 French francs	41.98
100 Bulgarian leva	10.00

The Albanian lek is not accepted in international transactions, and all accounts of the Albanian government with foreign countries, including the Soviet orbit countries, are settled in dollars and rubles, chiefly the latter. The Soviet Union and some of its captive states periodically announce an exchange rate for the lek, but that is only a courtesy gesture. At present only the Soviet Union, Bulgaria, Romania, and Eastern Germany quote the Albanian lek, the rates being as follows: 100 Albanian leks equal 8 rubles or 13.10 leva or 12 lei or 6.67 Eastern German marks.

15. TRANSPORTATION AND COMMUNICATIONS

Highway Transportation

Historical Background

During the Roman Empire, Albania, then part of Illyria, was a communication link between Rome and its far-flung colonies in the East. The Via Appia, which ended at Brindisium (Brindisi), on the west coast of the Adriatic, was continued on the eastern coast by the Via Egnatia, which ran from Dyrrhachium (Durrës) and Apollonia (Pojan) to Constantinople. The Romans also built a network of secondary roads in Albania for foot and horse, but probably not for vehicular traffic.

In the Christian era, the Via Egnatia and other roads in Albania were used by the Goths, Normans, and Angevins in their invasions. The Albanian road network was a part of the military system of the Byzantine Empire until the twelfth century, when Venetian control of some coastal cities and the Crusades gave the ancient road system a greater commercial purpose. Indeed, Albania became one of the links between East and West.

The Turkish invasions which began in the last quarter of the fourteenth century ended the normal development of commerce, and for the next five centuries very little was done to expand the road network in Albania. During the long period of Turkish domination, most Albanian roads were capable of handling only foot and pack transport. Caravans composed of 200 to 400 mules and horses, owned and driven by Vlachs, and accompanied by armed mercenaries were not uncommon during this period. Such caravans served Albania and the neighboring countries of Macedonia, Greece, Serbia, and Montenegro. They carried imported supplies (unloaded at the port of Vlorë) to the interior of the country and brought back wool, cheese, wax, and other agricultural products.

In the late nineteenth century, the Sublime Porte sought to build a few coach roads, usually employing forced labor or prisoners. These projects were either not finished, or were of small importance, so that when Albania became independent in 1912, the country had only 160 kilometers of road suitable for carriage travel.

Beginnings of the Modern Road System

The modern road system in Albania had its origins during World War I. Military necessity forced the Austro-Hungarian forces, which occupied nearly three-fourths of Albania, to construct a network of vehicular traffic roads and to institute a large-scale improvement of the communications system. Accordingly, a corps of capable army engineers began to build new roads capable of handling automotive traffic. A network of decauville (narrow-gauge demountable track) rail lines was also constructed by the Austro-Hungarians from Shkodër to Shëngjin, Lesh, and Vorrë, with a branch line from Ura e Bunës toward Shirokë. The Austro-Hungarians also built a cableway from Lesh to Vorrë capable of transporting materials as well as men. In addition, they constructed or repaired some harbors.

When the Austro-Hungarians evacuated Albania, they had constructed 650 kilometers of roads for vehicular traffic, 130 kilometers for lighter travel, and 450 kilometers of decauville railroads. However, on their retreat they destroyed many of the roads they had constructed, while the native population plundered the material on the decauville lines.

The Italian and French armies built a number of roads in the south for their military operations. The Italians constructed two automotive highways, one running from Vlorë–Tepelenë–Gjirokastër, and the other from Vlorë–Himarë–Sarandë. These roads were used by the Italians again in 1940 when they invaded Greece from Albania. The Italians also built 120 kilometers of decauville road from Vlorë in two directions: one line went from Vlorë–Qaf'e Koçiut (Babicë) down to Shushicë and Penkovë, where it divided into two branches, one passing along the Vlainë brook to Gernec, while the other continued along the bank of the Shushicë to Mavrovë. The other line went from Vlorë through Goricë to Panaja. The Italian-built decauvilles met the same fate as those constructed by the Austro-Hungarians.

The French occupied the Korçë area, where the roads built by the Turks were generally better than those in the rest of the country. The French occupation forces improved these roads for heavy vehicular and automotive traffic. They also upgraded the Korçë–Kapshticë–Florina (Greece) road and that from Korçë through Kolonjë to Ura e Peratit to handle heavy automotive traffic.

Road Construction by the Albanian and Italian Governments, 1920-1943

The network of highways constructed in Albania from 1920 to 1939 was based on the road system developed by the occupying powers during World War I. However, since most of the important bridges had been destroyed at the end of the war and most of the roads had become dilapidated, a new start had to be made by the Albanian government. With a few minor exceptions, travel in 1920 was possible only by foot and pack train. As the new government had neither the funds nor the technicians to launch a large-scale road-building program, in 1921 it passed a road law based on an old Turkish law which resembled Western feudal custom. This provided that all persons from eighteen to fifty-eight work ten days a year gratis on the roads, or pay a tax ranging from 2 per cent to 6 per cent on earnings over one hundred gold napoleons a year. This law made possible the building of a few new roads and the repair of the old ones. Thus, in 1921 the Elbasan–Peqin road, the Pogradec–Qaf'e Thanës road, and parts of the Elbasan–Qukës–Përrenjes road were constructed. The following year the Tirana–Durrës highway was completely repaired and put into operation for heavy vehicular traffic. In 1923, the government began to reconstruct the bridges and damaged portions of the Durrës–Elbasan–Korçë highway; the Durrës–Elbasan portion was opened to traffic in 1925, and the following year the Tirana–Durrës–Elbasan–Korçë road was opened to automobile traffic. This was one of the most significant achievements of the Albanian government, as these highways connected the major part of southern Albania with Durrës, the country's principal port. The reconstruction in 1925 of the Rrogozhinë–Lushnjë road also made possible vehicular traffic between the capital city and Vlorë, Berat, Gjirokastër, and Sarandë.

An important event occurred in 1925 in the development of roads and harbors in Albania, the formation of the Sviluppo Economico dell' Albania (SVEA) enterprise by Italian capital for the economic development of Albania. SVEA granted Albania fifty million gold francs, a large part for constructing roads and bridges. From 1926 to 1937, Italian and German concerns and technicians built a number of modern highways with SVEA funds, the most important of which were the Shkodër–Pukë–Kukës road to the Yugoslav frontier, and the Milot–Rreshen–Burrel–Klos–Bulqizë–Peshkopi, Krujë–Qaf'e Shtamës–Burrel, Tirana–Qaf'e Krabës–Elbasan, and the Lushnjë–Kolonjë–Fier roads. In addition, a number of large steel and concrete bridges were constructed. Thus, by the end of 1937, Albania had 2,224 kilometers of roads for automotive traffic, with 611 kilometers more under construction. There were 4,371 permanent bridges with a total length of 13,085 meters, and 1,234 temporary bridges with a total length of 4,793 meters.

Immediately upon their invasion of Albania in April 1939, the Italians launched a large-scale road-building program to prepare for their invasion of Greece and Yugoslavia. The Azienda Strade Albanesi (ASA) was created for this purpose, and a plan was drawn up to improve or rebuild 1,200 kilometers of Albanian road within the next two years.

The Italians have claimed that in September 1943, when Italy capitulated, Albania had 2,366 kilometers of roads capable of handling heavy automobile traffic, of which 467 kilometers were tar-surfaced, 629 were macadamized and most of the rest rolled. The Italians have claimed further that during the occupation of Albania they built 1,270 kilometers of new roads (besides modifying and improving 248 kilometers of the old ones) and built 1,998 culverts and 290 bridges with arches of more than three meters in width. In view of the fact that there were in Albania over 2,200 kilometers of automotive roads in 1937, the Italian claims appear exaggerated, although it is indisputable that the Italians did improve the Albanian road system.

Roads under the Communist Regime

The road system in Albania probably reached its zenith in 1942. Later, the civil war among nationalist and Communist formations and the guerrilla warfare against the German forces damaged or destroyed most of the large bridges and left some of the best highways in a state of dilapidation. Thus, when the Communists took over in November 1944, they faced a serious transportation problem. However, the large amount of reserve building supplies in the hands of the Italian construction concerns in Albania and the large number of Italian road engineers stranded in Albania were utilized to the full by the Communist regime, and by the summer of 1945 most of the principal highways and bridges had been repaired and put back into operation. In a report on the ten-year development of communications, Radio Tirana alleged on September 18, 1954 that since 1944 the Communist regime had built new roads to a length of 353 kilometers and had asphalted 350 kilometers more. During the same period, added the report, 7,000 linear meters of new or repaired bridges had been built. Among the more important roads claimed constructed by the Tirana regime are: Kukës–Peshkopi, 65 kilometers; Kolgecaj–Shëmëri, 70 kilometers; Berat–Çorovodë, 50 kilometers, and many shorter ones. The newly built roads are 6 to 7 meters wide, and the roadbeds are constructed of crushed stone covered with gravel or sand. Table 1 gives the principal roads currently in operation in Albania (see map, page 243).

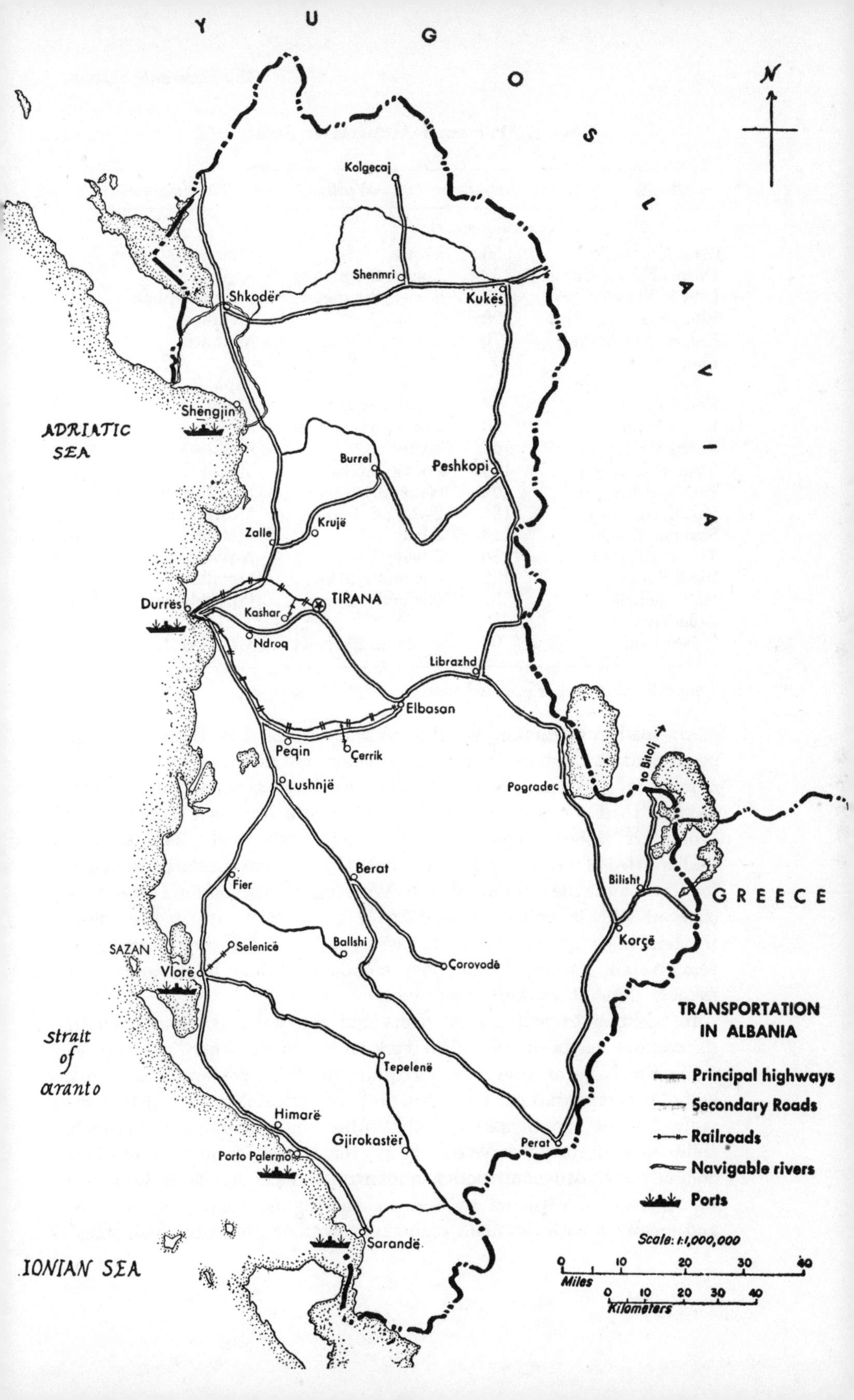

YUGOSLAVIA
N
ADRIATIC SEA
Strait of Otranto
IONIAN SEA
GREECE
SAZAN
Kolgecaj
Shenmri
Kukës
Shkodër
Shëngjin
Burrel
Peshkopi
Krujë
Zalle
Durrës
TIRANA
Kashar
Ndroq
Librazhd
Elbasan
Peqin
Çerrik
Lushnjë
Pogradec
To Bitolj
Berat
Fier
Bilisht
Korçë
Selenicë
Ballshi
Çorovodë
Vlorë
Tepelenë
Himarë
Gjirokastër
Perat
Porto Palermo
Sarandë
TRANSPORTATION IN ALBANIA
Principal highways
Secondary Roads
Railroads
Navigable rivers
Ports
Scale: 1:1,000,000
0 10 20 30 40
Miles
0 10 20 30 40
Kilometers

Table 1. PRINCIPAL AUTOMOTIVE ROADS, 1955

Road	*Length* (in kilometers)	*Width*	*Surface*
Berat-Çorovodë	50	1-way	Metalled [a]
Durrës-Ndroq-Tirana	38	2-way; 6-8 meters	Asphalt
Durrës-Vlorë	127	2-way; 6-8 meters	Mostly asphalt
Elbasan-Korçë	109	2-way	Metalled
Kolgecaj-Shëmërí	70	2-way	Metalled
Korçë-Bilisht-Greek Frontier	37	2-way	Asphalt
Korçë-Bitolj	74	Scant 2-way	Metalled
Korçë-Perat	90	2-way; 5.5 meters	Metalled
Kukës-Peshkopi	65	2-way	Metalled
Lushnjë-Berat-Perat	149	2-way; 6-8 meters	Metalled
Peshkopi-Librazhd	102	Generally 2-way	Probably asphalt
Shkodër-Durrës	133	2-way; 6-8 meters	Mostly asphalt
Shkodër-Kukës	114	2-way	Metalled
Tirana-Elbasan	56	2-way; 6-8 meters	Asphalt
Vlorë-Sarandë	133	Generally 2-way	Metalled
Vlorë-Tepelenë	82	Generally 2-way	Probably asphalt
Zallë-Krujë-Burrel-Peshkopi	96	2-way to Burgajet	Metalled to Burgajet

[a] Superficial gravel or crushed rock.

All road construction by the present regime has been done by penal and "voluntary" compulsory labor. In addition to the large number of political prisoners and inmates of concentration camps used on road construction, the country's youth has been mobilized in "voluntary" labor brigades to build and repair roads. The Kukës–Peshkopi road (Rruga e Rinisë–Youth Road) was declared a youth "action," and the Union of the Working Youth organization was charged with its construction. Since 1945, every youth in the country ten years of age or over has served at least three months a year, usually during the summer months, building roads under extremely difficult working conditions.

In addition to political prisoners and the youth, every citizen in the country has been obliged to work on the roads either "voluntarily" or on the basis of laws which require adults to perform road work without compensation. Law No. 747 of December 30, 1949 provides for the mobilization of the entire male population between eighteen and forty-five years of age for a certain number of days annually for road construction and maintenance. All short vehicular traffic roads constructed by the present regime connecting villages and localities with the main highways have been built by "voluntary" labor; that is, the peasants and villagers have been compelled to work without pay. To cite but one of the many examples, Radio Tirana on April 24, 1952 said that work on the Mes–Prekol road, 17 kilometers 500 meters long, had started, and that the Dukagjin citizens "will voluntarily contribute to building this road," which would help to exploit the forest reserve on Mount Cukali.

Road construction and maintenance are the responsibility of the Ministry of Communication, which has a Directorate of Roads and Bridges. The Directorate has under its authority a number of state road construction enterprises, known as Ndërmarje e Shtetit e Ndërtimevet-Rruga-Ura (State Enterprise of Road and Bridge Construction), in the principal cities. The Directorate is responsible for building and maintaining roads and bridges as outlined in the state plans, and for issuing directives to the various construction enterprises. The One-Year State Economic Plan for 1948 provided for an investment of 83,455,000 leks for constructing new roads and maintaining and asphalting older roads. The Two-Year State Economic Plan for 1949-50 provided for road investments of 92 million leks for 1949 and 86 million leks for 1950. It specified that only those roads used for heavy traffic to and from the mines should be asphalted; these roads included the Rrogozhinë–Lushnjë–Ura Vajgurore road (for the transport of petroleum products) and the Rubik–Vorrë–Shëngjin road (for the transport of copper and chrome ores). The Five-Year State Economic Plan (1951-55) provided for asphalting 140 kilometers of roads and constructing 300 kilometers of new roads, including the Kolgecaj–Shëmëri road with a length of 49 kilometers and the Gramsh–Lozhan road with a length of 70 kilometers. Investment for transportation and telecommunications for the duration of the Five-Year Plan was set as 3.2 billion leks, but no breakdown was given as to the amount assigned to road construction and maintenance.

Railroad Transportation

Projects for building railroads in Albania date back to the middle of the past century, when a number of proposals were made to the Turkish government for improving its transportation system, but none materialized. The large network of decauvilles built by the Austrians and Italians during World War I could not be considered a railroad network; the only permanent line that remained from these decauvilles was the Vlorë–Selenicë stretch. The first serious attempt to build a standard-gauge railroad line was made in 1927, when work began on the construction of a line between Durrës and

Tirana; the roadbed was prepared and all minor bridges were built by March 31, 1934, but the line was not completed until 1949.

The Italians made a serious attempt to build a railroad network in Albania to connect with the railroad networks of Greece and Yugoslavia. Work was started on a 83-kilometer line from Durrës to Labinot, principally to handle shipment of the iron ores of the Pogradec basin to the port of Durrës. The roadbed on this line was almost completed, some tunnels were dug, and most of the bridges were built. However, the Italians were unable to finish this line during their uneasy occupation of the country, and they left no completed railroad line in Albania, with the exception of the decauville from Vlorë to Selenicë.

Railroads Built since 1947

Early in 1945, Yugoslav engineers arrived in Albania to survey the railroad bridges, roadbeds, and tunnels built by the Italians and to make plans for continuing the work. On November 28, 1946 an agreement was signed in Belgrade between Albania and Yugoslavia for the formation of an Albanian-Yugoslav Company for the Building and Exploitation of Railroads; a protocol was signed on the same day providing for the building of railroad lines in Albania. Early in 1947, the joint Yugoslav-Albanian Railroad Company was formed, and plans were at once drawn for constructing a network of railroad lines along the roadbeds already prepared by the Italians. The following lines have so far been completed; they are all standard-gauge (4 feet 8 1/2 inches) single track.

Durrës–Peqin. Work on this line began in April 1947, but was officially inaugurated with a great deal of fanfare on May 1. The line, 43 kilometers long (26.7 miles), was officially opened on November 29, 1947. Its construction was entrusted to the Communist youth movement, and some 40,000 youths (including youth labor brigades from Yugoslavia and other countries) participated in the project on a "voluntary" basis.

Durrës–Tirana. Work on this line was inaugurated officially on April 11, 1948; it was opened on February 23, 1949 (Red Army Day). The line, 37 kilometers (23 miles) long, was built by "voluntary" youth labor brigades; some 30,000 boys and girls worked on it at one time or another. The construction of the road was under Soviet supervision.

The joint Yugoslav-Albanian Railroad Company finished the Durrës–Peqin line and started the Tirana–Durrës line. However, after the Tito-Cominform break, the enterprise was dissolved.

Kashar–Ysberish. This 7-kilometer line is a spur of the Durrës–Tirana line. It was officially opened on September 11, 1949.

Peqin–Elbasan. Work on this line was begun on April 16, 1950; it was officially opened on December 21, 1950 (Stalin's birthday). A total of 26,863 youths worked on the line, which is 35.5 kilometers (22 miles) long.

Although separately built, the three main branches, Tirana–Durrës, Durrës–Peqin, and Peqin–Elbasan, are now considered one line; it takes over five hours for the train to run the 115.5 kilometers from Tirana to Elbasan. (The direct automobile route from Tirana to Elbasan is a little over one hour.)

Albanian railroads are controlled and operated by the Albanian Ministry of Communications through Drejtoria e Hekurudhave (Directorate of Railroads). Rolling stock is small and in poor condition. Originally, it consisted of a few locomotives and some freight and passenger cars supplied by Yugoslavia, which had in turn obtained them from UNRRA. Later additional locomotives were sent from the Soviet Union, Romania, and Poland. The construction, operation, and maintenance of railroads in Albania are relatively primitive. There is only one repair shop, located in Durrës.

The Five-Year Plan (1951-55) provided for the construction of a 90-kilometer line from the coal mines at Memaliaj to Vlorë and a 7-kilometer spur from Paper to the new oil refinery at Çerrik. Work on the Memaliaj–Vlorë line started early in July 1955 but stopped at the end of the same month, probably as a result of the introduction of the "new economic course." Work on the Paper–Çerrik spur was started in 1952, and it was still continuing in the summer of 1953. No announcement of its completion has been made, although it probably has been finished.

The Albanian railroad network is very small; by the end of 1953, its total length was only 129 kilometers. It should be remembered, however, that the investments needed for the construction of a railroad line are so large that they can be justified economically only in especially favorable circumstances. Moreover, in Albania the mountainous structure of the country increases the cost of railroad building appreciably. It would appear probable that future emphasis will be given to road traffic and, to a certain degree, to development of air travel.

River and Sea Transportation

River and Canal System

There is no navigable river or canal system of any importance in Albania. Only the Drin and the Buenë (Bojanë) rivers are navigable, and they for only short distances. The Buenë is usually entered only by barges, landing craft, and small steamers drawing not more than five feet; these steamers formerly maintained service between Shkodër and Shëngjin. Depth at the bar is 405 feet, and depths in the river are from 7 to 8 feet in the summer and 15 to 16 feet in the winter. In summer, the current never exceeds 3 knots, but in winter it is as high as 7. The channel shifts from day to day. The three main lakes —Lake Shkodër, Lake Ohrid, and Lake Prespë (Prespa), which Albania shares with Yugoslavia and, in the case of Lake Prespë, with Greece as well—are navigable for small boats, but they have not been used for commercial shipping since the end of World War II.

Sea Transportation

There are five principal ports in Albania which have facilities for handling seagoing cargos; they are, in order of importance, Durrës, Vlorë, Sarandë, Shëngjin, and Porto Palermo.

Durrës, the chief port, was developed into a first-class harbor with Italian funds before World War II, and served as Italy's principal supply base for its military operations against Greece and Yugoslavia. The port possessed adequate warehouses and petroleum storage tanks with a capacity of 7,000 tons. However, the German command in Albania, fearing an Allied invasion, mined and destroyed the port completely in the summer of 1944. The present regime, with Soviet technical and material assistance, has done a good deal of reconstruction work and has restored it to use. It has also built a railroad spur to the docks and has installed large automatic fixed and movable cranes and winches for loading and unloading heavy cargos. In the past several years, the port has handled an average of 25 arrivals and departures of passenger ships, freighters, and tankers a month. Aside from the tankers, nearly all the ships serving Albania at present are of Soviet and Soviet-bloc registry. Shelter is good at this harbor, except from west and southwest winds. At least 200 acres have depths of 24 feet.

Vlorë, the second port in importance, is the best natural harbor in Albania; it commands the strategically important Island of Sazan (Saseno). Vlorë has a spacious bay, approximately 9 miles long and 3.5 to 5 miles wide, and at least 30 to 40 square miles with depths of more than 60 feet. Shelter is good throughout the bay, except from northwest winds; when these blow, ships anchor at Pasha Liman in the extreme south of the bay.

Before World War II, Albania had no merchant marine except for a limited number of very small craft engaged in coastal trade. Most shipping was handled by Italian shipping concerns; there was daily service between Bari and Durrës. The small shipyard at Durrës was capable of building small fishing boats.

The regime has increased coastal shipping and has maintained infrequent service with Trieste and some of the Italian ports on the Adriatic. The following motor vessels constituted the Albanian merchant marine in 1954:

Name of Vessel	*Size (in tons)*	*Speed (in knots)*
Teuta	500	8
Mesapliku	350	8
Qemal Stafa	350	8
Ylli i Kuq	100	5-6
Ali Kelmendi	600	5-6
Konferenca e Pezës	150	5-6
16 Tetori	200	5-6
Dalip Tabaku	250	5-6
Asim Zeneli	350	7
10 Korriku	150	5
Kurveleshi	500	6
Labinoti	70	4
Thoma Kàllefi	120	4
Shqipëria e Re	35	5
Dalip Noka	35	5
Mustafa Mataiti	70	5

Of the boats listed above, *Ali Kelmendi, 16 Tetori,* and *10 Korriku* were built at the Durrës shipyard between 1946 and 1953. Some of the smaller boats were also probably built there. *Teuta, Mesapliku, Qemal Stafa, Kurveleshi, Asim Zeneli,* and *Ylli i Kuq* have in the past several years sailed occasionally between Albanian ports and Trieste, Venice, and other Italian ports on the Adriatic.

There are also a few Albanian schooners, and a small number of fishing boats sail from Durrës, Vlorë, and Shëngjin.

Air Transportation

Adria-Aero-Lloyd Concession

Due to the lack of transportation facilities and the mountainous character of Albania, the necessity for air transportation was felt after World War I, despite the smallness of the country. Accordingly, a representative of the German Adria-Aero-Lloyd came to Tirana for negotiations with the Albanian government, and on November 2, 1924 an agreement was concluded granting the German concern a ten-year concession for an internal air service. Air service began at once, but it proved an unprofitable undertaking. Nevertheless, the company maintained the service. Finally, Adria-Aero-Lloyd, with the consent of the Albanian government, sold its concession to the Italian company Ala Littoria, S. A. In 1935, a ten-year agreement was signed between the Albanian government and the Italian company for civil aviation service in Albania. Ala Littoria instituted air service between Tirana and the country's principal cities: Shkodër, Kukës, Peshkopi, Kucovë, Vlorë, Gjirokastër, and Korçë. Tirana was also connected with Rome and Brindisi, and later with Salonica and Sofia.

Internal civil air transport was not restored after World War II. While Albania was under Yugoslav tutelage (1944-48), service was maintained by the Soviet-Yugoslav Air Transport Company between Belgrade and Tirana, and an occasional Soviet plane landed at the Tirana airport bringing in important Soviet officials. After the Tito-Cominform break, a semiweekly line was established by the MASZOVLET (Soviet-Hungarian Air Transport Company) between Budapest and Tirana. This line operated until the spring of 1953, when it discontinued the service because of the rigid restriction placed on flights by the Yugoslav government, which required every plane to stop at the Belgrade airport in order to fly over Yugoslav territory. After that, aside from sporadic Soviet flights, there was no air service between Albania and the outside world until February 1955, when, as a result of Soviet-Yugoslav rapprochement, regular air service was instituted between Tirana and Moscow and the other capitals of Eastern Europe.

Postal and Telecommunication System

Postal Service

The first Albanian Provisional Government formed by Ismail bey Kemal in Vlorë in December 1912 included a Ministry of Post and Telegraphs, headed by the well-known patriot, Lef Nosi. Attention was given to the development of postal-telegraph service from the very inception of the modern Albanian state. By 1927, there were in Albania fifty-three post offices covering all the country's regions and rendering fairly efficient postal service. As the country's highways from 1927 to 1938 were improved and made passable for vehicular traffic, the postal service improved accordingly, and by 1938, a twenty-four-hour service between the principal cities had become a reality.

The present regime inherited an excellent postal system in Albania. On December 15, 1944, the Presidium of the Anti-Fascist Council of National Liberation promulgated Law No. 23 with provisions for regulating the state's postal, telephone, and telegraph systems. Article 1 of the regulation provided that the "services of reception, transport, and delivery of the object of correspondence . . . are an exclusive privilege of the state." Postal service is run by the Directorate of

Post, Telephone, and Telegraph (PTT) in the Ministry of Communications.

Telegraph and Telephone System until 1944

During the period between the two wars, a fairly good system of telegraph and telephone communications was developed in Albania, linking nearly all towns, prefectures, and subprefectures. Due to the mountainous nature of the country, communications were difficult to maintain and were frequently damaged. The separate police telephone system linking various regions and districts with headquarters in Tirana was more efficient than the public system. In 1939, there were 56 hand-operated telephone exchanges with over 900 lines, and an automatic exchange in Tirana with 150 lines. Of some 1,000 telephones in the whole country in 1939, 400 were in Tirana and 200 in Durrës. The rest were scattered throughout the other larger towns. There were at the same time, 1,430 miles of telegraph line, 43 circuits, and 52 offices. During the four years of Italian occupation (1939-43), the public telegraph and telephone system was expanded greatly and its efficiency increased.

Until 1939, only the lines linking Tirana with Durrës were used exclusively as telephone lines; in all other cases, telegraphic lines also served for telephone communication.

Overland telegraphic communications until 1939 were maintained with Greece and Yugoslavia; there were two lines with Greece, and two lines with Yugoslavia. The Italians expanded the network considerably, especially to Yugoslavia, and instituted telephonic communications with Yugoslavia. In May 1943 a Rome-Tirana-Sofia telephone circuit was reported in operation.

Four submarine cables had been laid before World War II between Italy and Albania: Vlorë-Otranto; Vlorë-Island of Sazan-Brindisi; Durrës-Brindisi; and Durrës-Bari. There was also a cable between Sarandë and Corfu (Greece). In 1940, a new cable was laid by the Italians between Durrës and Brindisi. During the war, all the submarine cables were extensively used by the Italians, chiefly for military purposes, but they have not been operated since the advent of the Communist regime in Albania.

The Telephone and Telegraph System since 1944

The Communist regime inherited a well-established telegraph and telephone communication system from the defeated Italian and German forces. The lines destroyed during the last year of the war were quickly restored to operation by Italian civil and military technicians who were forcibly retained in Albania by the Communist government. There were also sufficient Italian reserves of telecommunications material for restoring the damaged lines. All telecommunications facilities are owned and operated by the state; they are directly controlled by the Directorate of Postal, Telephone, and Telegraph in the Ministry of Communications.

Although the regime has often made claims of having expanded post, telephone, and telegraph services in the past ten years, no detailed figures have been given. In a broadcast of September 19, 1954, Radio Tirana alleged that since the end of the war 2,250 kilometers of telephone and telegraph lines had been strung, and that a number of automatic telephone exchanges had been installed. Over the past several years, Albania has received considerable amounts of telecommunications material from the Soviet Union and the captive countries, especially Hungary and Czechoslovakia, including large quantities of cable of all types, electrical and telephone equipment, automatic switchboards, batteries, lamps, aluminum wire, and insulating tape. The 1948 State Economic Plan allotted 23 million leks for the development of postal-telephonic-telegraphic communications, including the stringing of 350 kilometers of new lines. The Two-Year Plan (1949-50) allocated only 14 million leks for the development of communications, and the Five-Year Plan (1951-55) provided for the extension of the telegraph and telephone communication system by the construction of 1,500 kilometers of new lines.

At present, Albania has some sixty telegraph and seventy-five telephone exchanges; the total number of telephone lines is not known. The Tirana press often carries accounts of the installation of automatic telephone exchanges in the larger cities; one such automatic switchboard for five hundred subscribers was reportedly inaugurated in Elbasan on March 15, 1954. Actually, the telephone and telegraph system is inefficient, and long-distance connections are made within this country only with difficulty. Aside from a few professional people, such as doctors, and the ranking Party and governmental officials, there are no private telephone subscribers. Persons desiring to make a telephone call must go to a postal-telegraph office. The whole telephone system is devoted to the service of the cumbersome bureaucracy that has developed to astounding proportions under the Communist regime.

Radio

The first radio station in Albania was inaugurated in November 1938; it was a 3-kilowatt short-wave station which broadcast a few hours daily and handled radio-telephonic and radio-telegraphic communications with Italy. During the war, the Italians built two other small experimental stations in Tirana and constructed smaller stations of medium frequency in Gjirokastër, Korçë, Vlorë, Peshkopi, Kuçovë, and Shkodër. The inadequacy of the wire telegraphic network led the Italians to erect a number of point-to-point radio-telegraphic stations throughout the country. They also built stations at Durrës, Sarandë, and the Island of Sazan for communications with ships.

The Communist regime found nearly all the Italian radio facilities intact, and the 3-kilowatt high frequency prewar Radio Tirana was used by the Tirana government until March 1952. The Constitution of 1946 provided that all telecommunications be owned and operated by the state. Order No. 57 issued by the Council of Ministers on November 30, 1950, created the Committee on Radio Broadcasting, a state agency attached to the Council of Ministers. The order provided that all radio stations and all radio-broadcasting facilities in the country be state property and be operated by the Committee on Radio Broadcasting, whose chief functions are described as the "organization of radiocasting for education, entertainment, and raising the political, cultural, and artistic standards of the masses, and for their mobilization in the performance of their duties assigned to them by the People's Authority" (*Gazeta Zyrtare,* December 27, 1950). On July 23, 1953 the Committee was merged with the Ministry of Education and Culture, but in 1955, it was again made a separate agency and was reattached to the Council of Ministers.

Under the direction of a Soviet engineer, work was begun on the construction of a 50-kilowatt medium frequency station at Kashar, near Tirana; broadcasting from the station was inaugurated on March 30, 1952. The equipment was supplied by the Soviet Union and Hungary. It was stated by Albanian officials that the station was a "gift" of the Soviet Union. The broadcasting activities of the Tirana regime were greatly increased with the completion of this station.

The Tirana government has also placed in operation local radio stations built by the Italians at Korçë, Gjirokastër, Shkodër, Kuçovë (Stalin Town), and Vlorë. As of the end of 1953, the following six radio broadcasting stations were in operation in Albania:

City	*Power (in kilowatts)*	*Frequency (in kilocycles)*
Tirana (Kashar)	50.00	1,358
	3.00	4,880, 6,084, 6,560, 7,210, 7,850, 9,960, 15,630
Shkodër	0.20	8,215
Kuçovë (Stalin Town)	0.10	1,200
Vlorë	0.10	8,500
Gjirokastër	0.25	1,430
Korçë	0.20	1,088
	0.10	5,820, 8,500

Public loudspeakers were installed by the Italians during the war and were greatly expanded by the present regime for propaganda purposes. A beginning has also been made in "radiofication" (wire-diffusion). According to an account in *Zëri i Popullit* of June 29, 1954, a small radio station was recently put in operation at the Stalin Textile Combine, near Tirana, for the "radiofication" of various parts of the plant, and workers' apartments were being "radiofied."

Part IV – Cultural and Social Developments

16. PUBLIC HEALTH

This short survey of Albania's public health illuminates the every-day struggle of a small people against extremely adverse circum-stances. Whatever the political complexion of the regime in power, each has had to meet the same difficulties in improving public welfare. Popular remedies and even sorcery were widely practiced in the villages and in the mountains until recent times. Disease has always taken a heavy toll. The death rate among adults has always been comparatively high by European standards, but the rate of infant mortality has been even more alarming. There has been a constant shortage of physicians and trained nurses, although during the years between the two world wars considerable progress was made. In addition, the lack of communications and transportation facilities have prevented doctors in the cities from visiting the villages and the highlands where most of the population live.

Generally speaking, health conditions have been somewhat better in the mountainous regions than in the lowlands, especially in the coastal plains, where malaria has always been prevalent. However, the mountaineers have had to contend with special adverse factors growing out of their physical environment and way of life. Their almost hermetical isolation has resulted in malnutrition; and diseases such as syphilis and tuberculosis, virtually untreated until the recent past, have been passed from generation to generation.

Despite the many hardships brought upon Albania by foreign military occupation, public health has sometimes profited. During World War I, the Italian, French, and Austro-Hungarian armies used their extensive medical facilities to help the civilian population. Dur-ing the years of Italian occupation (1939-43), sanitary conditions were considerably improved, and Italian specialists and doctors made a significant contribution to the country's public health service.

After the capitulation of Italy in 1943, guerrilla warfare against the Germans greatly reduced medical care. Antimalaria work, except in the larger civic centers, was abandoned. During the winter of 1944/45 the incidence of malnutrition, tuberculosis, and malaria greatly alarmed the Allied Military Liaison in Albania. The new

Communist regime had neither the means nor the experience to cope with the imminent disaster, and UNRRA during the years 1945-47 provided critical medical assistance.

In 1948, the Communist government initiated its first economic plan, the so-called One-Year Plan. This was followed by the Two-Year Plan (1949-50) and the Five-Year Plan (1951-55). Although these plans have all had programs for improvement of public health and general living conditions, there is not much information available on what has been accomplished. The vague official reports on the newly established social security system can only be accepted with reservations. Even if all figures and propaganda claims of the Communist regime are taken at face value, Albania still has a long way to go before one can really speak of "health" and "public welfare."

Factors Relative to Public Health

Food Consumption

Because of primitive farming techniques and the generally poor quality of the arable land, Albanian per capita food consumption has been low even by Balkan standards and barely above the subsistence level. Between 1936 and 1938, the average daily intake was approximately 2,000 calories. At about the same time, Yugoslavia and Hungary had a per capita average of roughly 2,800 calories, Greece 2,600, and Italy 2,500.

The diet was based largely on maize, which with other cereals accounted for approximately 80 per cent of the caloric intake. Animal proteins and fats were generally insufficient, except for the population of the towns and for those directly engaged in animal husbandry. In some places, olive oil replaced deficient animal fats, but its availability depended on local transportation facilities. The general shortage of transportation also limited the consumption of fresh vegetables, fish, and fruits. There was no method of home fruit conservation known to the population, and prewar Albania did not possess a commercial cannery. Undernourishment was paralleled by malnutrition.

At the end of World War II, famine threatened. According to the UNRRA report, during 1947 the average daily caloric intake was only 1,276, even though 1947 was the third year of UNRRA assistance and nearly 53,000 metric tons of cereals and 63,000 metric tons of other UNRRA food supplies with a total value of over ten million dollars had been delivered to Albania. In addition, UNRRA provided Albania with 162 metric tons of cod liver oil for children and nursing mothers.

Since the end of the UNRRA operation in 1947, Communist officials have avoided the publication of food consumption statistics, although a food rationing system is in effect based on political and economic considerations. Government employees, members of the Workers' (Communist) Party, and skilled workers belong to a so-called first category, with the rest of the population classified in the second category. Food allocation is about 15 to 20 per cent higher for the privileged first category than for the second, but there is not always enough food available to fill the rations. The official newspaper *Bashkimi* complained as late as May 22, 1953: "Ration cards give the workers the right to certain quantities of necessary food, but the people have been supplied very irregularly."

There is no reliable information concerning the current caloric intake. An official report of March 30, 1954 boasts of a health "Preventorium" for "weak"—apparently undernourished—"children at Sarandë, where the children receive 3,500 calories per day." The report makes clear that this caloric intake is "exceptionally" high. Furthermore, the Preventorium has only seventy-five beds. Enver Hoxha's speech to the Albanian People's Assembly on June 17, 1955 disclosed that in 1954 the people "received" (which may mean per capita consumption as well as production *in toto*) 78 per cent more sugar, 140 per cent more cheese, 99 per cent more fats, 41 per cent more macaroni, and 11 per cent more meat and fish than they had received in the course of 1950. This relatively great increase, if true, is principally due to the extremely low level of 1950. Taking into account the starvation level of the immediate postwar years and the slow progress made in the 1948-50 period, the average daily caloric intake may be estimated at about 2,200-2,300.

Housing, Water Supplies

Rural houses (which in Albania means most houses) are built of available materials, generally of stone. "Fortified" houses are occasionally found in the mountains. Housing does not measure up to Western standards, except in the major cities. In many areas the average rural dwelling is cramped and crowded, with the peasant's stock and domestic animals sharing the house in bad weather.

Electric power is available only in the larger cities. Water supplies are inadequate, and, except in the mountains, frequently contaminated and unfit for drinking. After World War II, when malnutrition, tuberculosis, and malaria threatened to become a national disaster, UNRRA provided pumping units and pipes for the Tirana waterworks, as well as two chlorinators and necessary spare parts for the waterworks of Tirana and Durrës.

Piped sewerage systems are almost nonexistent, and only the leading hotels, hospitals, and luxury apartment houses have flush toilets.

Sanitary legislation was introduced as late as 1947. Under the Five-Year Plan, a sewerage system was to be built for Tirana, but there is no evidence that the work has been completed. The Plan also had provisions for the construction of nine public baths in the main civic centers. Only three had been completed at the end of 1954.

In view of these circumstances, the 2,094,000,000 leks (approximately $41,880,000, roughly 10 per cent of the Plan's investment program) allocated for housing projects, improvement of drinking water, sewerage systems, and public baths seem strikingly inadequate. Enver Hoxha's address to the Albanian People's Assembly on June 17, 1955, also revealed that the improvement of living conditions is largely limited to the privileged classes of industrial labor and Communist officialdom.

Available plan reports indicate that the housing program has been concentrated on Tirana, Durrës, Pukë, and other places where new industrial establishments have been erected. Furthermore, the report emphasizes that out of 2,100 apartments in Tirana, 1,100 will be "permanent." This distinction seems to indicate that the housing program to a large degree consists of building temporary barrack-settlements around the industrial centers.

As to the general sanitary conditions, in a report of June 23, 1955, Enver Hoxha indirectly admitted that his government has done little or nothing insofar as the rural areas are concerned with the exception of the "mobilization of the Communist front organizations."

Clothing

Although the urban population has almost completely discarded the national dress for Western attire, nearly all Albanian peasants still make their own clothes and wear some part of their national dress both for work and on important occasions. This posed a particular difficulty during the period of UNRRA assistance, for some of the delivered clothing items were not considered suitable by the rural population. UNRRA shipped 3,739 metric tons of clothing items with a total value of $4,272,000. This helped to alleviate the clothing shortage of the desperately needy, but the overall clothing shortage was not solved. The Communist government has concentrated on providing the privileged class of Party and government officials and industrial laborers with the most needed items.

Endemic Diseases

The terrain, rural superstitions, and general illiteracy have prevented even the most ambitious administration from keeping adequate records on public health. Available statistics usually relate only to those people treated by the health organizations, and this category has always been a rather small segment of those who needed treatment.

Table 1, which shows the incidence of the three endemic diseases, malaria, syphilis, and tuberculosis, in per cent of all cases treated by the various organs of the Albanian Department of Health, gives a general idea of the situation in the interwar period. This table reveals that malaria has been by far the most prevalent disease in Albania. The number of people treated for malaria during the same six-year period is as follows: 29,659 persons in 1927; 23,443 in 1928; 25,863 in 1929; 22,209 in 1930; 21,145 in 1931; and 27,881 in 1932.

Table 1. INCIDENCE OF THREE ENDEMIC DISEASES, 1927-1932
(in per cent of patients treated by Department of Health)

Disesase	*1927*	*1928*	*1929*	*1930*	*1931*	*1932*
Malaria	42.0	41.0	40.5	33.0	31.0	34.0
Syphilis	2.8	2.3	2.3	1.8	1.5	1.5
Tuberculosis	1.5	2.0	1.5	1.3	1.3	1.2
Other	53.7	54.7	55.7	63.9	66.2	63.3
Total	100.0	100.0	100.0	100.0	100.0	100.0

Before the Second World War, Albanian health authorities concentrated upon malaria. The Department of Health distributed quinine regularly, approximately 20 pounds per year, and hospitals, dispensaries, and pharmacies also supplied quantities. The extermination of mosquitoes played a vitally important role in the course of the antimalaria campaign. The Rockefeller Foundation after nearly two years of exhaustive research established an antimalaria service in Albania in close cooperation with the country's Department of Health. The first antimalaria stations at Tirana and Durrës were established in 1929, and in the course of the following years additional stations were set up at Elbasan, Shkodër, Berat, and Vlorë. The stations came under the direction of the Albanian Director General of Health. At the same time, the engineering division of the Department of Health undertook to drain marshes, clean polluted rivers, and destroy mosquitoes and their larvae by chemical means.

Under Italian occupation, health conditions generally improved. The functions and organization of the Rockefeller Foundation were taken over by the Italian Marciafava Istituto Malariologico, which completed the most extensive malaria survey made in Albania. This survey showed that 12,855 children under ten years of age (approximately 5 per cent of this age group) were infected by malaria.

During the summer of 1945, typhoid fever broke out in Tirana. During the winter of the same year, malaria struck. Food shortages and malnutrition during the war years had undermined the physical resistance of the population and medicine had run short. UNRRA then came to the help of the Albanian people. UNRRA engineers drained polluted rivers; UNRRA airplanes sprayed DDT. By the end of 1946, UNRRA had shipped typhus vaccine for 30,000 people, sufficient DDT powder to protect the entire population for one year, and enough antidiphtheria serum to inoculate all children from one to ten years of age.

From 1947 until 1949, the number of malaria cases decreased slowly. In 1949, there were 238,266 malaria cases reported (of the total population of about 1,186,000), still well above the prewar level. Even in 1950, according to regime figures, 60 per cent of all children in the Vlorë and Durrës districts were infected with malaria. The year 1951 was apparently the first successful year of the antimalaria campaign, with reported cases of malaria not exceeding 75,000.

No statistical data are available for 1952, but it was officially reported that in 1953, 7.7 per cent of the total population was malaria-infected. The report emphasized that only 28,000 persons, approximately 2.2 per cent of the population, were new cases. This figure is somewhat higher but more realistic than a Moscow report, which estimated the number of malaria cases for the year at about one third that of 1938.

In 1954, the government planned further preventive measures, including the disinfection with DDT of 36 million square yards of building, 22 million square yards of stagnant waters, and 5,600 hectares of marshes. The government declared that in 1954 new malaria cases did not exceed 1 per cent of the total population (approximately 12,200 people), and that malaria had "ceased to be" the plague of Albania.

While it is impossible to check the accuracy of the quoted Communist reports, the following figures show the incidence of malaria cases in per cent of the total population for 1936 and 1938, and available postwar years: 1935, 26.0; 1938, 16.5; 1945-46, 70.0; 1947, 60.0; 1948, 41.0; 1949, 21.7; 1951, 6.5; 1953, 7.7.

The Communist government does not publish statistics on other diseases, but it claims that the incidence of tuberculosis and syphilis is also steadily receding. Reliable unofficial reports, however, indicate that an epidemic of typhoid fever which broke out during November and December of 1950 took an extremely heavy toll, particularly among children. Private reports of a polio epidemic in 1953 were corroborated by Enver Hoxha in a speech a year later. Private reports also indicate that tuberculosis is still widespread; some estimates run as high as 14.5 per cent of the total population.

Public Health Service

Medical Training

Albania received no medical inheritance from the Ottoman Empire. There were practically no doctors, nurses, dentists, or pharmacists. At the end of World War I, when military occupation ended, the Albanian state had no hospitals. In 1919, the American Red Cross dispatched a medical mission to Albania, composed of a physician and a few nurses. In 1920 there were 55 doctors, 32 pharmacists, 7 dental surgeons, and 5 midwives available for the Department of Health.

Since no medical school existed in the country, government scholarships were awarded for the study of medicine abroad. Approximately one third of the Albanian students abroad studied medicine, mostly in Italy, France, and Germany. The number of trained Albanian medical personnel slowly increased so that by 1938 there were 155 physicians, 44 dental surgeons, 99 pharmacists, and 29 midwives registered with the Department of Health. The Albanian Red Cross also contributed to medical training. It established a school for nurses in Tirana where annual classes of some thirty nurses obtained three-year training. The Italian occupation did not greatly change the picture.

After the war, the Communists removed or imprisoned all "unreliable" doctors. Italian physicians who had remained in Albania were taken prisoners, but in some cases they were reassigned to the new health organization.

In 1948, a three-year medical school was established in Tirana for the training of medical assistants. Under the Five-Year Plan, six "Night Medical Polytechnicums" were established in the major cities with evening classes for the training of assistant doctors, assistant midwives, and assistant pharmacists. The Albanian Red Cross apparently has continued its training of health service workers. Radio Tirana reported in 1952 that the Red Cross organized 347 "health courses" attended by 6,800 "workers." There is no indication, however, whether these were professional health service workers, or workers attending "first-aid" courses.

In 1952, a High Medical Institute was founded in Tirana. Students graduate as medical doctors after six years of study. The first class of doctors, probably of fifteen or twenty, will graduate in 1959. Professors include both Albanians and Russians. The system of government scholarships abroad has been maintained, most students being sent to the Soviet Union and the captive countries which have cultural agreements with Albania. During the period 1949-50, 18 scholarships were established by the Ministry of Health for medical students studying abroad, and 509 scholarships for nurses, medical assistants, and midwives.

Organization

Before World War II, responsibility for public health services rested with the Directorate General of Public Health, which was subordinate to the Ministry of the Interior. Since communities could not afford to contribute to service costs, all expenditures were met by the central government. The expenditures of the Department of Health in thousands of gold francs during the 1928/29-1932/33 period were as follows: 1928/29, 550; 1929/30, 519; 1930/31, 594; 1931/32, 524; 1932/33, 887.

The basic functions of the department were carried out through four principal organs: hospitals, dispensaries, ambulance stations, and traveling medical officers. Traveling medical service was instituted in 1932. Each traveling medical officer was assigned a number of villages, and completed a tour of his area once a month. Serious and contagious cases were sent to the nearest dispensary or hospital. Traveling medical officers were authorized to call on the police or gendarmery to take unwilling persons to the hospital. They also were authorized to issue free medicine and to supervise the health of schoolchildren. Prior to the Italian occupation, traveling medical officers were posted at Vlorë, Himarë, Kurvelesh, Gramsh, Shpat, Pukë, Mirditë, Kukës, and Malsi' e Madhe. Apparently this system of traveling medical officers established by the monarchy has remained basically unchanged.

Resident physicians of the health service were permanently stationed at Konispol, Tepelenë, Skrapar, Mallakastër, Mat, Zerqan, Lesh, and Frashër, while "communal doctors" were assigned to the communities of Reskovec, Këlcyrë, Libohovë, and Leskovik.

In 1945, the creation of the Ministry of Health gave cabinet rank to the head of the public health service. Following the pattern of the new administrative division of the country, Albania is now divided into ten regional health departments, 53 health districts, and 47 outlying health localities. Traveling medical personnel has been increased: instead of traveling doctors, there are "traveling sanitary teams," each consisting of a physician, a nurse, and one or two assistants. The teams tour an assigned area, visiting every locality at regular intervals. Radio Tirana claims that by the end of 1953 there was a health institution for every four villages, and one "medical cadre" for every 576 inhabitants.

The medical profession was "nationalized" by the Communist government. Classified as "workers of health" its members are now state employees. All physicians and dentists, as well as the newly trained assistant doctors, nurses, and other trained personnel, are required to work through the state's medical service, although they are allowed to undertake private practice in their spare time.

Hospitals and Dispensaries

The first Albanian hospital was established by the American Red Cross in 1919 and taken over by the Albanian government in 1920. The number of hospitals greatly increased in the interwar period, even though most of the new hospitals had a very small capacity. By the time of the Italian occupation, there were eight civilian hospitals, one military hospital, and a small mental hospital. Only the hospitals in Tirana, Korçë, and Vlorë were well designed and modern. The General Hospital in Tirana, by far the best in the country, posessed the only X-ray institute in Albania, and in 1938 acquired the services of several distinguished foreign specialists. Tirana was also the location of the Chemical and Bacteriological Institute of Albania.

Where most needed, the government also established dispensaries, usually as a temporary expedient, until a hospital was built. The army maintained dispensaries in all major cities where it had garrisons. Although a semiprivate institution, the Albanian Red Cross participated in the government's health program from 1922 onward. It established a dispensary and a dental clinic in Tirana and maintained an auto ambulance service.

Of the specialized health institutions, the Children's Ambulance Centers at Tirana, Korçë, and Shkodër should be mentioned. They were the forerunners of the maternity and children's hospitals. As part of the long-range antituberculosis campaign, two sanatoria were set up: one attached to the Tirana General Hospital, the other at Voskopojë. The number of patients treated in the hospitals, dispensaries, and ambulances increased steadily from 26,242 in 1925 to 169,800 in 1938.

During the Italian occupation, medical institutions were expanded. The Central Institute of Public Health in Tirana, which had been begun under the auspices of the Rockefeller Foundation, was completed in July 1940. The Italians also built a modern maternity and children's hospital in Tirana, which went into operation in December 1942. The Central Military Hospital was enlarged, a modern hospital was constructed in Kuçovë, and additional dispensaries were established at Selenicë and Rubik.

After the war, rehabilitation of the health service was greatly assisted by the UNRRA program. In addition to food, clothing, and drug supplies, UNRRA shipped the complete equipment for eight 200-bed hospitals, twelve 40-bed hospitals, two dental units, and 28 laboratory units. UNRRA also sent X-ray spare parts, surgical instruments, and many other items vitally important to the war-ravaged Albanian health service. However, much of the medical supplies and equipment were unfamiliar to the Albanian doctors, who had not kept up with Western medical progress during the war years. Serious problems were also posed by the primitive facilities of the hospitals. For example, the storage of UNRRA penicillin was possible only in Tirana and Durrës, where refrigerating facilities were available.

The Communist government apparently began its long-range hospital program with the introduction of the One-Year Plan in 1948 and continued it in the Two-Year and Five-Year Plans. Figures on the number of available beds in Albanian hospitals, from official Albanian and Soviet sources, are: 1948: 2,680; 1950: 3,120; 1953: 3,559; 1954: 3,557. The planned figure for 1955 was 3,953.

These figures reveal that no major expansion has occurred. The 49 hospitals and sanatoria with 3,557 beds in 1954 represent a ratio of one bed for every 371 persons, compared with one bed for every 1,266 persons in 1938. Plan reports claim that 77,000 people were treated in hospitals in the course of 1953, while the dispensaries and ambulance stations had a total turnover of 1,102,000 patients. According to Soviet sources, there were 478 dispensaries and ambulance stations at the beginning of 1954.

A State Pharmaceutical Laboratory was established in Tirana in 1948 for the manufacture of pharmaceuticals. According to official statements, the laboratory produced "more than 137 kinds of medicaments" in 1953 and more than 160 in 1954. There have been reports, however, of the unsatisfactory quality of Albanian pharmaceuticals. Albania still badly needs medicines. Most medicines are imported from the Soviet Union and the captive countries, although considerable quantities are sent by Albanians in the United States to their relatives in Albania.

It is difficult to determine the exact accomplishments of the Communist government in the field of public health, although the death rate seems to be decreasing. Actual accomplishments are exaggerated for propaganda purposes, and no objective analysis is possible without facts and figures. Recent official statements relating to the abovementioned State Pharmaceutical Laboratory illustrate the difficulties. The official *Zëri i Popullit* in an article on November 4, 1954 declared that production of this laboratory "will be increased after construction of a new building in 1954." A Radio Prague broadcast of December 8,

1954, however, referred to the "further expansion of the [Albanian pharmaceutical] industry" with the construction of another large pharmaceutical plant for which "much of the laboratory equipment and devices were furnished to Albania by the Soviet Union and the People's Democracies." According to a Radio Tirana broadcast of April 16, 1955, work on the new building did not begin until that month.

Social Insurance

According to the *Great Soviet Encyclopedia* (Vol. II, 2nd edition, 1950, p. 47), social insurance was first introduced by the Albanian Communist government in 1947. The initial social security scheme covered approximately 75,000 people, but it is not clear how many persons were actually insured, for the above figure includes eligible dependents. Social Assistance and Social Insurance, two independent organizations established in 1947, were merged into the State Social Security Organization. This organization is under the jurisdiction of the Ministry of Finance, which acts in consultation with the Ministries of Interior and Health, the Albanian Red Cross, and the trade unions.

The social insurance program enacted on March 5, 1953 closely resembles that of the Soviet Union and of the other captive states, although it covers an even smaller and more privileged segment of the population than do the other programs. According to the scheme, social insurance covers every state employee (including workers of the nationalized enterprises), all privately employed persons, and the members of the national security forces. The insurance scheme lists some fifteen types of benefits, grouped under five headings: medical care; compensation; old age pension; family allowances; and recreation. Payment is not deducted from wages and salaries. The entire scheme is financed by the state and by contributions from private employers.

Medical Care

Health insurance covers wage earners as well as their dependents, all "volunteer" workers during the period of their voluntary work, and students. In case of hospitalization, all expenses are covered by insurance. In cases of prolonged treatment not requiring hospitalization, coverage is determined by the Ministry of Finance.

Workman's Compensation

Compensation (sickness benefit) is due the wage earner for a certain period of sickness, or for the period of temporary disability caused by an accident on the job. In cases of work-connected permanent disability, the insured person becomes eligible to apply for pension.

The amount of compensation depends on the position held, the educational background, and "recommendation," that is, on one's political record.

Family Allowances

A special financial allowance is given the head of a family when a child is born. This apparently includes baby clothing and a special food ration. In case of death of the insured or a member of his household, a fixed sum is granted for burial expenses.

Pension

The insurance scheme establishes full pensions after twenty years of active employment, beginning with 1945. In case of invalidism, permanent disability, or retirement with less than twenty years of employment, the amount of the benefit is scaled down proportionately. The law also provides for widow's and orphan's pensions. Special consideration is given for "outstanding services to the State," which means that the families of leading military and police personnel, as well as those of the Party and government leaders, enjoy special privileges.

Recreation

All insured persons are entitled to a paid vacation, the duration of which depends on the length of active employment and the type of work. Workers and their children are also entitled to free recreation in government-owned rest houses. During the first four years of the Five-Year Plan, 23,995 workers and functionaries and 29,540 shock-workers were admitted to rest camps, according to official reports. In 1955 some 7,000 workers and 8,000 shock-workers were scheduled to spend their vacation in the camps. Expectant mothers are granted thirty-five days paid vacation prior to, and forty-two days after, childbirth.

Financing

Since there is no information concerning the exact number of persons covered by the insurance scheme and the exact benefits, it is impossible to evaluate the figures quoted by Enver Hoxha on June 17, 1955, when he stated that the budget for 1955 included 280 million leks (the official Albanian rate is 50 leks to one dollar) for social insurance, and that this was 15.5 per cent more than in 1954, when apparently the amount was roughly 240 million leks. In 1948, the administration of social security spent 191,600,000 leks on grants-in-aid, medical help, and pensions.

Hoxha also stated that during the 1948-54 period a total of 1,529,000,000 leks was received by beneficiaries from insurance funds. This represents a yearly average of 220 million leks. The Albanian Social Insurance Institute thus appears to be operating on a "hand-to-mouth" basis, and its funds are hardly sufficient to cope with any major disaster. Furthermore, old age benefits, and sickness and disability pensions must be set at an extremely low level, because social insurance expenditures have not greatly increased after ten years of accumulative rights or half-pensions.

Although the provisions of the social insurance law appear sweeping in scope and comprehensive in coverage, a closer examination indicates that such is not the case. At most, 25 per cent of the Albanian people are covered. The remaining three-quarters of the population is ineligible for social insurance benefits. Despite the intensive industrialization program, roughly 80 per cent of the people are still peasants and excluded from social security. They are entitled to free medical care and medicines from the public health service, but only upon the presentation of a certificate of indigence issued by the local Communist authorities. The issuance of such a certificate appears dependent upon the political background and reliability of the applicant, rather than upon his need of treatment.

An examination of the categories covered by social insurance shows that the entire program is designed to implement Communist economic and political planning. It covers workers in the nationalized enterprises, state employees, and members of the security forces. Even within these favored sectors, however, there are further inequalities. A law of December 3, 1949 giving free medical aid is illustrative of Communist welfare policy in Albania. The following seven categories receive free medical aid: (1) workers insured by social security; (2) state pensioners; (3) army officers and their families; (4) enlisted men; (5) volunteer workers; (6) members of the People's Police and their families (7) students with state scholarships. Discounting the first category, which is entitled to medical aid under the social security provisions, it is evident that the other categories are favored by the regime for political, economic, or security reasons. State pensioners are obviously those rewarded for their loyalty. Volunteer workers are those who "volunteer" to work on such "crash" economic projects as railroad construction, drainage canals, or agricultural work (i.e. schoolchildren and teachers who work during the summer vacation).

Students with state scholarships are the future elite, and the prime prerequisite for such scholarships is "political reliability." It is interesting to note that three of the seven favored categories represent the security forces. Even here, there is a most favored category. The families of all People's Police members are covered, but only the families of army officers, not those of enlisted men, are entitled to free medical aid.

17. EDUCATION

Albanian patriots in the second half of the last century faced the problem of creating national consciousness among the Albanian people, who had been under Turkish domination for over four centuries and had been divided by the conversion of the majority of the population to the Moslem faith. If there was to be a national resurgence, these patriots concluded, the mother tongue which had been neglected during Turkish rule must first be cultivated. Albanian was used in only two schools, both Catholic institutions in Shkodër, a Franciscan seminary founded in 1861 and a Jesuit school founded in 1877. These schools enjoyed the protection of Austria-Hungary, under whose auspices they had been created. The others were schools for the Moslem population conducted in Turkish, or Greek-language schools, which were under the control and supervision of the Patriarchate of Constantinople, for the Orthodox Christians. In the program of the League of Prizren (1878), it was agreed that the language of the administration of an autonomous Albania should be Albanian and that tax-supported Albanian schools should be opened. The Society for the Development of the Albanian Language, which was founded in Constantinople in 1879, had the objective of publishing educational books in Albanian. Schools were opened in the Albanian colonies of Romania, Bulgaria, Egypt, and, later, the United States.

It was difficult, however, to found Albanian schools in Albania proper. The Turkish authorities were opposed, and the Albanian schools could not compete with the Greek schools. Greek propaganda, spread through church and school, was a dangerous divisive influence in the country, its aim being to Hellenize the Orthodox Christians so that they would consider themselves Greeks. This aim was fulfilled to a certain extent, for many Christians opposed the creation of Albanian schools. The clergy of the Greek Church excommunicated the teachers of Albanian schools, and the language itself was prohibited and anathematized.

Toward the end of the nineteenth century, a few Albanian schools were opened in the district of Korçë. One was an institution for girls (1891), founded by Gerasim Qirias, an Albanian who had been educated by the American Board of Missions. However, these schools were dependent upon the influence Albanian Moslems could exercise on the Porte and on the domestic policy of the Ottoman government, which oscillated between reform and conservatism. Consequently, they were soon closed.

After the 1908 Young Turk Constitution, an upsurge of educational activity rose in Albania, especially in the south. A congress met in Monastir (Bitolj) in November of that year and decided upon a unified alphabet. Many Albanian schools were opened, even in villages. To fill the need for teachers, plans for a normal school were drawn at a congress held in Elbasan in 1909. However, national education was again short-lived. The Young Turks' real aim was not the free development of the nationalities within the Empire but their Ottomanization. They were alarmed by the progress of the Albanians, and by the end of 1910, the new Albanian schools were closed.

Education in Independent Albania, 1912-1939

Since World War I broke out shortly after Albania declared her independence in November 1912, there was little time for progress in national education. The belligerent powers—Austria-Hungary, Italy, France—which occupied the country opened a few schools in their zones, adapting their systems and programs and including their languages in the curricula.

Albanian national education really started with the Congress of Lushnjë (1920), when a Ministry of Public Instruction was created by the newly formed government. This Ministry faced enormous problems. Illiteracy was very high. As late as 1938, approximately 80 per cent of the population was illiterate. The new Ministry also faced the problem of creating an educational system for the entire country from the bits and scraps left over from the long Ottoman period.

Organization of the Educational System in 1934

The first radical change in education occurred in 1933, when on April 22 the nationalization of education and the suppression of private schools in Albania was decreed. Article 206 of the Constitution was amended to read: "The teaching and education of the Albanian citizens are an exclusive right of the state. They are given only in schools and various institutions of the state according to law. . . . Private schools of any category, which have functioned until now, are closed."

Private schools were suppressed on the grounds that they were financed from abroad and that they were of no benefit to the state. The government also maintained that private education fostered a separatist sentiment among the younger generation.

Following the nationalization of education, a decree-law was passed (September 26, 1934) reorganizing the educational system. Dr. Mirash Ivanaj, then Minister of Education, prepared the law, which is known in Albania simply as *Ligji i Ivanajt* (Ivanaj's law). It was the most important and complete "organic decree-law" ever made in Albania. It aimed to create an integrated national education program.

Elementary Education. Free elementary education was made obligatory for all children of Albanian citizens from the age of four to that of thirteen. In the villages, where there were no kindergartens, education began at the age of seven with elementary school. Five grades of instruction were given in elementary school. The first three grades constituted the lower division, the last two the upper division. Upon completion of elementary school, the student could enter a gymnasium, or other secondary school.

Secondary Education. The aim of secondary education was to give the student a general education, to prepare him for further study in universities or other institutions of higher learning, or to give him the necessary theoretical and practical knowledge for exercising a free profession. Albanian secondary schools consisted of the following types.

1. *Gymnasium,* eight years of instruction. This was divided into two levels, the lower comprising the first four classes, and the upper the last four. The lower level was the basis for all secondary schools. Those gymnasia that had no particular specialization emphasized a kind of general education. There was also a state secondary institution, the National Lycée of Korçë, in which the courses were conducted in French. The *lycée* program consisted of nine years of instruction, the first two preparatory. Its curriculum after the second year was that of all recognized French *lycées,* with the addition of Albanian language and literature.

2. *Normal School,* four years of instruction. There were two such schools, one in Elbasan which was coeducational, and one in Tirana for girls. The normal schools were intended to prepare the teaching body of the elementary schools and kindergartens. Students entered normal school after four years of a gymnasium.

3. *Town School* (*shkolla qytetse*), four years of instruction. This was a unit by itself and constituted the lower division of the professional schools; it corresponded to the lower level of the gymnasium.

4. *Commercial Institute,* four years of instruction of higher secon-

dary grade. Students were admitted after they had finished a town school, with a major in commerce.

5. *Technical School,* three to five years of instruction, depending on the field. This consisted of upper secondary grades. Its principal aim was the theoretical and practical teaching of agriculture and various crafts. The students entered a technical school after they had completed a town school.

The secondary schools had the following fields: (1) The gymnasia had classical and scientific divisions, beginning with the third year. The National Lycée of Korçë, according to the French system, had a liberal arts division and a science division. (2) The normal school trained teachers for elementary and kindergarten instruction, with a two-year curriculum for kindergarten training and a four-year program for elementary training. The normal school for girls was united with the gymnasium for girls, which was the Institute for Girls in Tirana. For their last two years, normal school students specializing in elementary education attended training schools (*shkolla ushtrimore*) to obtain practice training. (3) The branches of study in the town schools were business, wood-carving, dairy, agriculture, and housekeeping, depending on the needs of the localities. Specialization began in the third year.

Higher Education. There were no universities in prewar Albania, and advanced study had to be pursued outside the country.

Private and Minority Schools

There were several private schools in Albania prior to the suppression of private education in 1934. These included schools owned by private individuals, such as the Instituti Qirias, a secondary school for girls near Tirana; the schools, principally in Shkodër, founded by the Franciscan and Jesuit orders; a few schools belonging to religious communities, the *medreses* (religious schools) of the Moslem community, and the seminaries of the Orthodox Church. A few private schools were established by American organizations. The elementary school in Korçë, directed by the Reverend Phineas Kennedy and his wife, was the heir of the girls school opened in 1891, and was financed by the American Board of Missions. Of much greater importance was the Vocational School (*Shkolla Teknike*) of Tirana, founded in 1921 by the American Junior Red Cross, which offered courses in mechanics, agriculture, and elementary engineering. Some Italian schools, both elementary and secondary, financed by the Italian government, had also been created.

The only nonstate school (semiprivate) permitted after 1934, although under a new arrangement, was the Albanian-American Agricultural School of Kavajë, near Durrës. This school was founded in the 1920's by private American funds on lands granted by the Albanian government to Dr. Erickson and Dr. Erwin. In 1931, under a twenty-year agreement between the Near East Foundation of New York and the Albanian government, the school was put under the control of the government. It consisted of a boys school and a girls school. Farm work was the basis for the education received in the boys school. The girls school, formerly an institution training young women for teaching in village schools, later developed a "folk school" type of program. The school was closed in 1939, when Italy occupied the country.

The only minority schools were the Greek schools in the prefecture of Gjirokastër, where some 30-35,000 Greeks lived. When these schools were closed in 1933, the Greek government protested to the League of Nations, which referred the question to the Permanent Court of Justice at The Hague. The Albanian government contended that this involved no infraction of minority right, since all citizens were denied the right to private schools. However, in 1935 the Permanent Court of Justice decided in favor of the Greeks, and the Albanian government was obliged to restore the Greek schools. It is significant that during the Greco-Albanian contest the Italians made common cause with the Greeks. They were irritated by the closing of the Italian schools and believed that the educational decree-law was directed against them. In 1936, when Mehdi Frashëri's cabinet was in power, a bill was passed dividing schools into state schools and "authorized schools," the latter being another name for private schools. In addition to the Greek minority schools, the Franciscan gymnasium of Shkodër was reopened (the Franciscans were all Albanians) under government control.

Educational Reform of 1938

On May 6, 1938, a decree was promulgated reforming the secondary school system. The law was designed to replace certain academic and agricultural courses which predominated in the schools with vocational training. Under this reform, the work school *(shkolla e punës)* completed the education given in elementary schools. It offered two- or four-year courses and it was designed to train young Albanians for various useful arts and crafts, for farming and animal husbandry, and for small industrial and commercial enterprises. Courses offered in the schools were determined by the Ministry of Education according to the economic needs of the locality. However, this reform was short-lived, since a year later the Italians occupied Albania.

University Students, Teaching Personnel, and Number of Schools

As there were no institutions of higher learning in prewar Albania, students went abroad to pursue further studies, usually on government fellowships. The first groups were sent to Austria and Italy, since Albanians had the closest ties with these countries. When students began to graduate from the National Lycée of Korçë, a turn toward France began. As Italian penetration deepened in Albania, the number of students studying in Italian universities began to increase. A few government fellowships were given for studies in England, but not for the United States. The few graduates from American colleges had studied with American assistance or with private means. There were also some graduates from German universities. Those who attended the University of Athens were generally southerners and generally used their own funds. In 1936/37, 363 university students were abroad for study on private means, and 65 on government scholarships. French, German, and Austrian universities were held in highest esteem by the Albanians.

Secondary school teachers were selected from among university students. Not all had completed their studies, and they were engaged without competitive examination, since there was a scarcity of trained personnel. As the system improved, some competition developed and elementary school teachers were granted teaching certificates on the basis of examinations. Secondary school instructors especially were handicapped by a lack of textbooks. In the upper grades of the secondary schools, in particular, material for many subjects had to be dictated to, or mimeographed for, the students.

In 1938, there were 642 elementary schools in Albania in which 1,350 teachers taught about 54,000 pupils, and 7 boarding schools in mountainous regions with 450 boarders. There were 18 secondary schools: 3 gymnasia, 1 lycée, 2 normal schools, 1 commercial institute, 1 technical institute, 1 agricultural institute, and 9 "town schools," with a total of 5,677 students and 261 teachers. The girls' schools were separated from those for boys; only the National Lycée of Korçë and the Normal School in Elbasan were coeducational. In 1938, 30 per cent of the girls of school age were attending school; the corresponding figure for boys and girls together was 36.7 per cent. There were 1,425 girls in secondary institutions, 15,778 in elementary schools, and 318 women teachers in both elementary and secondary institutions.

A detailed picture of the school situation in Albania during 1938/39 is given in Map No. 10 of *Albania in 10 cartine dimostrative,* compiled by Francesco Pollastri, Chief of the Geographical Office of the Istituto Centrale di Statistica del Regno d'Italia (Rome: Tip. Failli,

1939). Because some of the figures do not seem reliable, the table is not included here. However, if the number of elementary school pupils, the number of girls, and the statistics for secondary education in the prefectures of Kukës (Kosovë) and Peshkopi (Dibër) are excluded, the rest of Map No. 10 on the school situation in Albania appears reasonably accurate.

Youth Organizations

In 1930, Enti Kombëtar Djelmënija Shqiptare (National Organization of Albanian Youth) was founded to direct the activities of all Albanian youth societies and to improve "the patriotic, moral, and physical education of the youth of the country," in school and out. This was a new departure in the Albanian educational system, and it reflected the increased control and regimentation of public activities by the state.

Five years later, representatives of the various cultural and sports societies of Albania created a federation named Vllaznija Shqiptare (Albanian Brotherhood). The federation, which was under the Ministry of Education, had its headquarters in Tirana. In February 1939, the Ministry of Popular Culture was established; its Directorate of Albanian Youth took control of the youth federation from the Ministry of Education. A month or so later, the entire situation was changed by the Italian invasion.

EDUCATION UNDER AXIS OCCUPATION, 1939-1944

With the occupation of Albania by Fascist Italy, education came completely under Italian control. Italian was introduced in all the secondary schools. As the Albanian government (under the Fascist regime) on July 19, 1939 stated to the authorities of the Albanian-American Agricultural School of Kavajë, it was necessary that all institutions, in keeping with the principle of fascism, "Everything for the State," be incorporated into the national system. It was at that time that the Kavajë school was transferred to the state. Italy sought the fascistization and Italianization of education in Albania.

In 1941, after the collapse of the Yugoslav state, Kosovo (Kosovo-Metohija in Yugoslavia)—a preponderantly Albanian province—was annexed to Albania. This proved an incentive to the spread of education and the founding of Albanian schools in that province, but there was an insufficient number of teachers.

With the strengthening of the resistance movement in 1941, paralysis ensued in education. Secondary schools became centers of guerrilla recruitment and resistance, and students as well as instructors took to the mountains. Many of those who remained engaged in subversive propaganda work. When the Germans entered Albania in September 1943, after the Italian capitulation, they recognized Albanian neutrality and left the Albanians free to run their own schools along nationalistic lines, but there was hardly any education.

Education under the Communist Regime, 1944-1954

Communist Philosophy and Methods of Education

When the Communists came to power in November 1944, one of their goals was the reorganization of education. As the former Minister of Education, Bedri Spahiu, wrote in 1950, they had to fight "bourgeois survivals in culture," "abolish backwardness," and "place at the disposal of the broad masses all the means for spreading and developing the new socialist culture and ideology."

Education in Albania was to be built on Marxist-Leninist foundations. At the First Congress of the Albanian Communist Party in 1948, Enver Hoxha, then Premier of Albania, made clear its function: "The school must transmit to the working masses the ideas and principles of the Party, its aims and duties; it must install the new socialist principles of education; it must educate the children of all the strata of the population on the basis of these principles; it must fight against any alien ideology and against any foreign influence on youth."

For any totalitarian system, especially the Communist system, youth is the property of the state. The school must serve to bring the child under the control of the state; every phase of his development should be under government control. Article 31 of the 1950 Constitution of the People's Republic of Albania reads: "The State takes especial care of the education of youth . . . The schools are under state management . . ."

According to Communist philosophy, economic forces determine the form of a society. Education is instrumental in the creation and development of that kind of industry and productive system which will lead to the building of the "new society." Communist education aims at training students in a very narrow field and to deprive them of well-rounded knowledge and an open inquiring mind. In his speech of March 24, 1946, Enver Hoxha said: "This culture and this education should no longer be only a worthless decoration, but should serve the general interest to produce more and better . . . We need that culture which will make the people more capable of working and producing, and we will make this culture and education a weapon of the broad working masses." The state has opened schools for early specialization in industry and agriculture as well as factory schools in order to carry out its two- and five-year plans. Obviously, such a program, by creating a new professional class, increases the number of supporters of the regime.

The conditioning of the child to Communist ideology begins in the lowest grades. In kindergarten and school, the child learns the Albanian alphabet under the eyes of Lenin, Stalin, Enver Hoxha, and now also Mehmet Shehu. At the outset of the regime, education was obligatory until the child finished elementary school (twelve years of age); by the decree of June 12, 1952, it was prolonged to include the first seven grades, which means three more years after elementary education.

Textbooks in all schools preach the teachings of Lenin and Stalin. The Tirana rulers themselves stated in the Educational Reform Law of 1946 that textbooks would be prepared which would contain Communist ideology as their main principle. Since communism as an ideal equals the Soviet Union as a realization, everything Russian is extolled and everything Western is ignored or minimized. Education is slanted to make the student identify himself with the world Communist movement and to demonstrate to him that communism represents the inevitable development of Albania's national heritage and culture. Endeavors are further made to identify that movement with progress and, strange as it may seem, with freedom.

In the classroom, lip service is paid to the idea that education be factual and objective, but there is no subject taught in schools in which the Marxist-Leninist ideology is not introduced. The work of writers of the pre-Communist Albanian national revival are distorted to fit the new appraisal on the basis of Marxist-Leninist principles. In his report of October 1950 before the General Council of Education, Kahreman Ylli, then Minister of Education, warned: "Against them [Western system and philosophy], we should establish the socialist principles of social relations which are meant to construct and strengthen socialism." When a teacher of a secondary school prepares his *pllan i punës* (work plan), according to a model furnished by the Ministry of Education, he must include in the proper column—under threat of harsh disciplinary measures—the ideological purpose of the subject developed in class.

Teachers are subject to indoctrination and must attend political seminars. It is the aim of the Ministry of Education that they should not only implicitly follow the principles and methods of Soviet pedagogy but that they also should acquire the Soviet outlook. In order to stimulate the instructors, the Ministry of Education has at various periods created such titles as *arësimtar i dalluar* (distinguished educator), *mësuës i dalluar* (distinguished teacher), *mësuës i merituar* (meritorious teacher), or *mësuës i popullit* (teacher of the people).

The Educational System

On March 25, 1946, Enver Hoxha, as head of the government, made known to the People's Assembly the Communist program for education. He said that one of the main goals was the fight against illiteracy. The government would increase the number of elementary schools and would take rigorous measures against those parents who would not observe the law that made elementary education obligatory. Enver Hoxha also declared that the doors of the secondary schools would be opened for the "broad masses of the country and town youth." He stressed that "the school reform and the change in program should suit the created conditions in our land and should comply with the needs for the building of a new Albania." Almost five months later (August 17, 1946), the Law on Educational Reform was passed. This law made learning to write obligatory for all persons from twelve to forty years of age, and created a pre-school system for the whole state. Under the jurisdiction of the Ministry of Health, the system began with nursery school; it continued through kindergarten and *shtëpitë e fëmijve* (houses for children) under the Ministry of Education.

General education schools (according to Soviet model, elementary, seven-year, and secondary) were made uniform throughout Albania. The gymnasia were preserved. The elementary schools consist of four grades, and the seven-year schools comprise seven grades (the first four corresponding to the elementary school). The secondary schools have four grades beyond the seven-year school. The Tirana government has preserved the seven-year schools of the Greek minority in the prefecture of Gjirokastër, but the Albanian language is also taught. These schools are of course under the same strict government control as are the general schools. The law also permitted the establishment of temporary schools composed of the first three elementary grades, completely separated from the regular elementary schools.

Professional education was introduced for the preparation of cadres "in the various fields of the economic, social, and cultural life of the country." It is under the jurisdiction of the Ministry of Education in collaboration with other ministries. The law also stated that there would be pedagogical and technical schools of four years, practical and professional schools of two years, schools of two years' duration for perfection in crafts, and "rapid courses" running from six to twelve months.

The Law on Educational Reform also established adult education, upon which only a start had been made in prewar Albania. Night schools were opened to give adults an opportunity to begin or to continue their education without leaving work.

Toward the end of 1946, the first Pedagogical Institute was founded in Tirana to provide two years training for teachers for secondary schools who had graduated from a secondary pedagogical school. By 1950, the Pedagogical Institute comprised five departments: Albanian language and literature, Russian language and literature, history and geography, physics and mathematics, biology and chemistry.

As time passed, however, greater emphasis was placed on professional and technical training. A law of January 29, 1948, had as objectives "(a) to increase the number of students . . . from whom the qualified workers will come; (b) to build a broad network of schools with professional courses in order to help the creation of technical cadres, skilled and semiskilled workers, who will bring about the realization of the plans; (c) to take all steps for the development of theoretical and professional knowledge of the qualified workers."

On October 10, 1950 a governmental decree established secondary professional schools called *teknikums* along Soviet lines. These are divided into "low" and "middle" schools. The courses in the low schools last from six months to two years; in the middle schools, four years. The *teknikums* are built and directed by the various ministries, according to an approved government plan. Students who have finished a seven-year school are eligible to enroll. The programs of these schools are determined by the ministry that manages them, in agreement with the Ministry of Education. During the four years of instruction, the number of hours for general education should be 25 to 40 per cent of the total number of hours; the number of hours of practical training in school and in production should not be less than 50 per cent of the number of hours devoted to theoretical professional education.

By 1950, Albania had professional schools for medicine (assistants to physicians), finance, commerce, the petroleum industry, and agriculture. The graduates of these schools, if they do not pursue further studies, are placed in sectors the government deems important.

A decision of the Council of Ministers on August 14, 1951, founded three institutes of higher learning called "high institutes" to give "to science, culture, and technique in our country broader perspectives and to create conditions for their further development, according to the example of science, culture, and technique of the Soviet Union, so that they may be of service to the working masses, [as well as] factors in the development of the economy of our country, and in order to form the intelligentsia of our land." These institutes offer a four-year course, and students are eligible to enter after they have completed secondary education. Three institutes were opened in Tirana on November 1, 1951: the High Pedagogical Institute, the High Polytechnical Institute, and the High Agricultural Institute. In 1952, the foundation of an economic and a medical high institute followed.

Teaching Personnel and School Statistics

According to the Five-Year Plan (1951-55), in 1950 the elementary schools numbered 2,000 with an enrollment of 150,800 pupils, as compared to 643 elementary schools with 52,000 pupils in 1938. From 11 secondary schools (the *Great Soviet Encyclopedia,* 2nd edition, 1950, says there were 18 such schools in 1938) with 6,300 students before World War II, the number rose by 1950 to 193 seven-year schools with 18,350 students, 23 secondary schools with 5,400 students, and a pedagogical institute with 130 students. The teaching staff increased from 1,620 in 1938 to 5,150 in 1950. (The prewar figures given in the Five-Year Plan differ from those on page 274, which were obtained from British sources.)

Even if these figures are accepted as true, it is questionable if the teaching staff is sufficiently qualified to maintain even a moderately high standard of instruction. In prewar Albania, there was a scarcity of teachers and few were well trained, particularly in secondary education. After the Communists came to power, the problem became even more serious, since some teachers had been killed during the war, others were living in exile, and still others were in prison or unemployed because they were not trusted.

To cope with the dearth of teachers, in 1947 the government opened schools for elementary school teachers which offered six-month courses. Any student could register who had completed elementary school and who was eighteen years of age. The quality of these teachers can readily be imagined. As for the training of instructors for secondary education, certainly the training of two years in the former Pedagogical Institute of Tirana was not sufficient. The three directors of the high institutes—Piro Dodbiba of the Agricultural, Zia Këlliçi of the Polytechnical, Hasan Dume of the Pedagogical—were appointed upon graduation from institutes of higher learning in Moscow, and have had no other training or experience. This is indicative of the low quality of the teaching personnel in Albania today.

The difficulties encountered in training teachers and in securing textbooks hamper the realization of the ambitious objectives of the Five-Year Plan for education. By 1955, the number of elementary schools was to increase to 2,158, thus insuring the application of the law on obligatory elementary education. Seven-year and secondary schools were to number 391 and to have an enrollment of 68,000 students, and there were to be 1,800 students in the high institutes. It is unlikely that the goals of 1955 were even approached. According to the report analyzing the results of the 1952/53 school year (*Arësimi Popullor* [Popular Education], August 1953), the plan for that year was not carried out, principally because of the "insufficient activity of the teachers, the organization of youth and the women," and "the little care of the executive organs." Kahreman Ylli, who served as Minister of Education for two years, was dismissed on May 10, 1952, "for having neglected the tasks entrusted to him by the government."

Although one might contest the figures on illiteracy as given in the Five-Year Plan—679,000 in 1945 reduced to 375,000 in 1950—there is no doubt that great progress has been made in this field. The regime is interested in bringing home to the people its ideology and policies, and the written word is one of the most effective methods. However, fulfillment of the Plan target against illiteracy is not expected. According to the report for 1952/53, the fight against illiteracy was not very successful because the necessity for the "liquidation of illiteracy" and the "responsibility for the materialization of the plan" had not been sufficiently appreciated.

Education is a very important factor in the regime's goal of "socialist construction." The regime's claim may even be true that it spent more than 310 million leks (at the official Albanian rate of 13.85 leks to one dollar) for 1946/47; 493 million leks for 1949 (at the official Albanian rate of 50 leks to one dollar since 1947); 663 million leks for 1950. For the 1951-55 period, on the basis of the Five-Year Plan, the government was to invest 3.46 billion leks in education.

Albanian teaching personnel are often criticized for harboring "bourgeois tendencies." When Kahreman Ylli was Minister of Education, he declared that the Albanian school system was infested with "reactionary ideology." In his report to the Second Nationalist Conference of the Albanian Workers' Party (Communist Party), held in Tirana in April 1950, Bedri Spahiu, then secretary of the Party's Politburo, attacked "the low ideological level" of Albanian teachers. In the resolution of July 25, 1953, which analyzed the results of the education plan for the period 1952/53, high educational officials stressed the need to raise "the scientific and ideological quality" of the teachers.

Party Education

Before the Tito-Cominform break in 1948, Albania was a sub-satellite. The real leaders of the Albanian Communist Party were the Communists of Yugoslavia, at that time still subservient to Moscow.

It was not until 1949 that a Central Party School was opened in Tirana to prepare leaders for the Party, for government organizations, and for the professional unions (*profsoiuzy*). A prominent place in the school program is given to the study of Marxist-Leninist-Stalinist teachings, the history of the Bolshevik Party, the history of the Albanian Workers' Party, and active training in Party and government organization. Other Party schools have the usual ideological courses and set an example for all other schools. On June 15, 1950, a Radio Tirana report stated that all 5,150 schoolteachers were taking training courses in ideology.

The professional unions also carry on cultural-educational work. They have created courses for the liquidation of illiteracy and have founded libraries. It was estimated at the second congress of the professional unions that 35 clubs, 212 libraries, 90 artists' collectives, 71 choirs, and 100 orchestras had been established in the country.

Another organization active in Party educational work is the Union of Working Youth of Albania. When a student leaves school, he is subjected to ideological indoctrination by members of this organization, which is under the direction of the Albanian Workers' Party. Albanian Pioneers, a Communist organization that embraces all children from seven to fourteen years of age, is under the supervision and control of the Working Youth.

Agents of the Union of Working Youth of Albania are everywhere seeing that the Party line is strictly followed. However, their work is especially useful in the villages, where they organize "circles" for the general and political education of the peasant youth. In the circles—there were 800 such circles in 1951—the young men of the villages are taught the Communist version of Albanian history, international questions, the Soviet Union, and the People's Democracies. They are assisted by the "Red Workers," whose function is to bring "socialist culture" to people in cooperatives, offices, plants, and schools.

Institute of Sciences

Prewar Albania had no learned societies. After her occupation by Fascist Italy, an Institute of Albanian Studies was created, which was replaced, following the Italian collapse and the occupation of Albania by Nazi Germany, by the Albanian Institute for Sciences and Arts.

When the Communists came to power, the name of the learned society was changed to Institute of Sciences. The aim of the Institute is the development of sciences, arts, and national culture. The scientific section of the Institute has made studies of the flora and fauna of the country and has directed a series of geological studies. For a long time, the history section has been working on a textbook of Albanian history and a collection of documents along Marxist-Leninist lines. The literary and linguistic section has carried on studies in the fields of Albanian literature, language, and folklore. It has finished the compilation of a Russian-Albanian dictionary, which is to be followed by an Albanian-Russian one, and it has also translated a number of Russian works into Albanian. In 1955, it published an excellent dictionary of the Albanian language.

It is significant that the first session (January 1952) of the Albanian Institute of Sciences was devoted to a discussion of Albanian linguistic problems in the light of Stalin's work on linguistics.

Russification of Education

As long as relations between the Soviet Union and Yugoslavia were friendly, Albania was subject mainly to Yugoslav influence. Serbocroatian was introduced in Albanian schools, and Yugoslav instructors came to teach. The greatest number of fellowships for studies were given by the government of Belgrade. According to Yugoslav statistics, there were 730 young Albanians studying in technical, industrial and professional schools in Yugoslavia in 1948. There were also students in military schools and academies, and more than 200 Albanians were given fellowships for studies in Yugoslav universities. However, after the 1948 rupture, Albania came completely under the control of the Soviet Union.

The Albanian educational system has been patterned on that of the Soviet Union. The Russian language has been introduced in all secondary schools. One of the departments of the Pedagogical Institute (now the High Pedagogical Institute) is that of Russian language and literature, and on September 19, 1950, Comrade Olga Smirnova, a Soviet educator, was its head. The Albanian Telegraphic Agency reported on October 15, 1950 that 60 Russian language courses attended by 1,484 workers were being given in various industrial plants under the supervision of Soviet instructors. In his speech of July 1, 1955, Mehmet Shehu thanked the Soviet teachers "Rudenko, Anikin, Arzanosevov, Vulkanov, Tononov and others who have rendered a very precious contribution in organizing and developing" the higher institutes. In fact, the vice directors of these institutes are Russian.

Most Albanian students who study abroad go to the Soviet Union. A few study in universities in People's Democracies, with which Albania has cultural agreements. According to the Five-Year Plan, the 900 young Albanians studying abroad are to occupy high positions in education. They adopt Russian programs, apply Russian methods in teaching, use Russian texts. The Moscow-trained director of the High Agricultural Institute, Piro Dodbiba, declared: "Our instruction has as its basis the school plans and programs of the higher institutes of the Soviet Union. Our task is to give our students solid knowledge of the theory of Marxism-Leninism, the agrobiology of the USSR, and the achievements of Soviet scholars."

The Albanian-Soviet Friendship Society is also carrying out a Russification program. Although the society was founded in 1945, it did not develop until 1948. In the summer of 1953, it held its third congress, which was attended by 400 delegates, representing 210,000 members, a great increase compared to the 7,000 members in 1947 and 120,000 in 1951. The society has established courses for teaching the Russian language in all parts of the country. In September 1953, which was dedicated to the celebration of the Albanian-Soviet friendship, 34 new courses in Russian were opened. In 1953 a two-year Russian language night school was established in Tirana. It was reported on July 10, 1955 that 43 people graduated and another 121 completed the first year of this school. In the 1955/56 school year, the Albanian-Soviet Friendship Society plans to increase the number of students in the Russian language school. (For other activities of the Albanian-Soviet Friendship Society, see page 133.)

Administrative Changes

On May 7, 1947, the Committee of Arts and Culture was founded by the Tirana government. On June 24, 1948, this committee was united with the office of Premier, while the National Library and the Ethnographical and Archeological Museum (both in Tirana) were detached from this office and placed under the jurisdication of the Institute of Sciences. On August 1, 1953, the Committee of Arts and Culture, the Radio Broadcast Committee, and the Direction of Publications were united with the Ministry of Education, which now bears the title Ministry of Education and Culture; its head is Ramis Alija.

18. RELIGION

A Historical Survey up to 1912

Christianity appeared in Albania in the first centuries of the Christian era, with Durrës on the Adriatic Coast an important Christian center. When the Roman Empire was divided into East and West (395), the province of Praevalis (Doclea-Scodra) in the north and the rest of Albania, although politically part of the Eastern Empire, ecclesiastically remained dependent on Rome. However, in 732, Leo the Isaurian detached these lands from Rome and subordinated them to the Patriarchate of Constantinople. The situation changed in the following centuries when the two churches were drifting apart, but in general Albania tended to follow Constantinople. When the definite schism occurred in 1054, the northern part of the country was placed under the jurisdiction of Rome.

For almost four centuries after the schism, Albania was a battleground between East and West, with the boundaries of the Roman Catholic Church and of the Orthodox Church reflecting the fortunes of the political powers supporting them. As such Western powers as the Normans of Sicily, the Venetians, and the Angevins of Naples expanded in Albania, the frontiers of the Orthodox Church receded. When the Byzantines or the Serbs pushed back the Western forces, the Catholic Church retreated. The local Albanian lords could not escape the effect of these changes, which compelled them to lead confessionally a vacillating life between the two churches. The distribution of Catholicism and Orthodoxy in Albania is the heritage of these four centuries of East-West struggle.

With the arrival of the Turks toward the end of the fourteenth century, Mohammedanism was introduced into Albania. The conversion of the people to the faith of the invaders was a slow process. In the north, the propagation of Mohammedanism met Roman Catholic opposition. However, the ignorance of the population, the absence of a capable clergy, and especially the material advantages of conversion weakened resistance. Waves of conversion occurred when Catholic powers such as Venice and Austria were at war with the Ottoman Empire. By the close of the seventeenth century, the Catholics were outnumbered by the Mohammedans.

The Orthodox Christians in the south suffered a different fate during the first centuries of Turkish domination. After the fall of

Constantinople in 1453, Mehmed II, in order to secure the allegiance of the Orthodox Christians in the Balkans, proclaimed himself the protector of the Greek Church, and a decree secured the old rights and privileges for the newly elected Patriarch and his successors. This policy made conditions for the Orthodox Church easier than for the Catholic north.

Large-scale conversions did not occur among the Orthodox Albanians in the early years of the Ottoman occupation, when the Turks did not fear intervention from an Orthodox Christian state and were not inclined to use force for apostasy. However, Islamic pressure was felt when the Russo-Turkish wars of the eighteenth century began, because the Ottomans considered the Orthodox Christian allies of Russia. The situation of the Albanian Orthodox Christians was temporarily improved by the Treaty of Küçük Kaynarci (1774), when Russia became the protector of all Orthodox Christians in the Ottoman Empire.

In certain parts of Albania, crypto-Christianity developed, a phenomenon rarely noticed elsewhere in the Balkans. The crypto-Christians were Christians living in regions bordering Moslem areas who openly professed Islam, while practicing Christianity in private. They apparently flowered in periods of outbursts of anti-Christian fanaticism. In the north, these crypto-Christians were called *laramanë* (motley), and lived particularly around Peć and in the plain of Kosovo (Yugoslavia). In south-central Albania, their counterparts were inhabitants of Shpat, a region comprising several villages between Elbasan and Berat. With the end of Ottoman rule, crypto-Christianity disappeared.

Religion in Independent Albania, 1912-1939

Albania emerged from Turkish domination in 1912 as a predominantly Moslem nation, with about two thirds of the population followers of Islam. Whereas for other Balkan peoples religion became a very strong stimulus to nationalism, as religion and nationality coincided, it was an obstacle for the Albanians.

As the economic-political basis of the Ottoman Empire had been religion, all positions in the Empire were open to Moslem Albanians. Since many Albanians showed great ability and rose to prominent positions, a certain community of interest had been built between the Albanians and the Turks. This helps to explain why Albania achieved independence so late and why the Albanians were not assimilated by their neighbors. Consequently, when the Albanian state was created, the Moslems who had held high positions in the Ottoman Empire, mostly beys, came to power. However, religious affiliation was not of great importance in the political life of independent Albania, for Roman Catholics and Orthodox Christians also played a prominent role. The religious groupings, which in the past often distinguished the social and political categories into which the population fell, were gradually losing their political influence after 1912.

Independent Albania did not adopt a state religion. The constitutions of the Republic and of the kingdom both declared that the Albanian state had no official religion, that all religions and faiths were respected, and that their liberty of practice was assured. They expressed the true feelings of the Albanian people, who whether Moslems, Orthodox, or Roman Catholics, are tolerant in religious matters or rather generally lack strong religious convictions.

Moslems

Official 1937 figures gave the Moslem population of Albania as 719,878, or 69.3 per cent of the population. This number includes both the Sunni and the Bektashi Moslems, who are not reckoned in the census separately. In Islam, there are two main branches, Sunni and Shiah, Bektashism being an offshoot of the latter. The relations between the Bektashis and the Sunnis in Albania remained somewhat strained until 1929, when the organization of the Moslem community was studied by the government. The Bektashis demanded complete independence in the Congress of Korçë in 1929, wanting to create a community of their own, but the Sunnis were too strong and they gained only spiritual and executive autonomy within the Moslem community.

Sunnis. The Sunnis are conservative and known as the traditional followers of Islam. They constitute the great majority of the Moslem population and are found throughout Albania, being strongest in the central part.

Before 1929, the Sunnis were headed by the Grand Mufti of Tirana, who presided over the Supreme Council of the Sheriat (Divine Laws of Islam), composed of five members, whose task was to regulate matters relating to religion and the *vakëfe* (property belonging to religious bodies). After 1929, when a new constitution of the Albanian Moslem community was established, the supreme authority of the community lay in the General Council, which consisted of the Chief of the community, the four Grand Muftis of the four zones, and a delegate for each prefecture of Albania. The Chief, who held the title Head of the Moslem Community, was Dr. Rexhep Shapati; he was elected by secret ballot cast by the members of the General Council. The four zones into which the Moslem community was divided, and in each of which a Grand Mufti resided, were Shkodër (prefectures of Kosovë and Shkodër); Tirana (prefectures of Peshkopi, Tirana, Durrës, and Berat); Korçë (prefectures of Elbasan and Korçë); and Gjirokastër (prefectures of Vlorë and Gjirokastër). The Grand Muftis were chosen by the General Council. There were muftis in the centers of the prefectures and sub-muftis in those of the subprefectures.

Significant for the trends of the time are some duties of the muftis prescribed by the organization law: "to encourage national brotherhood among Albanians of all beliefs; to urge Moslems to become informed concerning modern civilization." Polygamy, which had seldom been practiced by Albanian Moslems, was officially abolished and the wearing of veils by women was abandoned.

On March 3, 1936, the delegates of the sects (Kadiri, Rifai, Saadi, Tidjani) of the Moslem Community of Albania met at Tirana and formed a common organization called Drita Hyjnore (The Divine Light), which aimed to secure "the exercise of spiritual duties" and "to strengthen the morals of the faithful through sermons." The founding of this organization indicated a wide-felt need for a more educated Moslem clergy.

The Moslem community possessed a General Medrese (Moslem seminary) and published a periodical called *Zâni i Naltë* (The Supreme Voice).

Bektashis. The Bektashis are a sect often considered heretic by Orthodox Mohammedans. They take their name from the saint Hadji Bektash. The religious doctrines of Bektashism are devised to appeal to all intellects and temperaments. Like other mystic religions, Bektashism includes a gradual initiation to secret knowledge through a number of steps. These form a series of grades between a crude and unsophisticated religion, in which saint-worship is important, to an emancipated, and in some respects enlightened, philisophy of pantheism. Its doctrine and ritual, as far as the latter is known, have points of contact with Christianity.

Bektashism emphasizes ethics. It preaches abstinence from violence and charity to all men. The Bektashi should make no distinction in his conduct between Moslems and non-Moslems, and members of non-Islamic religions may be admitted to the order. The Bektashis are also allowed more liberty in such details of daily observance as veiling of women and abstention from strong drink, and instead of Ramazan they keep the less vigorous Persian fast which commemorates the murdered sons of Ali. This greater freedom and Bektashism's relationship to Christianity have appealed to Albanians.

Bektashism originated in the thirteenth century in a frontier region of Anatolia, where Christianity, Islamism, and paganism coexisted. It appears to have been introduced in Albania sometime in the fifteenth century by the Janissaries of the Ottoman army. Bektashism greatly expanded in southern Albania during the time of Ali Pasha Tepelena, the ruler of Yannina, who is believed to have been a Bektashi himself.

The Bektashis are strongest in the south, but they also wield some influence in the north, at Krujë. Owing to the influence of Naim Frashëri, the Bektashi apostle-poet of Albanian nationalism, Bektashism among the Albanians followed patriotic and nationalistic lines and played a prominent role in the movement for Albanian independence. In his *Notebook of the Bektashis,* Frashëri wrote: "The Bektashis are brothers not only among themselves but with all humanity as well. They love the rest of the Moslems and the Christians as their soul and they get along well with all men. But above all, they love their fatherland and their countrymen, this being the highest of all virtues."

In the 1920's, when the Albanian state re-emerged after World War I, the Moslems tended to break their former religious ties with Turkey. In January 1922, an assembly of five hundred Bektashi resolved to abolish the tutelage of Ankara; and the *Dede* (the supreme Bektashi), an Albanian, left Turkey and settled in Tirana. When the Turkish Republican Government in 1925 suppressed religious orders of dervishes in Turkey and closed the Bektashi tekkes (monasteries), the headquarters of the sect was transferred to Tirana.

According to the statute drawn up at the Congress of Korçë in 1929, the sect of the Bektashis was composed of clergy, confirmed members, and laity. At the top of the clergy was the *Dede* or *Kryegjysh* (Chief Grandfather); under him were five *gjyshë* (grandfathers), followed by *baballarë* (fathers) and dervishes. The clergy lived in tekkes.

The figures about the Bektashis vary greatly. Before World War II, the number of Bektashis in the world was estimated at 7,370,000 of whom 200,000 were Albanians.

Orthodox Christians

In 1937, the Orthodox Christians in Albania numbered 212,233, or 20.4 per cent of the entire population. They reside mostly south of the Shkumbî River, particularly in the prefectures of Gjirokastër and Korçë.

In the Orthodox Church, each state enjoys an independent or autocephalous national church. This means that in matters of doctrine each national Church subordinates itself to the Ecumenical Patriarch of Constantinople and the Holy Synod (the general church council), but that in its internal organization, it is independent. After their political liberation, all the Orthodox Balkan peoples achieved ecclesiastical independence, and each national church received in turn a *tomos,* or decree of autocephaly, from the Ecumenical Patriarch. At the end of World War I, only Albania still lacked a *tomos* (Bulgaria was considered schismatic until 1945) and her own independent Church.

Even under Ottoman rule, nationalist Orthodox Albanians in the United States, afraid of the great Greek influence exercised on the churches of their mother country, detached themselves from the Patriarchate of Constantinople and established the Albanial National Independent Church in Boston (1908). Upon the re-establishment of the Albanian independent state after the First World War, efforts were made for an independent Albanian Orthodox Church.

At the outset, one of the major obstacles was the presence of Monsignor Jakovos, a zealous Greek and an able politician, as Metropolitan of Korçë. In 1921, an Orthodox Congress held in that city arbitrarily declared the independence of the Albanian Orthodox Church, and the Tirana government ordered the expulsion of the Greek archbishop. On September 12, 1922, another Orthodox Congress convened in Berat proclaimed the autocephaly of the Church and elected a Church Council to function *ad interim* at Korçë. Attempts to negotiate with the Constantinople Patriarchate also began. There was need for a Synod, but there were only three bishops in Albania, Fan Noli, who had come from America to become Bishop of Durrës; Hierotheos of Korçë, and Monsignor Kristofor (Kisi); and four bishops were needed to constitute the Synod. At this juncture, a revolution took place which overthrew Bishop Noli as head of the Albanian government and forced him to leave the country.

The negotiations with the Patriarchate at Constantinople were resumed during Zog's regime. In the beginning, the Patriarchate did not approve of the Albanian Orthodox hierarchy. The Patriarchate also had misgivings about the independence of the Albanian Orthodox Church, a minority church within a Moslem majority. However, the real cause of the difficulties raised by the Patriarchate lay in the pressure exercised by the Greek government. In 1927, the independence of the Albanian Orthodox Church was declared again, but the Patriarchate did not recognize it.

On August 14, 1929, the constitution of the Autocephalous Orthodox Church of Albania was published. The Church was divided into four bishoprics: Korçë, Durrës and Tirana, Berat, and Gjirokastër. The bishopric of Durrës and Tirana bore the title of Metropolis and its head that of Metropolitan of the diocese and Archbishop of Albania. Supreme authority was vested in an Albanian Episcopal Holy Synod, composed of the active bishops of each diocese and the Great Mitred Economus. The Synod superintended the religious acts of the Church and was responsible for the religious education of the clergy and the Orthodox Christians, for which it had the right to found and maintain schools. A "Mixed Council," consisting of the members of the Synod and four laymen, one for each diocese, was created for the administration and control of church property, churches, and monasteries. This council met at Tirana under the presidency of the Archbishop.

Negotiations with the Constantinople Patriarchate were reopened in the 1930's, when Monsignor Kristofor Kisi, duly consecrated bishop in Constantinople before World War I, became head of the Albanian Orthodox Church. An agreement was reached in February, 1937. Two bishops were recognized by the Patriarch. For the remaining bishops, two Albanian theologians, a monk and a preacher, were found in Greece; they were consecrated by the Patriarchate, and the Albanians' Synod was thus made complete. In April 1937, the Ecumenical Patriarch duly issued the decree, or *tomos,* establishing the Church of Albania, under the control of the Synod of four bishops. The Synod elected Kristofor Kisi, Bishop of Tirana and Durrës, president; he thus became Archbishop of Tirana and Primate of the Autocephalous Albanian Orthodox Church.

Roman Catholics

According to official Albanian figures, the Roman Catholic Church in 1937 had 105,609 adherents, or 10.2 per cent of the population. The Catholics live principally in the north, and their center is Shkodër. Most of the mountaineers around Shkodër are Catholic. Because of their educated clergy, their organization, and the support they received from the Vatican and Italy, Albanian Catholics have played a role disproportionate to their number.

The Catholic church in Albania was composed of six dioceses, organized in two archbishoprics, those of Shkodër and Durrës, and the abbacy of Orosh. The smaller archbishopric, Durrës, consisted of a single diocese, that of the archbishop who resided at Korbin, near Krujë. The larger archbishopric, Shkodër, comprised four dioceses: Shkodër, Lesh (Alessio), Zadrimë (Sappa), and Pulat (Pulti). The archbishop himself was the bishop of the diocese of Shkodër. The bishopric of Pulat, which covers the mountainous Dukagjin territory, was usually occupied by a Franciscan. The sixth diocese, that of Mirditë, remained known by the title employed before the Italian Benedictines left Albania in the eighteenth century; the incumbent was called the Abbot of Orosh. He was a Mitred Abbot, an *Abbas Nullius,* which means that he came directly under the jurisdiction of the Vatican.

Two orders existed in pre-Communist Albania, the Franciscans and the Jesuits. The Franciscans had come in the thirteenth century, and in the middle of the seventeenth century they saved Albanian Catholicism from ruin. The Jesuits did not settle in Albania until the latter half of the nineteenth century. The Provincial of the Franciscans and the Rector of the Jesuit Order, both appointed by their own communities, resided at Shkodër, and participated with the archbishop in the submission to the Vatican of nominations to livings. Both orders had their own seminaries. The secular priests who occupied the non-Franciscan parishes were trained in the Jesuit seminary; those who belonged to the Franciscan order were trained in the Franciscan seminary.

A minority surrounded by Moslems and Serbian Orthodox and isolated from the Catholic West, the Catholics were among the first to take part in nationalistic movements. The Albanian language was taught in the Franciscan seminary, founded in 1861 under the auspices of Austria-Hungary, and in that of the Jesuits, established in 1877 under the sponsorship of the same power. The Franciscans have particularly distinguished themselves among Albanian writers, and the Albanian national epic poet, Father Gjergj Fishta, was a Franciscan. The periodical, *Hylli i Dritës* (The Star of Light) published by the Franciscans, tackled Albanian problems and spread its influence far beyond the Catholic minority. The Catholic orders also maintained elementary and secondary private schools until their schools were closed when the Albanian state nationalized education in 1933. The Franciscans, who were Albanians, accepted state control and inspection, and their institutions were reopened in 1936.

Religion under the Axis Powers, 1939-1944

The Italians maintained religious toleration, with no established state church. However, they revised the organization of the Moslem community, inducing the Moslems to create a Council of Ulemas, with a president to head their community. Ulemas from the "Liberated Areas" (Kosovo, Metohija, and parts of Macedonia), which were annexed to Albania after the collapse of the Yugoslav state, were added. No changes were made in the Orthodox and Catholic communities.

The Italians used different policies from group to group. They tried to win over the Catholics by favoring them, and they supported the Uniate Church—insignificant in prewar Albania—to proselytize Orthodox Christians. The Uniates are sometimes known as Greek Catholics; their services resemble the Orthodox, but they recognize the dogmas and the supremacy of the Vatican. In general, the Italians attempted to play the Christians against the Moslems. While Zog, a Moslem, as a rule employed Christian Prime Ministers, Catholic King Victor Emmanuel III used Moslems.

When the Germans entered Albania in September 1943, they made no changes in the organization of religious communities. However, the Albanian regency in a decree of April 4, 1944, extended the constitution of the Albanian Orthodox Church to include the "Liberated Areas," which meant that the Albanian Orthodox Church took under its jurisdiction the bishopric of Prizren and created two new bishoprics, one in Peshkopi and the other in Strugë (Yugoslavia).

Religion under the Communists

Organization

With the Communists' advent to power in November 1944, changes in the religious communities were expected, since the Communists seek the destruction of religion. Because of the diversity and loose organization of churches—except for the Roman Catholic Church—the task of the Communist government in Albania was easier than in other captive countries, but the process was gradual.

Moslems. The Tirana regime began church reorganization with the Moslem community, probably because it was less organized than the Christian churches. Under the May 5, 1945 constitution of the Albanian Moslem community, the Moslems again form a community, but the Bektashis are not included. The Moslems are led and represented by the Head of the Moslem Community, who is elected by secret ballot of the General Council. However, according to the constitution, the Head of the Moslem Community cannot function until the Chief of the State has issued his decree of approval, and the Chief of the State also has the right to discharge him. Until 1955, the Head of the Moslem Community was Hafëz Musa Haxhi Ali, an insignificant religious figure but a pliant Communist instrument.[1] The authority of the Moslem community is vested in the General Council, composed of the President of the Community, the four Grand Muftis, and a lay delegate-representative from each prefecture.

The statute of the Moslem community divides Albania into four zones, with a Grand Mufti for each. The Tirana zone comprises the prefectures of Peshkopi, Tirana, Durrës, and Berat, with Tirana as a center; that of Shkodër includes the prefectures of Kosovë and Shkodër, the latter the center; the zone of Korçë consists of the prefectures of Elbasan and Korçë, with the latter the center; that of Gjirokastër is composed of the prefectures of Gjirokastër and Vlorë,

[1] Since 1955, the head of the Moslem community has been Hafëz Suljeman Myrto.

the former the center. The Grand Muftis are elected by the General Council, but they take possession of their zones only with the approval of the Chief of the State.

The other organs of the Moslem community are (1) the Ordinary Council, composed of the Grand Mufti of the capital and two laymen appointed by the General Council, which decides the ordinary questions of the community; (2) the chief of the financial and ecclesiastical administration; and (3) the muftis and the regional councils.

The Bektashis constitute a community of their own. In this way, the government, while ostensibly satisfying the Bektashis' desire for independence, succeeded in accentuating the Sunni-Bektashi conflict.

The Bektashi community is composed of "families with Bektashi tradition," the *ashikë* and *muhibë* (degrees of initiation), and the "clergy." The clergy is composed of the Head of the Community, the World *Kryegjysh* (Chief Grandfather) of the Bektashis, who today is Ahmet Myftar Dede, the *gjyshë* (grandfathers), the *prindë* or *baballarë* (fathers), the dervishes, and servants of religious service. Since Albania is now the seat of Bektashism, the Communists seized the opportunity to declare the Head of the Community the "World Grandfather of the Bektashis."

The Bektashi community is divided into six zones or grandfatherships: (1) the grandfathership of Krujë, with a seat at Fusha e Krujës, having under its jurisdiction the prefectures of Durrës and Shkodër; (2) the zone of Elbasan, with headquarters at the tekke of Xhefai Baba in Krastë, containing the prefectures of Elbasan and Peshkopi; (3) the grandfathership of Korçë, with the tekke of Melçan as its seat, having under its jurisdiction the prefecture of Korçë; (4) the zone of Gjirokastër, with its seat at the tekke Asim Baba, which comprises the prefecture of Gjirokastër; (5) the grandfathership of Prishtë, which comprises the prefecture of Berat and the subprefecture of Përmet; and (6) the zone of Vlorë, with its seat at the tekke of Frashëri, composed of the prefecture of Vlorë and a subprefecture of Berat.

According to the constitution, Albanian is not only the official but also the religious language of the Bektashis. The community of the Bektashis has a school for the education of its clergy. The government has officially recognized the other dervish orders as independent religious communities; the head of the Halvetis is Sheh Ali Hormova; Sheh Besim Selimi heads the Kadiris; and Ilias Prishta, the Saadis.

Orthodox Christians. The Orthodox Church was not reorganized until some years after the Communist regime came to power. On August 28, 1949, Radio Tirana announced that the Orthodox Archbishop of Albania, Kristofor Kisi, had been deposed for "Fascist activities" and for plotting to detach the Church from the Eastern Orthodox faith and surrender it to the Vatican; Bishop Pashko Vodica of Korçë who assumed the name of Pais was named his successor and head of the Church. In February 1950, a congress held in Tirana voted on the new constitution of the Albanian Orthodox Church.

According to the new charter, the Church is officially called "The Autocephalous Orthodox Church of Albania." It is headed by the Archbishop of Albania, who at the same time is the Metropolitan of Tirana and Durrës. The bishoprics have remained the same: Berat, Gjirokastër, and Korçë. The Synod, composed of the archbishop and the bishops, decides on religious matters. Administrative and economic matters are still entrusted to the Mixed Council.

Some significant articles, however, have been introduced into the new constitution. The Church is obliged to develop in its adherents a sense of loyalty to the "people's power" and the People's Republic of Albania. It is also to collaborate more intensively with the Communist-controlled or infiltrated Orthodox Churches, "which interpret and practice rightly the high principles of the Gospels, peace, and brotherhood among men, and denounce every activity and attempt to destroy peace . . . in the world." "The official language of the Church is Albanian, but in the religious services other languages [Russian Church Slavonic] may be used."

Catholics. As early as 1945, the Catholic Church in Albania was attacked as an instrument of the Vatican. Monsignor Leone G. B. Nigris, the Apostolic Nuncio to Albania, was arrested in May 1945 and expelled, after being denounced as an agent who fomented anti-Communist reaction. In 1946, a number of prominent Albanian Catholic clergymen were brought to trial, accused of distributing leaflets against the regime and organizing guerrilla bands in the mountains. In this way the Tirana regime executed or imprisoned the most distinguished members of the Catholic hierarchy and destroyed the orders. However, it was not until 1951 that the great transformation of the Catholic Church in Albania occurred.

On June 26, 1951, a "general assembly" of Catholic clergymen was convened at Shkodër. Shortly thereafter in August 1951, the Presidium of the People's Assembly approved the "decisions" of the "general assembly," which meant, in effect, a new constitution for the Albanian Catholic Church.

According to the new "constitution," the Albanian Catholic Church is directed both in religious and administrative matters by the Albanian Catholic Episcopate, composed of the religious heads (archbishops, bishops, or their vicars) of the dioceses. Its seat is in Shkodër, and its head is the Metropolitan of that city. The dioceses of the Albanian Catholic Church are the following: the archdiocese of

Shkodër; the archdiocese of Durrës; the dioceses of Lesh, Zadrimë, Pulat; and the abbacy of Orosh (Mirditë). The Albanian Catholic Episcopate is responsible to the state for the acts of the Albanian Catholic Church.

The constitution further states that the Catholic Church of Albania has no organizational, political, or economic ties with the Vatican, and that relations concerning religious questions may be established only through government channels. The Catholic Church submits to the canon law of the world Catholic Church, if the provisions of this law do not contradict the laws of the Albanian People's Republic, public order, and public morality. The priests are to celebrate Mass and perform functions according to the dogmas, canons, and state laws in force. They will be trained in seminaries "created and administered" with the approval of the Tirana government. In exchange, the government undertakes to subsidize the Catholic Church, according to its abilities. Archbishops, bishops, and other religious leaders may be appointed and consecrated by the Catholic Church in Albania only with the approval of the Albanian government. In short, the Catholic Church in Albania is now a national church.

Dom Mark Bushi was first placed in charge of the fettered Albanian Catholic Church, but now Father Bernardin Shllaku, an eighty-year-old Franciscan brother, is its nominal leader.

Church and State

Even in the past, the Albanian religious groups were not independent of the state. No head of a religious community (Moslem or Orthodox Christian) could exercise his functions unless his appointment had been approved by the King; the budgets and regulations of religious communities had to receive the approval of the Ministry of Justice, which also reserved the right of inspection. However, under the Communist regime all religious bodies have been brought completely under the control of the government. "Freedom of conscience and religion," "liberty of religious communities," and "separation of Church and State" are merely paper guarantees. To achieve this control, the Communists have used various legislative acts, the elimination of distinguished clergymen who were uncooperative, and their replacement by willing tools.

On November 26, 1949, a law was enacted requiring all religious communities to develop among their members the feeling of loyalty toward "people's power" and the People's Republic of Albania. The heads of the religious communities, as well as the chiefs of the various sects must receive the approval of the Council of Ministers, after election by their respective competent organs.

Among the Sunni Moslems, those who were unwilling to work with the Communists, such as the old mufti of Shkodër and the respected mufti of Durrës, Mustafa effendi Varoshi, were liquidated, while others were imprisoned. Hafëz Musa Haxhi Ali, who formerly headed the Moslem community, was completely subservient to the government. In 1950, he led a Moslem delegation to the Soviet Union, visiting Uzbekistan and the religious monuments of Samarkand and Tashkent and meeting the "Red Mufti," Abdul Medjid Baba Djan. Hafëz Musa Haxhi Ali has also played an active role in meetings for the "preservation of freedom"—the Moscow freedom campaign—held in Tirana in August 1951 and June 1952.

For the Bektashis, the Communists had their own man, Mustafa Faja i Marteneshit, a Bektashi *baba* (father), who had fought on their side during the resistance against the Axis Powers. The Communists apparently selected him as Chief Grandfather of the Bektashis, but he and Baba Fejzo, another Communist sympathizer, were murdered as traitors in March 1947, in a Bektashi tekke near Tirana by dervishes of their own order. He had gone there, as the Tirana regime put it, in order "to discuss [with Dede Abazi, the Bektashi Chief] the democratization of their religious organization" (*Bashkimi,* March 20, 1947). The present Bektashi leader, Ahmed Myftar Dede, offers no resistance to the regime. As Primate of World Bektashism, he made an appeal to adherents in Albania and elsewhere to support the Stockholm Peace Appeal.

The Albanian Orthodox Church has also felt the heavy hand of Communist oppression. When the archbishops and the bishops did not yield to the demands of the regime, the leadership of the church was destroyed. Archbishop Kristofor Kisi, Primate of the Orthodox Church. Bishop Irenei, Deputy Metropolitan of Korcë and Gjirokastër, and Bishop Agathangjel of Berat were interned.

Pashko Vodica had been an ardent supporter of the Communists during the resistance movement, and his village, Vodica, was called "Little Moscow." After their advent to power the Communists made him the Bishop of Korçë. Archbishop Pais played a role for the Tirana regime and Moscow which his predecessor had refused to play. At the 1950 Orthodox Congress at Tirana, he delivered a speech clearly stating the present position of the Albanian Orthodox Church and defining the new relationship between Church and government. In this speech, he stated that it was the Church's duty to be faithful to the People's Republic of Albania and the "people's power," to preach the unity of the people, and to fight for the defense of the frontiers and the territorial integrity of the country.

Pashko Vodica further declared: "Our Church must also be faithful to the great camp of Peace, to the great anti-imperialist and democratic camp, to the unique camp of socialism, led brilliantly by the glorious Soviet Union and the Great Stalin against every attempt undertaken by enslaving imperialism in order to undermine international peace and throw the world into another butchery and new catastrophe." He then added that the Albanian Orthodox Church should stand in the unified camp of peace, which all progressive Orthodox Churches of the world joined, led by the Great Russian Church. Pais Vodica said that it was an honor for the Albanian Orthodox Church to be bound with the Great Orthodox Church of Russia, which correctly interpreted the high principles of the Gospels on love, brotherhood, and peace, and which was led by the great prelate, Patriarch Aleksei.

In the resolution approved by the Congress in 1950, the Synod was asked to direct all its activities toward the "camp of peace," in which participate "all the progressive Churches," headed by the Russian Orthodox Church.

The ties between the Albanian Orthodox Church and the Russian Patriarchate became closer in spring of 1951, when a delegation of Soviet religious leaders, headed by Bishop Nikon of Odessa, visited Tirana. The convocation of the Catholic "general assembly" of 1951 followed discussions which took place at that time.

The persecution of the Catholic clergy by the Tirana government has become more drastic in recent years. According to a document published in 1953 by the National Committee for a Free Albania, out of ninety-three Catholic clergymen in Albania in 1945, ten remain free; twenty-four have been murdered; thirty-five have been imprisoned; ten have died or disappeared; eleven have been drafted; and three have escaped abroad. The only remaining bishop is the octogenarian Monsignor Bernardin Shllaku, and he is kept under constant surveillance.

Article 26 of the law on religious communities (November 26, 1949) was aimed primarily at the Catholic community. It reads: "The religious communities or their branches (orders, societies, religious missions, etc.) which have their headquarters outside the state are not allowed to open branches (orders, missions, philanthropic institutions, etc.), and those which exist will be closed within a month from the date of the entrance into power of this law." The Jesuit and Franciscan orders were thus eliminated.

The land reform law of August 29, 1945 deprived the various churches of almost all their property. According to the National Committee for a Free Albania, in 1945 the Catholic institutions were as follows: 253 churches and chapels, 2 seminaries, 10 monasteries, 20 convents, 15 orphanages and asylums, 16 church schools, and 10 charitable institutions. By 1953, only 100 of the churches and chapels and 2 of the monasteries were still in existence; all the other institutions had been destroyed or confiscated. The two printing presses belonging to the Church had been confiscated, and the seven religious periodicals had been suppressed.

19. LITERATURE AND THE ARTS

Language

Origin and Records. Before the ancient Greeks, a great part of the Balkan Peninsula was inhabited by Illyrians and Thracians, both of whom spoke Indo-European languages. The Illyrian tribes occupied the western part of the peninsula from Epirus to the Danube and beyond, into Austria. The Adriatic was their western frontier and the Morava and Vardar rivers formed their eastern frontier. There were also Illyrians in Italy. The Thracian tribes spread to the east of the Illyrians, from the Vardar and Morava rivers to the Black Sea, and from the Carpathian Mountains to the Aegean. Illyrians and Thracians intermingled and influenced each other.

The Albanian language is an independent member of the Indo-European family of languages, and is related to the languages spoken by these two peoples. There are three theories about its origin: that it stems from ancient Illyrian, that it derives from ancient Thracian, and that it originates in both Illyrian and Thracian. Recent historical and philological research indicates that both Illyrian and Thracian contributed to the formation of the Albanian language.

Some misinformation still exists with regard to the first written documents in the Albanian language, and some scholars still maintain that Albanian dates only from the seventeenth century. However, the first records in Albanian date from the fifteenth century. They are a baptismal formula in the Roman Catholic rite, dating from 1462 (manuscript in Biblioteca Laurenziana, Florence), and a fragment of the New Testament in the Byzantine rite (manuscript in Biblioteca Ambrosiana, Milan), also dating from the fifteenth century, and according to some scholars perhaps from the fourteenth century.

Distribution. The Albanian language is spoken today in a zone whose boundaries do not correspond with those of the present Albanian state. The language frontiers border those of modern Greek between Sarandë and Kastoria, of Arumanian in the Grammos Mountains, of Macedonian in the east, and of Serbian more to the north.

The number of those who speak Albanian is not easy to estimate, because statistics on minorities in the Balkan States must be accepted with great caution. The Yugoslav government maintains that there are 750,431 Albanians living in Yugoslavia, according to the 1948 census. The Albanian minority in Greece before World War II was estimated by the Balkanologist C. Tagliavini at about 100,000, comprising the Albanians of Çamëri (Tsamouria) and those of the colonies founded in the middle of the fourteenth century and later.

Albanian settlements in Italy are also very old. Albanians began to emigrate to Italy before the time of Skënderbeg (1405-68), but the great emigrations followed his death, when Albania fell under Ottoman rule. The census of 1921 reckoned 20,113 families and 80,282 individuals who spoke Albanian in the south of Italy in Cosenza, Campobasso, Potenza, and Catanzaro, and in Sicily in the province of Palermo. An Albanian colony was established in Borgo Erizzo (present Arbanasi) near Zara (Zadar), in Dalmatia, in the middle of the eighteenth century, and there is an Albanian village, Vulkanesti, in Bessarabia.

Albanians have also emigrated to other parts of the world, especially Turkey, Egypt, Syria, Bulgaria, Romania, Argentina, and Australia. A considerable number, estimated at from 40,000 to 50,000, live in the United States, their center being Boston.

Dialects. More than 2,000,000 people speak Albanian. Albanian is divided into two main dialects, the Geg (Gheg) in the north, and the Tosk in the south. The approximate frontier between the two dialects is the Shkumbî River, which runs across central Albania, but the Geg dialect is also spoken south of that river. The difference between these dialects is not too great: southern and northern Albanians understand each other. The dialect spoken in the Albanian settlements of Greece and Italy is Tosk. In Borgo Errizzo, however, it is Geg; in fact, this is the only Albanian colony where Geg is spoken.

Written Language. There is still no common literary Albanian language, and it was not until November 1908 that a common alphabet was established by a congress of Albanian intellectuals who met at Monastir (Bitolj) and decided on a common Latin alphabet. Albanian is written as it is pronounced. Efforts were made before 1944 to establish a common written language, with the dialect of Elbasan on the Shkumbî River chosen for this purpose. This dialect is a Geg dialect bordering on the Tosk. However, the Elbasan dialect was dropped, and both officials and authors soon wrote again in their own dialects.

Geg and Tosk competed for supremacy in prewar Albania, the former with Shkodër as a center and the latter centering in Korçë and Gjirokastër. With the Communists' advent to power, the Tosk dialect got the upper hand. The Communist movement emerged in the south and most of the leaders of the Albanian Workers' Party (Communist Party) came from southern Albania. Another reason for the predominance of the Tosk dialect is the destruction of Catholic

Shkodër as a cultural center and the persecution and execution of the Catholic clergy (see page 298). A meeting of the Albanian Writers' Union, a Communist front organization, held in Tirana in 1952, "resolved" that only the Tosk dialect be used in publications.

Oral Literature

Albanian oral literature is a living and relatively rich literature of lyric songs, proverbs, tales, and especially heroic songs.

Oral literature may be divided into that of diaspora and that of Albania proper. The songs of the Italo-Albanians are old. They are reflections of the society and the times when these Albanians left after the death of Skënderbeg. In fact, their most important cycle tells of the wars of the Albanians against the Turks, the heroism of Skënderbeg and his fellow lords, and the hatred of the "enemy Turk." They reveal a semifeudal and Christian environment. The Albanians of Italy also have lyric poems which sing of love for wife and mother and of strong jealousy. One of their most beautiful songs is "Oh Dear Morea," which shows the love for the country where they left their beloved—some of the Italo-Albanians came from the colonies of Peloponnesus. A traditional poem influenced by Akritic songs is "Constantine the Small," which has acquired a ritual character among the Albanians of southern Italy and is sung at every wedding.

Little can be said, on the other hand, about the songs of the Albanian settlements in Greece. The Rheinhold collection, *Noctes Pelasgicae* (1855), and the smaller one by Sotiriou (*Laographia,* I [1909], 82-92) contain a few lyric songs but no heroic poems. In the beginning of the nineteenth century, however, we have a few beautiful heroic songs of the Albanian inhabitants of Epirus, especially of the village of Suli, who fought against Ali Pasha Tepelena for their freedom and the preservation of their Christian Orthodox religion.

In Albania proper, there are many love songs and wedding songs, but the bulk of Albanian oral poetry is composed of heroic songs. In the northern part of Albania, the latter are generally called *kângë trimnije* (songs of valor); in southern Albania, their name is *këngë pleqërishte* (ancient songs) or *këngë trimash* (songs of brave men). They are chronicle-like, telling of events and episodes in a particular section of the Albanian world, chiefly of vendetta murder, but there are occasional songs about murder for the protection of women. In most of the heroic songs, the underlying motif is honor; murder is committed in order to regain lost honor.

Most of the Albanian heroic songs are found in the northern part of the country, where there is a strong heroic milieu. They are of particular interest because they reveal a society permeated by the old traditional law of the mountains, the Kanum i Lekë Dukagjinit (The Code of Lekë Dukagjini). Since honor is the highest ideal in this environment and shame is regarded as worse than death, it is natural that people should prize a heroic death. A common saying among the mountaineers of northern Albania is "better dead than to become a woman [coward]."

However, several other Albanian heroic songs are interpretations of history and describe the role played by Albanians in the Ottoman Empire or the battles of the Albanians against the Montenegrins across the border. The Albanian songs of the wars against Montenegro reveal in general a hatred of the Shkje, as the Slavs are called by the northern highlanders. There is no oral heroic poetry dealing with frontier wars in the southern part of Albania.

In the mountains of northern Albania and in Kosovo and Metohija (Yugoslav regions inhabited mostly by Albanians), the Mujo-Halil cycle contains some of the most beautiful epic songs. These songs concerning the brothers Mujo and Halil are called *kângë kreshnikësh* (songs of heroes). They are also known as *kângë lahute* (lahuta songs), for they are always sung to the accompaniment of the *lahuta,* the Albanian musical instrument of the highlanders similar to the Yugoslav *gusle.*

In this Albanian cycle, the main subjects are the wars between the agas of Judbina, led by Mujo, against the Christian Slavs beyond the border over the abduction of women or the plundering of castles and towns. Disputes and imprisonments are not rare, but duels are more frequent. In all the wars and duels, Mujo is the victor, either by his own ability or with the help of the *zânë* and *orë* (Albanian mountain fairies). Judbina, where the fortress of Mujo is situated, is never conquered by fighting, but from time to time the Slavs penetrate into the town by treasonous means and set fire to Mujo's castle.

During the resistance movement against the Axis powers and later in the fratricidal fight, members of both the National Front and the National Liberation Movement improvised songs, but apparently there have been no collections.

The present Communist regime in Albania encourages the production of folk songs to spread the slogans and ideas of the Party. The subjects now are the Party, Comrade Enver, the Soviet Union and Stalin, the People's Democracies, and hatred of the Anglo-American "Imperialists." As Shefqet Musaraj, a prominent Communist writer, has put it: "We may say without any fear that folklore has marched hand in hand with the development and the great transformations which Albania has made in these ten years of Party leadership" (*Letërsia Jonë* [Our Literature], October 10, 1951). This is not exactly folklore since the basic element of spontaneity is missing—this is folklore to order.

Written Literature

The first documents in the Albanian language date from the fifteenth century and are religious in character. The writings in Albanian of the following three and a half centuries are almost all religious books or dictionaries. The oldest published work is Gjon Buzuku's *Meshari* (Missal) (1555), the language of which reveals contacts between southern and northern Albanian.

Religious subjects also characterized the Albanian works of this period written by Albanians in Italy. The oldest of these appeared in 1592 when Llukë Matranga published his catechism, *E mbsuame e Krështerë* (Christian Doctrine), the first document in the dialect of the Italo-Albanians.

Before Independence, 1850-1912

It was not until the middle of the nineteenth century that an Albanian literature with nationalist tendencies emerged. This could not and did not originate in Albania proper, where over two thirds of the population had been converted to Islam. Moreover, the schools which functioned in Albania were Turkish for the Moslems and Greek for the Orthodox Christians, and there was a ban by the Turkish government on written Albanian (the works of the early period were published in Italy). Therefore, Albanian literature of nationalist character first appeared in Italy, where the Italo-Albanians had preserved the language, customs, and traditions of their fatherland and had founded schools. Thus, in 1794 they possessed an excellent institution, Collegio di San Demetrio Corone, in Calabria, where Albanian was taught. No doubt the movements for the liberation and union of Italy served as a stimulus to nationalist literary and cultural works among the Italo-Albanians.

The two great initiators of the nationalist trend in Italy were Girolamo de Rada (1814-1903) and Demetrio Camarda (1821-82). De Rada's best poetic creation, *Milosaat* (Milosao), an idyll inspired by Italo-Albanian folk songs, was published in 1836. In his *Rhapsodies of an Albanian Poem* (1866), based on Italo-Albanian popular songs, he lauded the pre-Turkish freedom of the Albanians and their wars against the Ottoman invaders, and told of their surrender and exile. In *Scanderbeccu i pafaan* (The Hapless Skënderbeg) (1872), he dealt with the struggle of the Albanians under the leadership of their hero against the Turks, and with their national revival. De Rada was a poet under the influence of European romanticism.

Camarda laid stress on language. In his *Saggio di grammatologia comparata della lingua albanese* (1864), he made a scientific study of the Albanian language, demonstrating its antiquity. In the Appendix to his work, Camarda included specimens of prose and particularly folk songs from Sicily and Calabria, Albania proper, and Albanian settlements in Greece. He also tackled the problem of a common Albanian language.

Another writer of the Albanians of Italy was Giuseppe Serembe (1843-91), whose *Vjershe* (Poems), published posthumously, sing of love, friendship, religion, and the high ideals of freedom and humanity. Giuseppe Schirò published *Mili and Haidhia,* an idyll composed of eighteen songs, in which the life of an Italo-Albanian village is described through a sentimental story. However, his masterpiece is *Te dheu i huaj* (In the Foreign Land) (1900), in which Albanian historical figures are drawn within a framework of legend and history. His periodical, *Arbri i rii* (The Young Albanian), published in 1887, was predominantly literary, and aimed at contributing to Albanian national union.

The Treaty of San Stefano, which Russia imposed upon Turkey in 1878, accorded the Balkan Slavic nations large territories inhabited by Albanians and considered Albanian. When the Great Powers refused to accept this treaty and convened the Congress of Berlin (1878) in order to consider its revision, Albanian leaders met at Prizren, in Kosovo, and created the Albanian League, often called the League of Prizren. The patriots sought to defend the territorial integrity of their country and to establish an autonomous Albania within the framework of the Ottoman Empire, with Albanian schools and with Albanian as a language of administration. The League of Prizren naturally provided a great incentive to Albanian nationalist tendencies in literature.

To strengthen the work of the League, Albanian intellectuals in Constantinople in 1879 founded the first literary club, Society for the Development of the Albanian Language. Pashko Vasa Pasha (1827-92), the author of the touching elegy, "Oh, Albania, Unfortunate Albania," and Naim Frashëri (1846-1900), destined to become the apostle-poet of Albanian nationalism, belonged to this society. Through the initiative of the latter, a periodical *Drita* (The Light), was published in Constantinople, and there his first writings appeared.

Naim Frashëri was a relatively productive writer. Since he desired to stimulate the spirit of nationalism among the Albanians, he published several educational books. Among his literary creations, *Bagëti e Bujqësi* (Cattle and Land) (1886) is considered best. His *Lulet e Verës* (Spring Flowers) (1890), a collection of short poems, comprises some of the finest pieces in Albanian literature. The poet's love for his country shines brilliantly in *Istori e Skënderbeut* (History of

Skënderbeg) (1899), a long poem in which the battles of the Albanians against the Turks are described.

A religious person, Naim Frashëri belonged to the Islamic sect of Bektashism (sse page 288). In *Qerbelaja* (1898), named for a plain in Mesopotamia, he sang of the civil and religious wars among the Arabs after the death of Mohammed. In the *Fletore e Bektashinjet* (Notebook of the Bektashis) (1896), he expressed religious and moral ideas. Owing to his influence, Bektashism in Albania followed a patriotic and nationalistic trend.

Naim Frashëri was a romantic poet under the influence of Islamic religion. Several poems in his *Lulet e verës* (Spring Flowers) are imbued with Persian mysticism. However, all his work is completely Albanian in tone and execution. His love for the purity of the Albanian language was so great that in his religious works he even translated the established Oriental terms. Naim Frashëri is regarded a national poet in Albania.

Even earlier than Frashëri, Kostandin Kristoforidhi (1827-95) of Elbasan had published translations of the Old and New Testaments (1867) in a literary prose that has become classic. Kristoforidhi went from town to town and from village to village to study the dialects of his country. The material he collected was published in a posthumous volume entitled *Dictionary of the Albanian Language* (1904), which is regarded as a fundamental work on the subject. *Gjàja e Malësorvet* (Mountain Hunt) and *Hieja e Tomorit* (The Shade of Tomor) were published posthumously.

Faik Konitza (1875-1942), prewar Albanian Minister to Washington, has greatly influenced Albanian letters, and his pure and simple language has become a model for many Albanian writers. From 1897 to 1909, he published, in Brussels and later in London, the review *Albania,* with articles on literature, language, and folklore, in addition to historical and political studies. This periodical became the focal publication for all Albanian writers. Konitza developed his literary style primarily by journalistic writing.

Lumo Skendo, which was the pen name of Midhat Frashëri (1880-1949), did not produce many literary works, but he is known in Albanian literature as a translator of works of European literature and as a publisher of periodicals. His *Kalendari Kombiar* (National Calendar) (1897-1928) and his *Dituria* (Knowledge), published from 1909 to 1916 and again from 1926 to 1929, are invaluable for a study of Albanian letters. His most outstanding literary work is *Hi dhe shpuzë* (Ash and Ember) (1915), a collection of short stories.

Çajupi (pen name of Andon Çako) (1866-1930) was another lyric poet. In 1902, he published *Baba Tomorri* (Father Tomorri), a collection of poems in which he sings of love and fatherland. Many years later in 1921, he adapted La Fontaine's *Les Fables,* including with this a section entitled "Flowers of India," translations of Sanskritic poems. He also wrote a tragedy, *Burri i Dheut* (The Man of the Earth). Çajupi's popular rhythm and meter have appealed to the young Albanian writers.

Above all the writers of this era stands the imposing figure of Father Gjergj Fishta (1871-1940), who took part in the patriotic movement and was active in various political and literary congresses. Born in the mountains of northern Albania, he could not but be influenced by the heroic songs of the highlanders.

The battles of the Albanian mountaineers with the neighboring Slavs inspired this Franciscan Brother in the writing of his powerful epic *Lahuta e Malcís* (The Lute of the Mountains). In the first volume, *Te ura e Rzhanicës* (At the Bridge of Rzhanica) (1905), the poet extols in pure and forceful language the fight of the Albanians against the Montenegrins. Another volume, *Vranina,* which appeared a year later, describes the battle between Albanian highlanders and Montenegrins in 1858. In 1931, Fishta published another volume of his epic called *Lidhja e Prizrenit* (The League of Prizren), which deals with the Congress of Berlin, Ali Pasha Gucija, a hero and commander of the forces of the League, the League itself, and Mehmet Ali Pasha.

In 1935, Fishta wrote of his own work: "There are more than thirteen thousand verses, published up to now, of the *Lahuta e Malcís* which, in bloody battles against the Slav, at the time of the Congress of Berlin and later, and against the Young Turks, show the revival of national consciousness among the Albanian people and their happy triumph in the freedom and independence of Albania." (Gj. Fishta, "Vjersha heroike shqyptare" [The Albanian Heroic Song], *Hylli i Dritës,* XI [1935], 146.) Fishta's language is the pure Albanian used by the mountaineers, and his octosyllabic meter is characteristic of Albanian heroic poetry. It is considered the masterpiece of Albanian literature (parts have been translated into German), and Fishta has been called a "national poet."

Fishta was not only a great epic poet, he was also an outstanding satirical poet. He made use of his satirical talent in poems published in Konitza's *Albania.* In 1907, he wrote *Anzat e Parnasit* (Wasps of Parnassus), a collection of sixteen satirical poems, and in 1923 *Gomari i Babatasit* (Babatasi's Ass), a comedy in verse. In these works, he satirized European power politics, the venality and ignorance of politicians, petty-minded bureaucrats, and especially the pseudo-patriots.

Fishta also excelled in lyric poetry. In 1909, he published *Pika voeset* (Dew Drops), a collection of lyric poems, and in 1913 *Mrizi i*

Zânavet (Muses' Arbor), lyric poems on patriotic subjects. His *Vallja e Parrizit* (Dance of Paradise) (1925) contains religious songs.

Independent Albania, 1913-1939

The independence of Albania was proclaimed on November 28, 1912, but it was short-lived because World War I soon broke out and Albania was occupied by the belligerent powers. The dream of the patriotic writers was shattered, but the romantic patriotic tradition of which Girolamo de Rada and Naim Frashëri had been the leading exponents continued to live. Fishta, more than other writers, was aware of the changes which were taking place in Albanian society, but he still followed the tradition and preserved the high Albanian values, *besë* (loyalty), honor, manliness, which in his belief had saved Albania through the centuries.

P. Vinçenc Prennushi (1885-1954), a lyric poet, published his first literary creations in various reviews. In 1911, his important collection of folk songs, *Kangë popullore gegnishte* (Popular Geg Songs), appeared. *Fjala e Zotit* (The Word of God) (1918) is a book of sermons and *Quo Vadis?* (1932-35) a translation of Sienkiewicz's work. He also wrote plays and short stories. His best lyric work is *Gjeth e Lule* (Leaves and Flowers) (1925), which contains original and translated poems. He remained in Albania after World War II and fell a victim to the Communist regime.

Dom Ndre Mjeda (1866-1937) was a poet of the Catholic north. He had begun his writing and philological activity in the pre-Independence period. In 1917, he published *Juvenilia,* a collection of original and translated lyric poems; *Lissus* (Lesh) in 1928 tells of Illyrian bravery and the fortunes of the city of Lesh until the time of Skënderbeg.

A lyric poet of the south is Asdreni (pen name of Aleks Sotir Drenova) (1872-?), who lived in Romania and whose poems and prose writings were published in periodicals. Many of his lyrics have been collected in three volumes: *Rreze dielli* (Sunbeams) (1904), *Endra e lotë* (Dreams and Tears) (1912), and *Psalme Murgu* (Psalms of a Monk) (1930). His poems are characterized by perfect form.

Bishop Fan S. Noli (1880—) has spent most of his life in the United States. While still a priest, he published a play in three acts, *Israelites and Philistines* (1907), based on ancient Hebrew History. Although he has translated a number of liturgical books, the works that have given him a prominent place in Albanian literature are his translations of masterpieces of world literature: Shakespeare's *Othello* (1916), *Hamlet, Julius Caesar,* and *Macbeth* (1926); Ibsen's *Lady*

Inger of Ostrat and *An Enemy of the People;* Blasco Ibáñez's *The Hut;* and Cervantes' *Don Quixote.* Bishop Noli has translated in a masterly fashion *The Rubáiyát of Omar Khayyám,* based mainly on FitzGerald's translation. His poetic talent is also manifested in some short poems, and in translations of Longfellow's "Scanderbeg" (from *Tales of a Wayside Inn*), and Poe's "Annabel Lee" and "The Raven"; this latter translation is one of the pearls of Albanian literature.

Lasgush Poradeci (1899—–) was a new voice in this period. In the early twenties, a group of Albanian students in Vienna published a periodical called *Djalëria* (Youth), in which the first fine lyric poems of Poradeci appeared. They were reprinted in periodicals and newspapers published in Albania, and the young people fell under his spell. In 1933, he published *Vallje e Yjve* (The Dance of the Stars), a collection of his previously published poems and many new ones. His subject matter was different from those of other writers, for he wrote of sunsets and lakes, childhood memories and love, cool springs and birds, the soul and ideas. His poetry also had a new form, both musical and artistic in its construction. Poradeci has also rewritten several popular songs of southern Albania, turning them into works of art without altering their intrinsic character. In 1937, he published *Ylli i Zemrës* (The Star of the Heart). One of the finest Albanian lyric poets, he has greatly influenced the younger generation and raised the level of lyric verse in Albania.

In the twenties Ernest Koliqi (1900—–) appeared on the Albanian literary scene with *Kushtrimi i Skanderbeut* (Skënderbeg's Call to Arms) (1924), a dramatic poem. *Hija e Maleve* (The Shade of Mountains) (1929) and *Tregtar Flamujsh* (Merchant of Flags) (1935) are among the most beautiful collections of short stories in the language. Other publications of his are *Gjurmat e Stinve* (Tracks of Seasons) (1933), a collection of his lyric poems describing the local color of certain scenes of Shkodër, *Symfonija e Shqypeve* (The Symphony of Eagles) (1936), and *Quattuor* (1935), a melodramatic composition. Among his translations, his two-volume anthology, *Poetët e mëdhej t'Italis* (The Great Poets of Italy) (I, 1932; II, 1936), should be mentioned. His latest poetic compositions, apparently written in exile, are *The Song of Captain Mark* and *The Bard and the Hero,* inspired by popular epic poetry.

Koliqi's work is significant because it is that of a modern writer who, confronted with the old and the new, has strongly endeavored to combine them into a fruitful unity. It was a blow to Albanian literature when this gifted writer, who has contributed so much to the progress of Albanian literature, joined the Fascist movement after the Italian occupation of Albania.

The early thirties were a period of great intellectual ferment and excitement. Many young Albanians who had studied abroad—in Austria, France, Italy—returned home with new ideas which conflicted with those held by the older generation. In fact, the new generation was in a mild and confused state of rebellion against some of the old values and aspects of the romantic tradition. Contributing factors were the dictatorial regime of King Zog, which had opened the way for Italian penetration, and the constant threat of Fascist Italy to the country's independence. The world depression also keenly affected people's lives and consequently the literature of the time.

The new trends were chiefly noted in two periodicals, *Illyria* (1934-36) and *Përpjekja Shqiptare* (The Albanian Effort) (1936-38). A group of intellectuals of different cultural levels published the first journal, with the most influential member of the group Ernest Koliqi. The second periodical was published by Branko Merxhani, a proponent of philosophical and sociological studies, who printed the works of the best writers of the time. Vangjel Koça, a capable popularizer of the most modern trends of thought, was a regular contributor. Without neglecting ethnic traditionalism, *Illyria* and *Përpjekja Shqiptare* considered current problems. Both journals are a representative anthology of the literature of the period in which the restlessness and the conflict of ideas, as well as the aspirations of the new generation, are reflected.

The conflict between the "old" and the "new" in Albanian society was also reflected in the poems of Ali Asllani (1884–), which were first published in newspapers and reviews and later in a volume bearing the title *Hanko Halla* (Lady Aunt) (1942). It is also the theme of the more satirical poems by Kapa (pen name of Kostaq Cepa) published in the mid-thirties in various reviews. Satirical and cynical are the short prose writings of Chri-Chri (pen name of Nonda Bulka) collected in the volume *Kur qan e qesh bilbili* (When the Nightingale Weeps and Laughs) (1934).

Some young writers who began to distinguish themselves in the thirties were Mitrush Kuteli (pen name for Dhimitri Pasko), with short stories collected under the title *Netë shqiptare* (Albanian Nights); Nologus (pen name for Anton Logoreci), whose short stories were published in magazines; Llazar Efthimiadhi with some short stories; Vedad Kokona with *Dritë e Hije* (Light and Shadow), a collection of poems; Nexhat Haki with his poems in *Këngët e Ambares* (Ambare's Songs); Sterjo Spasse, who published the novel *Pse?* (Why?), based on social environment; and Ethem Haxhiademi, who wrote several plays, most of them based on classical themes (see page 317).

Under Axis Occupation, 1939-1944

After the Italian occupation (April 7, 1939), efforts were made for the propagation of Italian language and culture. Fascism, however, did not attract Albanian youth, both because it was antagonistic to their individualism and was identified with the invader. In 1940, the only Albanian periodical published was the literary review, *Shkëndija* (The Spark), under the editorship of Ernest Koliqi who had turned to fascism. Musine Kokalari became immediately known as a capable writer with her *Siç më thotë nëna plakë* (As My Old Mother Tells Me) (1941), a collection of short stories valuable for their descriptions of Albanian customs and traditions. Soon, however, a resistance literature began to emerge.

The great literary inspiration of the resistance movement was Midhat Frashëri, the tireless nationalist writer, who in June 1939 laid the foundations of the nationalist-democratic organization Balli Kombëtar (National Front), and in August 1949 formed in exile the National Committee for a Free Albania. However, the first open resistance in the press against the Italian occupation appeared in the review *Hylli i Dritës* (The Star of Light), organ of the Franciscan Brothers in Shkodër, which had played an important cultural and political role in the life of Albania since 1913. In addition to the editorials of P. Gjon Shllaku, the able and patriotic editor who was executed in 1946 by the Communists, *Hylli i Dritës* published literary writings with patriotic content. In 1941, the journal was closed by the Fascist authorities.

From 1942 on, the number of underground leaflets, clandestine reviews, and later, newspapers began to increase. These were published by the two resistance organizations, the National Liberation Movement (camouflage of the Albanian Communist Party) and the National Front.

The publications of the National Front, during the period 1942-44, were *Zâni i Lirisë* (The Voice of Freedom), later changed to *Robni o Liri* (Slavery or Freedom); *Lufta e Çlirimit Kombëtar* (The War of National Liberation); *Rini Përpara* (Forward, Youth); *Luftëtari* (The Fighter); *Oshëtima e Korçës* (The Echo of Korçë). Until the fall of 1943, the subject matter of these publications was nationalistic and anti-Italian. However, when the civil war broke out in the fall of 1943, most of the literature became anti-Communist. A few of the poems that appeared at this time were "Fratricide" by Hekuran Zhiti, "The Dictator" by Bardhyl Pogoni, and Luigj Toni's "Treason's Allegiance," all directed against those who joined the Communists.

As the Communist resistance movement grew, tracts, bulletins, and regular organs of the Communist Party—often camouflaged under the name National Liberation Movement—began to appear. *Zëri i Popullit* (The Voice of the People) and *Kushtrimi i Lirisë* (The Call of Liberty) in 1942, and *Bashkimi* (The Union) and *Gruaja Antifashiste* (The Anti-Fascist Woman) in 1943. Revolutionary in character, the writing dealt with Partisan heroes and martyrs; a brave mother who was shot by the Italian Fascists while demonstrating against the internment of her children, a Partisan who fought the invaders with "a bag or cartridges and a rifle." Adaptations and translations of Soviet songs were the strongest literary means of fomenting civil war. Among the writers who contributed to the Communist publications and identified themselves to a degree with the Communists in the pre-resistance period were Shefqet Musaraj, Dhimitër Shuteriqi, Andrea Varfi, and Aleks Çaçi.

In general, the literature of the resistance was of low artistic quality, with that of the nationalists a shade higher than that of the Communists, but its subject matter was new.

Under the Communist Regime, 1944-1954

In November 1944, the Communists entered Tirana and established their government. Literature now was made to conform to Communist doctrine. This task was entrusted to Sejfulla Malëshova, Minister of Culture and Propaganda, and the top Communist theoretician.

Malëshova, whose pen name was Lame Kodra, was a veteran Communist who had gone to Russia to study sometime in the mid-1920's and had returned in 1942. On June 10, 1945, he expressed his ideas on literature and culture in general in a lecture delivered in Tirana and published soon after under the title *Roli i kulturës në Shqipërinë e sotme* (The Role of Culture in Today's Albania). He indicated that the new culture would concentrate on political and economic problems. He attacked the principle of "art for art's sake," and asked for a close relationship between the artist, the poet, and the people. He advocated a "revolutionary realism" in art and literature. In regard to tradition, Malëshova's opinion was that there should be a re-evaluation of the authors of past generations—Konitza, Fishta, Noli, Kristoforidhi, N. Frashëri—discarding what was "reactionary" and retaining only what was "progressive."

To put his ideas into effect, Malëshova organized the Albanian writers into a union. In October 1945, he invited seventy-four writers, many of whom were non-Communists who had not collaborated with the invaders, and founded the Union of Albanian Writers. Malëshova did not restrict membership to the Union to Communist writers, perhaps because there were then only a few, and the new writers were as yet not Communist indoctrinated. On the day of its foundation, the young Communist writer, Dhimitër Shuteriqi, declared that the union sought that writers should come to know each other, discuss together questions of art and literature, and create a new unity of thought and action. In reality, it sought Party control of writers and literature. Malëshova was elected president of the Union of Albanian Writers.

The organ of the Albanian Writers' Union became *Bota e Re* (The New World) (July 1945–February 1946). In it appeared, side by side with the writings of Communist authors, those of non-Communist authors, such as Mitrush Kuteli, Kostaq Cipo, Nonda Bulka, Sterjo Spasse, and Arshi Pipa. It represented what was called an "All-Albanian Cultural Front." The works of Malëshova, commonly known as the Red Poet, naturally exercised great influence. His poems, published in a collection under the title *Vjersha* (Poems), were taken as examples by the younger generation. His language is pure and fluent.

A writer whose work came to prominence posthumously during the first years of Communist rule was Migjeni, pen name of Millosh Gjergj Nikollaj (1910-38). Migjeni's poems, *Vargje të lira* (Free Verses) (1942), were hailed because of their social content, because he placed much stress on the misery of the people. His characters were generally the outcasts of society, but he sought justice, not pity. The Communists, however, neglected to stress Migjeni's other demand: "Victory of Conscience and Free Thought."

The cultural line traced by Sejfulla Malëshova did not last long. In 1946, he came under attack by the Communist Party leaders, for causes which were both personal and political. Koci Xoxe, Vice Premier of Albania and the most influential member of the Party at that time, distrusted him because of his intellectual capacity and his support of non-Communist patriots. Malëshova favored relations with the Western powers, and the Albanian Writers' Union in October 1945 wired Truman and Attlee, calling for recognition of the Albanian government. However, by mid-1946 it became evident that the West did not intend to grant recognition, and Western-Albanian relations were becoming tense. Yugoslavia, which at this time had control over Albania, was not in favor of an "All-Albanian Cultural Front," which was an obstacle to the propagation of Yugoslav culture in Albania.

The man who most harshly attacked Malëshova was Bedri Spahiu of the Central Committee of the Albanian Communist Party. He delivered the official accusation, the substance of which later appeared in an article in *For a Lasting Peace, for a People's Democracy* on December 1, 1950:

> Sejfulla Malëshova—spokesman of the Right deviation—sought to turn our people's cultural front into an "all-Albanian cultural front," membership of which would be open without any restrictions to intellectuals who, during the war, acted as leaders of fascist ideology, as bitter enemies of the people and their culture . . . Paying lip-service to a critical assimilation of the cultural achievements of the old society, Sejfulla Malëshova smuggled in and lauded decadent culture and bourgeois ideology. He gave the "all-Albanian culture front" and all the intelligentsia the task of establishing close cultural relations with the U.S.A. and Great Britain.

After the attacks from the Party on "the opportunistic" views of Malëshova, the second conference of writers in June 1946 took a number of decisions against the positions of the Albanian Communist theoretician. Malëshova was assailed in the First Congress of the Albanian Communist Party (1948) for his "anti-people" views, and attacked again in the Conference of Albanian Writers in August 1949. He was expelled from the Central Committee of the Communist Party in 1946 and subsequently ceased to be a member of the Albanian Writers' Union. His supporters, Communist and non-Communist, such as Skënder Luarasi and Mitrush Kuteli, suffered with him.

Meanwhile, some original works were published by young Communist writers who mainly used themes of the war of national liberation, but who also produced some works dealing with postwar reconstruction. Zihni Sako, Fatmir Gjata, and Jakov Xoxe published short stories; Aleks Çaçi, Mark Ndoja, and Llazar Siliqi wrote poems; narratives and poems by Luan Qafëzezi and Dalan Shapllo appeared; Ibrahim Uruçi published his diaries, while Gjergj Komnino, Zisa Cikuli, and Vehbi Skënderi published poetry.

The 1944-48 period witnessed a few translations from Serbo-Croatian and a number of books translated from Russian, including Ilya Ehrenburg's *100 Letters, Destroyers of Quietness* by V. Solovyev, *The Unconquered* by B. Corbatov, Maxim Gorky's *Mother* (previously translated by T. Zavalani), *Chapaev* by D. Furmanov, and M. Sholokhov's *The Upturned Soil.*

In June 1948, the Tito-Cominform rupture brought about a complete break in Albanian-Yugoslav cultural relations. At the third conference of writers in October 1949, literature came completely under the control of the Party and turned toward the Soviet Union for guidance. Stalin and the Soviet Union became prominent subjects for Albanian writers. Half of the December 1950 issue of *Letërsia Jonë* (Our Literature), the new organ of the Albanian Writers' Union, consisted of poems dedicated to Stalin on his seventy-first birthday. Of course, Enver Hoxha and the Communist Party were not neglected, and many works were dedicated to the Albanian Communist dictator. The theme of socialist morality, which should characterize the attitude of a member of the party toward work, was frequent, and class struggle in the village also appears as a favorite theme. When the Moscow "peace campaign" was launched, the theme of the Albanian writers became peace and socialist construction.

When a literary "jubilee" was celebrated in 1950, the Communists tried to appropriate the great writers of the Albanian revival. Works by Kristoforidhi, Naim Frashëri, Sami Frashëri, Çajupi, and others were published under the sponsorship of the Writers' Union. In Tirana, a monument was erected to Naim Frashëri. In the lectures and the writings of this jubilee, their works were appraised in the light of Marxist-Leninist ideology, and past regimes were attacked on the ground that they had employed "formalistic criticism." However, Gjergj Fishta, the Franciscan friar who had contributed so much to Albanian cultural renaissance, was not even mentioned.

On the tenth anniversary of the Party's founding, which coincided with the first year of the Five-Year Plan, an editorial in the December 1951 issue of *Letërsia Jonë* stated:

> Mobilized around the Party and dear Enver [Hoxha], living intensely the life and efforts of our people in the struggle for the realization of the Five-Year Plan, with the glorious Soviet Union and the Great Stalin in their hearts, with love for the sister countries of people's democracies and for the peace camp, with limitless hatred against the aggressive American-English imperialists, Titoites, Monarcho-Fascists, and the Neo-Fascists of Rome, the Albanian writers, following the example of the Soviet writers, will know how to give—as it fits them—their contribution in the great fight for the realization of the Five-Year Plan, which is at the same time [a fight] for peace and socialism.

It was during this period that Dh. Shuteriqi published the first volume of his novel *Çlirimtarët* (The Liberators), which won a Prize of the Republic in 1952. This evoked the year 1941, beginning with the day the Soviet Union entered the war and closing with the formation of the Albanian Communist Party. Mark Ndoja, who was later purged, wrote the play, *The Dawning of the Day,* and F. Gjata published a novel, *Sons of People,* which used the theme of the war of national liberation. Andrea Varfi published his collection of poems, *To the Sounds of the Revolution,* and M. Myftiu the short story entitled *The Mine Was Not Closed.*

Although the peasant and his life is the most common theme, a new topic, that of work and workers, has recently appeared in Communist literature. The railroad and the road from Kukës to Peshkopi, the first significant acts in socialist construction, gave rise to a series of poems, sketches, and narratives. More important from a regime viewpoint are writings dealing with the worker in combines, factories, and hydroelectric plants, who typifies the working class in Communist literature. In the poem "Song for the Weaving Shock-Worker" Dh. Shuteriqi tells of a girl who renounces such traditions as the wearing of the veil and jumps from the primitive loom to the textile factory. Vedad Kokona portrays the worker who comes from far away Kukës to Ysberishë in order to build the Stalin Textile Combine. It has been estimated that the theme of work and the worker comprises only a third of the total literary effort. The Communist Party seeks to increase this proportion, but it is not an easy matter, since few talented writers are interested in the theme.

The translations of Soviet literature which began soon after the seizure of power by the Communists have continued through the years. Poems by Mayakovsky were translated by Zihni Sako and Lasgush Poradeci. N. Ostrovsky's *The Tempering of Steel,* A. Fadeyev's *The Young Guard,* M. Sholokhov's *And Quiet Flows the Don* have also been translated. Of course, the Soviet translations are intended to develop Albanian literature along the lines of Soviet socialist realism. Some works by writers of the sister "popular democracies" have also been translated into Albanian. In return, several Albanian literary productions have appeared in the periodicals and literary newspapers of the Soviet Union and the People's Democracies.

Although the Communist regime maintains that it has prepared better material conditions for creative writers, few literary creations of the last decade in Albania have any literary value. The poems which compose the bulk of the literary production are primarily versification rather than true poetry. There are few prose works of any length—two or three novels and some long short stories. The best writers still are those who are not Communists—Lasgush Poradeci, Vedad Kokona, Nonda Bulka, and Sterjo Spasse—but who are compelled, because of the conditions in which they live, to follow the Party line. Among the Communist writers, the best remain those of the prewar days: Dhimitër Shuteriqi, Aleks Çaçi, and Shefqet Musaraj. Only Fatmir Gjata and Kol Jakova seem to show promise as writers of the younger generation.

Yet the Communist regime has provided the writers with several new themes. They are the same topics to be found in Soviet literature. In Albania, according to the principle of "socialist realism," they should have "national form and socialist content." However, Albanian writers seem to find it difficult to follow this Communist literary principle; at times the socialist content is lost, while through imitation of Soviet works, the national form is often vitiated.

Theater

Prewar Theater

The theater played an unimportant role in prewar Albania, and even the capital had no professional theater. A few amateur groups in schools or towns occasionally presented comedies or plays of romantic patriotic content. In the thirties, Sokrat Mijo, a young Albanian who had studied dramatic art in Paris, tried to create a professional theater. However, the government was disinterested, and the people were prejudiced against the appearance of women on the stage. Even in performances of amateur groups, a feminine role was frequently played by a man disguised as a woman. Although Albanian authors were poor playwrights, for they had little knowledge of the construction of a play or the requirements of the stage, their plays attracted readers.

The first Albanian play was written by the Italo-Albanian Anton Santori and was entitled *Emira* (1887), depicting some of the customs of the Albanians living in Calabria. Sami Frashëri's (1850-1901) theme in his *Besa* (The Pledge) was about life and customs in Albania. Nationalism was upheld by Kristo Floqi (1873-?), the most productive Albanian playwright, in plays like *Religion and Nationality* and *Triumph of Liberty,* in P. Vinçenc Prennushi's (see page 308) *From Slavery to Freedom,* or in Foqion Petro Postoli's (1890-1927) *Mother's Duty.* Father Gj. Fishta (see page 307) wrote *The Civilized Albanian, The Civilized Albanian Woman,* and *Judas Maccabaeus* based on a Biblical subject. Don Ndre Zadeja (1890-1945) wrote a number of melodramas about Albanian life: *Ora e Shqypnis* (The Mountain Fairy of Albania); *The Siege of Shkodër; The Black Shadows; Rozafa* (the name of the fortress of Shkodër); and *Oso Kuka,* an Albanian hero of the Albano-Montenegrin wars. Ilo Mitkë Qafëzezi (1889—) published *Dhaskal Gjoka* (The Teacher Gjoka), a comedy about the schools in Korçë from 1830 to 1926. Of greater literary value were the dramatic compositions of Ernest Koliqi (see page 309), *Quattuor,* a conversation among four musical instruments each praising its own qualities, and *The Symphony of Eagles.* Haki Stërmilli (1895-1953) wrote *The Unfortunate Dibrane, Love and Faithfulness,* and *Happy Dawn.* Ethem Haxhiademi (1920—) has been prolific in tragedies based on either mythological or historical characters: *Ulysses, Achilles, Alexander, Pyrrhus, Skënderbeg, Diomedes,* and *Abel.* Classical drama and some of the most significant plays of the eighteenth and nineteenth centuries were translated. Fan S. Noli (see page 308) distinguished himself with translations of two of Ibsen's plays and some of Shakespeare's masterpieces.

Albanian prewar drama did not realistically portray Albanian life, but rather depicted a romantic patriotism or a romantic revival of the historic past. All the authors strove for purity of language—a cause for which Father Gj. Fishta had appealed to his countrymen in "The Albanian Language."

Under the Communist Regime

The theater can be a powerful propaganda weapon, and the Communists encouraged the creation of theaters and the production of plays of a political-social nature, following the Party line. The plays have been mostly translations from Russian.

Soon after they came to power, the Communists invited Boza Nikolić, president of the Society of Yugoslav Actors, to organize a professional Albanian theatrical group. In 1945, with the collaboration of Sokrat Mijo, director of the dramatic school in Tirana, the Yugoslav expert managed to form a group composed partly of former amateur players and partly of talented young men and women. On September 26, 1945, this new theatrical group presented *The Lover,* an adaptation of a play by the Yugoslav playwrights Veselinović and Barsak. In addition to the theater at Tirana, two other theaters were founded, one in Shkodër (1949) and another in Korçë (1950).

The two main approved themes of current Albanian plays are the war of national liberation and events and situations of tactical interest to the Party. Thus, Aleks Çaçi wrote *Margarita Titulani,* a play about a girl who was killed during the resistance against Italian Fascists. *Father Deni* is a play attempting to show the intrigues of the "reactionary" upper Catholic clergy. Besim Lëvonja wrote *The Prefect* to attack collaborators with the Axis powers. Kol Jakova's *Hajrija and Halili* endeavors to show the patriotism of the Albanian people in the war against Turkey for the liberation and independence of their country. Jakova also wrote *Our Land,* dealing with the agrarian reform, and the comedy *The Milk Jug.* Fatmir Gjata wrote *The Peasant Girl* to describe the life of Albanian girls working in the Stalin Textile Combine.

A few translations from the Russian are from pre-Communist playwrights, such as Gogol's *The Inspector-General* and Ostrovsky's *Christmas Comes But Once a Year,* but the majority are Soviet plays. During the theatrical festival which celebrated the tenth anniversary of the founding of the Albanian Communist Party (the so-called theatrical olympiad, August 4-13, 1951), several Soviet plays of a propagandist character were produced in Albanian. Twenty-one groups with 250 amateur actors from all parts of Albania took part in this olympiad. In the article "A Great Success for Our Theater," which appeared in *Letërsia Jonë* in August 1951, it was maintained that, while the Albanian actors learned a great deal from Soviet theatrical art, "which is the most developed art in the world," they also educated the Albanian working masses "with the qualities of the Soviet people." Yet the article complained that only one Albanian play—A. Malo's *But Where Are They?*—had been presented.

The Albanian theater after the Tito-Cominform rupture was taken over by Russian experts, and it is now under the direction of a Soviet citizen, Andrei Ivanovich Krichko. In June 1950, the Russians created a puppet theater, the first performance of which was *The Tale of Lost Time,* by the Soviet writer Evgeni Shvare. Interest in the theater has increased, but interest in artistic quality is nonexistent. The only plays produced are those whose subject matter conforms to the Party line.

Fine Arts

In prewar Albania, drawing was required in elementary and secondary schools, but there was no art school until the thirties, when a rudimentary art school was opened in Tirana. Talented students wishing advanced training had to pursue their studies abroad.

Two young artists, Vangjush Mijo and Androniqi Zengo, broke with tradition and introduced "impressionism" in Albania. In fact, painting, in the modern sense, was born with them. Vangjush Mijo is primarily a landscape painter. He studied in Italy and painted many Venetian landscapes. "Autumn Impressions," a series of canvases conveying an autumn mood, is generally considered his masterpiece. Androniqi Zengo studied in Athens. Although her father was an icon painter, she broke from this stylized form and depicted sensual nudes and carefully articulated still lifes.

The only Albanian sculptor of note is Odhise Paskal from Përmet. Paskal has a higher concept of art than many of his fellow artists, for he studied sculpture in Florence and was also well versed in literature. His sculptures are generally of Albanian heroes. He created the monument "Skënderbeg" in Tirana, and those of the "National Warrior" and "Themistokli Gërmënji" (a patriot) in Korçë.

In 1950, Androniqi Zengo painted a portrait of Naim Frashëri, the poet of Albanian renaissance, and Odhise Paskal did a bust of Frashëri, which was placed before the house of the Committee for Arts and Culture in Tirana. Paskal has also worked on monuments to Lenin and Stalin. There is an art school in Tirana, but it is not known whether any new artists have emerged in the Communist state. Arts are under the control of the Committee for Arts and Culture and must follow the Party line.

In prewar Albania, two important archeological excavations were carried on, the first in Pojan, which is near the town of Fier. Pojan was the ancient Apollonia, a Greek colony founded in 588 B.C. and an intellectual center (Emperor Augustus studied there) during the Roman Empire. The Pojan excavations were under the direction of a French archeological expedition headed by Léon Rey. The ruins in Pojan show buildings and sculptures of Greek and Roman civilizations. The second excavations were made in Butrint (Butrinto), the ancient Greek colony of Buthrotum opposite Corfu, under the direction of an Italian archeological mission led by Luigi Ugolini. Layers of several civilizations were revealed: Greek, Roman, Byzantine, and Venetian. The statues and other works of art which were discovered were exhibited at the National Museum in Tirana or in small museums built at the sites of excavation. A beautiful statue, called "Venus of Butrinto," was given to Mussolini as a present by King Zog. The Tirana regime has not allowed the French and Italian archeological missions to resume their excavations.

Music

There has always been great variety in Albanian folk music; the songs are heroic or lyric; some are sung to instrumental accompaniment. The people of the mountains of northern Albania produced heroic songs sung to the accompaniment of a primitive string instrument called the *lahutë* (lute), similar to the South Slavic *gusle*. In the towns of the south there were some orchestras, called *saze,* composed of four or five instruments, which played musical tunes accompanying folk dances on particular occasions, such as weddings. These styles of music were connected with Albanian regions and were called: Lapçe (in the district of Gjirokastër); Shkodrançe (Shkodër); Dibrançe (in Dibër); Devolliçe (in the region of the Devoll River, near Korçë); and Beratçe (in Berat).

Before the Communist Regime

Western music was little known in the country prior to World War I. Its diffusion began with the twenties, when a brass band composed of Albanians who had been trained in the United States came to Albania, toured the major towns, and settled in Korçë, where it gave regular concerts of popular and classical music. The so-called "Royal Band," which also played Western compositions, was later founded in Tirana.

In the middle thirties, young native artists, mostly singers who had studied music abroad, began to appear. Three young Albanian sopranos particularly distinguished themselves: Tefta Tashko, Maria Paluca, and Gjorgjija Filçe. Besides operatic pieces and *lieder,* they also sang Albanian folk songs popularizing Tosk songs among the Gegs and Geg songs among the Tosks. Some of these were highly stylized, Paluca excelling in the songs of Shkodër. Kristaq Antoniu was a rising young Albanian tenor. However, in instrumental music, only Antonin Guraziu, a pianist, made a name for himself. The late Sotir Kozmo was active in the musical life of Albania; he was a choir director and a capable organizer of concerts and recitals.

The only Albanian composer worth mentioning was Kristo Kono, who studied in Italy. He adapted several folk songs from the south, and composed some instrumental works based on traditional folk motifs. Bishop Fan S. Noli proved his versatility with the composition of *Byzantine Concerto,* after he took up residence in the United States.

Under Communism

Music, like every other cultural activity in a Communist country, is subject to vigilant and vigorous Party control. Acceptable subject matter for songs and compositions include Communist leaders, socialist construction, and topics of political interest to the Party. Songs hold by far the first place because they are extremely effective in bringing home to the masses Party campaigns and slogans. Of the best known pre-Communist singers, Gjorgjija Filçe, Maria Paluca (now Kraja), and K. Antoniu are employed by the new regime.

Among composers, Kristo Kono holds first place. He was one of the first musicians to put his talents at the disposal of the regime, and he is the composer of "Zemra e Maleve" (The Heart of the Mountains), dedicated to his friend Enver Hoxha, and of "Dhuratë Stalinit" (Gift to Stalin). He has produced special songs for such Party occasions as May Day, the elections of May 28, 1950, and the folklore festival. He has also put Communist propaganda to music in such songs as "Populli korean lufton" (The Korean People Fight). During the campaign for increased agricultural production, Kono composed the song "Let Us Sow," based on folk motifs and possessing a gay rhythm. He is also the composer of a more ambitious work for orchestra, entitled *Fantazi shqiptare* (Albanian Phantasies). His composition of 1954, *Agimi* (The Dawn), was given a command performance in Tirana in that year. Next to Kono in importance and prestige among Communist composers is Konstantin Trako.

The Committee for Arts and Sciences is the government authority which passes judgment on new Albanian compositions. Its evaluation of Communist music in an article in *Bashkimi* of September 14, 1950 is significant. The article complained that some composers did not know how to make use of the motifs in folk music and dance; that others did not know how to interpret Albanian folk songs; that texts with "decadent" contents, which did not reflect the reality of the new life and "had nothing positive but pessimism," were set to music; that Albanian musicians must profit from the experience of Soviet composers.

There are Albanian songs dedicated to Lenin, Stalin, Moscow, and the Soviet Union, and Russian songs are very popular, sung both in Russian and in Albanian translation. During September, Albanian-Soviet Friendship month, visiting artists from the Soviet Union give highly publicized government-sponsored musical performances in Albania. Western music was formerly held in high esteem, but in Communist Albania it is now disdained as "bourgeois" and "decadent," and Soviet music is held up as the paramount achievement in world music and the only acceptable model for Albanian musicians.

For education in the arts, the Tirana government has built the Lycée Jordan Misija, named in honor of a young artist who fell in the resistance movement. This *lycée* has both vocal and instrumental sections.

Public Libraries and Museums

According to an official acount (March 19, 1954 issue of the *Bulletin d' Informations de L'Agence Télégraphique Albanaise*), Albania now possesses thirteen main public libraries, as compared with five in 1938. The most important is the National Library in Tirana, which is said to have 156,000 volumes, compared with 12,000 when the Communists took over in 1944. Its collection now comprises 26,000 volumes in the Russian language, including the "great classics" on Marxism-Leninism.

The spectacular growth of the National Library in Tirana since 1944 is partly due to Communist confiscation of all important private libraries, including that of Midhat Frashëri, who was a well-known bibliophile reputed to have owned one of the finest private libraries in the Balkans. A large number of the books in the National Library in Tirana dealing with Western culture and the development of Albanian national consciousness are said to be restricted to trustworthy Party members, or kept in locked rooms to which the public has no access.

The prewar National Museum, which contained several excavated *objets d'art,* is still in Tirana. Two additional museums have been built in Tirana since the establishment of the Communist regime: the Museum of National History, and in 1954 the Lenin-Stalin Museum.

Appendix

BIOGRAPHICAL SKETCHES
of Leading Figures of the Communist Regime

RAMIZ ALIJA
Born October 1925 in Shkodër, of poor family. Rel. Background: Moslem. Educ.: Graduated from secondary school in Tirana.

Chronological Data

1939-40: Member of the Albanian Youth of the Lictor (Albanian Fascist Youth).

1942: Joined the Albanian Communist Youth while still in school; arrested in August but released after nine days in prison.

1943: Became member of the Albanian Communist Party, April; finished school in June and was sent by the Party to the Regional Committee of the Communist Youth in Berat, where as organizational secretary of this committee, he organized the youth of that area for Communist activities.

1944: Became member of the political section of the Seventh Partisan Brigade, March; elected candidate member of the Central Committee of Communist Youth at its First Congress in August, as well as a member of the Secretariat of the Anti-Fascist Youth during the same month; member of political section of Second Combat Division, also in August; political commissar of the Fifth Combat Division with rank of lieutenant colonel, November; fought with this division in Yugoslavia.

1945: Member of Central Committee of Albanian Communist Youth, elected at its Second Congress in April; re-elected member of the Secretariat of the Anti-Fascist Youth.

1946: Organizational Secretary of the Albanian Communist Youth.

1947: Secretary General of the People's Youth of Albania, September, which position he held until February 1948.

1948: Transferred to the Office of Propaganda and Agitation of the Party's Central Committee, February; member of the Party's Central Committee, November, which position he still holds.

1949: President of the People's Youth, February.

1950——: Deputy to the People's Assembly.

1950——: Member of the General Council of the Democratic Front.

1952——: First Secretary of the Secretariat of the Union of Working Youth of Albania and member of Politburo of the Central Committee of the Union of Working Youth.

1954: Member of the Presidium of the People's Assembly, July.

1955——: Minister of Education and Culture, June.

LIEUTENANT GENERAL BEQIR BALLUKU

Born 1917 in Tirana. Rel. Background: Moslem. Married. Educ.: A few years of grammar school. Decoration: Order of Skënderbeg First Class.

Chronological Data

1935-39: Metal worker in Tirana; at that time had the reputation of being lazy and a petty thief.

1939: Conscripted into the army, in which he began carrying on subversive activities.

1940-41: Demobilized in 1940 and joined resistance movement; in 1941 helped found the Albanian Communist Party.

1942: Joined the Partisan units in the Tirana area and became political commissar of the Third Partisan Brigade; later chief of staff of various brigades.

1944: Deputy commissar, Third Army Corps.

1945: Political commissar, First Army Corps; member of the Special Court to try "war criminals and enemies of the people"; Vice President of the General Council of the Democratic Front.

1947: Appointed Commander of the Second Infantry Division, with the rank of colonel.

1948: Promoted to Major General, February, and appointed Chief of Staff of the People's Army, which position he held until he was appointed Minister of People's Defense in July 1953.

1948——: Member of the Central Committee of the Albanian Workers' Party and member of Politburo in November; re-elected in April 1952 and July 1954.

1952-53: Attended Voroshilov Military Academy, August 1952–August 1953; member of Albanian delegation to Stalin's funeral in March.

1954——: Appointed First Deputy Premier and reappointed Minister of People's Defense, July 20.

MADAME LIRI BELISHOVA

Born *ca.* 1923 in Belishovë village, Skrapar district. Rel. Background: Moslem. Married Nako Spiru in 1945, but never used his name; he committed suicide in 1947. Educ.: Graduate of the Girls Pedagogical Institute in Tirana in the late 1930's; studied nursing in Tirana; probably attended school on Marxism-Leninism in Moscow from August 1952 to August 1954.

Chronological Data

1941-44: Active in the Albanian Communist Youth in Berat district; participated actively in the Partisan formations, and lost one eye. A fanatic Communist and effective agitator. Evacuated to Bari (Italy) in fall of 1944 for medical treatment at Allied field hospital.

1944-48: Member of the Secretariat of Albanian Anti-Fascist Youth.

1945: Member of Albanian Youth delegation to World Youth Conference, London, November.

1945——: Member of the General Council of the Democratic Front.

1946: Head of Albanian delegation to Third Congress of Yugoslav Youth, Zagreb, May; head of Albanian delegation to Soviet Physical Cultural Festival in Moscow, July.

1946-47: President of People's Youth; dismissed after the suicide of her husband, Nako Spiru, and banished to Berat as a school teacher; also dismissed from the Party's Central Committee.

1948——: Regained her position after the purge of Koci Xoxe in November and elected to Party's Central Committee and Politburo by Party's First Congress; re-elected by Second Party Congress in April 1952 and again in July 1954.

1950: Member of the Presidium of the People's Assembly, July; has also been a deputy to the People's Assembly since 1950.

1952-54: In Moscow, probably studying, from August 1952 to August 1954.

1953: A member of the Albanian delegation to Stalin's funeral, March.

1954——: Elected Secretary of the Party's Secretariat, July 12.

SIRI ÇARÇANI

Born 1918 in Fush-Bardhë village, Kurvelesh district, son of a landowner. Rel. Background: Moslem. Married. Educ.: Attended state gymnasium in Shkodër; was a very poor student.

Chronological Data

1941: Served as informer for his uncle, Daut Çarçani, who was Prefect of Gjirokastër under the Italians.

1942-44: Joined the Partisan forces; later appointed assistant commissar of "Asim Zeneli" Battalion.

1945-50: Military Prosecutor in the security forces; often served as state prosecutor in military tribunals trying nationalists and anti-Communists, most of whom were given death sentences and executed.

1951——: Appointed Prosecutor General of the People's Republic of Albania, June 12, 1951.

MAJOR GENERAL KADRI HASBIU

Born *ca.* 1920 in Mavrovë village, Vlorë region. Rel. Background: Moslem. Educ.: Graduated from Commercial High School in Vlorë; attended military school in Moscow; speaks Italian and Russian.

Chronological Data

1942: Graduated from Commerical High School in Vlorë.

1942-45: Joined the Partisans after graduation and became member of the Communist Party; served as commissar in the Fifth Partisan Brigade and was given the rank of captain.

1946-47: Appointed Deputy Chief and, later, Chief of Military Security Section in the Directorate of State Security.

1948-50: Studied in the Soviet Union.

1950-54: Assistant Minister of the Interior, in charge of state security.

1950——: Elected candidate member of the Party's Central Committee in April 1950; became a full member in April 1952.

1954——: Appointed Minister of the Interior, July 1954.

GENERAL OF THE ARMY ENVER HOXHA

Born October 16, 1908 in Gjirokastër. Rel. Background: Moslem. Married Nexhmije Xhuglini, former school teacher, in February 1945; they have two sons. Educ.: Grammar school in Gjirokastër; National Lycée in Korçë: one year (1930-31) at University of Montpellier (France) on state scholarship; studied law in Paris and Brussels, but received no degree; thorough knowledge of French, and has studied Russian, English, Serbo-Croatian, and Italian. Decorations: Foreign: Yugoslav Partisan Star, Yugoslav Order of National Hero, USSR Order of Suvarov; Albanian: Albanian Partisan Star First Class, Order of the Albanian Flag, Memorial Medal, Order of Liberty First Class, and Order of National Hero.

Chronological Data

1930-33: Attended the Faculty of Natural Sciençes at the University of Montpellier on Albanian state scholarship (1930-31); scholarship discontinued because of failure in studies. He then proceeded to Paris in search of work.

1933-36: Private secretary of the honorary consul of Albania in Brussels, Belgium. He also studied law at the local university, but never graduated.

1936-39: Returned to Albania and was appointed teacher of French at the State Gymnasium in Tirana; after four months, was transferred to the National Lycée in Korçë to teach the same subject. Late in 1939, he was to be transferred to the secondary school of Gjirokastër, but refused to go.

1940-41: Operated a tobacco store in Tirana, which became a Communist cell and meeting place of anti-Fascist (Communist) resistance.

1941: Present at the founding of the Albanian Communist Party on November 8 in Tirana; elected member of the provisional Central Committee of the Party and its provisional Secretary General; in the meantime, he was sentenced to death *in absentia.*

1942: One of the organizers of Conference of Pezë (September 16), which founded the Abanian National Liberation Movement, and became member of the General Council of National Liberation.

1943: Elected to the Central Committee of the Albanian Communist Party (which since November 1948 has been known as the Albanian Workers' Party) and appointed Secretary General by the Party's First National Conference held at Labinot in March; he held this latter position until July 1954.

1943: Re-elected member of the General Council of National Liberation Movement at Conference of Labinot, held in July, as well as political commissar of the Abanian Army of National Liberation (ANLA).

1944: President, Anti-Fascist Committee of National Liberation, and Comander in Chief with rank of colonel general, appointed at Conference of Përmet, May 24; Prime Minister of the Provisional Democratic Government of Albania, appointed at Conference of Berat, October.

1945: President of the Democratic Front (successor to the National Liberation Front), which position he still holds; elected Deputy to the Constituent (later People's) Assembly, December 2, and re-elected in May 1950 and May 1954.

1946: Premier, Minister of Foreign Affairs, Minister of People's Defense, and Commander in Chief, appointed by the People's Assembly in March; also elected member of the Presidium of the People's Assembly.

1946: Headed Albanian delegation to Yugoslavia in July and to the Paris Peace Conference from August to October.

1947: Headed Albanian delegation to Moscow in July and to Bulgaria in December.

1948: Attended conference of foreign ministers of the Soviet Union and the People's Democracies held at Warsaw; elected member of the Party's Politburo, which position he had held since November 1941 but never revealed publicly until the Party's First Congress in November of 1948; he still holds this position.

1949: Headed Albanian delegation to Moscow in March and April; promoted to General of the Army in November.

1952: Headed Albanian delegation to the Nineteenth Congress of the Communist Party of the Soviet Union in Moscow, October.

1953: Relinquished posts of Minister of People's Defense and Minister of Foreign Affairs, July 23.

1954: Relinquished position of Premier and Secretary General of the Party, the latter office having been abolished.

1954——: Appointed First Secretary of the Party's Central Committee, July 12.

MADAME NEXHMIJE HOXHA

Born 1921 in Dibër; her maiden name was Xhuglini. Rel. Background: Moslem. Married Enver Hoxha in January 1945. Educ.: Graduated from Girls Pedagogical Institute in Tirana in 1941.

Chronological Data

1941: Graduated from Girls Pedagogical Institute in Tirana, which she attended on govenrment scholarship; joined the Albanian Communist Party upon its formation in November, and became a member of the Central Committee of the Communist Youth of Albania during the same month.

1941-42: Taught elementary school while engaged in clandestine Communist activities; became member of the Party's Regional Committee in Tirana, with special emphasis on the mobilization and Communist orientation of young women and girls; attended the Conference of Pezë (September 1942); tried by a Tirana court *in absentia* and given twelve years in prison; never apprehended, although she was in Tirana all the time.

1944: Left Tirana in March and was assigned by the Central Committee of the Albanian Communist Youth to the Vlorë-Gjirokastër zone; later attached to the First Combat Division to attend to the indoctrination of women in central Albania; participated in the Congress of Përmet (May) and in the Youth Congress at Panarit (August), where she was elected a member of the Secretariat of the General Youth Council; attended the First Congress of the Albanian Anti-Fascist Women in Berat (November), where she was also elected a member of the Secretariat.

1945-46: Albanian delegate to the Anti-Fascist Women Congress in Belgrade; President of Mother and Child, an affiliate of the Union of Albanian Women.

1946-55: President of the Union of Albanian Women; replaced in October 1955 by Vito Kapo.

1948: Attended Second Congress of Anti-Fascist Women in Belgrade, January, and Second Congress of International Women's Federation in Budapest, December.

1948-55: Elected member of the Party's Central Committee and deputy to the People's Assembly.

1949: Head of Albanian delegation to meeting of International Federation of Democratic Women in Moscow, November.

1950——: Elected Vice President of the Albanian-Soviet Friendship Society, October, and member of the Presidium of the People's Assembly.

1952: Headed Albanian delegation to thirteenth session of the Executive Committee of Women's International Democratic Federation in Bucharest, July.

1952——: Head of Agitation and Propaganda Directorate of the Party's Central Committee.

MAJOR GENERAL TUK JAKOVA

Born April 26, 1914 in Shkodër. Rel. Background: Roman Catholic. Married in 1945; one daughter. Educ.: Elementary school and two years in Shkodër gymnasium. Decorations: Yugoslav Partisan Star, Albanian Order of National Hero, and Order of Skënderbeg First Class.

Chronological Data

Until 1940: Carpenter by trade in Shkodër.

1937: As labor leader in Shkodër, published clandestine anti-Zog bulletin for workers.

1938: One of the seventy youths (trial of youths) arrested for Communist activities. Brought to trial in Tirana on December 15 and sentenced to four years confinement at Berat.

1939: Released when Italy invaded Albania on April 7. Fled to Yugoslavia, but returned to Albania in the same year.

1940-1942: Engaged in resistance activities in Tirana with such Communist colleagues as Qemal Stafa and Vasil Shanto; one of the founders of the Albanian Communist Party (November 8, 1941); went from city to city organizing Party committees; nearly captured in Shkodër on June 5, 1942 but managed to escape; tried *in absentia* twice in Tirana and Shkodër and condemned to death; attended Conference of Pezë, which founded the National Liberation Movement.

1943: Attended First Party Conference at Labinot, March; present at the National Liberation Conference in Labinot in July, where he was elected member of the General Council and of the ANLA *Shtab;* present at the founding of the First Partisan Brigade at Vithkuq (August 15), and was named one of its commissars.

1944-45: Attended Conferences of Përmet, May, and was elected member of the Anti-Fascist Council of National Liberation; political commissar of First Combat Division, Second Combat Division, and finally of First Army Corps; attended Conference of Berat, October 1944.

1945: Albanian representative at the World Trade Union Conference in Paris; President of the Albanian Trade Unions, which position he held until 1947.

1945——: Deputy to the People's Assembly; served as President of the Assembly from January to March 1946.

1946-47: Minister without Portfolio, March 1946—February 1947; Head of Albanian delegation to he United Nations Health Conference in New York, June 1946, and observer at the United Nations Security Council, August 1946.

1947-48: Minister to Yugoslavia, and also accredited Minister to Hungary, March 1947—October 1948.

1948: Minister of Industry, February-October head of delegation to Moscow to seek economic assistance and permission to purge Koci Xoxe, September; Orgburo Secretary of the Party, replacing Xoxe, October; Second Secretary of Party's Central Committee and member of Politburo, elected by Party's First Congress, November; Vice Premier, November 28.

1949: Headed various trade and political delegations to Hungary, Czechoslovakia, Bulgaria, and Romania.

1950: Minister of Industry, March-July.

1951: Removed as member of Politburo and Orgburo in February, and as president of the Albanian-Soviet Friendship Society, June.

1952: Accused by Hoxha at the Second Party Congress (March-April) of right-wing deviation and of disobeying Party orders vis-à-vis religion. Jakova admitted his "grave" errors, and was re-elected to the Party's Central Committee, but not to the Politburo.

1953-54: Released as Vice Premier and appointed Minister of Finance, July 1953, from which position he was released and re-appointed Vice Premier in July 1954. Discharged from this position, June 24, 1955 (purged).

MAJOR GENERAL HYSNI KAPO

Born 1915 in Tërbaç village, Vlorë region. Rel. Background: Moslem. Left first wife in 1945 and married Vito Kondi, sister of Alqi Kondi. Educ.: Commercial School in Vlorë. Decorations: Memorial Medal, Liberation Medal, Order of the Albanian Flag, Order of Freedom Second Class, Order of Skënderbeg Second Class, Partisan Star First Class, Order of the People's Hero, and the Yugoslav Unity and Brotherhood First Class, and Service of the People.

Chronological Data

1936-40: Nurse at State Hospital in Vlorë.

1941: Joined the Albanian Communist Party when it was formed on November 8 and was immediately appointed political secretary of the Party Committee for Vlorë region; in the same year formed the first Partisan resistance group known as "Çeta Plakë," in which he served as commissar.

1941-43: Held the position of military "responsible" for the whole Vlorë area; commissar of the *Shtab* (General Headquarters) of the first operational zone Vlorë-Gjirokastër, and commissar of the Fifth Partisan Brigade.

1943: Became member of the General *Shtab* of the ANLA and member of the General Council of the National Liberation Movement; in March 1943 was elected member of the Central Committee of the Albanian Communist Party, a position he still holds.

1944: Member of the Presidency of the Anti-Fascist Council of National Liberation; Chief of Staff, First Combat Division; political commissar, First Army Corps; Inspector General of ANLA, with rank of colonel.

1945: Member of the Special Court to try "war criminals and enemies of the peope," formed in January.

1945-47: Minister to Yugoslavia, July 1945–February 1947.

1945——: Member of the People's Assembly.

1946: Co-opted member of the Party's Politburo; became full member, April 2, 1952, and re-elected July 1954; elected Secretary General of the Democratic Front; served as head of the Abanian delegation to the War Reparations Conference in Paris; member of the Albanian delegation to the Paris Peace Conference; head of Albanian delegation to the United Nations General Assembly.

1947-49: Assistant Minister of Foreign Affairs; member of Albanian delegations to Moscow, July, and Sofia, December.

1949-50: Director of Political Directorate of the People's Army.

1949: Promoted to Major General, July 8.

1950: Appointed Vice Premier, July 4.

1951: Appointed Minister of Agriculture and Procurements, September 6.

1954: First Vice Premier and Minister of Agriculture, July 20.

1955——: Released from Ministry of Agriculture, June 6; appointed President of Albanian Soviet Friendship Society, August 15.

ABDYL KELLEZI

Born 1919 in Tirana. Rel. Background: Moslem. Married. Educ.: Secondary school in Tirana and secondary military school in Rome, Italy; speaks French and Italian.

Chronological Data

1939: Arrested in Tirana for anti-Fascist activities.

1939-41: Interned at Ventotene Island, Italy.

1942: Arrested in Tirana for anti-Fascist activities, August; Secretary of the Tirana National Liberation Council.

1943: Attended Conference of National Liberation Movement at Labinot and elected member of the General Council of National Liberation.

1944: Commissar of the Sixteenth Partisan Brigade; member of ANLA's General Staff; member of the Council for Administration of the State Bank and member of its Board of Directors.

1945: Member of the Executive Committee of the General Council of Democratic Front; member of Commission for Investigation of War Profits in Tirana.

1945——: Deputy to the People's Assembly.

1945-46: Managing Director of the State Bank.

1946-48: Assistant Minister of Finance.

1948-53: Minister of Finance, until July 1953, when he was demoted to Assistant Minister of Finance.

1949--53: Headed various trade delegations to the Soviet Union, Romania, Bulgaria, East Germany, and concluded trade and payments agreements with these countries.

1953: Member of Albanian delegation to Stalin's funeral, March.

1954——: Reappointed Minister of Finance, July.

BILBIL KLOSI

Born 1919 in Mallakastër. Rel. Background: Moslem. Married Yollanda Xhuvani, daughter of Aleksander Xhuvani, in 1945. Educ.: Graduated from National Lycée in Korçë, and received law degree in France; speaks fluent French and Italian.

Chronological Data

ca. 1938: Graduated from National Lycée in Korçë.

1938-42: Studied law in France.

1942-43: Partisan of the "Old Band" of Mallakastër; on the political staff of the Fifth Partisan Brigade.

1944: Commissar of the Third Combat Division, November; President of the Military Tribunal of the First Corps, with rank of lieutenant colonel.

1945: Secretary of the Ministry of the Interior; elected deputy to the People's Assembly, representing Vlorë region, Mallakastër district; re-elected in 1950 and 1954.

1946: Appointed second assistant to the State General Prosecutor, March 26; also member of the Constitutional Committee of the People's Assembly.

1950: Appointed Assistant State General Prosecutor, July.

1951——: Appointed Minister of Justice, September 6, 1951; reappointed in July 1953 and July 1954.

1952: President of Albanian Lawyers Association, May.

SPIRO KOLEKA

Born July 8, 1908 in Himarë. Rel. Background: Orthodox. Married. Educ.: San Demetrio Corone, 1928-29; University of Pisa, 1930-34, degree in civil engineering; speaks Greek, Italian, French, a little English. Decoration: Yugoslav Partisan Star.

Chronological Data

1935-36: With Italian engineering firm in Shkodër.

1936: Arrested on charges of having participated in Fier revolt of 1935 against Zog.

1937-39: Director of Public Works Office in Shkodër, Albanian Ministry of Public Works; traveled extensively in Italy; took active part in resistance to Italian occupation; fled to Yugoslavia, but returned in December 1939.

1940-41: Began cooperating with resistance underground; organized the Mani and Koleka Engineering Company.

1943: Elected member of the General Council of the National Liberation Movement and of the ANLA General Staff at Conference of Labinot, July.

1944-48: Minister of Public Works in the Anti-Fascist Committee of National Liberation, appointed by the Congress of Përmet, May 1944; reappointed to same position by the Congress of Berat, October 1944, and relieved in November 1948.

1945——: Deputy to the People's Assembly, December 1945; re-elected in May 1950 and May 1954.

1946: Concluded Maritime Agreement with Yugoslavia, September.

1948-49: Minister of Communications, October 1948–August 1949.

1948-50: President of State Planning Commission, November 28, 1948–July 5, 1950.

1948——: Member of the Party's Central Committee and Politburo.

1949: Member of Albanian delegation to Moscow led by Hoxha, March-April; head of Albanian trade delegation to the Soviet Union, November-December.

1949-53: Vice Premier, appointed November 1949, relieved July 1953.
1950: Minister of Public Works, March-July.
1951: Head of Albanian trade delegation to Poland, January.
1953: Minister of Industry and Construction, July.
1954——: Appointed President of State Planning Commission with rank of Minister, July 20.
1955——: Vice Premier, June.

MAJOR GENERAL HAXHI LLESHI

Born 1913 in Reshen, Dibër region. Rel. Background: Moslem. Married, no children. Educ.: Grammar school and private tutoring; speaks Serbo-Croatian.

Chronological Data

1941-43: Head of resistance group in Dibër area; attended Conference of Pezë, September 1942; enrolled member of the Albanian Communist Party in 1943.
1943-44: Elected member of General Council of National Liberation Movement and of ANLA's General Staff by Conference of Labinot, July 1943; given the rank of colonel at Congress of Berat, May, 1944.
1944-46: Minister of the Interior, May 1944–January 1946; appointed Minister without Portfolio, March 12, 1946.
1945——: Deputy to the People's Assembly.
1946: Headed Albanian delegation to Belgrade to deposit ratified copy of Treaty of Friendship and Mutual Assistance Pact with Yugoslavia, September.
1948——: Candidate member of the Party's Central Committee.
1948-49: Acting President of the State Control Commission, November 1948–November 1949.
1949: Promoted to Major General.
1950——: Member of General Council of Democratic Front, and member of Presidium of People's Assembly from July 1950 to July 1953.
1953——: Elected President of the Presidium of the People's Assembly, August 1.

RITA MARKO

Born 1920 in Korçë. Rel. Background: Orthodox. Educ.: Attended grammar school in Korçë.

1936: Participated in the strike staged by Puna organization in Korçë in February
1939-42: Active in the Communist resistance in Korçë; joined Partisan formations in 1942 in the Korçë district, and also became a Party member.

1942-44: Company commissar and, later, batallion commissar of the Fourth Partisan Brigade.

1944-48: Commissar of the Twelfth Partisan Brigade, commissar of the Eighth People's Defense Brigade (Security Brigade), and finally regimental commissar in the Security Forces with the rank of major.

1949-50: First Secretary of the Party Committee in Korçë district; elected candidate member of the Party's Central Committee in April 1950.

1950——: Deputy to the People's Assembly.

1950: Minister of Industry, July; released in March 1951.

1951——: Secretary of the Party's Central Committee, March.

1952: Appointed member of the Presidium of the People's Assembly, March; reappointed Secretary of the Party's Central Committee; member of the Central Committee, and candidate member of the Politburo, April; member of the Central Committee of the Union of Trade Unions; member of the Albanian delegation to the Nineteenth Congress of the Communist Party of the Soviet Union in Moscow, October.

1954: Member of the Central Electoral Commission for election to People's Assembly, representing the trade unions.

MANUSH MYFTIU

Born 1919 in Vlorë. Rel. Background: Moslem. Single. Educ.: Graduated from Vlorë elementary school and Classical Lycée in Rome (1939), and attended the Medical Faculty in Turin, Italy, but did not complete his studies; knows Italian well.

1939: Graduated from Classical Lycée in Rome; member of a Communist cell in Vlorë.

1940-41: University of Turin; returned to Vlorë and became a member of the Albanian Youth of the Lictor (Albanian Fascist Youth); at the same time, member of a Communist cell.

1941: Became a member of the Albanian Communist Party after it was founded on November 8; chosen member of the Vlorë Party District Committee and one of its leaders for the next three years.

1944: Commissar of Fifth Partisan Brigade; commissar of First Combat Division; attached to the Fifth and Eigth Brigades of the First Army Corps.

1945——: Deputy to the People's Assembly.

1946: Director of the Political Directorate of the People's Army, with rank of colonel.

1947: Member of Commission for Improvement and Organization of State.

1947-49: President of the People's Assembly.

1948——: Member of the Central Committee of the Albanian Workers' Party.

1949: Deputy Minister of Foreign Affairs.

1949-50: Minister without Portfolio, November 1949–July 1950.

1941-51: President of State Control Commission with rank of Minister, November 1949–April 1951.

1950——: Vice President of the Albanian-Soviet Friendship Society.

1951: Acting Minister of Justice, March-September; head of Albanian cultural delegation to Moscow, arrived December 15.

1951-52: Vice Premier, April 1951–April 1952.

1952: Candidate member of the Party's Politburo, which position he still holds, and Secretary of the Party's Secretariat until July 12, 1954.

1954——: Appointed a Vice Premier, July 20.

KIÇO NGJELA

Born 1920 in Shepër village, Gjirokastër region. Rel. Background: Orthodox. Married. Educ.: Graduated from secondary school in Albania and studied in Rome; speaks Greek and Italian.

Chronological Data

1940-42: School teacher; joined the resistance movement in 1941 and operated chiefly in the Tirana area.

1946: Elected member of the General Council of the Democratic Front in October.

1946-47: Assistant Minister of National Economy and Assistant President of the State Economic Planning Commission.

1948: Appointed Minister of Finance, February; Acting President of the State Economic Planning Commission, October; relinquished above two posts and appointed Minister of Domestic Trade, November.

1950——: Deputy to the People's Assembly.

1950: Member of an Albanian trade delegation to Rome, May; reappointed Minister of Domestic Trade, July.

1951: Member of Albanian trade delegation to Moscow.

1952: Elected candidate member of Party's Central Committee, April; President of the Albanian Preparatory Committee for the International Economic Conference in Moscow.

1953: Relinquished post of Minister of Domestic Trade and appointed President of the Union of Consumers' Cooperatives, July.

1954——: Appointed Minister of Trade, July.

GOGO NUSHI

Born December 15, 1913 in Vuno village, Himarë district. Rel. Background: Orthodox. Married, two children. Educ.: Grammar school; learned Greek in his native village, and Italian and French while working in France.

Chronological Data

1928-40: In 1928 emigrated with his father to Lyons, France, where he worked as a laborer in factories and came under the influence of the French Communist Party; collaborated with left-wing Albanian intellectuals in France and Switzerland and participated in the publication of such pro-Communist publications as *Populli* and *Sazani.* In 1933, helped to organize in Lyons a branch of the National Liberation Committee, an Albanian pro-Communist organization with headquarters in Paris; also became member of the Albanian Federation in Paris, which was under the influence of such Communists as Sejfulla Malëshova and Ymer Dishnica.

1940: Returned to Albania, allegedly "lent" to the Albanian National Liberation from the Albanian Liberation Committee of France; on his return engaged in the transport business in Tirana with his brother, who was later killed in underground activity.

1941: One of the founders of the Albanian Communist Party, November 8.

1941-43: Became active in the Communist resistance movement, and was intermittently arrested and released; his experience among the French workers pre-eminently qualified him for organizing the labor movement in Albania; recruited a large number of youth and workers in the Communist movement.

1944: Elected member of the Presidium of the Anti-Fascist National Liberation Council, Congress of Përmet, May; also served in a political capacity in the First, Second, and Fourth Combat Divisions; at the end of the year became member of the Tirana Economic Commission Board.

1945——: Elected member of the General Council of the Albanian Trade Unions, February, and deputy to the Constituent (later People's) Assembly from Tirana, December; re-elected to the People's Assembly in May 1950 and May 1954.

1946——: Elected member of the General Council of the Democratic Front, October; in 1950 was elected Vice President of the Presidium of the Democratic front, which position he still holds.

1947: Member of the Albanian Economic Mission to Belgrade, June; Minister of Trade, February 2, 1947 to November 1948.

1948-49: Minister of Industry, October 1948–November 1949.

1948——: Member of the Party's Central Committee and Politburo, elected by Party's First Congress in November 1948 and re-elected to the same positions by the Party's Second Congress in April 1952.

1949: Elected President of Albanian Trade Unions in October; held this position until September 1951.

1950: Represented the Albanian Workers' Party at the Twelfth Congress of the French Communist Party in Paris, April; elected member of the Presidium of the People's Assembly in July, and re-elected in July 1954.

1951: Appointed Vice Premier, September.

1954——: Appointed Secretary in the Party Secretariat.

FADIL PACRAMI

Born 1922 in Shkodër. Rel. Background: Moslem. Educ.: Graduated from gymnasium in Shkodër and studied medicine for two years in Italy; speaks French, Italian, and probably Russian.

Chronological Data

1941-42: Graduated from Shkodër Gymnasium and went to Italy to attend medical school.

1942: Returned to Albania and joined the resistance through the Communist-controlled youth organization in Tirana.

1943: Appointed chief of the youth organization in Tirana and continued his Communist resistance activities.

1944: Elected member of a ten-man Secretariat of the Albanian Anti-Fascist Youth by the Youth Congress held at Panarit, August 8-10; also elected member of the Albanian Anti-Fascist National Liberation Council.

1945-46: Elected Vice President of the Albanian Anti-Fascist Youth, April 1945, and member of Secretariat of Democratic Front, August 1945.

1945: Member of the General Council of the Albanian-Soviet Friendship Society; head of Albanian delegation to World Youth Congress, London, where he was elected member of the General Council of the World Federation of Democratic Youth.

1946: Albanian delegate to the Balkan Youth Congress, Sofia, February; member of Albanian delegation to Soviet Physical Culture Festival in Moscow, July; elected member of the Presidium of the Albanian Anti-Fascist Youth, October.

1946-53: Assistant Minister of Education.

1947——: Deputy to the People's Assembly.

1949——: Editor in Chief of *Zëri i Popullit;* President of Union of Albanian Journalists, elected February 1949.

1949-52: Member of the Directorate of Society for Aid to Army and for Defense (SHNUM), December 1949–May 1952.

1950: Secretary of Central Electoral Commission for May 28 general elections; candidate member of the Party's Central Committee, April.

1950——: Elected member of General Council of Democratic Front, May 1950.

1952——: Elected member of the Party's Central Committee by Second Party Congress, April 1952.

1952: Member of Albanian delegation to the Nineteenth Congress of the Communist Party of the Soviet Union, October.

1953: Elected President of Committee for Cultural Relations with Foreign Countries, February; head of Albanian cultural delegation to the Soviet Union, December.

1954: Appointed Secretary of the Central Electoral Commission for the general elections of May 20; appointed President of the Foreign Affairs Commission of the People'sAssembly.

1955: Headed cultural delegation to Red China and North Korea.

JOSIF PASHKO

Born 1916 in Vodicë (Ersekë), son of Pashko Vodica, now Archbishop Paisi, Primate of the Albanian Orthodox Church. Rel. Background: Orthodox. Married. Educ.: Graduated from Normal School in Elbasan, 1938.

Chronological Data

1939-42: Elementary school teacher in Elbasan area.

1942-44: Joined Partisan bands with his pro-Communist father, then an Orthodox priest in Ersekë; became political commissar in various Partisan brigades and finally a lieutenant colonel in the DMP (security division).

1945-46: A security officer in the Ministry of the Interior; on March 26, 1946 became second assistant to the State General Prosecutor, in charge of security matters.

1950-51: Relieved from his post as Deputy General Prosecutor, July 1950, and appointed Assistant Minister of the Interior.

1950——: Deputy to the People's Assembly.

1951-52: Minister of State Control, September 1951–April 1952; Secretary of the Party's Secretariat and member of Central Committee, April 1952.

1954: Released as Secretary of the Central Committee and appointed Minister of Construction and Communications.

1955——: Appointed Minister of Construction, June 6.

MAJOR GENERAL SHEFQET PECI

Born 1906 in Picar village, Kurvelesh district. Rel. Background: Moslem. Married and has children. Educ.: Elementary school in his village and attended artillery school in Tirana; speaks Italian. Decorations: Partisan Star First Class, Order of the Albanian Flag, Order of Valor, Order of Skënderbeg Third Class, Memorial Medal, and Liberation Medal.

Chronological Data

1925: Became a noncommissioned officer in the Albanian Army.

1927-31: Attended artillery course in Tirana, and in 1931 was promoted to rank of second lieutenant in the artillery.

1932-36: Regular army officer.

1937: Accused of seditious activities against the Zog regime, arrested and imprisoned, but released after four months.

1938: Appointed custodian of one of the dormitories of the Normal School in Elbasan.

1939-42: Organized the students of the Normal School for anti-Italian demonstrations; arrested and imprisoned in 1942, but released after four months; joined the Albanian Communist Party when it was formed; joined the underground movement and was sent to Gjirokastër as a member of the Party Committee; at the end of 1942, appointed commissar of the "Çerçis Topulli" Partisan group.

1943: Commissar of "Asim Zeneli" Battalion; commissar of the First Mixed Group; in December, commander of the Fifth Partisan Brigade.

1944: Member of the General Liberation Council, May; Deputy Commander of the First Combat Division, with rank of major; Chief of Operational Staff of the Third and Twenty-Fifth Brigades, October; Commander of the Third Army Corps, with rank of colonel, November.

1945: Inspector General of the Albanian People's Army.

1945——: Deputy to the People's Assembly.

1946: Commander of the Third Infantry Division, March; Commander of the Fifth Infantry Division, May.

1948: Director of Combat Training in the General Staff; Commander of the DMP (security division).

1948——: Elected candidate member of the Party's Central Committee in November 1948; elected full member of the Central Committee in April 1950; re-elected in April 1952.

1949: Director of Lines of Communications of the People's Army; promoted to Major General, July 8.

1949-51: Minister of Communications, August 1949–November 1951.

1951-54: Appointed Minister of Mines, November 1951.

1953——: Appointed President of the State Control Commission in July 1953 and again in July 1954.

PILO PERISTERE

Born 1909 in Korçë. Rel. Background: Orthodox. Educ.: Attended elementary school in Korçë; speaks Greek and Italian.

Chronological Data

Until 1940: Metal (tinsmith) worker in Korçë and a professional soccer player.

1932-40: Became active in labor syndicates in Korçë and worked closely with Koci Xoxe and the Puna group (the Korçë Communist group).

1940: Moved to Tirana and began collaborating with Enver Hoxha, with whom he had worked in Korçë.

1941-42: Joined the Communist resistance movement, and organized Partisan forces in Korçë and Vlorë; in 1942, became commissar of the "Mokra" Partisan group in Pogradec.

1943: Attended the First Party Conference held in Labinot, March; became commissar of the Second Battalion of the Fourth Brigade, December.

1945: Vice President and Chief of Internal Section (Security) of the Executive Committee of the People's Council in Korçë; later chief of the Public Works Section in the same committee.

1948——: Elected member of the Central Committee of the Albanian Workers' Party by the First Party Congress, November.

1949: Vice President of the Union of the Albanian Trade Unions; member of the Albanian delegation to the Tenth Congress of Soviet Trade Unions in Moscow, April.

1949-51: Secretary General of the Union of Albanian Trade Unions, October 1949–September 1951.

1950——: Deputy to the People's Assembly.

1950——: Deputy member of the Executive Committee of World Federation of Trade Unions.

1951——: Elected President of the Central Council of Trade Unions of Albania, September 21, 1951; re-elected in August 1952 and July 1954.

1952: Candidate member of the Party's Politburo, April 1952.

1954——: Appointed Vice President of the People's Assembly, July 20.

MIHAL PRIFTI

Born September 25, 1918 in Gjatë village, Gjirokastër district. Rel. Background: Orthodox. Married. Educ.: Completed secondary studies in Greece; attended Faculty of Physics and Mathematics at University of Athens, 1939-40, and Faculty of Engineering at University of Rome, March-June 1941; speaks Greek, Italian, and Russian.

Chronological Data

1929: Went to Greece to join father who had emigrated there.

1929-40: Attended school in Greece.

1940: Returned to Albania.

1941: Studied for a few months in Rome; returned to Albania and joined the Albanian Communist Party.

1942: Professor at Commercial School in Vlorë.

1942-43: Political Secretary of the Party Committee in Vlorë and member of the Anti-Fascist National Liberation Council in the Vlorë region; assigned to the political section of the First Partisan Brigade, December 1943.

1943-45: Acting commissar of the First Partisan Brigade; instructor in the political section of the First Combat Division; later commissar of the Second Combat Division with rank of lieutenant colonel.

1945: Separated from the Army and appointed Secretary General to the Office of the Premier.

1947: Chief of the Ministerial Committee for receiving UNRRA supplies.

1947-49: Albanian Minister to the Soviet Union, April 1947-September 1949.

1948——: Elected member of the Party's Central Committee by First Party Congress, November 1948; re-elected in April 1952.

1949: Accredited Albanian Minister to Poland, April; head of Albanian observers at the United Nations General Assembly in New York, October.

1950: Visited Rome to investigate defection of the security officer of the Albanian legation in that city.

1950——: Deputy to the People's Assembly; member of the General Council of the Democratic Front.

1953——: Appointed Albanian Ambassador to Moscow, August.

MADAME FIQRETE SHEHU

Born *ca.* 1920 in Berat, daughter of a former government employee named Sanxhaktari. Rel. Background: Moslem. Married Mehmet Shehu (now Premier) in 1945. Educ.: Attended the Girls Pedagogical Institute in Tirana, but did not graduate.

1940-41: A clerk in the postal service in Tirana; joined the Communist Party when it was founded in November 1941.

1942-43: Mobilized youth in Tirana for Communist subversive activities; joined the First Partisan Brigade, August 1943, as a recruit and there met her future husband, who commanded the brigade.

1944-45: Assistant political commissar of the First Partisan Brigade, and later member of the political bureau of the First Combat Division; one of the leaders in the Anti-Fascist Women of Albania.

1946-49: Member of the political bureau of the Union of Albanian Women; member of the political bureau of the People's Youth Union; secretary of the Party Committee in Tirana; member of the Albanian delegation to World Congress of Partisans of Peace in Paris, April 1949.

1950: First Secretary of the Party Provisional Bureau for Tirana and candidate member of the Party's Central Committee, April; member of the General Council of the Democratic Front, May; First Secretary of the Politburo of the Tirana district Party Committee, July.

1950——: Deputy to the People's Assembly.

1950: Vice President of the People's Assembly, June; Vice President of Union of Albanian Women, October.

1951: Member of Editorial Board of *Shiqipëri-BRSS* (Albanian-USSR); Vice President of the Albania Committee for the Defense of Peace, which position she still holds.

1952——: Elected full member of the Party's Central Committee by Second Party Congress, April 1952; member of Commission to Fight Illiteracy, May 1952.

1952: Member of Executive Committee of the People's Council of the city of Tirana, October; headed delegation of Albanian Peace Committee to Vienna Peace Congress, November; President of the Tirana branch of the Albanian-Soviet Friendship Society.

LIEUTENANT GENERAL MEHMET SHEHU

Born January 10, 1913 in Çorush village, Mallakastër. Rel. Background: Moslem, son of a sheik (Moslem priest). Married Fiqrete Sanxhaktari, a former school teacher and government employee, in 1945. Educ.: Graduated from American Vocational School in Tirana, 1932; attended military college in Naples, 1935; officers' training school in Tirana, 1936; Voroshilov Military Academy in Moscow, 1945-46; speaks fluent English, Italian, and Russian, and knows some French and Serbo-Croatian. Decorations: Yugoslav Partisan

Star, Bulgarian Order of September 9, 1944, Order of Skënderbeg First and Second Class, Order of Albanian Flag, Order of Freedom Second Class, Partisan Star First Class, Order of Valor, Memorial Medal, Liberation Medal, Order of People's Hero.

Chronological Data

1932: Graduated from American Vocational School in Tirana.

1935: Granted scholarship to attend military college in Naples, but recalled after four months because of pro-Communist activities.

1936: Attended officers' school in Tirana.

1938: Went to Spain and in November joined the "Garibaldi" International Brigade XII, later becoming Acting Commander of its Fourth Battalion; joined the Spanish Communist Party, December.

1939: On withdrawal of International Brigade into France on February 2, 1939, interned in a French concentration camp, where he remained for three years and four months; during this period he joined the Italian Communist Party and was a member of the camp's Communist Party.

1942: Released from the camp in France; on August 10, arrived in Albania under Italian escort and remained under arrest in Tirana for twenty-four hours; on his release, returned to his native Mallakastër, joined the Partisan underground movement, and became a member of the Communist Party Committee for Vlorë district; later its Organizing Secretary.

1943: Appointed leader of the first Communist resistance group to be formed in Mallakastër, February 4; appointed Commander of the First Partisan Brigade, which he organized at Vithkuq, August 15.

1944: Elected member of the Anti-Fascist General Council and given rank of colonel by Congress of Përmet, May; appointed second-in-command of the First Combat Division, and in August, Commander; on November 28, promoted to Major General and appointed second deputy for operations of the Chief of Staff; sent to Shkodër area to put down an anti-Communist revolt.

1945-46: Attended Voroshilov Military Academy, September 1945–August 1946; on his return appointed Chief of Staff of the Albanian Army; also elected member of the General Council and of the Executive Committee of the Democratic Front, which positions he still holds.

1947: Elected deputy to the People's Assembly; re-elected in 1950 and 1954.

1948: Dismissed as Chief of Staff and also from the Party's Central Committe in February, reportedly because of his opposition to Tito's demand for the stationing of two Yugoslavian divisions on Albanian soil; appointed to the newly-created but insignificant Ministry of Post, Telegraph, and Telephone. During the next five months (February-June) under close surveillance by Lieutenant General Koci Xoxe, then

Minister of the Interior, and spent most of his time chaffing in his native village in Mallakastër. The Tito-Cominform break saved him from final purge, and in October he was appointed Minister of the Interior; the following month he arrested his predecessor, Koci Xoxe. He was also appointed Vice Premier, a member of the Party's Politburo, and Secretary of the Party's Secretariat, thus becoming the number two man in the Party and government hierarchy.

1949: Promoted to Lieutenant General, July 8.

1953: Relieved of his position as Secretary of the Party's Secretariat, July 23.

1954——: Appointed Premier, replacing Enver Hoxha, July 20.

BEHAR SHTYLLA

Born May 11, 1918 in Korçë. Rel. Background: Moslem. Married Valentina, daughter of Engineer Jovan Adam. Educ.: Graduated from National Lycée in Korçë and studied in Italy; speaks French and Italian.

Chronological Data

1938: Graduated from National Lycée in Korçë and went to Italy to study.

1940-44: Returned from Italy in 1940 and joined the Albanian Youth of the Lictor (Albanian Fascist Youth), later joined the Communist underground and became a member of the Albanian Communist Youth.

1944-45: Elected Secretary of the National Liberation Council in Korçë; later was called to Tirana and appointed successively Secretary General of the Ministry of the Interior and Secretary General of the Ministry of Foreign Affairs; member of Albanian Youth delegation to World Youth Conference in London, November 1945.

1946: Member of Albanian delegation to the United Nations Health Conference in New York, June; member of Albanian delegation to Paris Peace Conference, July; member of Albanian delegation to observe United Nations General Assembly, October.

1948: President of Albanian delegation to World Health Organization in Geneva, June.

1949-52: Albanian Minister to France, February 1949–June 1952; member of Albanian delegation to observe United Nations General Assembly in New York, September 1949.

1952-53: Albanian Minister to Italy, June 1952–July 1953.

1953——: Appointed Minister of Foreign Affairs, July 1953 and July 1954.

MAJOR GENERAL BEDRI SPAHIU

Born 1906 in Gjirokastër. Rel. Background: Moslem, Bektashi sect. Married, one child. Educ.: Attended high school in Gjirokastër and Shkodër, and military schools in Tirana and Turin, Italy; speaks French and Italian. Decorations: Yugoslav Partisan Star, Albanian Partisan Star, and Order of Skënderbeg First Class.

Chronological Data

1927-30: Artillery School in Tirana, commissioned first lieutenant.

1932-35: Member of subversive clandestine officer group in the Albanian Army; participated in the Fieri revolt against Zog's regime; dismissed from the service and imprisoned.

1937-41: After release from prison, became automobile sales agent in Gjirokastër; in 1939-40 member of the Albanian Fascist Party, but in 1941 joined the Communist resistance movement in his native city.

1943: Elected member of the Presidium of General Council of National Liberation and Chief Administrative Officer of ANLA's General Staff at Conference of Labinot.

1944: Appointed Minister of Economic Reconstruction in the Anti-Fascist Committee of National Liberation at Conference of Përmet, May; given rank of Major General; headed the ANLA delegation to ask for military supplies at Allied Headquarters in Bari, August-September.

1944-46: Minister of Reconstruction, appointed at Congress of Berat in October 1944; Minister of Social Assistance, appointed January 1945.

1945: Appointed Public Prosecutor of the Special Court to try "war criminals and enemies of the people," March-April; became a member of the Bektashi General Council; visited Belgrade and Moscow.

1945-47: Assistant Chief of Staff dealing with administrative matters.

1945——: Deputy to the People's Assembly.

1946: General Purchasing Agent of the Albanian Army; member of the Albanian delegation in Belgrade which concluded the mutual assistance pact with Yugoslavia.

1948-54: Member of the Presidium of the People's Assembly; member of the Party's Central Committee and, until April 1952, member of the Politburo and Secretary of the Central Committee in charge of propaganda and agitation.

1948-49: State Public Prosecutor, May 1948–March 1949.

1949: President of Committee appointed by the Presidium of the People's Assembly to investigate Koci Xoxe's case, January-April; State Prosecutor at trial of Xoxe and his followers, May-June.

1950——: Member of General Council of the Democratic Front.

1951-55: Elected President of the Albanian-Soviet Friendship Society in June; released from position, August 15, 1955.

1951-53: Appointed Vice Premier and Minister of Education in April 1952.

1953-55: Appointed Minister of Education and Culture in July 1953 and again in July 1954; released from position, June 21, 1955 (purged).

KOÇO THEODOSI

Born 1913 in Korçë, of a middle class family. Rel. Background: Orthodox. Married. Educ.: Graduated from National Lycée in Korçë, and studied mining engineering in Belgium and France; has a good Western cultural background; speaks French and Italian.

Chronological Data

1934-41: Graduated from National Lycée in Korçë; studied in Belgium and later in Lyons; became member of Federation of Albanians in France; graduated from University of Lyons and returned to Albania in 1941.

1941: Member of the Albanian Communist Party in Korçë, December 1941, and worked clandestinely in that area until 1943, when he left for the mountains to join the Partisans.

1944: Attended Congress of Përmet, May; state commissar of the oil fields at Kuçovë, November.

1945: Headed Albanian economic delegation to Bulgaria and Romania.

1946: Member of the State Planning Commission and Assistant Minister of Public Works.

1949: Member of Albanian delegation to Moscow headed by Hoxha, March-April; Vice President of State Planning Commission.

1950——: Deputy to the People's Assembly.

1950-53: President of the State Planning Commission, July 1950–July 1953.

1952: Elected member of the Party's Central Commission, April.

1955——: Appointed Vice Premier, June 24.

A BRIEF CHRONOLOGY, 1944–1955

1944

November 28

The National Liberation Movement, self-proclaimed provisional government of Albania at Berat, October 20-23, installs itself in Tirana as the government of Albania, with Enver Hoxha as Premier.

November 29

Albania is declared "liberated" (complete seizure of power by the Communist regime).

1945

January 4

The Albanian Government requests recognition on the part of the United States, the United Kingdom, and the Soviet Union.

January 27

A special tribunal opens in Tirana (others are created throughout the country) with the alleged object of trying "war criminals" and the "people's enemies." The tribunals condemned hundreds to death and thousands to prison and hard labor.

February 11

Albanian trade unions are created, comprising workers in industry, agriculture, mining, civil service, etc.

March 14

An UNRRA delegation arrives in Tirana to arrange numerous shipments of aid in the form of food, clothing, medicines, etc.

March 22

A tax of 7,250,000,000 leks is imposed on businessmen for war profits. Through this device, the merchant class was liquidated.

April 29

Yugoslavia recognizes the Albanian regime.

May 8

American unofficial mission to Albania enters Tirana to survey conditions.

July 14

Consumer goods cooperatives are formed, followed by similar organizations for tailors, barbers, bakers, shoemakers, and other small tradespeople.

August 1

Agreement signed in Tirana between the Albanian regime and UNRRA for sending supplies to Albania.

August 2

Transportation is nationalized. Nationalization of industry and of individual factories followed.

August 5

First Congress of National Liberation Front held; name changed to Democratic Front.

August 29

The Agrarian Reform Law is promulgated.

November 10

Establishment of diplomatic relations between Albania and the Soviet Union. United States and British Governments send note with conditions for American recognition of the Albanian Government.

December 2

Elections to the Constituent National Assembly take place.

1946

January 11

The Constituent Assembly proclaims Albania a republic.

January 17

The Albanian Government closes all Roman Catholic cultural institutions and starts mass arrests of priests and persecution of laymen.

January 25

Albania applies for United Nations membership.

February 10

The Ministry of Education begins special courses in Serbo-Croatian, which later become compulsory in all secondary and night schools, marking the beginning of close cultural cooperation between Yugoslavia and Albania.

March 14

The new Albanian constitution patterned on the Yugoslav is adopted, establishing a People's Republic.

April 17

General Myslim Peza, a Vice Premier, threatens drastic measures against persons opposing government plans. Mass arrests follow within the Army, Democratic Front, government, Party, intelligentsia.

June 1

The Agrarian Reform Law of August 1945 is amended and amplified.

July 9

Yugoslav-Albanian Treaty of Friendship, Collaboration, and Mutual Aid is concluded in Tirana.

August 29

U.N. Security Council rejects Albania's application for United Nations membership.

October 22

Two British destroyers are damaged by undeclared mines in the channel northeast of Corfu off the Albanian coast. Casualties are high: an officer and 37 ratings killed and 43 ratings injured.

November 15

Informal United States mission leaves Albania, because the Albanian Government refused to recognize the prewar treaties between the United States and Albania.

1947

March 25

A majority of the United Nations Security Council condemns Albania for connivance in the sinking of two British destroyers which struck mines off Sarandë (Corfu Channel) on October 22, 1946. Soviet veto blocks a decision.

May 27

Report of the Commission of Investigation of the United Nations Security Council concludes by majority vote that Albania together with Yugoslavia and Bulgaria supports guerrilla warfare in Greece.

July 10

Albanian Government refuses invitation to participate in the Marshall Plan.

August 9

Tirana announces the introduction of forced labor throughout the country.

September 28

Sixteen persons are sentenced to death by the supreme military court in Tirana for having allegedly worked as foreign agents for the United Kingdom and the United States with the aim of overthrowing the regime. Others are imprisoned.

1948

July 1

The Albanian Communist Party, in accordance with the Cominform resolution, breaks off economic relations with Yugoslavia and expels from the country Yugoslav experts sent to Albania under the "economic union" treaty of 1946.

October 3

Koci Xoxe is suspended as Vice Premier and later denounced as an anti-Marxist, Trotskyite, and Titoist. He was executed June 11, 1949.

October 5

The opening of the week of Soviet-Albanian Friendship marks the first intensive direct cooperation with the Soviet Union, which replaced Yugoslavia as "adviser."

November 8

First Communist Party Congress, which changed the name of the Albanian Communist Party to Albanian Workers' Party.

1949

February 8

Albania becomes member of Council of Mutual Economic Assistance.

April 9

International Court of Justice enters judgment establishing Albania's responsibility for the explosions of October 22, 1946 in the Corfu channel.

May 2

The Italian Foreign Office announces the resumption of diplomatic relations with Albania, which had been interrupted since the invasion in 1939.

June 2

The Two-Year Plan (1949-50) is approved by the Assembly.

August 26

Formation in Paris of the National Committee for a Free Albania, headed by Midhat Frashëri.

August 28

Archbishop Kristofor Kisi, head of the Albanian Autocephalous Orthodox Church, is removed from his post. He was imprisoned some months later.

September 21

United Nations Special Balkan Commission report is published advising the General Assembly that Albania was the principal source of material assistance to the Greek guerrilla movement, and to call on Albania and Bulgaria to cease aiding the Greek guerrillas.

November 12

Yugoslavia denounces the Friendship and Mutual Assistance Pact with Albania, the only pact not denounced by Albania after the Tito-Cominform break.

November 26

Adoption of the law on religious communities obliging them to develop among members loyalty toward "the people's power" and the People's Republic of Albania.

December 15

Judgment of the International Court of Justice awarding Great Britain damages of £843,947 against Albania resulting from the Corfu incident. This was never paid.

1950

June 29

The newly elected People's Assembly convenes.

July 4

The new constitution of the People's Republic of Albania is approved by the Assembly.

1951

February 19

A bomb explodes outside the Soviet Legation in Tirana. As a consequence, mass arrests and purges in the Party take place.

August 3

Following a Church Statute, approved by the National Assembly in June, the Roman Catholic Church in Albania is forced by the government to sever connections with the Vatican.

November 2

Three institutes of higher learning – pedagogical, polytechnical, and agricultural–are established at Tirana.

1952

March 31

The Second Party Congress convenes with Hoxha maintaining that the Two-Year Plan was only 91.4 per cent fulfilled, while Mehmed Shehu outlines the program for the first Five-Year Plan (1951-55).

July 1

Stakhanovism is introduced.

September 1

The new Penal Code, harsher than its Soviet counterpart, becomes effective.

1953

July 11

Declaration of the Foreign Ministers of Greece, Turkey, and Yugoslavia that "the independence of Albania would constitute an important element for the peace and stability of the Balkans."

July 24

Government changes take place, reducing the Cabinet seats from 19 to 10. Omer Nishani resigns as President of the Presidium of the National Assembly and is replaced by Haxhi Lleshi.

August 4

Albania and the Soviet Union raise their respective legations to the status of embassies.

August 26

Secretary John Foster Dulles' letter to the President of the National Committee for a Free Albania clarifying American policy toward Albania.

December 21

Diplomatic relations between Albania and Yugoslavia are resumed.

1954

July 20

Hoxha resigns as Premier, retaining his position as head of the Communist Party. He is replaced by Moscow-trained General Mehmed Shehu.

November 23

Albania's application for membership in UNESCO is rejected.

1955

March 4

President Eisenhower offers $850,000 worth of food to ease food shortages in Albania. The Albanian Government on March 7 rejected the offer.

May 14

Albania signs the Eastern security treaty in Warsaw.

June 24

Changes take place in the government. Tuk Jakova, Vice Premier, and Bedri Spahiu, Minister of Education and Culture, both veteran Communists, are relieved of their posts for inefficiency.

July 3

The Albanian Minister of Foreign Affairs, in a message to Greece through the Secretary General of the United Nations, expresses the desire to establish normal diplomatic and good neighborly relations.

August 3

The Greek Government, replying to the Albanian message, expresses willingness to establish normal diplomatic relations subject to certain conditions: end of the state of war with Albania linked with a frontier agreement, Greece reserving the right to seek a settlement of "pending territorial issues"; the Albanian Government should cease aiding and abetting Greek Communist agents across the border; Albania should return the Greek hostages taken into Albania during the Greek rebellion.

December 15

Albania is admitted as a member in the United Nations. The United States government abstains from voting.

TREATIES AND AGREEMENTS

Bulgaria	*Date of Signing*
Convention on Cultural Cooperation	December 16, 1947
Friendship, Collaboration, and Mutual Aid Treaty	December 16, 1947
Trade Agreement for 1948 (repeated every year)	August 4, 1947
Traffic and Communications Agreement	July 21, 1949
Agreement for Political and Social Cooperation	October 13, 1949
Long-Term Credit Agreement (granted to Albania from Bulgaria)	October 30, 1954
Communist China	
Cultural Cooperation Agreement	October 16, 1954
Scientific and Technical Cooperation Agreement	October 16, 1954
Long-Term Credit Agreement (granted to Albania by China)	December 3, 1954
Protocol for Exchange of Goods and Payments for 1955	December 3, 1954
Cultural Cooperation Protocol	March 2, 1955
Czechoslovakia	
Trade Agreement for 1949 (repeated every year)	March 12, 1949
Cultural and Radio Broadcasting Cooperation Agreement	December 4, 1952
Scientific and Technical Cooperation Agreement	September 11, 1953
Eastern Germany	
Trade Agreement for 1951 (repeated every year)	April 4, 1951
Cultural Cooperation Agreement	August 1, 1953
Scientific and Technical Cooperation Agreement	October 28, 1953

Hungary	*Date of Signing*
Trade Agreement for $1,730,000's worth of goods (repeated every year without mentioning specific sum)	March 16, 1949
Air Traffic Agreement	March 31, 1949
Cultural Cooperation Agreement	November 20, 1951
Italy	
Trade Treaty for 1955	December 17, 1954
Poland	
Trade Agreement for 1949 (repeated every year)	January 25, 1949
Cultural Cooperation Agreement	December 6, 1950
Radio Broadcasting Cooperation Agreement	January 21, 1951
Economic Agreement	January 27, 1951
Romania	
Trade Agreement for 1949 (repeated every year)	April 2, 1949
Radio Broadcasting and Cultural Cooperation Agreement	September 12, 1951
Scientific and Technical Cooperation Agreement	April 14, 1954
Soviet Union	
Trade Agreement for 1949 (repeated every year)	April 10, 1949
Radio Broadcasting Cooperation Agreement	June 28, 1950
Economic Mutual Help Agreement	February 18, 1951
Scientific and Technical Cooperation Agreement	April 22, 1952
Yugoslavia	
Border Traffic Agreement	April 17, 1946
Trade and Payments Agreement	July 1, 1946
Friendship, Collaboration, and Mutual Aid Treaty	July 9, 1946
Civil Aviation Convention	July 11, 1946

	Date of Signing
Maritime Transport Agreement	September 11, 1946
Joint Companies Agreements	November 28, 1946
Economic and Financial Cooperation Agreements	November 28, 1946
Credit Agreement	June 12, 1947
Cultural Convention	July 9, 1947
(All the above Agreements were denounced by Albania immediately after the Tito-Cominform split; the treaty of Friendship, Collaboration, and Mutual Aid, however, was denounced by Yugoslavia on November 12, 1949.)	
Border Traffic Protocol	December 11, 1953

Soviet Union-People's Democracies

Council for Mutual Economic Aid (CEMA)	February 8, 1949
Eastern Security Treaty (Warsaw Pact)	May 14, 1955

BIBLIOGRAPHY

Bibliographical Works

Armao, Ermano. *Catalogo ragionato della mia biblioteca.* Florence: G. Barbèra, 1953. Part D, pp. 126-79, comprises books on Albania.

Bibliografia geologica e geografico-fisica della regione albanese. Rome: Istituto Politico dello Stato, 1939. Accurate and complete.

Guys, Henri. *Bibliographie albanaise. Description raisonnée des ouvrages publiés en albanais ou relatifs à l'Albanie de 1900 à 1910.* Tirana: K. Luarasi, 1938. A supplement to *Bibliographie albanaise* by E. Legrand.

Jokl, Norbert. Albanian bibliographies in *Indogermanisches Jahrbuch.* Leipzig, 1917——. Some 140 pages in all by this famous Albanologist.

Kersopoulos, Jean G. *Albanie: ouvrages et articles de revue parus de 1555 à 1934.* Bibliographie No. 1 in Série de Bibliographies Françaises sur les Nations Balkaniques. Reprint from *Les Balkans.* Athens: Editions Flamma, 1934.

Legrand, Emile Louis Jean. *Bibliographie albanaise: description raisonnée des ouvrages publiés en albanais ou relatifs a l'Albanie, du quinzième siècle à l'année 1900.* Completed and published by Henri Guys. Paris: H. Walter, 1912.

Manek, F., Pekmezi, G., and Stotz, A. (comps.). *Albanesische Bibliographie.* Vienna: Selbstverlag des Vereins "Dija," 1909.

Sevadjian, Léon. *Bibliographie balkanique, 1920-1938.* 8 vols. Paris, 1931-1939. Each volume has a section on Albania.

United States, Library of Congress, Division of Bibliography. *The Balkans: II. Albania.* Compiled by Helen F. Conover under the direction of Florence S. Hellman. Washington, D. C., 1943. A selected list, 24 pages, of references.

General

Albania, Ministry of Interior Affairs. *Shqipria më 1927* (Albania in 1927), by T. Selenica. Tirana: Shtypshkronja "Tirana," 1928. The statistics are valuable; otherwise, to be read with caution.

———. *Shqipënija më 1937* (Albania in 1937). In the series "Publications of the Committee for the Celebration of the 25th Anniversary of Independence, 1912-1937." Tirana: Kristo Luarasi. 1937. The work deals with the activity of government departments during the first twenty-five years of Albanian independence.

L'Albania. Sponsored by the Reale Società Geografica Italiana. Bologna: Zanichelli, 1943. Studies by various Italian men of science.

"Albaniia," *Bolshaia Sovetskaia Entsiklopediia* (Great Soviet Encyclopedia). 2nd ed., Vol. II, 1950, pp. 33-51.

Almagià, Roberto. *L'Albania.* Rome: P. Cremonese, 1930. A good concise book, containing a bibliography, pp. 287-91.

Baldacci, Antonio. *L'Albania.* Rome: Istituto per l'Europa Orientale, 1930. Dealing mainly with physical geography, this book is written by an authority on Albania.

———. *Studi speciali albanesi.* 3 vols. Rome: Anonima Romana Editrice, 1932, 1933, 1938. The work contains, in addition to new studies, many articles published in various reviews by the author.

Bourcart, Jacques. *L'Albanie et les Albanais.* Paris: Bossart, 1921. A good book written by a French scholar who lived in Albania during World War I.

Busch-Zantner, Richard. *Albanien; neues Land im Imperium.* Leipzig: W. Goldmann, 1939. This deals with Albania under fascism.

A Chronology of Events in Albania, 1942-1952. New York: Free Europe Press, Free Europe Committee, Inc., 1955.

Great Britain, Economic Warfare Ministry. *Albania, Basic Handbook.* 3 pts., 2 suppls. [London], August 1943.

Hahn, Johann G. von. *Albanesische Studien.* Vienna: Aus der Kaiserlich-Königlichen Hof- und Staatsdruckerei, 1853. In spite of its date, this is still a very important work.

Konstitutsia i osnovnye zakonodatelnye akti narodnoi respubliki Albanii (Constitution and Basic Legislative Acts of the People's Republic of Albania). Translation from Albanian. Edited by N. Ia. Kupritsa. Moscow: Izdatel'stvo inostrannoi literaturi, 1951.

Redlich, Marcellus D. A. von. *Albania Yesterday and Today.* Worcester, Mass.: The Albanian Messenger, 1936.

Shatilov, A. *Narodnaia respublika Albaniia* (People's Republic of Albania). Moscow: Voennoe izdatel'stvo ministerstva oborony soiuza SSR, 1954.

LAND AND PEOPLE

Albania, Drejtorija e përgjithëshme e shëndetsisë (General Directorate of Health). *Statistikë e lëvizjes demografike dhe gjendjes shëndetsore në periudhën 1927-1932* (Statistics of the Demographic Movement and Health Situation in the Period 1927-1932). Tirana: K. P. Luarasi, 1933.

———. *Statistikë e përgjithëshme shëndetsore. 1925-1929* (General Health Statistics, 1925-1929). Tirana, 1926-1930.

Albania, Drejtoria e përgjithëshme e shëndetsisë (Direction générale de la santé publique). *Rapport, 1912-1937.* Tirana 1938.

Baldacci, Antonio. "Le città dell'Albania," *Nuova Antologia* (Rome), CCLXVII (September 16, 1929), 255-61.

Burenko, S. F. *Izvestiia vsesoiuznogo geograficheskogo obshchestva* (Proceedings of the All-Union Geographical Society), No. 1 (January-February 1952), pp. 53-58. Pages noted deal with Albania.

Çabej, Eqrem. "Sitten und Gebräuche der Albaner," *Revue Internationale des Etudes Balkaniques,* I-II (1934-1935), 556-70.

Coon, Carleton S. *The Mountains of Giants: A Racial and Cultural Study of the North Albanian Mountain Ghegs.* Papers of the Peabody Museum of American Archaeology and Ethnology, Harvard University, XXIII, No. 3. Cambridge, Mass.: Peabody Museum, 1950. This work is a well-known American anthropologist's report on his field work in Albania.

Durham, Mary Edith. "Albania," *Geography* (Manchester, England), XXVI (March 1941), 18-24.

———. *High Albania.* London: E. Arnold, 1909.

Frashëri, Stavre, Th. *Permës Mirditës në dimër* (Through Mirditë in Winter). Korçë: Peppo-Marko, 1930.

Gjeçov, A. Shtjefen Konst. *Kanuni i Lekë Dukagjinit* (The Code of Lekë Dukagjini). Shkodër: Shtypshkroja Françeskane, 1933. There is an Italian translation. published by the Reale Accademia d'Italia, of this important traditional code.

Haigh, William Edwin. *Paludizma në Shqipni* (Malaria in Albania). Translated from the French by Dhimitër Beratti. Tirana: K. P. Luarasi, 1927. Report presented to the League of Nations.

Hasluck, Margaret. *The Unwritten Law in Albania.* Cambridge, England: University Press, 1954.

Hecquard, Hyacinthe. *Histoire et description de la Haute-Albanie ou Ghégarie.* Paris: A. Bertrand, 1908.

Kirk, Dudley. *Europe's Population in the Interwar Years.* New York: Columbia University Press, 1946.

Louis, Herbert. *Albanien; eine Landeskunde vornehmlich auf Grund eigener Reisen.* Stuttgart: J. Engelhorn, 1927. A very good book with a bibliography.

Markgraf, Friedrich. *Pflanzengeographie von Albanien: ihre Bedeutung für Vegetation und Flora der Mittelmeerländer.* Stuttgart: Schweizerbart, 1932.

Moore, Wilbert Ellis. *Economic Demography of Eastern and Southern Europe.* League of Nations Publication, 1945. II. A. 9. New York: Columbia University Press; London: Allen and Unwin, 1946.

Mosely, Philip E. *The Distribution of the Zadruga Within South-Eastern Europe.* Reprint from *The Joshua Starr Memorial Volume.* pp. 219-30. Jewish Social Studies, Publication Vol. V. New York, 1953. Albania is included in this original contribution which is based on field work.

Nopsca, Baron Franz. *Zur Geschichte der Kartographie Nordalbaniens.* Reprint from *Mitteilungen der K.K. Geographischen Gesellschaft in Wien,* 1916, pp. 520-85. A fundamental study of the cartography and geography of Albania.

Sestini, Aldo. *Le pianure costiere dell'Albania.* Reprint from *Bolletino della Società Geografica Italiana* (Rome), 1940, pp. 513-27. Very good.

Statistical Handbook of the Soviet Bloc. New York: Free Europe Press, Free Europe Committee, Inc., 1954.

United Nations, Statistical Office of the United Nations, Department of Economic Affairs. *Demographic Yearbook 1952*. New York, 1952.

———. *Demographic Yearbook 1953*. New York, 1953.

Urban, Martin. *Die Siedlungen Südalbaniens*, Tübinger geographische und geologische Abhandlungen, Reihe II, Hft. 4. Ohringen, 1938.

Valentini, P. Giuseppe. *La famiglia nel diritto tradizionale albanese*. Vatican City: Tipografia Poliglotta Vaticana, 1945.

"Die Verwaltungseinstellung und die Entwicklung der Bevölkerung in Albanien," Südost-Institut, *Wissenschaftlicher Dienst Südosteuropa* (Munich), III, No. 10 (1954), 211-16.

Wolff, Robert Lee. *The Balkans in Our Time*. Cambridge, Mass.: Harvard University Press, 1956. In several chapters there are useful sections on Albania.

History and Politics

Amery, Julian. *Sons of the Eagle: A Study in Guerrilla War*. New York: Macmillan, 1949. Wartime resistance movements in Albania, particularly during the German occupation, as seen by a member of the British Military Mission attached to the Legality Movement.

Ancel, Jacques. *Les Balkans face à l'Italie*. Paris: Delagrave, 1928.

Archer, Laird. *Balkan Journal*. New York: W. W. Norton, 1944.

Armstrong, Hamilton Fish. "Italy, Jugoslavia and Lilliputia [Albania]," *Foreign Affairs*, VI (January 1928), 191-202.

———. *Tito and Goliath*. New York: Macmillan, 1951.

Babinger, Franz. *Ewlijâ Tschelebi's Reisewege in Albanien*. Berlin: Reichsdruckerei, 1930. A good summary of the Albanian sections in the work of a seventeenth-century high Ottoman official.

Bernard, Roland. *Essai sur l'histoire de l'Albanie moderne*. Paris: Les Editions Domat-Montchretien, F. Loviton, 1935.

Bumçi, Mgr. "Qui sont les Albanais et que veulent-ils?" *Réforme Sociale* (Paris), Series 8, IX (1920), 69-81. The author was an Albanian Catholic prelate and representative at the Paris Peace Conference of 1920.

C. H. G. "Greek Claims in Southern Albania," *The World Today* (London), New Series, II (October 1946), 488-94.

Ciano, Galeazzo. *L'Europa verso la catastrofe*. [Milan]: Arnaldo Mondadori Editore, 1948. Ciano's report on Albania in 1938 is an important part of the book.

The Ciano Diaries, 1939-1943. Edited by Hugh Gibson. Garden City, N.Y.: Doubleday, 1946.

"Constitution of 1946 of the People's Republic of Albania," *Gazeta Zyrtare* (Official Gazette) (Tirana), March 19, 1946, No. 19. An English translation of this constitution was made by Bishop Fan S. Noli and published in Boston by the Committee for the Defense of Albania.

"Constitution of 1950 of the People's Republic of Albania," *Bashkimi* (The Union), Tirana Government daily, July 28, 1950. The amendments made to the Constitution of 1946 and incorporated into that of 1950 may be found in *Gazeta Zyrtare* (Official Gazette) (Tirana), August 4, 1950, No. 51.

Dako, Christo A. *Albania: The Master Key to the Near East.* Boston, Mass.: E. L. Grimes Co., 1919. Contains a biblography.

Davies, "Trotsky." *Illyrian Venture: The Story of the British Military Mission to Enemy-Occupied Albania, 1943-44.* London: The Bodley Head, 1952. The author was the chief of the British Military Mission.

Dedijer, Vladimir. "Albania, Soviet Pawn," *Foreign Affairs,* XXX (October 1951), 103-11

Dedijer, Vladimir, (ed.). *Il sangue tradito; relazioni jugoslavo-albanesi, 1938-1949. Documenti ufficiali, lettere, fotografie, memoriali coordinati ed elaborati. . . .*Varese: Editoriale Periodici Italiana,1949. A Yugoslav account of Yugoslav-Albanian relations, mainly before the Tito-Cominform break, containing some important documents. This is a translation from Serbo-Croatian.

Evelpidi, C. *Les états balkaniques; étude comparée, politique, sociale, économique et financière.* Paris: Rousseau, 1930. Contains bibliography.

Federal Writers' Project, Massachusetts. *The Albanian Struggle in the Old World and New.* Sponsored by the Albanian Historical Society of Massachusetts. Boston: The Writer, 1939.

Fraschery, Sch. Samy, bey. *Was war Albanien, was ist es, was wird es werden?* Translated from the Turkish by A. Traxler. Vienna: A. Hölder, 1919. A booklet which describes Albanian political thought toward the end of the nineteenth century.

Frashëri, Mehdi. *Nacionalizma shqipëtare dhe faktorët ngatrestarë të brendëshmë dhe të jashtmë* (Albanian Nationalism and Troublesome Internal and External Factors). Tirana, 1943. The author was Premier of Albania several times.

Fultz, Joan. "The Origins and Nature of the People's Republic of Albania." Unpublished Master's Thesis, University of Chicago, 1948.

Gegaj, Athanase. *L'Albanie et l'invasion turque au XVe siècle.* Louvain: Bureaux du Recueil, Bibliothèque de l'Université, 1937.

Giannini, Amadeo. *L'Albania, dall'independenza all'unione con l'Italia 1913-1939.* Milan: Istituto per gli Studi di Politica Internazionale, 1940. This contains the constitutions of the Albanian state from its foundation to the occupation by Fascist Italy.

———. *La questione albanese alla Conferenza della Pace.* Naples: R. Ricciardi, 1922.

Glasgow, George. "Italy, Albania and the Mediterranean," *The Contemporary Review* (London), CLV (May 1939), 540-51.

Godart, Justin. *L'Albanie en 1921.* Report presented to the Directors of the Foundation. Paris: Centre Européen de la Fondation Carnegie. 1922.

Godart, Justin. *L'Albanie en 1922*. Enquête de la Société des Nations. Paris: Publication de la Conciliation Internationale, 1922.

Greece, Hypourgeion ton exoterikon. *The Greek White Book. Diplomatic documents relating to Italy's aggression against Greece, with a preface by Emmanuel Tsouderos, Prime Minister of Greece.* London, New York: Published for the Royal Greek Ministry for Foreign Affairs by Hutchinson and Co., 1942.

"History of the Albanian Communist Party," *News from Behind the Iron Curtain*, Pt. 1, IV, No. 11 (November 1955), 3-10; Pt. 2, V, No. 1 (January 1956).

Hoxha, Enver. "Successes of the Albanian People's Republic," *For a Lasting Peace, for a People's Democracy* (Bucharest), XXXII (92) August 11, 1950, 4-5.

Inalcik, H. "Timariotes chrétiens en Albanie au XVe siècle," *Mitteilungen des Oesterreichischen Staatsarchivs* (Vienna), IV (1952), 118-38.

J., B.F.T. "The New Government in Albania," *The World Today* (London), II (March 1946), 122-31.

Libardi, P. Camillo. O.M. *I primi moti patriotici albanesi nel 1910, 1911, 1912, specie nei Ducagini.* Pts. 1 and 2. Trento: A. Ardesi, 1935. There is a good collection of documents at the end of Part 2.

Logoreci, Anton, "Albania" [annexation by Italy], *The Contemporary Review* (London), CLXII (July 1942), 42-48.

———. "Albania and Yugoslavia," *The Contemporary Review* (London), CLXXVII (June 1950), 360-64.

Lorecchio, Anselmo. *Il pensiero politico albanese in rapporto agli interessi italiani.* Rome: Tipografia Operaia Romana, 1904. This book by an exponent of the Italo-Albanians contains many documents.

Lucatello, Guido. *La natura giuridica dell'unione italo-albanese.* Padova: CEDAM, 1943.

MacColl, René. "Albania and the British Mission," *Quarterly Review* (London), CCLXXI (October 1938), 301-15.

Manchkha, P. *Albaniia na puti k sotsializmu* (Albania on the Road to Socialism). Moscow: Gospolitizdat, 1951.

Martin, William. "Petit pays, grand problème: l'Albanie," *Revue de Paris*, XXXIX (September-October 1932), 27-44. An intelligent evaluation of the Albanian situation in the early 1930's.

Miller, William. "Albania and her Protectress [Italy]," *Foreign Affairs*, V (April 1927), 438-55.

Mousset, Albert. *L'Albanie devant l'Europe (1912-1929).* Paris: Delagrave, 1930. A good booklet.

Noli, Fan S. *George Castrioti Scanderbeg (1405-1468).* New York: International Universities Press, 1947.

Pipineles, P. *Europe and the Albanian Question.* New York: Greek Government Office of Information, [1944]. A Greek viewpoint by one of Greece's well-known diplomats.

"The Political and International Reorganization of Albania; the Personal Union Between Albania and Italy," *Völkerbund* (Geneva), VIII (April 20, 1939), 170-84. Text in English and Italian.

Programi i Kabinetit të Mitrovicës (Program of Premier Mitrovica's Cabinet). Tirana, December 1943. This document contains the measures taken by the German-sponsored National Assembly of October 16, 1943.

Radio Free Europe, Information and Reference Department. *Political Attitudes in Albania.* New York: National Committee for a Free Europe, 1952.

Remérand, Gabriel. *Ali de Tébélen, Pacha de Janina, 1744-1822.* Paris: Librairie Orientaliste Paul Geuthner, 1928. A good work, based on Turkish sources as well as Western.

"La République Populaire d'Albanie: L'Évolution politique," La Documenlaire d'Albanie (July 1950)," La Documentation Française, *Notes et Etudes Documentaires* (Paris), March 4, 1954, No. 1844.

"La République Populaire d'Albanie: L'Evolution politique," La Documentation Française, *Notes et Etudes Documentaires* (Paris), March 2, 1954, No. 1843.

Robinson, Vandeleur. *Albania's Road to Freedom.* London: Allen and Unwin, 1941. An account of Albania under King Zog and Italian influence.

Saikowski, Charlotte. "Albania in Soviet Satellite Policy, 1945-1953." Unpublished thesis for the Certificate of the Russian Institute, Columbia University, 1954.

Scaglione, Pietro. *Historia e Shqipëtarëvet t'Italisë* (History of the Albanians of Italy). New York: Emporium Press, 1921.

Schirò, Giuseppe. *Gli Albanesi e la questione balcanica.* Naples: Ferd. Bideri, 1904.

Self, George Moore. "Foreign Relations of Albania." Unpublished Ph.D. dissertation, University of Chicago, 1943.

Sereni, Angelo P. "Legal Status of Albania." *American Political Science Review,* XXXV (April 1941), 311-17.

Seton-Watson, Hugh. *The East European Revolution.* New York: Frederick A. Praeger, 1951.

Shmelev, N. S. *Novaia Albaniia* (New Albania). Moscow: Molodaia gvardiia, 1951.

Skendi, Stavro. "Albania Within the Slav Orbit: Advent to Power of the Communist Party," *Political Science Quarterly,* LXIII (June 1948), 257-74.

———. "Albanian Political Thought and Revolutionary Activity, 1881-1912," *Südost Forschungen* (Munich), XIII (1954), 159-99.

———. "Beginnings of Albanian Nationalist and Autonomous Trends: The Albanian League, 1878-1881," *American Slavic and East European Review,* XII (1953), 219-32.

———. "The Northern Epirus Question Reconsidered," *Journal of Central European Affairs,* XIV (July 1954), 143-53.

———. *The Political Evolution of Albania, 1912-1944.* Mimeographed Series, No. 19, March 8, 1954. New York: Mid-European Studies Center, Free Europe Committee, Inc., 1954.

Stadtmüller, Georg. "Die albanische Volkstumsgeschichte als Forschungsproblem," *Leipziger Vierteljahrsschrift für Südosteuropa* V (1941), 58-80.

Stickney, Edith Pierpont. *Southern Albania or Northern Epirus in European International Affairs, 1912-1923.* Stanford University, Calif.: Stanford University Press, 1926. An excellent work; bibliography pp. 173-91.

Story, Someville, (ed). *Memoirs of Ismail Kemal Bey.* New York: E. P. Dutton, [n.d.]. Ismail Kemal Bey was the Albanian who declared the independence of his country.

Sufflay, Milan. *Srbi i Arbanasi* (Serbs and Albanians). Belgrade: Izdanje Seminara za Arbanasku Filologiju, 1925. Symbiosis of Serbs and Albanians during the Middle Ages.

Sulser, Jack Arnold. "Some Chapters in Albanian-American Relations." Unpublished Master's Thesis, University of Wisconsin, 1950.

Swire, Joseph. *Albania: The Rise of a Kingdom.* London: Williams and Norgate, 1929. A detailed account by an intelligent journalist who spent some years in Albania; bibliography.

———. *King Zog's Albania.* London: R. Hale, 1937.

Thallóczy, Ludwig von, (ed.). *Illyrisch-albanische Forschungen.* Vols. I and II. Munich and Leipzig: Duncker and Humblot. 1916. A fundamental work on Albania; Vol. I mainly comprises historical studies.

Umiltá, Carlo. *Jugoslavia e Albania.* Milan: Garzanti, 1947. An account by an Italian diplomat on Kosovo-Metohija, particularly after the annexation of this region to Albania in 1941.

United States Congress, House of Representatives. Select Committee on Communist Aggression. *Communist Takeover and Occupation of Albania.* Special report No. 13. 83rd. Cong., 2nd. Sess. Washington, D.C.: Government Printing Office. 1954.

United States Congress, Senate. *Tensions Within the Soviet Captive Countries, Albania.* Document No. 70, Pt. 6. Prepared at the request of the Committee on Foreign Relations by the Legislative Reference Service of the Library of Congress. 83rd. Cong., 1st Sess. Washington, D.C.: Government Printing Office, 1954.

V., E. b. *Die Wahrheit über das Vorgehen der Jungtürken in Albanien.* Vienna: C. Fromme, 1911.

Volpe, Gioacchino. "Formazione storica dell'Albania," *Nuova Antologia* (Rome), CCCCVI (December 16, 1939), 313-32.

Vucinich, W. S. "Communism Gains in Albania," *Current History,* XXI (October and December 1951), 212-19, 345-52.

Wassa (Effendi). *La vérité sur l'Albanie et les Albanais.* Paris: Imprimerie de la Société Anonyme de Publications Périodiques, 1879. The author is an Albanian who held high positions in the Ottoman administration.

Weigand, Gustav. "Sind die Albaner die Nachkommen der Illyrer oder der Thraker," *Balkan-Archiv* (Leipzig), III(1927), 227-51.

Yugoslavia, Ministry of Foreign Affairs of the Federal People's Republic of Yugoslavia. *White Book.* Belgrade, 1951.

ECONOMICS

Adam, Eng. Jovan. "Historia e Rrugëve të Shqipërisë" (The History of the Roads of Albania), published serially in issues 1, 3, and 4 of *Buletini për Shkencat Shoqërore* (Bulletin for Social Sciences) (Tirana), 1953.

Albania. *Act. Hours of Work* (women and children). International Labour Office. Legislative Series, 1936, Alb. 1. Geneva, October 1938.

———. *Kodi Penal i Repubikës Popullore të Shqipërisë* (Penal Code of of the People's Republic of Albania). Law No. 1470 of May 23, 1952, published in full in *Gazeta Zyrtare* (Official Gazette) (Tirana), August 1, 1952, No. 15.

Albania, Ministry of Economic Affairs. *Relacioni 1928-1929.* (Report 1928-1929). Tirana, 1931.

Albania, Ministry of Finance. *Tableau du Commerce Extérieur du Royaume d'Albanie.* In French and Albanian. Tirana, 1938.

"L'Albania economica," *Rivista di Politica Economica* (Rome), XXX (February 1940), 142-46

L'Albania economica. Sponsored by the Camera di Commercio Italo-Orientale di Bari. Bari: Soc. Ed. Tip., 1927. This treats such subjects as agriculture, mineral resources, communications, foreign trade, and the Italo-Albanian treaty.

The Albanian Working Class Organized in Trade Unions Struggles for Building the Bases of Socialism. Budapest: Athenaeum Nyomda U.V., for the Presidency of the Albanian Trade Unions Council, Tirana, [1947?].

American Petroleum Institute. *Petroleum Facts and Figures,* 11th ed. New York: American Petroleum Institute, 1954.

Archetti, Sandro. "Sulla pescosità delle acque interne e sull'industria peschereccia in Albania," *Atti dell'Accademia Veneto-Trentino-Istriana* (Venice), 1932, pp. 119-27.

Baldacci, Antonio. *Itinerari albanesi (1892-1902) con uno sguardo generale all'Albania e alle sue communicazioni stradali.* Rome: Reale Società Geografica Italiana, 1917.

The Balkan States. 2 pts. Pt. 1: *Economic: A Review of the Economic and Financial Development of Albania, Bulgaria, Greece, Rumania and Yugoslavia since 1919.* Papers, No. 18, Pt. 1. New York: Oxford University Press, for the Royal Institute of International Affairs, 1936.

Belishova, L. "Stroitel'stvo osnov sotsializma v Albanii" (The Building of the Foundations of Socialism in Albania), *Bol'shevik* (Moscow), XXIX (January 1952), 44.

Bell, E. A. "Italians Process Albanian Heavy Oil to Aviation Gasoline," *Oil Weekly,* XCVIII (July 22, 1940), 28-30.

Benini, Zenone. *Albania fascista.* Florence: Marzocco, anno XVIII [i.e. 1940]. The author was Undersecretary for Albania in the Italian government during the Fascist occupation.

Borgatta, Gino. "L'economia albanese e la collaborazione dell'Italia," *Nuova Antologia* (Rome), CCCXCIV (December 1, 1937), 343-46.

Bourcart, Jacques. *Les confins albanais administrés par la France (1916-1920); contribution à la géographie et à la géologie de l'Albanie moyenne*. Paris: Delagrave, 1922.

Calmès, Albert. *The Economic and Financial Situation of Albania.* Annex to the Report presented to the Council by the Financial Committee of the Provisional Economic and Financial Committee on its eighth session, Geneva, September 1922. Geneva: Imp. A. Kundig, 1922.

"Control of Albanian Oilfields Assures 4 Percent of Italy's Crude Requirements," *World Petroleum,* X (May 1939), 26-27.

"Economic Report: Albania," Free Europe Committee, *News from Behind the Iron Curtain,* III, No. 5 (May 1954), 12-22.

Gasser, E. "Present Position of the Dairying Industry in the Different Countries: Albania," *International Review of Agriculture* (Rome), XXX (April 1939), 144T-151T.

Gross, Hermann. "Wirtschaftsstruktur und Wirtschaftsbeziehungen Albaniens," *Weltwirtschaftliches Archiv* (Jena), XXXVIII (October 1933), 505-51.

Gurakuqi, Luigj. *Çështja e Vajgjgurit* (The Oil Question). Shkodër, 1923.

Histori e shkurtër e lëvizies punëtore në Shqipëri (A Brief History of the Labor Movement in Albania). Tirana, 1946.

Holmes, J. C., and Jordan, R. R. "Economic Developments in Albania," U. S. Bureau of Foreign and Domestic Commerce *Reports,* XXXII (August 11, 1930), 372-74.

Inalcik, Halil. *Hicrî 835 tarihli sûret-i defter-i sancak-i Arvanid* (Copy of a Record Book of the Sandjak of Albania Dating from 835 of the Hegira [1432 A.D.]). Ankara: Türk Tarih Kurumu Basimevi, 1954.

Italian Center of Studies and Publications. *What Italy Has Done for Albania.* Rome: S.A. Grafiche Penetto and Petrelli, [1946?].

Kategorizimi i Punëtorëve (Workers' Classification). Issued as supplement to *Gazeta Zyrtare* (Official Gazette) (Tirana), April 30, 1950.

"Kodi i Punës" (Labor Code), in *Gazeta Zyrtare* (Official Gazette) (Tirana), September 16, 1947. An English translation is in the Legislative Series, for May-June, 1948 of the International Labour Office.

Lorenzoni, Giovanni. *La Questione agraria albanese; studi, inchieste e proposte per una riforma agraria in Albania.* Bari: G. Laterza 1930. An important work by an expert.

Magnani, Mario. "Risorse minerarie dell'Albania," *Le Vie d'Italia* (Milan), XLV (November 1939), 1450-63.

Michelangeli, Mario. *Il problema forestale albanese.* Rome: Reale Accademia d' Italia, 1940.

Milone, Ferdinando. *L'Albania economica.* Padua: CEDAM, 1941.

Moschetti, A. "Le miniere in Albania," *L'Industria Mineraria d'Italia* (Rome), IV (September 1930), 409-32.

Nechaeva, R. "'Ekonomika Albanii na podëme" (Albania's Economy on the Rise), *Vneshniaia Torgovlia* (Foreign Trade) (Moscow), XX (September 1950), 1-6.

Nicholas, Edward E. "Economic Potentials of Albania." Unpublished Master's Thesis, Columbia University, June 1950.

Nopcsa, Báró Ferencz. "Zur Geologie der Küstenketten Nordalbaniens," *Mitteilungen aus dem Jahrbuch der Kgl. ungarischen geologischen Anstalt,* XXIV, No. 4, 131-65. Budapest: Kgl. ung. Universitäts Buchdruckerei, 1925.

Nowack, Ernst. *Beiträge zur Geologie von Albanien.* Stuttgart: E. Schweizerbart, 1923-1926. An important work by a well-known specialist.

———. *Die geologische Karte von Albanien.* Publication of the Militaergeograpsisches Institut. Vienna, 1928.

———. *Geologische Übersicht von Albanien.* Innsbruck, 1929.

Perović, Marko. *Ekonomski Odnosi Jugoslavije i Albanije (1947-1948)* (Economic Relations Between Yugoslavia and Albania). Belgrade, 1951.

Perrin, Bernard. "Le pétrole d'Albanie," *Revue des Deux Mondes* (Paris), 8th Series, LVII (May 1, 1940), 148-60.

Polacco, F. "Organization of Agricultural Statistics in Albania," *International Review of Agriculture* (Rome), XXXI (February 1940), 161S-164S.

"La République Populaire d'Albanie: Évolution économique et sociale," La Documentation Française, *Notes et Etudes Documentaires* (Paris), March 6, 1954, No. 1845.

Ronart, Otto. "L' évolution économique de l' Albanie," *Revue Economique Internationale* (Brussels), XXVIII (December 1936), 581-97.

Shvets, V. "Dvukhletnii gosudarstvennyi plan razvitiia narodnogo Khoziaistva Albanii" (Two-Year State Plan of the Development of People's Economy in Albania), *Vneshniaia Torgovlia* (Foreign Trade) (Moscow), XIX (August 1949), 1.

———. "Uspekhi Albanskoi narodnoi respubliki" (Successes of the Albanian People's Republic), *Vneshniaia Torgovlia* (Foreign Trade) (Moscow), XXI (February 1951), 7.

Società Italiana per il progresso delle Scienze, Commissione per lo Studio dell'Albania. *Relazione.* Pts. 1 and 2. Rome, 1915. Scientific studies by various scholars.

Società Italiana per lo Svilupo Economico dell' Albania. *Un decennio di vita della* "S.V.E.A." Rome: Libreria dello Stato, 1936.

Stanley, Eugene. "Italy's Financial Stake in Albania," *Foreign Policy Reports,* VIII (June 8, 1932), 79-86.

Stepanov, D. "Bor'ba albanskikh trudiashchikhsia za demokratiu i sotslialism" (The Struggle of Albanian Working Masses for Democracy and Socialism), *Voprosy ekonomiki* (Economic Questions) (Moscow), XIII (November 1950), 41.

Twelfth Report to Congress on Operations of UNRRA. Washington, D.C.: Government Printing Office, 1948.

UNRRA, *Economic Rehabilitation in Albania.* In *UNRRA Operational Analysis Papers, 1-53.* No. 46 of series. 53 nos. in 6 vols. London: UNRRA European Regional Office, 1947.

United States, Department of Interior. *The Mineral Resources of Albania.* Washington, D. C.: Bureau of Mines, 1944.

United States, Department of the Interior. *Minerals Yearbook 1949*. Washington, D.C.: Government Printing Office, 1951.

United States, General Counsel of the Treasury, Office of Preliminary Study of Certain Financial Laws and Institutions. *Albania*. Prepared by Nelson Lancione. Treasury Department, Office of the General Counsel. Washington, D.C., 1944.

"Via Egnatia," *Blackwood's Magazine* (London), CCXLVI (September 1939), 440-48.

Vlora, Ekrem. "Reforma agrare në Shqipëri" (Land Reform in Albania), *L'Albanie Libre* (Rome), Organ of the [Albanian] National Independent Bloc, issues 15-32 (1950-1951). Studies by a former Albanian landlord.

Whistler, H. "Further Observations on the Birds of Albania," *Ibis* (London), Series 13, VI (April 1936), 335-56.

World Production of Raw Materials. London: Royal Institute of International Affairs, 1941.

Zavalani, Dalib. *Die Landwirtschaftlichen Verhältnisse Albaniens*. Berlin: P. Parey, 1938. A valuable work.

Zuccari, G. C. "I prodotti petroliferi albanesi," *Strade* (Milan), XXI (May 1939), 218-88.

CULTURE

Albania; revue d'archéologie, d'histoire, d'art et des sciences appliquées en Albanie et dans les Balkans. Years: 1925-1928, 1932, 1935, 1936, 1939. Milan: Bestelli and Tumminelli, 1925-[1939].

"Analyzohen rezultatet e vitit shkollor 1952-1953" (The Results of the School-Year 1952-1953 Are Analyzed). Report of Comrade Qibrie Ciu, report of Comrade Kadri Baboçi, resolution, *Arësimi Popullor* (Popular Education) (Tirana), VIII (August 1953), 18-27.

Arnold, T. W. *The Preaching of Islam: A History of the Propagation of Muslim Faith*. London: Luzac and Co., 1935. The part on Albania principally refers to Catholicism.

Astakhov, S. "Deiatel'nost' Vatikana v Albanii" (Vatican Activity in Albania) *Novoe Vremia* (New Times) (Moscow), September 10, 1947, No. 37, pp. 12-15.

Barić, Henrik. *Albanorumänische Studien*. Zur Kunde der Balkanhalbinsel, II, Quellen und Forschungen, 7. Sarajevo: Institut für Balkanforschung, 1919.

Birge, John K. *The Bektashi Order of Dervishes*. Hartford, Conn.: Hartford Seminary Press, 1937. The author, who visited Albania, writes about Albanian Bektashism.

Burgess, Aline. "Home Economics in an Albanian School," *Journal of Home Economics*, XXIII (June 1931), 532-34.

Çabej, Eqrem. "Die albanische Volksdichtung," *Leipziger Vierteljahrsschrift für Südosteuropa*, III (1939), 194-213.

———. *Elemente të gjuhësisë e të literaturës shqipe* (Elements of Albanian Linguistics and Literature). Tirana: Shtypshkroja e Ministrisë s'Arësimit, 1936.

Çabej, Eqrem. "Për gjenezën e literaturës shqipe" (On the Genesis of Albanian Literature), *Hylli i Dritës* (The Star of Light) Shkodër, XIV (1939), 647-61; XV (1939), 8-15, 84-93, 149-80.

"College of Albania [Tirana]," *School and Society,* XXX (December 28, 1929), 876-77.

Il Collegio Saveriano di Scutari d' Albania nei primi cinquant' anni (*1877/8-1927/8*). Chieri: G. Atesano, 1928.

Cordignano, P. Fulvio. *L'Albania atraverso l'opera e gli scritti di un grande Missionario italiano, il P. Domenico Pasi S.J.* (*1847-1914*). Vols. I and II. Rome: Istituto per l'Europa Orientale, 1933-1934.

———. *Geografia ecclesiastica dell' Albania dagli ultimi decenni del secolo XVI alla metà del secolo XVII.* Reprint from Orientalia Christiana 1934. Rome: Pont. Institutum Orientalium Studiorum, 1943.

———. *La poesia epica di confine nell'Albania del nord.* Pt. 1a. "Studio critico-letterario," of Collana studi sui paesi dell' "Illyricum," No. 5. Venice: Tipografia Libreria Emiliana, 1943.

"Education in Albania," *School and Society,* XLIX (May 6, 1939), 566-67.

Elbin, N. "Kulturnoe stroitel'stvo v stranakh novoi demokratii" (Cultural Formation in Countries of the New Democracy), *Novoe Vremia* (New Times) (Moscow), XXXIV (August 20, 1947), 11-17.

Fishta, P. Gjergj. "Vjersha heroike shqyptare" (The Albanian Heroic Song), *Hylli i Dritës* (The Star of Light) (Shkodër), XI (1935), 142-52.

"Fjala e shokut Enver në Sesionin e V-të të Kuvendit Popullor" (Comrade Enver [Hoxha]'s Speech During the Fifth Session of the People's Assembly). *Arësimi Popullor* (Popular Education) (Tirana), VIII (August 1953), 1-15.

Frashëri, N. *Fletore e Bektashinjet* (Notebook of the Bektashis), as republished in *Balkan Archiv* (Leipzig), II (1926), 226-56. A booklet by the apostle-poet of Albanian nationalism which has been influential among Albanian Bektashis.

Hasluck, F. W. *Christianity and Islam under the Sultans.* Vol. 1 and II. Oxford: Clarendon Press, 1929. There are parts on Albanian Bektashism and Sunnism.

Hasluck, Margaret. "The Nonconformist Moslems of Albania," *The Contemporary Review* (London), CXXVII (May 1925), 599-606.

Ippen, Th. "Das religiöse Protektorat Oesterreich-Ungarns in der Türkei," *Die Kultur* (Vienna), III (1902), 298-310.

Jacques, Edwin E. "Islam in Albania," *Moslem World,* XXVIII (July 1938), 313-14.

Jokl, Norbert. *Linguistisch-kulturhistorische Untersuchungen aus dem Bereiche des Albanischen.* Untersuchungen zur indogermanischen Sprach- und Kulturwissenschaft . . .8. Berlin and Leipzig: W. de Gruyter, 1923.

Juhasz, William. *Blueprint for a Red Generation.* New York: Mid-European Studies Center, Free Europe Committee, Inc., 1952.

Kennedy, Phineas B. (Rev. and Mrs.). "Politics and Religion in Albania," *Missionary Review of the World,* LXII (July 1939), 359-60.

Kodra, Lame. *Roli i Kulturës në Shqipërinë e sotme* (The Role of Culture in Albania Today). Tirana, 1945.

Koliqi, Ernesto. *Epica popolare albanese.* Padua: Gruppo Universitario Fascista, 1937.

———. "Influenze orientali sulla letterature albanese." *Oriente Moderno* (Rome), XXXIV (Gennaio 1954), 25-42. The author finds that the poet Naim Frashëri is the only Albanian author influenced by Persian poetry.

———. "Nuove correnti della moderna letterature albanese," *L'Albanie Libre* (Rome), November 28, 1953, p. 3.

Konidare, G. I. *Hellenike ekklesia os politistike dynamis en te historia tes hersonesou tou Haimou* (The Greek Church as a Civilizing Force in the History of the Balkan Peninsula). Athens, 1948. The study in this work is the most extensive on the Christian Orthodox Church in Albania; however, it lacks strict scholarship

Kremnev. P. "Podëm prosveshcheniia i kul'turi v narodnoi respublike Albanii" (The Rise of Education and Culture in the People's Republic of Albania), *Sovetskaia Pedagogika* (Soviet Pedagogy) (Moscow), VII (1952), 111-14.

Lambertz, Maximilian. *Die Volkspoesie der Albaner, eine einführende Studie.* Sarajevo: J. Studnicka, 1917. A good introductory study.

———. "Das Werden der albanischen Literatur," *Leipziger Vierteljahrsschrift für Südosteuropa,* VII (1943), 160-74.

Logoreci, Anton. "The Dialogue of Modern Albanian Writing," *Books Abroad,* Vol. 3 (Spring, 1956), 155-159.

Mann, Stuart E. *Albanian Literature.* London: Bernard Quaritch, 1955.

Mborja, Perikli D. "La peinture moderne en Albanie," *Revue Internationale des Etudes Balkaniques* (Belgrade), III-IV (1936), 555-58.

Mladenov, St. "Bemerkungen über die Albaner und das Albanische in Nordmazedonien und Altserbien," *Balkan Archiv* (Leipzig), I (1925), 43-70.

Musaraj Ševtet. "Deset let literatury v Albánské lidové republice" (Ten Years of Literature in the Albanian People's Republic), *Literární Noviny* (Literary News) (Prague), November 27, 1954, p. 8.

Musaraj, Shefqet. Dhjetë vjetë letërsi nënë drejtimin e Partisë" (Ten Years of Literature under the Leadership of the Party), *Letërsia Jonë* (Our Literature) (Tirana), X (October 1951), 48-62.

"Nga referati i shokut Kahreman Ylli përpara Këshillit të Përgjithëshmë Arësimor" (From the Report of Comrade Kahreman Ylli before the General Council of Education), *Zëri i Popullit* (The Voice of the People) (Tirana), October 18, 1950, p. 2.

"Partija–organizatore udhëheqëse dhe edukatore e rinisë" (The Party–Leader in the Organization and Education of Youth), *Bashkimi* (The Union) (Tirana), September 15, 1951, p. 3.

Pedersen, Holger. *Zur albanesischen Volkskunde.* Copenhagen: S. Michaelsens Nachfolger, 1898.

Petrotta, Gaetano. *Svolgimento storico della cultura e della letterature albanese.* Palermo, 1950.

Petrotta, Pappas Gaetano. *Popolo, lingua e letteratura albanese.* 2nd. ed. with additions and corrections. Palermo, 1932.

Praschniker, C., and Schober, A. *Archäologische Forschungen in Albanien und Montenegro.* Akademie der Wissenschaften in Vienna. Schriften der Balkankommission. Vienna: H. Hölder, 1919.

Rey, Léon. "Seize années de fouilles en Albanie," *Revue de Paris,* XLVI (August 1, 1939), 685-96. Archeological discoveries of French expedition described by their leader.

Rossi, E. "Saggio sul dominio turco e l'introduzione dell'Islam in Albania," *Rivista d'Albania* (Rome), III (1942), 200-13. The author was a well-known Turkologist.

Schirò, Giuseppe. "Della lingua albanese e della sua letteratura, anche in rapporto alle colonie albanesi d'Italia," as republished in *Studi Albanesi* (Rome), II (1932), 74-127.

Scura, Antonio. *Gli Albanesi in Italia e i loro canti tradizionali.* New York: F. Tocci, 1912.

Skendi, Stavro. *Albanian and South Slavic Oral Epic Poetry.* Memoirs of the American Folklore Society, Vol. 44. Philadelphia: American Folklore Society, 1954.

———. "Beginnings of Albanian Nationalist Trends in Culture and Education (1878-1912)," *Journal of Central European Affairs,* XII (1953), 356-67.

———. "The South Slavic Decasyllable in Albanian Oral Epic Poetry," *Slavic Word,* IX, No. 4 (December), 339-49.

Spahiu, Bedri. "Cultural Revolution in Albania and the Struggle in the Ideological Front," *For a Lasting Peace, for a People's Democracy* (Bucharest), XLVIII (December 1, 1950), 2.

Šufflay Milan. "Die Kirchenzustände im vortürkischen Albanien. Die orthodoxe Durchbruchszone im katholischen Dame," in *Illyrisch-albanische Forschungen,* I, pp. 188-282. Munich and Leipzig: Duncker and Humblot, 1916. An excellent study.

Sulzberger, C. L. "Red Pattern Seen in Albania to Capture Catholic Church," *The New York Times, September* 21, 1951.

Tagliavini, Carlo. "La lingua Albanese," *Studi Albanesi.* (Rome), V-VI (1935-1936), 5-33. An excellent study.

Ugolini, Luigi M. *Albania antica.* Rome: Società Editrice d' Arte Illustrata, 1927.

———. *L'antica Albania nelle ricerche archeologiche italiane.* Rome: E.N.I.T., 1928.

———. "L'attività archeologica dell'Italia in Albania," *Nuova Antologia* (Rome), CCLXIV (March 1, 1929), 88-101.

———. "How I found New Troy," *The World Today* (London), LVI (September 1930), 342-47. Excavations in Albania, described by the head of the Italian Archeological Mission.

Weigand, Gustav. "Das Albanische in Attika," *Balkan Archiv* (Leipzig), II (1926), 167-225.

Zankow, Stefan. "Albanskata pravoslavna tsurkva i neinata uredba" (The Albanian Orthodox Church and Its Organization), Faculty of Theology of the University of Sofia, *Godishnik* (Yearbook), XII (1934-1935), 1-66.

PERIODICALS

Albania; revue mensuelle albanaise de littérature, linguistique, histoire, sociologie. This was published in Brussels, 1897-1902, and in London, 1903-1909. Most Albanian intellectuals contributed to this review, which contains valuable articles.

Arësimi Popullor (Popular Education) (Tirana). Monthly organ of the Ministry of Education of the Communist regime, 1946——.

Arhiv za arbanasku starinu, jezik i etnologiju (Archives for Albanian Antiquity, Language and Ethnology) (Belgrade). Complete collection 1923-1926. This contains some important articles.

Bashkimi (The Union) (Tirana). Daily organ of the Democratic Front (Government) of the Communist regime, 1944——.

Bota e Re (The New World) (Tirana). Monthly organ of the Writers' Union of Albania from 1944 to 1946.

Buletin për Shkencat Shoqërore (Bulletin of Social Sciences) (Tirana). Current publication of the Institute of Sciences, Tirana.

Fletorja Zyrtare (The Official Gazette) (Tirana). Published periodically by the prewar and war Albanian governments until 1944.

Gazeta Zyrtare (The Official Gazette) (Tirana). Published periodically after 1944 by the Albanian Communist government.

Hylli i Dritës (The Star of Light) (Shkodër). Published monthly in Shkodër by the Franciscan Brothers, 1933-1939. Very valuable.

Krediti dhe Financat (Kredit and Finance) (Tirana). Monthly organ of the Ministry of Finance of the Communist regime.

Leka (Shkodër). Published periodically in the prewar period by the Jesuits in Shkodër. It contains some valuable articles.

Letërsia Jonë (Our Literature) (Tirana). Monthly organ of the Writers' Union of Albania from 1946-1953.

Nëntori (November) (Tirana). Monthly organ of the Writers' Union of Albania since 1953.

News from Behind the Iron Curtain. Published monthly since 1952 by The Free Europe Press, Free Europe Committee, Inc., New York.

Përpjekja Shqiptare (The Albanian Effort) (Tirana). Published monthly in the late 1930's. Very valuable.

Rivista d'Albania (Rome). A publication of the Studies Center for Albania, Royal Academy of Italy, I (1940), II (1941), III (1942), and IV 1943). This contains important articles by Italian and some Albanian scholars.

Studi Albanesi (Rome). Published annually by the Istituto per l'Europa Orientale (Vol. I, 1930; Vol. II, 1932; Vols. III-IV, 1933-1934; Vols. V-VI, 1935-36). These volumes contain a variety of studies by Italian scholars; important.

Zëri i Popullit (The Voice of the People) (Tirana). Organ of the Workers' (Communist) Party of Albania, 1944——.

Index

Note: Numbers in italics refer to maps and tables.